THOU SHALL PROSPER

Ten Commandments for Making Money

Rabbi Daniel Lapin

John Wiley & Sons, Inc.

Published by John Wiley & Sons, Inc., Hoboken, New Jersey.
Published simultaneously in Canada.

This publication is designed to provide accurate and authoritative information in regard to the subject
matter covered. It is sold with the understanding that the publisher is not engaged in rendering
professional services. If professional advice or other expert assistance is required, the services of a
competent professional person should be sought.

Wiley also publishes its books in a variety of electronic formats. Some content that appears in print
may not be available in electronic books. For more information about Wiley products, visit our Web
site at www.wiley.com.

Library of Congress Cataloging-in-Publication Data:

Lapin, Daniel (Daniel E.)
  Thou shall prosper : ten commandments for making money / by Rabbi Daniel Lapin.
    p. cm.
  Includes bibliographical references and index.
  ISBN 0-471-21868-5 (cloth: alk. paper)
    1. Wealth—Religious aspects—Judaism. 2. Finance, Personal—Religious aspects—Judaism.
    3. Money—Religious aspects—Judaism. I. Title.
  BM538.W4 L37 2002
  296.3'64—dc21

                                                                    2002008986

Printed in the United States of America.

10 9 8 7 6

Contents

Introduction

Mark Twain once wrote: "The Jews constitute but one percent of the human race. Properly the Jew ought hardly to be heard of; but he is heard of, has always been heard of. He is a successful businessman, the immense wholesale business of Broadway is substantially in his hands. Eighty-five percent of the great and lucrative businesses of Germany are in the hands of the Jewish race. The Jew is a money-getter."[1]

In reality, Jews do not constitute even one tenth of one percent of the human race. Mark Twain may have grossly overestimated the size of the world's Jewish population, but he was quite right to observe that Jews are disproportionately successful in business. From notorious Nazis to Hassidic scholars, from Japan's cultural commentators to conspiracy theorists who have never met a Jew, all who have examined the historic and current identity of the Jewish people acknowledge one simple truth—Jews are good at business.

This is true not only in the United States of the twenty-first century, but also in many countries over many centuries. Whether in Europe, North Africa, or the United States, Jews have always been both reviled and admired. Jews are hated and envied; they are despised and loved. For people that make up only a little over two percent of the U.S. population, they are disproportionately influential in so many areas of American life. They are spoken of, written about, and depicted far more than other groups of similar size. Part of the reason for this is surely their conspicuous economic success.

I hope that this observation does not make you squeamish. I am not trying to affirm anti-Semitic stereotypes of the money-grabbing Jew. On the contrary, I am dispelling the anti-Semitic canard. Remember that Judaism itself has never seen wealth as evidence of misdeed. In fact this book will show that although there are obvious exceptions found in all faiths, for the most part people prosper when they live among many others, all behaving decently and honorably toward one another.

As an Orthodox rabbi, I have devoted much of my research to studying and isolating those characteristics that have helped Jews excel in business. This book makes these characteristics available in usable form for all readers, regardless of faith. You might be wondering, "If he knows the secrets of wealth creation, why doesn't he just get on with creating wealth instead of writing the secrets down for others?" The answer, as you shall see in the pages ahead, is that your prosperity does not mean that there is any less for me. My lengthy investigation into the accumulated wisdom of three thousand years of Jewish scholarship reveals precisely the reverse. The more wealth that the people around me create, the more I shall benefit, too.

YOU DO WANT MORE MONEY, DON'T YOU?

Don't be embarrassed to admit that you want more money. Think of all the good things you could do if you had more discretionary income and more accumulated assets. I am not suggesting that you corrode your soul with a deep sense of discontent. You can be very happy with your life and grateful for its many blessings while simultaneously desiring more. That doesn't make you an ungrateful whiny person. So would you like more money? Just say, "Yes, I would like more money than I now have." Not only do I *think* you want more money, I sincerely *hope* you want more money. The more money you want, the more you will be willing to work and produce for me and for countless other people.

It makes me happy to know that there are many humans just like you out there, all eager to have more money and therefore all eager to do things for me. One of the ancient Jewish sages, Ben Zomah, once found himself in a crowd of people. Some around him were probably complaining about being jostled by the masses. Ben Zomah laughed joyously and said, "Blessed is the Creator who has created all these people to serve me." Continuing, he mused aloud, "Think what Adam had to endure before he could eat bread. He ploughed, he planted, he reaped, he bound the sheaves, he threshed and winnowed, he ground the ears, and he sifted the flour. He then kneaded and baked, and then, at last, he ate, whereas I get up each morning and find all these things done for me. How much did Adam have to do to obtain clothing? He had to shear sheep, wash the wool, comb it, spin it, and weave it. I get up each morning and find all these done for me. All kinds of craftsmen come to the very door of my house and supply me with whatever I need."[2] Like Ben Zoma, I see other people as vital contributors to my well-being.

However, all this is true only if you want more money. If you are living on a park bench, panhandling passersby and feeling quite content with your life, you are unlikely to be motivated to do anything for me. If you feel that struggling through the month trying to figure out which bills to pay is just the way things are, you are unlikely to expend any energies trying to figure out how to supply some of the things that everyone else would like to have. If you feel you have made more than enough money and that now you should devote your years to improving your golf handicap, well, you aren't much good to me either. Although many different kinds of people in diverse situations are helpful in one way or another to their fellow humans, there is one group of people that is truly useful to everyone else—those people eager to earn more money. If you are in that group, then this book is for you.

THE RECIPE

You don't have to aspire to drive the Indianapolis 500 to learn valuable life lessons from the great racing driver Mario Andretti. He could probably teach you much about handling stress in everyday life and extracting peak performance from yourself. Likewise, you don't have to be Jewish to have access to the lessons of wealth that have been a part of traditional Jewish culture for centuries.

Take a look at the magazine racks next time you have a few minutes to visit a large book store. You will notice at least two or three monthly magazines catering to each and every interest, no matter how narrow or esoteric. Interested in learning more about model railroading? Start picking up those two or three journals each month and read them. Then visit your library and explore its section on trains. Sooner or later you will find yourself immersed in a new world with its own language, its own skills, its own merchants, and its own universe of enthusiasts. Soon your friends will notice that you have absorbed a new culture. New things interest you. You now choose to spend your time and money on model train layouts instead of on whatever used to excite you. Similarly, should you desire to find out more about body building, bicycling, or owning BMW motor cars, there is a world of wisdom out there and an entire culture awaiting you.

Making money is not so different from other interests. It, too, involves skills and requires immersion in a new culture. The one difference between making money, on the one hand, and bicycling or collecting model trains, on the other hand, is that the latter are some of the things you might choose to do with some of your time. You might take slices out of your life to indulge your hobby. You might devote an hour each day to working out at a gym. Although these activities enrich your life, they occupy separate little cubbyholes in your existence. They don't much shape how you live the rest of your life. If you play in a bowling league each Tuesday evening or race your sailboat on Saturdays, well, these activities also play little role in the rest of your life.

However, learning how to increase your ability to make money and produce wealth suffuses every aspect of your existence. It sometimes turns things on their heads. For instance, whenever I ask university students why they are studying, their answers invariably revolve around increasing their ability to earn money. Is gaining wisdom all about increasing wealth? No, of course not. The reverse is far truer. Gaining wealth is about increasing wisdom. You could be a hermit with no visible social life at all yet build and operate a remarkable model train layout. Very rarely does a person accumulate wealth without acquiring social skills. Does this mean that you should learn to get along with people in order to make money? No, of course not. But learning how to make money does inevitably improve your relationship with others.

This book makes the Jewish approach to money and wealth accessible and useful to anyone. It will describe some of the secrets of Jewish business success and will show how they can be adopted by all people, regardless of faith or background. You will explore this culture that has produced such disproportionate wealth; and you will find the tips, tools, and techniques that you will apply to your life. And the best part of it is that by doing so you will be helping those around you just as much as you help yourself.

Before identifying the powerful wealth-producing concepts that lie at the root of success, I need to dispel some incorrect notions.

FOUR FALSE THEORIES ABOUT JEWISH BUSINESS SUCCESS

There are four popular but false theories that are frequently advanced to account for Jewish business success. I will debunk each in turn, and then explore the truth. As with most falsehoods that endure, tiny kernels of truth are found in some of them. The falsehoods gain credibility and currency from the tiny truths they contain, but they obscure our investigation until put to rest. These four popular theories are:

1. Spurred by anti-Semitic persecution, Jews evolved by natural selection into a race of money-making geniuses.
2. Jews cheat. The 1971 edition of the *Oxford English Dictionary* sitting on my bookshelf defines the word *jew* as a verb meaning "to cheat or overreach in the way attributed to Jewish traders."
3. Jews secretly network and devotedly advance one another's interests.
4. The high average intelligence of Jews accounts for their fiscal talent.

Each of these four mistaken explanations can be refuted.

False Theory #1: Jews Learned How to Make Money Because of Natural Selection

This first explanation suggests that, wherever Jews were persecuted, poor Jews, unable to bribe their way to freedom, were caught and killed by tormentors, whereas rich Jews procured their escape and survived, free to breed. In order to take this explanation seriously, it would be necessary to believe in a sort of "money gene" buried in the DNA of Jews. Much in the way that the Darwinian theory of natural selection is believed to work, the money gene theory would mean that those with the gene were able to breed and retain the money gene in the Jewish gene pool. The only problem with this manifestly racist explanation is that no such gene exists.

False Theory #2: Jews Cheat to Get Ahead

The second fallacious theory suggests that Jews seize an advantage in business by cheating or by using excessively aggressive business practices. Although the occasional Jew may be dishonest, something that is true for every ethnic, religious, and racial group in the world, duplicity and obnoxiousness are hardly broad-based Jewish characteristics. And although it is true that in earlier times people disparagingly used the expression, "He jewed me down"—frequently without ever having met a Jew—nonetheless, I don't think that language usage reliably points to a Jewish cultural trait.

The Jewish guidebook, known in its totality as the Torah, a comprehensive blueprint of reality whose foundation is the Bible contains over five times as many laws dealing with *honesty in business* as it has laws concerning the kosher dietary rules. Furthermore, to accept the theory that Jews prosper primarily by cheating, we would have to accept that cheating, or being obnoxious, confers an advantage in business. But dishonesty and loathsome behavior only pay off in the very short term. Reputation is key. Sooner or later, the cheating, dishonest, and unpleasant business professional runs out of people with whom to conduct business.

In contrast, the story told to me by Southern California investor and health care entrepreneur David Holder is typical. David became his family's breadwinner at the age of 13 when his mother was abandoned in the small town of Moorhead, Mississippi. Its population then was 1500; you get to know folks pretty well in small towns. Struggling to support her family, Mrs. Holder worked as a waitress in the local café. David remembers being 13 years old when his mother sent him out to seek work. "You must find work with one of the four Jewish families in town," she insisted. "Start off by asking Harry Diamond to give you a chance." Harry Diamond, member of the Moorhead city council, ran the haberdashery store, Diamond's Department Store, that his late father, old Mr. Diamond, had started decades earlier. Harry hired the young boy and became his mentor, friend, and boss. David worked for him until he was 18 and to this day, David credits Harry Diamond's lessons and generosity with much of the enormous success that he has since enjoyed in business.

As I have traveled the country on business, many people have shared similar fond memories of warm friendships and honorable partnerships with Jews. Given the large number of long-term partnerships and business relationships that people of all backgrounds have enjoyed with Jews over the years, I have to dismiss this second theory.

Fasle Theory #3: All Jews Belong to a Secret Network

The third false theory hangs on the quaint notion that all Jews really do love one another and constantly seek opportunities to help one another.

This absurdity is about as true for all Jews as it is for all Christians, all tennis players, or all bald-headed men. It is certainly true that any large and united group of people who devotedly advance one another's interests would prosper. As a rabbi, I would have to admit sadly that as desirable as such fraternal feeling would be, it is simply not the case in the American Jewish community. Jews argue about everything. Somehow the more involved in Judaism and the Jewish community that Jews are, the more frenetic and intense their arguments seem to become. As the following joke illustrates, Jewish argumentativeness is so well known that it is central to the culture.

A young scholar was invited to become the new rabbi of a little old synagogue. During his very first Sabbath service, a hot debate erupted as to whether people should stand or sit during the reading of the Ten Commandments. Next day, the rabbi visited 98-year-old Mr. Katz in a local nursing home.

"Mr. Katz, I'm asking you as the oldest member of the community," said the rabbi, "what is our synagogue's custom during the reading of the Ten Commandments?"

"Why do you ask?" asked Mr. Katz.

"Yesterday we read the Ten Commandments. Some people stood, some people sat. The ones standing started screaming at the ones sitting, telling them to stand up. The ones sitting started screaming at the ones standing, telling them to sit down."

"That," said the old man "is our custom."

Here is another story about two Jews; unfortunately this one is not a joke. It is just as typical of what happens to Jewish partnerships that sour as it is of what happens to such partnerships between people of any faiths. Jeffrey Katzenberg, former studio chief at Disney, left his old friend, Michael Eisner, chief executive officer (CEO), in 1994 after Disney chairman Eisner denied him a sought-after promotion. The hostility escalated for about five years until it exploded into a court case. Katzenberg filed a civil lawsuit against Disney and sat quietly as the man who was once considered his closest friend, Michael Eisner, was forced to admit that he had probably said of Mr. Katzenberg, "I hate the little midget."[3]

Like everyone else, Jews do business with people they like and trust regardless of religious and ethnic background.

False Theory #4: Jews are Smarter than Everyone Else

The fourth false theory for Jewish business success is that, as a group, Jews possess unusually high intelligence. Whether that is true is unimportant; what is important is that it just doesn't matter. Outside of a broad range of acceptability, IQ is almost irrelevant to business success. Being super smart is as detrimental to success in business as is being just plain dumb. The story of Forrest Gump becoming a business mogul is just that—a movie story. It would not happen in real life. Someone whose IQ is simply too low for him or her to function may be a loving person and a fine worker, but not someone who is going to succeed as an entrepreneur in business or anywhere else. That is a sad fact of life. An IQ that slides way down the left-hand slope of the IQ bell curve, toward the low numbers, condemns you to fail in business.

That should not surprise you. However, here is the shocker: After decades in the rabbinate and around business, during which time I carefully and closely observed hundreds of people in dozens of occupations, it became quite clear to me that an IQ that slides down the right-hand slope of the IQ bell curve into the upper triple digits just as likely condemns you to fail in business. But wait! Isn't Bill Gates of Microsoft reputed to possess an unusually high IQ? Certainly he does; but remember, this book is not about becoming Bill Gates. Bill Gates is a rare aberration. He is an event that occurs only once or twice in any epoch when absolutely everything lines up perfectly. To be Bill Gates requires a very high IQ. However, to be astoundingly successful in business, say as successful as Sam Walton of Wal-Mart, one need only possess an IQ that falls within a very broad range of acceptability.

If indeed Jews as a group do enjoy exceptionally high intelligence, they succeed in business in spite of those scores, not because of them. Superbrilliant intellectuals become idiosyncratic chess players, or they tend to gravitate to the faculties of major universities. For the most part, they are notoriously inept at business and seldom become tycoons. They are often seen as brilliant, but not quite with it. To succeed in business, it is far more important to know how the world really works than it is to be brilliant. For every Thomas Edison, who both was brilliant and became affluent through his brilliance, there are many stories of creative inventors who died penniless and whose invention was later utilized and marketed by a much more normal person, who made his or her own fortune. The good news is that although it is very difficult to increase one's native intelligence, it is considerably easier to learn how the world works.

THE TRUE EXPLANATION FOR JEWISH SUCCESS IN BUSINESS AND MONEY MATTERS

If these four theories are false, what then does account for the fact that in country after country, century after century, Jews have consistently been at the top of the economic scale, despite battling prejudice and roadblocks every step of the way? Before I answer that, I should tell you a little more of what you can gain from this book. Although Americans believe in each person's ability to carve out his or her own life, it is childlike not to acknowledge that each person is born with certain gifts and blessings.

People like to think that everyone is born equal. However, some win the geographic lottery by being born in a free and prosperous country while others lose. Some win the genetic lottery in looks or athletic skills while others do not stand out in these areas. No matter how wonderful a human being I might be, I am never going to be chosen to succeed Queen Elizabeth as England's next monarch. No matter how much I love music and no matter how hard I practice on my piano, I am unlikely to succeed in becoming the conductor of the Vienna Philharmonic Orchestra. My son may enjoy sports; but with genetically determined height limitations, he is not going to be able to go one on one with Michael Jordan. These limitations condemn nobody to a life without power, music, or athletics, but each person begins life with a head start in some area and a handicap in other areas.

I had the great blessing and advantage of being born into a family that took God's word, the Torah, most seriously. Also, for generations, my family has devoted itself to probing and understanding thousands of years of Jewish scholarship that has emanated from the oral tradition of the written Torah. Most everything of value that I have learned about money and economic success is derived not just from my very limited personal experience, but chiefly from history's most enduring longitudinal study of the psychology and sociology of a financially successful people.

The principle foundations of this 3,000-year-long study are captured in Talmudic and Kabbalistic sources that can be fully comprehended only in their original Aramaic and Hebrew. They form the bedrock of my own belief system. It is the prism that resolves reality for me into its principle colors. It has deeply influenced my values and professional opinions, and I never try to conceal that. The Torah has much to say about financial interactions. Although originally delivered to the Jewish people, many of the principles are universal and are as true for any one individual as they are for any other, regardless of religious affiliation or lack thereof. These ideas constitute the core of this book and can be useful to you regardless of your background.

I have no ability to make you wealthy enough to find your way onto the *Forbes* magazine list of the 400 wealthiest Americans. I cannot rule it out either, but I would be foolish to guarantee you that stratospheric level of financial success. The techniques of this book will put you on to the road to maximizing what you can accomplish. You take it from there on your own. I don't believe that you can train to become Bill Gates or Warren Buffett. These are unique individuals for whom many factors of talent and timing came together in an almost magical way.

Similarly, I don't believe that anyone can promise a budding artist that he or she will be the next Michelangelo or guarantee that following a certain set of rules will make you president of the United States. But, there are very specific steps one can take that will help one become a better artist or a more successful politician than one might otherwise have been. In the same way, there are certain steps one can take that will lead one to greater financial achievement. Considering the disproportionate number of Jews on the Forbes 400 list each year, it seems that Jews do possess knowledge of the steps to take in creating wealth. Jews constitute about 2.3 percent of the U.S. population. That means that there should be about nine Jews on the Forbes 400 list. In reality, depending on the year, there are between 60 and 100 Jews on this prestigious list. Similar data for the more average population reveal that the percentage of Jewish households with income greater than $50,000 is double that of non-Jews.[4] I shall identify those steps that have made this success possible and present them for you. Following those steps may not bring you to the attention of *Forbes* magazine, but doing so will help you make far more money than you would otherwise.

KNOWING HOW THE WORLD REALLY WORKS

Certain fundamental principles detailing how the world works have been deeply ingrained in the Jewish people since the time of Abraham. Over the generations, even as many Jews have abandoned their spiritual source and forsaken their religious practices, these illustrative principles have lingered and remained powerful shapers of a people.

Let me give you an example. The Jewish people are known worldwide as "the people of the Book." This originally referred to the Bible. But a side benefit of the fact that Judaism always expected every Jew to be literate in order to read "The Book" was that Jews have always had a disproportionately high literacy rate and a respect for education. Howard Schultz, the CEO and chairman of the Starbucks coffee empire, describes how his parents scrimped and saved in order to send him to college. He wrote: "After four years, I became the first college graduate in my family. To my parents, I had attained the big prize: a diploma. But I had no direction. No one ever helped me see the value in the knowledge I was gaining. I've often joked since then: If someone had provided me with direction and guidance, I really could have been somebody."[5] Well, guess what, Howard? Someone did provide you with direction and guidance. It was those people who scrimped and saved in order to send you to college—your parents. They did implant in you traditional Jewish direction and guidance. They injected you with two ideas: (1) the conviction that one sacrifices present pleasures for future benefits and (2) a respect for the value of education. And they were pretty darn successful. You know how I know? It's easy. As a business consultant, I have studied your leadership of Starbucks. I know how many times you have sacrificed your present pleasures for the long-term good of your company, and I also know how much emphasis you place on and how much money you dedicate to education. Yes, I'd say your Jewish parents deserve much credit for your success.

Bookshelves and books are such an identifiable feature of a Jewish home that an acquaintance of mine tells the story of how, one day, she rebelled against the piles of books all over her family's living room. In a frenzy of orderliness, she banished all the books to other areas of the house desiring to have at least one neat room. A young man who had been courting her daughter visited their home for the first time. He was welcomed and invited to enjoy a cup of tea in this newly tidied room. Later, after the subsequent marriage, the young man informed his chagrined mother-in-law that on seeing no books, he almost turned around and walked back out the door that first night. His immediate conclusion had been that he couldn't possibly have anything in common with such a strange bookless family.

Just as cherishing books has remained a characteristic of Jewish homes, even of those homes not strongly identified as religious or even Jewish, there are many other characteristics that remain deeply imbedded in the Jewish psyche. These are characteristics that everyone seeking success should emulate until they become second nature.

Jewish tradition teaches that after you have done new things consistently for a while, you can feel yourself to have become a different person. One example that probably everyone has experienced is contrasting how you feel at the beginning of an exercise regimen with how you feel once you have been at it for a few months. What was an almost unendurable daily burden gradually stopped being painful and finally became an essential part of having a good day. The strenuous daily program started to give you a high of good feeling. You didn't just start feeling differently about an exercise workout, your very muscles, tendons, and tissues, your heart, and your lungs changed. One way of looking at it, and a fairly accurate way at that, is that you became a different person.

You probably already realize that acquiring more money will require that you learn not only new facts, but also new intuitions and new ways of responding to situations. Seeing oneself as having become an entirely new and different person is essential to any major growth step. It is an accurate perception. If you really grew, then you really changed. It is as simple as that. It is no accident that many fervent religious believers describe their spiritual advances in terms of being *born again*. Becoming a different person is not nearly as formidable as it sounds. Before I show you how to do it, let me show you why doing so is necessary.

SUCCESS REQUIRES LEARNING AND PRACTICE

Suppose you were interested in becoming proficient in self-defense. You might start by reading several excellent books on martial arts. Will you now be ready to fearlessly tread the mean streets after dark? Of course not. Imagine this scenario. As a malevolent arm snakes around your neck from the rear and a hard and cold object prods you in the ribs, you bravely reach into your hip pocket to locate your well-worn copy of *Everyone's Guide to Self-Defense*. You try to flip through the pages as you gasp for breath. Chapter seven, you recall, describes suitable responses to attacks from behind. Unfortunately, by that time the sad outcome of the unpleasant encounter will be difficult to change. It would not even have helped much had you memorized the contents of the book. The only way to improve your confidence on the streets in a meaningful way is to attend classes regularly and practice the moves until they become second nature to you. That way, when attacked, your body will automatically respond in mere milliseconds. You will react instantly, powerfully, and effectively because you bypassed the slow logic centers of your brain. To the utter dismay of your assailant, you will have become a new person—quite different from the fearful old victim he mugged last year.

The parallel to business will become clear when you recall some negotiation or other in which you thought of dozens of brilliant and inspired thrusts and counterthrusts. The only problem was that you thought of these illuminating points during the ride back from the meeting well after its conclusion. During the very transaction itself, you were so busy trying to keep up your side of the negotiation that you had no chance to let your genius shine forth. You obviously would have done better had you just been a different, more experienced negotiator.

How does one become a better negotiator? In much the same three-phase method that one becomes better at judo, better at omelet cooking, and better at writing poetry: (1) learn, (2) understand, (3) practice. Phase one is learning the techniques. Phase two is understanding those principles that lie behind the techniques. Understanding how those techniques work provides assurance that that they will work. Gaining confidence in the ultimate effectiveness of those techniques is important because it helps to provide the motivation to keep going with phase three. Phase three is doggedly and determinedly practicing, not only to become proficient in the technique, but also to become a different person.

When I emphasize the need for practice, I do so in the same spirit as the piano teacher urging her student to practice—it is how the material becomes part of you. This could be why I sometimes refer to myself as a *practicing Jew*. The implication is not that with enough practice I might one day get it right, although that may well be true, but that by consistently practicing the religiously mandated behaviors, by doing different things, I will integrate the desired habits into myself, eventually becoming a new person. You should feel comfortable with the idea of constantly practicing the techniques that will be discussed here and making them a regular component of your daily life.

WHAT MADE ME WRITE THIS BOOK

In 1978 I had the privilege of participating in the founding of a congregation in Los Angeles, which I then served for 15 years. For the most part, most rabbis who accept positions in existing congregations must adjust themselves to existing patterns and customs for fear of antagonizing longtime members. As the founding rabbi of Pacific Jewish Center, I was fortunate in that I was able to set the customs and the patterns that would shape the synagogue's future.

Hoping to emulate the patterns from ancient Jewish tradition, in which the community's leaders and teachers were themselves also engaged in earning their own livings, I too declined to accept a salary from the congregation. I look back on those years and sometimes think I may have been wrong about this; but I decided that instead of being a paid rabbi, I would take a job in business. I worked for several companies, including Merrill Lynch, supporting my family while gaining business experience, and later opened my own real estate finance company.

I well recalled the story my father would relate so frequently about the famous eighteenth-century preacher, Rabbi Jacob Kranz of Dubno, Lithuania. Shortly before the high holy days one year, Rabbi Kranz found himself visiting his friend and colleague, the equally famous Rabbi Elijah of Vilna, later known as the genius of Vilna. The latter invited his trusted guest, Rabbi Kranz, to help him probe his own moral shortcomings in anticipation of the forthcoming Day of Atonement. Rabbi Kranz thought for a moment and asked, "Are you really sure you want me to offer you criticism?" Rabbi Elijah answered that in his hometown of Vilna, he was held in such high esteem that nobody would dare help him confront the areas in which he could personally improve.

Somewhat reassured but still apprehensive, Rabbi Kranz obeyed the request and criticized his venerable host. "As the respected and well-compensated leader of the entire Vilna Jewish community, you enjoy the benefits of being able to spend your days in rabbinic research, prayer, and answering questions. You seldom even have to leave your home other than to attend services in the nearby synagogue. Obviously everyone thinks you are a saint. Why shouldn't you be? What real challenges do you ever have to confront? You have absolutely no idea at all of what life is like for ordinary people who have to struggle in the marketplace each day in pursuit of a livelihood. In the midst of a hundred daily opportunities for dishonesty and discourtesy, they still conduct their affairs honorably. During the coming Ten Days of Penitence, you cannot even begin to compare yourself with those members of your synagogue who are earning a living in business, raising their families, and are engaged in communal welfare."

As he reached the punch line to the often-told tale, a profoundly sad expression would always steal across my father's features. Looking much the way I imagined that Rabbi Elijah of Vilna looked on hearing those penetrating words of disparagement two centuries ago, my father would end the story thus: "And the genius of Vilna broke down and wept inconsolably." As his eldest son, I always sensed that my father, having spent his entire life in the rabbinate, felt that he too deserved the same censure. Certainly on some subconscious level, this part of my background played a role in influencing my decision to devote myself to two simultaneous careers, congregational rabbi and Los Angeles business professional.

In this way, my wife, Susan, and I enjoyed the enormous benefits of being our congregants' friends rather than their employees. This rabbinic status, common in Talmudic times but rare today, also granted me some other valuable benefits. I was able to regulate admission to my Torah study lectures, of which I delivered about seven each week. Because I was not a congregational employee, I chose to welcome only those who stimulated me and those whose presence contributed to the intellectual excitement of the sessions. Not surprisingly, most of the 60 or 70 attendees at each session were considerably more accomplished than I was. Some were directors of investment banking houses like Bear Stearns and Drexel Burnham, others were scientists at local aerospace concerns like TRW and Hughes, and some were well known in Hollywood's entertainment industry. I quickly discovered the truth of the Talmudic dictum of Rabbi Hanina, who said, "I have learned much from my teachers, even more from my colleagues, but I have learned most by far from my students."[6]

I carried the principle of rabbinic financial independence still further, maybe too much further. I declined to participate in what I felt was the somewhat clumsy arrangement whereby the clergy are usually proffered a check after officiating at a wedding or a funeral. I had noticed the discomfort experienced by my rabbinic colleagues at these life-cycle events when a proud bridegroom or a mourning relative would press an envelope into the rabbi's hands. The rabbi would furtively slip the envelope into a breast pocket, to be glanced at later. To me it seemed almost like a tip. My feeling was that the amount was seldom enough to compensate me at what I considered to be my hourly value but just enough to deprive me of the feeling of being a giver. When the well-intentioned tried to press the envelope into my reluctant fingers, I would awkwardly decline wishing that the circumstances would allow a full explanation for what might have sometimes appeared to be my churlishness.

Later it became clear to me that clergy in general, along with so many other people, feel uncomfortable with money. They feel demeaned by it instead of feeling proud of supplying another person's needs. Jews often recite a well-known blessing after enjoying the food purchased with the work of their hands. The ancient words express gratitude to God for creating human beings with deficiencies and needs. That blessing reminds Jews that helping other people make up for those deficiencies by supplying their needs is how one makes an honorable living. When you receive payment after supplying the needs of a client, a customer, your boss, or, if you are a member of the clergy, even a congregant, that money is testament to your having pleased another human being.

I realized that in spite of having possessed some theoretical knowledge of money, business, finance, and economics, I had utterly failed to internalize it and make it part of my worldview. In discussions with business professionals around the country, it became clear to me that I was not alone. Like them, my business performance was far below where it might have been had I only absorbed and applied all the spiritual rules of financial success. The business failures I suffered were all directly related to ignoring the principles of this book. I knew the commandments and rules in theory. I also knew that the exercise of writing this book would help me absorb these principles and make them part of my day-to-day living. I know that reading it will help you do the same.

The Torah, which is the basis of my knowledge of this subject, comprises 613 separate principles. These are categorized into 10 broad headings that we refer to as "the Ten Commandments." I have arranged the material that you need to be prosperous into a similar format of 10 broad headings, each of which encompasses many separate principles.

Believe in the Dignity and Morality of Business

Making money is much harder to do if, deep down, you suspect it to be a morally reprehensible activity.

If there is one Jewish attribute more directly responsible for Jewish success in business than any other, it is this one: Jewish tradition views a person's quest for profit and wealth to be inherently moral. How could it be otherwise? As I explained in the Introduction, who I am and how I earn my living are inextricably bound together. If your chosen means of contributing to the world, and incidentally providing for your needs and desires, is immoral, then you must stop doing it because it will inevitably taint your entire existence. If your life is bifurcated into the work arena and the social arena with the two never meeting, not even in your own mind, then that is one of the first repair jobs you should undertake. Step one in the process of increasing your income is to begin wrapping yourself around these two related notions: (1) you are in business, and (2) the occupation of business is moral, noble, and worthy.

As you will see, that view of business is not universally shared. Generally speaking, media, entertainment, and public education in the United States all subtly denigrate business. They tend to suggest that government and non-profit organizations do more for poor people than the private sector does and that business professionals need to be restrained from committing crimes in their single-minded pursuit of profit. It is not surprising that many other large groups in the United States have come to believe the same. This campaign has been so pervasive that everyone has inevitably been conditioned to believe it, at least to some extent. Believing that making money is a selfish activity will undermine anyone's chances of success.

FEEL VIRTUOUS, GROW WEALTHY

Most people understand that they enjoy greater success when they feel good about their activities. For example, in martial conflict, the defender's advantage is acknowledged by most military experts to be as much as five to one. This means that the defender's *conviction* of being *right* is enough to require a five-to-one superiority on the part of the invader in order for the attack to stand a good chance of success. That is because people tend to feel morally justified in defending their homes and families, whereas an attacker often *doubts* the righteousness of the cause. It follows that you would have vast additional power to inject into your enterprise if you could simply develop a deep conviction of its intrinsic morality.

This is how people are created. For better or worse, humans are holistic. Even the human body does best when its spiritual and physical sides are synchronized. Consider the role of placebos in modern medicine. Against their rational instincts, physicians are forced to recognize that placebos have some effect. Drugs are a vital element of medicine; the patient's mind is the second vital element. Considering placebos to be effective may seem primitive. Primitive beliefs that have been categorically refuted, such as the flat earth theory, are seldom controversial. The very fact that placebos are controversial tells me that a sizable number of credible physicians are persuaded of their efficaciousness. That is what makes the issue controversial. If all doctors agreed that placebos were worthless, the debate would be over. Why would a placebo have any therapeutic impact at all? People's bodies perform better when their brains and souls are on board with the program. This is why most people choose doctors in whom they have confidence. A patient's recovery is directly linked to how much confidence that patient has in his or her medical advisers. It is almost as if your body knows what is in your mind and responds accordingly. Helping your mind to know and believe that what you do professionally is good, noble, and worthwhile in itself helps to fuel your energies and propel your efforts.

If you feel really good about your profession, you sweep others along with you on the waves of your enthusiasm for what you do. You will become known for telling entertaining accounts of amusing incidents in your professional life. Stories about events in your business day can inspire others, and they will be moved by poignant interactions you relate. These natural and positive aspects of your public persona flow inevitably from feeling pride and passion for your work.

You see, increasing your ability to create wealth is not just a matter of knowing a technology. It is not just a matter of knowing what kind of investments to seek or knowing how to write a resume. Having additional money in your pocket, real spendable money, is not the same as having a pen or a cigar lighter in your pocket. A substantial and meaningful increase in the amount of money you own changes you. You become a slightly different person, and people notice the change. Now if extra money makes a new person of you, it easily follows that making a new person of you is a step on the road to having more money.

This is what it might look like expressed as a mathematical equation:

$$\text{Old you} + \text{More money} = \text{New you}$$

Now, subtracting "Old you" from both sides of the equation (remember that whatever you do to one side of the equal sign you must also do to the other), we have

$$\text{More money} = \text{New you} - \text{Old you}$$

In other words, in order to acquire more money, you need to work on far more than merely learning new skills. You have to work on changing yourself. It may not be easy, but it can certainly be done, and it works.

As a rabbi, I have always seen the Torah as a comprehensive guide to how the world *really* works. For instance, I expect no conflict between Torah wisdom and chemistry, and I find none. Both, after all, are instruments that explain how the world works, each from its own perspective. Thus chemistry might remind me that just as two atoms of hydrogen combined with one atom of oxygen results in one molecule of water, so can a molecule of water be split into its constituents, hydrogen and oxygen. In other words, in the real world equations can be read both forward and backward.

Similarly, if feeling passion and pride for my work helps me talk enthusiastically about what I do, so does talking excitedly about my work increase the passion and the pride I feel for it. This is why ancient Jewish wisdom insists that approval of our friends is an important aid to a person's business success; and likewise, people are stimulated and encouraged by their friends' approval. Even more important, this approval helps people find passion and enthusiasm in what they do.

Conversely, if you are embarrassed about your business, you set yourself up to fail. Few sales professionals wholeheartedly and effectively promote products or services they feel to be shoddy or overpriced. Not only does your moral ambivalence inhibit all-out effort, but it also triggers a shame reflex. Instead of winning the approval of people whose opinions you value, you feel them radiating an almost palpable disapproval for your profession. You shrink into yourself and appear apologetic and embarrassed. This is hardly the posture of success. As a result, you will fail to talk about your work, thus forfeiting the everpresent advertising opportunities that present themselves in ordinary social interaction.

Feeling virtuous about what you do is an enormous advantage and one that has been a part of Jewish tradition since time immemorial. Developing a deep conviction of the intrinsic morality and dignity of business injects vast power into any enterprise undertaken. There is a very real and practical reason that companies engage me to teach their executives and employees that the process and practice of business, although as vulnerable to misdeed as any other, is inherently dignified and moral. People who view themselves as ethical and virtuous are far less likely to step over a legal line than are people who feel that they are already deeply involved in improper conduct.

Have you ever cheated on a diet to which you were committed? I know that I have, and I recall how much easier it was to raid the refrigerator the *second* time. I remembered how I had vacillated back and forth three hours earlier. "How could I ruin the good efforts of the past week?" I had asked myself. My yearnings for that chocolate cream pie were strongly countered by the realization that if I yielded to temptation, I would be turning the entire previous week of discipline into a farce. That held me off for a while, but then my stomach enzymes began howling in chorus for just a taste of that chocolate cream pie. As my fevered imagination recalled the delicious taste, I blocked out the disturbing but ever-weaker calls of my conscience, and, I am sorry to confess, I yielded. The delicious taste, I discovered, was tempered by the slightly bitter taste of failure.

However, three hours later, when I found myself again lusting for just one more slice of the same pie, the voice of conscience was far weaker. After all, this time I would not be destroying a perfect record of disciplined restraint. I had already done that three hours earlier. What is one more little slice? Nothing really. One more little slice is never very much when you already consider yourself to have been slicing off more than you ought to have.

The Jewish principle underpinning this observation is found in *Sayings of the Fathers*: "Ben Azzai said, hasten to commit good acts and flee from misdeed since every good act encourages another in its wake, while every misdeed eases the way to the next."[1] This is one reason for the enormous emphasis that Judaism places on atonement. The origin of the word *atone* was when one viewed oneself as being *at one* with God. The annual observance of Yom Kippur, the Day of Atonement, allows Jews to reset the odometer of one's moral self-evaluation back to zero, as it were. God can once again regard us as being at one with Him. Turning over a new leaf and making a fresh start is enormously liberating. It allows one to recover one's morally driven self-restraint that might otherwise have eroded beyond the point of usefulness.

Similarly, in business everyone encounters numerous opportunities to slice off a piece of pie that would best be left alone. Everyone finds frequent opportunities to cross the line in pursuit of just a little more. Some businessman who sees himself as already a swindling rogue just by virtue of his occupation—a greedy business professional profiting by seizing the earnings of gullible fools—should have little trouble seizing just a little more.

No, you are not a swindling rogue. In reality, you are a noble person providing for others in a marvelous environment that benevolently rewards you for your consideration. You may find yourself smiling at these words; but once you have overcome your skepticism, you will have taken a giant step toward increasing your revenue.

MONEY IS HOLY, AND HOLIDAYS ARE LINKED TO MONEY

Indeed, overcoming one's skepticism about the nobility of money seems to be an intrinsic part of the original Divine plan for Jews as reflected in some of the Jewish holidays.

One Jewish holiday in particular seems to focus on money. Almost everyone knows that Jews observe Chanukah by lighting candles on each of the eight nights of the holiday. Far less familiar are two details concerning the celebration:

1. Part of the observance is for the light from those candles to have no utilitarian purpose. For this reason, they are customarily lit in a room in which other lighting, perhaps the regular electric lighting, is blazing. This allows the candles to serve their exclusive symbolic function and perhaps stimulate a discussion among family members. Someone may well ask, "Why do we have candles lit if there is already plenty of light in the room?" Another may inquire, "Can we turn off the lights so we can see the candles better?"

2. There is a custom of giving children monetary gifts on Chanukah. Like other people, Jews enjoy giving gifts of various kinds on all sorts of occasions. For instance, on Purim, the feast of Esther, people give gifts of food delicacies to one another. However, Chanukah is the only holiday on which not only is it not distasteful to give a gift of money, but it is viewed quite positively, especially for children.

These two quirks of observance are linked by their explanation. The definitive *Code of Jewish Law*, compiled in 1563 by Rabbi Joseph Karo of Safed in the Holy Land, emphasizes that absolutely no benefit should be obtained from using the light of the Chanukah candles. Then, conjuring up what we ought surely to condemn as an anti-Semitic stereotype, the Code declares, "And even to examine your money and to count how much money you have may not be done by the light of the Chanukah candles."[2] What! And I suppose that on all other occasions on which Jews light celebratory candles, such as those that usher in the Sabbath each Friday night, the first thing they choose to do is count their money? Hardly. The point is that on Chanukah you are supposed to be supersensitive to your money and particularly grateful for it. This is so central a feature of the Chanukah holiday that you might have been forgiven for supposing that counting your money in front of the holiday candles would be a way of enhancing the link between Chanukah and your money. Thus the *Code of Jewish Law* warns that you must not count your money by the light of the candles, even though you might have imagined that especially on this holiday that is exactly what you should do. You should certainly count your money on Chanukah, just not by the light of those special candles. They have a special symbolism that is linked to the money but just a little loftier. What does light symbolize to people? Well, if you aren't sure, take a glance at your Sunday comics and see what a light bulb shown above the head of one of the characters means. It usually suggests that Dagwood has just had a bright idea. That is why folks sometimes say, "I have seen the light," when what they really mean is, "Oh yes, I understand perfectly." Or someone might ask the person to whom he is patiently explaining something, "Do you see?" In reality, Chanukah candles are intended for only one purpose, and that is to signify education and understanding. Even the name of the holiday, *Chanukah*, is an expansion of the Hebrew word for education. This word comprises the first four out of the five letters making up the Hebrew word *Chanukah*. Yes, education and money are very closely linked, but who doesn't know that? Quite a few people in the United States today, it turns out.

Joining together the themes of the candles and the money, we find the reason for the custom of giving children money for each of the eight nights of Chanukah in amounts that are proportional to the success of their studies. The money is a reward for the *light* they have gained during the past year. In this way, early in their development, children are inculcated with the idea that not only is money not bad, but it often can be a result of self-improvement. You receive money in proportion to how helpful you can make yourself to other people. Chanukah is a reminder that educating oneself is surely one of the best ways of increasing one's potential to be helpful to others.

JEWS BECAME BANKERS TO HELP OTHERS, NOT AS A LAST RESORT

In Western culture, the term "moneylender" has come to be an insult and an indictment. Obviously people who view money lending, banking, or finance as sleazy and unworthy occupations are hardly likely to engage in them, let alone flourish in them. By contrast, Jews always viewed putting one's capital at risk to enable someone else to make a profit as an honorable way to earn a living and to help others. The Jewish hierarchy of charity regards lending someone money to go into business as more noble than simply giving him the money. The latter condemns the recipient to be a beggar without enough self-respect to launch his or her own enterprise. However, lending money to a needy man elevates him into an independent businessman. This way his dignity is preserved, and he retains the psychological self-image so necessary to conducting business successfully.

There is a popular historic misconception regarding how Jews in medieval Europe found themselves reluctantly thrust into banking. The theory argues that Jews turned to finance because of oppression and anti-Semitism on the part of the locals who denied Jews access to the various artisan guilds and other more desirable professions, such as farming. Left without alternative, claims this incorrect theory, Jews reluctantly turned to banking. In reality, this is not why Jews became bankers. In many enlightened Islamic countries during the same period, although there were few restrictions on Jewish occupations, Jews also found themselves engaged in banking and finance. Jews did not flee toward finance, they selected it at the outset. Although Jews were not driven into banking by anti-Semitism, there is nonetheless an interesting link between Jewish bankers and anti-Semitism, as Winston Churchill described in England at the end of the thirteenth century.

> In those days, when the greatest princes were pitifully starved in cash, there was already in England one spring of credit bubbling feebly. The Jews had unseen and noiselessly lodged themselves in the social fabric of that fierce age. . . . From time to time they could be most helpful to personages in urgent need of money. This led the English Jews into a course of shocking imprudence. Land began to pass into the hand of Israel, either by direct sale or more often by mortgage. For some time past there had been growing a wrathful reaction. Small landowners oppressed by mortgages, spendthrift nobles who had made bad bargains, were united in their complaints. . . . [King] Edward saw himself able to conciliate powerful elements and escape from awkward debts, by the simple and well-trodden path of anti-Semitism. . . . The Jews [were] held up to universal hatred, were pillaged, maltreated, and finally expelled from the realm. . . . Not until four centuries had elapsed was Oliver Cromwell by furtive contacts with a moneyed Israelite to open again the coasts of England to the enterprise of the Jewish race.[3]

Debtors discovered an easy way to escape their obligations. It was simple: Get rid of the Jews. With the departing Jews went the inconvenient debts. It may not be a coincidence that in 1925, Adolf Hitler penned these words in his book *Mein Kampf* (in English, *My Struggle*): "The best way to know the Jew is to study the road he takes. He comes as a merchant and with his thousand-year-old mercantile dexterity he quickly becomes active in finance and economics which soon become his monopoly."

Certainly Jews in Weimar Germany, between the two World Wars, did dominate the fields of banking and finance. This may have had something to do with their subsequent fate in that bloodstained land. However, the comfortable relationship Jews enjoyed with banking was far older than the Weimar Republic. The most famous Jewish banking house in Europe was that of the Rothschilds. Its reason for success is illustrated by the story of Prince William of Hesse-Cassel who in the very early 1800s needed to remain invisible while lending a large sum of money to the Danish court. Using Mayer Amschel Rothschild as an intermediary allowed the prince to remain anonymous. Denmark paid the interest regularly to Rothschild,[4] who reliably transferred it to the prince.

A few years later, Napoleon announced that the house of Hesse-Cassel would no longer exist. This conveniently meant that all money owed to the prince was to be paid to the French treasury. The French did not know the identity of the prince's debtors, but they suspected correctly that Rothschild did. Although they offered Rothschild a 25 percent commission on debts he collected and handed over, the old man remained scrupulously loyal to his royal client. Rothschild and his two sons surreptitiously traveled throughout Germany collecting all the debts due to His Serene Highness. It was not because of anti-Semitism that Rothschild became a wealthy banker; it was because he acquired a reputation of utter trustworthiness.

You see that although, historically, anti-Semitism may have been a consequence of Jewish domination of finance, it was hardly the cause. If it wasn't anti-Semitic oppression that drove Jews into banking, what was it? The main reasons that Jews found their way into the fields of finance were undoubtedly trustworthiness and their conviction that they were fulfilling a necessary need in society. When a merchant in Venice gave a sum of money to a local Jewish banker, the merchant could rest assured that his supplier in Amsterdam would receive the equivalent funds from another Jewish banker in Holland. What was so vital was that the two Jewish bankers trusted one another. It was this intangible system of trust that made commerce and wealth creation possible, but there was another reason, too.

Both Christians and Moslems accepted a rather literal interpretation of the Bible's prohibition against charging interest to borrowers. This absolutist view effectively eliminated banking as a profession for the faithful of those religions. A Jewish understanding of the Bible on the other hand, depends on what Jews refer to as the "Oral Torah," whose ecclesiastical authority fully matches that of its written counterpart. Jews believe that God taught the Oral Torah to Moses during the 40 days he spent on the summit of Sinai. It is from the oral Torah that Jews were able to learn under exactly which circumstances God permitted interest to be levied against a loan and precisely how that loan contract needed to be drawn.

As a result, Jews felt no compunction about earning their livings by brokering and providing capital loans. On the contrary, they felt that they were providing a vital and valued service. Obviously the field of banking, like any other field, presents its moral challenges. Some financiers have become notorious for extorting usurious rates of interest, but Judaism explicitly prohibits that kind of exploitation of unfortunate people. Some have violated the rules, but this indicts them alone and not the occupation. The fabulous profits that banking has generated for its many Jewish practitioners over the centuries came chiefly from Jews feeling that the profession was honorable and helpful to society. They were not only *willing* to become bankers; they were also *proud* and *eager* to do so.

GOLD IS GOOD: GOD SAID SO

Judaism literally bequeaths wealth to its adherents by communicating moral enthusiasm for the profession of business. One can find the roots of Jewish conviction in the morality of business right at the start of the Torah. Almost any child raised in a home that took Jewish scholarship seriously would have studied the first few chapters of the Bible before his or her tenth birthday, and the message of those chapters lies deep in the Jewish psyche.

During the seven days of Creation, the word *good* is used seven times as God brings various parts of the world into being and expresses profound satisfaction at how they came out, as it were. Amazingly, the eighth appearance of the word *good* is applied to nothing other than the eternal symbol of money—gold.[5] Right there, in the very beginning of the vast volume of the Torah, no more than 43 verses into the constitution of the Jewish people, gold, the ultimate medium of exchange, the metal of monetization, is described as good by God Himself.

As you can imagine, that verse not only made Jews very comfortable in the jewelry business, another profession where Jews have excelled in many countries; but the verse also established within the collective Jewish subconscious the idea that gold, a metaphor for money and wealth, is good. Although Jews have certainly experienced more than their fair share of poverty through the centuries, often arriving on new shores as penniless refugees, wealth was always seen to be a blessing. In a well-loved monthly prayer regularly recited on the eve of each new moon, Jews feel quite comfortable asking God not only for health and peace but also for prosperity.

It is perfectly kosher to ask God for money. If you are comfortable with prayer, go ahead and include a request for prosperity in your prayers. What you are really asking for is the opportunity to serve your fellow human beings. The Talmud advises worshippers in the Jerusalem temple who wish to increase their wealth to pray facing the south, toward the direction of the table that held the ceremonial bread, because the bread was mystically linked to money. The mystical master and thirteenth-century Kabbalist, Nachmanides, wrote of the ceremonial temple table and its showbread: "From the showbread upon the table came material blessings and economic abundance to all Israel."[6] He described the bread as a sort of economic kick start. (Strangely enough, even today, the idea linking money and bread lingers with us as we colloquially refer to money as *bread* or *dough*.)

Deep within traditional Jewish culture lies the conviction that the only real way to achieve wealth is to attend diligently to the needs of others and to conduct oneself in an honorable and trustworthy fashion. Jews feel at ease blessing children each Sabbath with the words: "May God make you like Ephraim and like Menasseh."[7] The Oral Torah fills in the gaps by explaining that Ephraim represents spiritual steadfastness and Menasseh represents economic creativity. The two belong together, and Jews wish their children to embody both.

The Sabbath blessing to Jewish children continues with the Biblical priestly blessing: "May the Lord bless you and safeguard you."[8] Again the Oral Torah, quoted by the authoritative commentator Rashi as well as by the nineteenth-century leader of German Jewry, Rabbi Samson Raphael Hirsch, explains the blessing to be for material wealth. The astounding news for the Jews was that God wants humans to be wealthy because wealth follows large-scale righteous conduct, which is His ultimate goal for His children.

As Tevye the milkman put it in the play *Fiddler on the Roof,* "I know it's no great shame to be poor; but it's no great honor either." In fact, the Bible emphasized the wealth of the Patriarchs; and along with other requirements, being rich was necessary for being chosen as a prophet during Biblical times. For instance, the Talmud records that not only did Moses himself possess enormous wealth, but so did most of the subsequent prophets of Israel: "Rabbi Yochanan in the Talmud said, God only allows his Divine Presence to rest on someone who is strong, wealthy, wise, and humble."[9] The wise King Solomon said: "The crown of the wise is their wealth";[10] and Jews have always understood that sentence to mean that God is happy with wise behavior and rewards it with wealth.

Not only does the Bible commence with an account that includes God's warm and positive opinion of gold, but as you read further, you can see that the story about the origins of ancient Israel reaffirms the theme. Again the Bible describes to its devotees the healthy outlook that legitimately acquiring money pleases God and is a positive experience.

Ancient Israel as a nation had its beginnings in Egypt. Each Passover Jews celebrate the Exodus from Egypt, highlighting the evening with a recitation of that escape. There is much emphasis on the haste in which they left the land of their subjugation, hence the unleavened matzos that are eaten because there was no time for the bread to rise. Yet in spite of their haste, it is clear that the ancient Israelites had ample time to take care of business. There may not have been time for bread to rise, but there was time for something far more important—obeying the Lord's instruction to Moses: "Let each Israelite request of the Egyptians silver and gold."[11] Later one reads: "The Children of Israel carried out the word of Moses; they requested from the Egyptians silver, gold, and fabrics. . . . the Egyptians granted their request and they emptied Egypt."[12]

Formed in the crucible of hundreds of years of Egyptian slavery, ancient Israel finally experienced the Exodus, departing into the desert with sufficient gold and silver to later construct the tabernacle and to establish their own Promised Land. This theme linking redemption and wealth constantly reappears in Jewish culture. Money certainly isn't everything, but it mustn't be underrated either. In fact, it is a legitimate component of any Divine redemption. It is no surprise that Jews have never been handicapped in business by feelings of moral confusion about money.

I realize that the fact that Jews possess this extensive cultural reservoir affirming the morality of business is not necessarily of help to everyone. You might regard the Torah and its prescriptions as irrelevant to a modern business practitioner, certainly to a non-Jewish one. But my purpose has been merely to demonstrate how the Jewish people, throughout their often difficult history, derived real business effectiveness and economic power from possessing a deep *conviction* about business being an honorable profession. This is what allowed them and, indeed, spurred them to succeed.

My task is to mark the path toward similar conviction for you. In my Introduction, I said that you must be more than a mere reader. You need to be an active participant in your own "redemption." You will need to walk your own path to conviction. The first marker on that path is to see most clearly how today's cultural forces defy your purpose. In that fashion, you will be able to design your own campaign to defeat those forces.

"CHARITY IS GOOD; BUSINESS IS SELFISH"— A POPULAR MISCONCEPTION

As a business consultant, I spend considerable time in the offices of men and women who guide the destinies of great companies. On entering a client's office, I nearly always try to examine the plaques and testimonials on the wall. Among other citations, I have discovered awards from local Rotary clubs, photographs of hospitals to which my clients have donated funds, and thank-yous for teaching classes to underprivileged youngsters. I make it a point to always identify at least one tribute that catches my eye. After studying it, I inquire about it in order to enjoy hearing the story behind the pictured benevolence. The business professionals are obviously proud of their philanthropic activity and, I believe, suitably so. They can be cajoled into talking about their pet causes and usually do so eloquently and passionately.

But I have noticed that it is much easier to persuade business professionals to talk about the good they do *outside* the office than about the immeasurable good for society they do by running their businesses. For example, John Walton is a son of the late Sam Walton, the founder of the highly successful Wal-Mart chain. John, himself high on the Forbes 400 list of wealthiest Americans, joined another tycoon, Theodore J. Forstmann, founding partner of the investment banking concern Forstmann Little, in setting up the Children's Scholarship Fund. This charity offers partial tuition scholarships for kindergarten through grade 12 to low-income families who want to send their children to a private school or educate them at home. The fund currently helps about 34,000 poor children in 47 states attend 7,000 private schools. Walton and Forstmann are rightly proud of what they have achieved and are not only attempting to vastly increase the fund's capacity to provide yet more scholarships but also actively encouraging others to do the same thing.

Seattle business professional and Jewish philanthropist Stuart Sloan has created and built several large and successful commercial enterprises, including the much-praised QFC regional supermarket company, of which he is the former chairman. In what is thought to be the largest gift to a single U.S. public school, Sloan is giving $1 million a year for eight years to the T. T. Minor Elementary School in Seattle's central area. Sloan wanted to transform the long-neglected school by focusing on "the whole child for the whole year, creating a year-round school with a strong academic program and enough staff to tackle issues that get in the way of learning."[13] Stuart Sloan is justifiably proud of what he is doing.

Do Walton, Forstmann, and Sloan and thousands of less well known good Samaritans feel the same pride about the good they do in their day-to-day activities? Tens of thousands of people are able to take care of their families because they have a good job at Wal-Mart. In addition, millions of U.S. families acquire their household needs at fair and advantageous prices.

Under Ted Forstmann's leadership, Gulfstream developed the new ultra-long-range business jet, the Gulfstream V, which not only enabled people to travel faster and accomplish more, but also provided jobs and security to thousands of workers.[14] I hope he feels as much pride in the success of the Gulfstream Aerospace Corporation as he does in the Children's Scholarship Fund he started. He ought to; those accomplishments are praiseworthy. Is Sloan as proud of the good he has done helping people through his commercial activities as he is of his achievements at the T. T. Minor Elementary School? More to the point, do the vast majority of Americans understand and appreciate what business contributes to their well-being? Do you feel the same pride in the good you accomplish merely by running your business as you do in the civic and charitable work you do?

YOU CAN'T EARN AN HONEST LIVING WITHOUT PLEASING OTHERS

Here's another example: I knew a young woman who made a fairly good living for herself and her daughter as a pharmaceutical company representative. She visited doctors' offices and introduced the caregivers to her company's new medications. She often would relate to me the sheer terror she felt on walking into a doctor's office in her sales district.

Then one day while visiting her office, I overheard her on the phone. She sounded brutal. First she begged, and then she threatened. She obviously wasn't going to take "no" for an answer. After a few minutes, she hung up the phone with a triumphant grin. "Got him to give a thousand dollars," she crowed. It turned out that she was raising funds for breast cancer research. When I asked why she felt so much more comfortable browbeating a contractor into a donation than a doctor into a pharmaceutical purchase, her shocking answer was "But this is for a good cause!"

Few people can truly excel at occupations about which they entertain moral reservations. That woman was convinced that raising money for medical research was good and worthy, while selling pharmaceuticals was selfish; it made her uneasy. When asked about her occupation, she tried to disguise it as something other than what it was. However, she frequently related how much money she had raised for charity. Why would she never have considered boasting about the commissions she earned the previous month? She was shocked when I suggested to her that her monthly commission check was a measure of how helpful she had been to the doctor, his patients, her own company, and the hundreds of other employees of her company who depended on her sales efforts. Deep down she must have felt that selling medicine clearly did nothing for anyone else. She might even have suspected that she was helping her company earn the kind of obscene profits that television pundits constantly condemn. She had no confidence that her method of earning a living was more moral than that of a snake oil salesman of yesteryear. Deep down she did not believe that she was doing the doctor and his patients a favor, while at the same time, of course, benefiting herself.

Consider this final example. A rabbinic colleague recently consulted with me. He wanted to know whether I thought he could augment his income by joining a multilevel marketing company in which his neighbor had been trying to interest him. I asked him if he understood what it would really entail on a practical level. I saw him shift uneasily from foot to foot for a moment before answering. He would have to try to "lure" all his friends, relatives, and associates making them consumers and distributors of his products, he explained. He saw himself as "using" his friends to further his own self-interests. It did not occur to him that he might just be the same answer to their dreams as his sponsor was to his own aspirations. It was clear to me that he would approach people as a *supplicant,* not as a *benefactor.*

My answer to him was that although many succeed, some brilliantly, in multilevel marketing companies, he was unsuited to the enterprise. Those who do succeed are filled to the brim with passion, enthusiasm, and conviction. I reasoned that my rabbinic friend's demeanor and his very words indicated to me that he would feel *uncomfortable* involving his social circle in his business endeavors. I told him that it seemed to me as if he thought he would be *exploiting* them. He nodded his assent. Continuing, I explained that unless he was capable of believing that by involving his friends and relatives, he was doing them the biggest favor imaginable, he should best seek an alternative avenue of enrichment. To really succeed in whatever is the business of your choice, you have to come to understand and utterly absorb into your being the fundamentally true idea that your activities in your business are *virtuous* and *moral,* provided of course that you conduct your business affairs honestly and honorably. Absorb this lesson into your heart and into your soul, and you will have overcome a major hurdle on your road to financial achievement.

You must respect the dignity and the morality of business. This is one of the most important reasons why Jews have enjoyed economic success over the generations, and it is one that, regardless of your own background, you can use, too. You will just need to find your own way to seeing the beauty and the nobility in how you earn your living. It is far more than merely seeing yourself as an honest and good person. You must come to see that part of your goodness, part of the benefit you bring to others, is your daily conduct in operating your business enterprise. Whether you work in forestry, pharmaceuticals, or other industries that incur the wrath of the culture, whether you make widgets or run a small flower shop, you must understand the nobility inherent in going to work each day. The rule is that people seldom excel at any occupation that deep down they consider unworthy; and even if they are neutral about the morality of business, that neutrality is a weak reed on which to build success.

HOW WE ARE ALL PERSUADED THAT BUSINESS IS EVIL

If at this point you are wondering how anyone could feel that making money is immoral, let me assure you that everyone is subtly influenced by the culture surrounding us. More and more, that culture has been beaming out a negative view of business and businesspeople. Even the pro-business *Hi and Lois* cartoon presupposes that Lois's son has never been exposed through school, reading, or television to the shocking idea that business professionals like his dad can be heroic. Increasing numbers of Americans view wealth not as the morally legitimate rewards of risk, innovation, and effort, but as an unjust and morally suspect outcome. So pervasive is the message that almost nobody is completely immune to its insidious effects. And it comes from a broad cross section of sources: education, the media, even business professionals themselves.

Reprinted with special Permission of North American Syndicate.

HOW WE ARE TAUGHT THAT BUSINESS IS BAD, FROM EARLY EDUCATION

It is sad that everyone seems to have been conditioned to moral skepticism regarding business. Imagine watching a high school teacher asking each of her students in turn to tell the class what career path they were interested in selecting and the reasons why. One boy stands up and announces, "I want to become an environmental consultant so I can ensure clean air and water for all." Everyone cheers. The next student informs the class that she wants to become a medical researcher in order to find a cure for AIDS. Everyone applauds wildly. Another student reveals that his dream is to become a teacher, ". . . so that I can help poor youngsters step on to the elevator of the American dream." Everyone gasps in admiration at the idealism of the future educator. Finally, the last girl is asked of her plans. She furrows her brow for a few moments and then slowly and clearly says, "I want to become a highly successful business executive so I can improve the world and make a difference in many people's lives." I think that in most schools guffaws of raucous laughter would greet this perfectly reasonable statement.

This is not such an imaginary lesson. Between 1990 and 1995, Germany lost nearly half a million jobs. Although some of the economic battering experienced by the Germans during this period might be attributable to costs incurred in the reunification of East and West Germany, the German weekly magazine *Wirtschaftswoche* presented a different explanation. It claimed that the sad economic performance of the country whose industry gave the world the term "Economic Miracle" was due to Germany's educational establishment spending the previous three decades *teaching kids that money is a bad thing!*

Wirtschaftswoche surveyed the country and revealed that 40 percent of Germans say they regard entrepreneurs as "exploiters," up from 17 percent since the last poll in 1965. They discovered that a majority of 16- to 19-year-olds, presumably an age group ready for risk, says "no thanks" to the idea of starting a business. The older age groups who attended school prior to those years and escaped the educational antibusiness indoctrination showed far more enthusiasm for entrepreneurial activity.[15] When organizations, countries, or companies allow themselves to believe that making money lacks social value, they should not be surprised to see their economic performance decline. The same holds true for individuals.

MOVIES AND TELEVISION CONSPIRE
TO MAKE YOU POOR

In his book *Hollywood vs. America,* my long-time friend Michael Medved wrote that prior to 1965, television shows portrayed businessmen as good guys twice as often as bad guys. This ratio was reversed in the 1970s, when audiences were treated to two business villains for every good guy. Medved points out that during Hollywood's Golden Age in the 1930s and 1940s, businessmen frequently appeared in a highly sympathetic light. "In the 1933 George Cukor classic *Dinner at Eight,* Lionel Barrymore played a decent and dignified shipping magnate, struggling to keep his company afloat,"[16] and in the cherished family film *It's a Wonderful Life,* Jimmy Stewart's character George Bailey is a humane, compassionate, and likeable *banker*. Today, the very idea of a likable banker has become unthinkable. Big business has become the media's favorite villain.

This evolution was noted by business columnist Daniel Seligman in his *Forbes* magazine article, "Tom Cruise versus Corporate Evil."[17] Seligman wrote that the movie *Mission: Impossible 2*, the number-one movie of summer 2000 in 25 countries, was also the new number-one "prototypical antibusiness movie." *Mission: Impossible 2*'s villains set up an elaborate scheme to get rich off "stock . . . stock options, to be a little more precise"—at which point, Seligman wrote, "we know we are dealing with ultimate evil."

An exhaustive analysis of prime time television by sociologists Robert Lichter, Linda Lichter, and Stanley Rothman concluded: "Clearly the business of TV's businessman is crime. In fact, this is the only occupational group on television that is disporportionately involved in crime."[18] Even television children get the message that business professionals are evil. Lichter, Lichter, and Rothman describe an episode of *Diff'rent Strokes* in which two brothers go into business selling brownies. After accepting an order too large for their fledgling business to fulfill, they enlist the help of their sister. Instead of accepting her wish to be made a full partner in their business, they offer her a meager salary as their employee. "That's what business is all about," the boys tell her. "You do the work and we get the profits."[19]

Journalist Marc Gunther put it this way: "Power crazed media moguls blackmail members of Congress. An agribusiness giant poisons an Indian reservation. A famed Texas CEO hires a hit man to gun down his ex-girlfriend. If you missed these stories from the world of commerce, you haven't been watching television lately. They're examples of an unmistakable trend: the rise of corporate villainy in prime time."[20]

In one television episode of *Walker Texas Ranger*, the CEO of fictional Agri-Feed Company foists an untested animal feed additive onto a Native American reservation, murders his corporate counsel, wipes out dozens of Native Americans, and sends in a private army to cover up the mess. "Billions in future profits, for the lives of a few Cherokees," the CEO sums up.

How about the 1997 "fact-based" movie called *Two Voices* about two women who heroically exposed the dangers of silicone breast implants. Forget about a fictional villain. This cable television movie demonized a real corporation, Dow Corning, which the Food and Drug Administration (FDA) and the Justice Department had investigated and exonerated. Dow, it turned out, had indeed disclosed all known safety risks associated with implants. Furthermore, mainstream science has now debunked the central claim that silicone implants cause terrible diseases. In the movie with an agenda, one of the noble heroines asked, "How do these guys at Dow Corning sleep at night?" Her husband helpfully explained, "Dow is like any other corporate entity. Their board answers to the stockholders."

For further evidence, peruse a special report on television (TV) programming from the Media Research Center in Alexandria, Virginia, whose researchers watched a mind-numbing 863 sitcoms, dramas, and TV movies broadcast by ABC, CBS, NBC, and Fox. The researchers' findings: "Businesspeople tend to be portrayed as venal and unscrupulous. They engage in criminal behavior. As a group, corporate types commit more murders on TV than any other occupational category—even career criminals. Heroic CEOs, meanwhile, are scarce. You see lawyer heroes and cop heroes, but it's hard to do a TV show about job creation or investment, laments Tim Lamer, co-author of the report titled *Businessmen Behaving Badly*."[21]

In Michael Pack's brilliant, made-for-PBS (Public Broadcasting System) special, *Hollywood's Favorite Heavy: Businessmen on Prime Time Television*, one screen writer, Philip De Guere, creator of the television series *Simon and Simon*, admitted that not only had he been making villains of businesspeople but that he was "going to do more of it." He wasn't done. "It's something that everybody can identify with and is consequently probably pretty close to the truth," he said. The narrator of *Hollywood's Favorite Heavy*, Eli Wallach, noted that corporate executives on TV "seem to make an awful lot of money, without ever having to work hard or produce useful products. To succeed, all they seem to do is lie, cheat, blackmail, even murder."

In one of his articles decrying the popular culture's tendency to demonize business professionals, journalist and author Michael Fumento pointed out that businesspeople are portrayed as greedy:

> "Greed—for lack of a better word—is good," proclaimed corporate raider Gordon Gekko in Oliver Stone's *Wall Street*. This is Hollywood's vision of the businessman. And whether it's on the big screen or on the boob tube, businessmen applying Gekko's vision of the world regularly shoot, slash, poison, blackmail, extort, and smear their way to the top. And businessmen, Hollywood style, aren't getting any better. In the second *Aliens* movie, Sigourney Weaver's character, Ripley, accuses the representative of the otherwise unnamed entity "The Company" of sending 157 colonists to a horrible death of being cocooned and ripped apart by vicious alien creatures. The representative simply replies that, "It was a bad call." Later he tries to block the attempt of other people in his party to avoid hand-to-hand combat with the aliens by going into orbit and blasting the planet, explaining that along with the aliens, they would be destroying a facility with a "significant dollar value." Finally he attempts to have Ripley and a little girl impregnated with the horrible alien embryos in order to slip the alien creatures past quarantine and be rewarded by The Company. Back here in the twentieth century, the Washington-based Media Institute has found that by the age of 18, the average TV viewer has seen businessmen attempt more than ten thousand murders and countless lesser offenses, all in the name of greed.[22]

And although *Wall Street* represents the "go-go" 1980s and even though *Aliens II* is not a recent film, this trend continues. Playing to the culture's antibusiness mood, Hollywood continues to routinely cast business professionals negatively. *Wall Street, Boiler Room, Tomorrow Never Dies,* and 2002's summer hit movie, *Spiderman* feature business moguls as villains. It is difficult to think of movies or TV shows that depict business professionals as heroic or even morally neutral. You might remember the hilarious and popular hit *Trading Places,* starring Eddie Murphy, that Paramount Pictures made in 1983.

The villains of the piece were two brothers, businessmen who ran a large securities and commodities trading company. They were depicted as a pair of heartless, racist, swindling tycoons. In general, our entertainment establishment seems intent on portraying those who successfully earn their living in business as evil, psychotic, or both.

Listen to *Vanity Fair* columnist Christopher Hitchens: "At least in fiction and in motion pictures, the businessman is most commonly cast as a villain. . . . In the movies, the instant the camera pans up the towering and glittering skyscraper, you just know that there is a corporate villain lurking on the top floor."[23]

Perhaps you are saying to yourself, "Who cares what entertainment shows? Everyone knows that the movies are fiction."

WE CAN'T HELP BELIEVING SOME OF WHAT PEOPLE TELL US

Let me tell you a Bible story, from the second book of Samuel, that you may never have heard. Its entire purpose is to educate the Bible reader to this one simple and inescapable fact: You cannot help believing some of what people tell you.

Once on a time, a long while ago in a far off land, there lived a great and good king called David. When he was not winning wars or growing his nation's economy, he was composing beautiful music and writing the book of Psalms. God was so proud of him that He decreed that the future Messianic line would descend from His favorite ruler, David.

Many years earlier, long before he became king, David had a dear friend, crown prince Jonathan, who was the son of King Saul. Although King Saul made several attempts on the life of David whom he rightly saw as his son's rival for the crown, David's affection for Jonathan never wavered. And although Jonathan knew he would never be king after his father, he displayed no petulance and loved his old friend as before. Not surprisingly, the names Jonathan and David became synonymous with true friendship.

After the collapse of the royal house of Saul, instead of executing his former enemies as was the charming custom of the day, David was careful to treat all the now unemployed appointees and officials of Saul's court with dignity and magnanimity.

"Are there any survivors of the House of Saul for me to rescue and help for the sake of my old friend Jonathan?" asked King David. A fellow by the name of Ziva informed the king that an infirm son of Jonathan had survived. David summoned the poor cripple, Mephiboshet, for whom Ziva was now working, and said:

"Don't be afraid. I will deal kindly with you for the sake of your late father Jonathan. I will restore to you the entire estate that belonged to your grandfather, King Saul, and you will always be welcome in my palace." You can imagine how relieved and grateful Mephiboshet must have felt toward the new king, and he pledged eternal loyalty to his benefactor.

Soon after David became king of Israel, his own son, Absalom, launched a rebellion. Messengers came to David with the news that large numbers of the population had joined Absalom. Aware of his son's ruthlessness, David assembled his loyalists and called out, "Arise, let us flee, there will be no escape or mercy from Absalom."

Unbeknown to David, as an act of loyalty, Mephiboshet tried to accompany the king, but was hindered by his handicap. Instead, he sent his employee, Ziva, to transmit his pledge of support. A day or two later, while on the run, David spotted the crafty old courtier. Calling to him, David asked Ziva how his boss, Mephiboshet, was doing.

The treacherous villain responded, "I come alone bearing gifts for you, oh, King. Mephiboshet remains in Jerusalem hoping to exploit the chaos by restoring himself to the throne of his grandfather. He is part of the plot against you."

"Is that so?" thundered the angry king. "From today, all of Mephiboshet's estates are now yours." Ziva could scarcely conceal his glee at how well his plot had succeeded.

The rebellion finally ended and King David returned to Jerusalem. Mephiboshet visited the king and hobbled into the throne room.

"Why didn't you go with me when I fled from Absalom? Did you join my late son, Absalom?" King David sadly accused the son of his old friend.

"Of course not, my dear king" said Mephiboshet. "At the time of the crisis, Ziva advised me to stay home on account of my physical handicap, while he would join you and lend his support on my behalf. Then the perfidious scoundrel slandered me to you, telling you that I had betrayed you and joined the rebellion. Heaven forbid, I would never have done such a thing. I remain deeply indebted to you for all you have done. Please don't believe this story."

King David held up his hand and said, "Say no more, my dear Mephiboshet. I am assured of your good faith. Tell you what, why don't you and Ziva share the estate of your late grandfather."

"Let him just have it all" answered Mephiboshet despondently.[24]

Needless to say, Jewish tradition lavishes pages of attention to the unexpected end of this story. Why didn't David yank the estate back from the wicked Ziva, punish his duplicity, and return the entire property to Mephiboshet, its rightful owner? Why, instead, did David leave the rogue with half his ill-gotten gains and restore only half to the good and loyal Mephiboshet? The Talmud regards this as an enormous failure on the part of King David. For this mistake in judgment, God later punished David by splitting his land into two during the days of his grandson Rehoboam. But the question of how David misjudged the situation remains.

David was a smart and effective ruler. How could one as familiar with human nature as he was have said to the faithful Mephiboshet, "Why don't you and Ziva share the estate of your late grandfather?" The Talmud provides an answer that is a frightening glimpse into human nature: Once you admit a lie or a slander into your ears, you can never totally rid yourself of its effects. You may think that you have expunged the information from your memory, but its impact will be with you forever.

Intellectually, David knew that Ziva had misled him with that vicious slander of Mephiboshet. However the *emotional* impact of the anger he had originally felt on hearing that Jonathan's son had betrayed him lingered within him. Although he knew in his head what had really happened, the judgment of his heart was impaired by his having once heard the slander. This is the lesson of that story and the main reason it is recounted in such Biblical detail. You may think that you can remain uninfluenced by the things you hear, but it just isn't so.

MANY PEOPLE BELIEVE THAT BUSINESS IS INHERENTLY BAD

Understand that it is very unlikely that you have not been at least slightly impacted by the culture's slander of business. If the story of King David doesn't persuade you that everything seen and heard on television profoundly, if subconsciously, affects all viewers, perhaps the billions of dollars spent on advertising will do so. Shrewd corporate executives would hardly invest the unimaginable sums they do in television advertising if doing so played no role at all in influencing the way people thought.

For those doubtful of how successful the campaign to discredit the worthiness of business has been, *Business Week* featured a cover story entitled "Too Much Corporate Power?"[25] that quantified American attitudes toward business with poll numbers:

- 72 percent of Americans agree that business has gained too much power over too many aspects of American life.
- Only 47 percent agree that "in general, what is good for business is good for most Americans" (down from 71 percent in 1996).
- 66 percent agree that "large profits are more important to business than developing safe, reliable, quality products."
- Only 27 percent thought that business had "fair and reasonable prices, relative to their profits."

While certainly admiring the achievements of many of today's wildly successful young entrepreneurs, many Americans have become conditioned to distrust the morality of business. One can almost hear the popular applause when large companies have their wrists slapped by government bureaucracies. Individuals possessing little familiarity with the complexities of antitrust law, for instance, enthusiastically encourage legal action against conspicuously successful enterprises. Some of this can be seen as requiting of envy, which is in itself destructive. But much also springs from widespread sentiment that both companies and individuals only prosper at the expense of other invisible victims. When companies are penalized by obscure governmental regulations, they are surely only getting what they deserve.

Even those champions of business whom one would expect to be defending the institution of business shy away from insisting on its intrinsic capacity for virtue and morality and, instead, concede the altogether false point that business is about greed. The twist they introduce is brazenly proclaiming greed to be good. *Industry Standard* magazine once featured an article called "The Gospel of Greed,"[26] which observed the growing popularity of Ayn Rand's theories of Objectivism, based on turning selfishness into a virtue.

There is an overwhelming problem with simply dismissing business as being an expression of greed—a reprehensible greed but one that somehow also helps a few lucky but unworthy people. The majority of decent, hardworking Americans regard greed and selfishness not as virtues but as vices. For this reason, attempting to defend business by conceding that business is about greed—but, never mind, greed is actually good—is doomed to fail. The notion that business is good because it is greedy will never win people's hearts and minds. Foolishly claiming that business is about greed merely confirms the growing cultural conviction that business is, at root, fundamentally immoral—that even if commerce may be necessary for a healthy economy, it is a necessary evil. Best-selling author Dinesh D'Souza sums up this idea: "Capitalism has won the economic war, but it has not yet won the moral war."[27]

POPULAR CULTURE SUPPORTS IMMORAL "LOVE": MONEY IS BAD, BUT SEX IS GOOD?

What I find most amazing is how the U.S. culture encourages people to take a far sterner and more judgmental view of business and our appetite for money than of any other human appetite. You may or may not read *People* magazine, but any journal with such a large circulation cannot be totally ignored. It does reflect the values of a large part of the United States. It is amazing that to celebrate Valentine's Day in 1996, *People*'s cover story was "The Greatest Love Stories of the Century,"[28] which described some of the legendary couples of the century. Try and fill in the missing names: Richard Burton and . . . yes, that's right, Elizabeth Taylor. How about the future King Edward VIII of England and . . . Wallis Simpson. Frank Sinatra and Ava Gardner, Clark Gable and Carole Lombard, and Spencer Tracy and Katharine Hepburn were some of the other couples recognized as "the greatest love stories of the century."

It is interesting that the magazine failed to mention that at the time of his great love story with Liz, Richard Burton was married to Sybil, the mother of his two young daughters. It also neglected to note the fact that Wallis Simpson was inconveniently married to her husband, Ernest, when she met her prince. Somehow, Frank Sinatra's wife and three children at the time of his adulterous relationship with Ava Gardner also didn't make it into the article. When mentioning Clark Gable's greatest love story, the magazine does confirm that it was not with his wife at the time, Ria Gable, but with Carole Lombard. Likewise, Spencer Tracy's great love story was not with his wife, Louise Tracy, but with Katharine Hepburn. In fact, more than half the couples being lauded in this remarkable cover story were committing the old-fashioned sin of adultery.[29] Do I really need to mention that not only were these relationships not condemned, they were being presented as romantic tales?

As these things sometimes happen, it was exactly two weeks later when another magazine ran a contrasting cover story. This one was not about love, romance, and sex, it was about business and money. It was not an objective view. Instead, the *Newsweek* cover story entitled "Corporate Killers" featured photographs of business leaders like Louis Gerstner of IBM and Robert Allen of AT&T that had been doctored to resemble police mug shots. The story concerned layoffs. "Call it 'in-your-face capitalism.' You lose your job, your ex-employer's stock price rises, and the CEO gets a fat raise. Something is just plain wrong when stock prices keep rising on Wall Street while Main Street is littered with the bodies of workers discarded by the big companies."[30]

Journalist James Glassman rightly pointed out that although the story was chock-full of anecdotes and opinion, *there was not a single employment statistic.*[31] No wonder! Between 1991 and 1995, the number of Americans newly employed had grown by 7.2 million. In other words, while some companies were shedding workers, other companies were hiring workers; and far more people were being newly hired than fired. *Newsweek* stated that a total of 137,000 workers had lost their jobs in the companies highlighted in the story and held the story's Corporate Killers responsible for the loss. Yet *Newsweek* failed to mention that the U.S. economy during that period was adding 137,000 new jobs every three weeks!

Depending on your outlook, you might feel that the actions of *Newsweek*'s featured CEOs, the Corporate Killers of the article, were indeed evil. Or, you might be among those who feel they were doing what was necessary to ensure their companies' survival and the preservation of many more jobs that would have been lost had the companies foundered. Whichever way you feel, it is clear that *Newsweek* offered only one side of the story—the CEOs were evil. Clearly *Newsweek* felt confident that its readers would not protest and, indeed, few did.

Two kinds of men cause pain. One is the corporate chieftain who fires an employee, and the other is a man who commits adultery. Who inflicts more pain? Who has caused more irreparable harm? Who has grievously damaged more people? Is it not true that a betrayed spouse suffers more pain than a fired employee does? Is it not also true that it is more likely that a fired employee will find other employment equal to or superior to his or her ex-job than it is that a betrayed spouse will recover a happy marriage? Is it not obvious that in most cases when an adulterer destroys a marriage, more people are damaged than when a person loses a job? It would seem clear that a compassionate culture ought to censure more vigorously someone who commits adultery than it does the department head who fires unneeded employees.

Yet *Newsweek* and the *Weekly Standard* make it clear that the opposite is true. Adultery, betrayal, and shattered futures are merely irrelevant collateral damage to the great love stories. But lost jobs, in an environment that created thousands of new jobs for every one terminated job, is reason to condemn those executives as corporate killers. Here is the message that the culture is broadcasting: If you cause unbearable pain to others while in pursuit of your sexual pleasure, you will find understanding and sympathy. However, if you are a businessperson causing even the slightest tinge of discomfort to others while in pursuit of profit and wealth, you will immediately and unconditionally be condemned as immoral.

It is actually even worse that this. Academics such as David Waldstreicher, a history professor at Yale University, considers profit to be altogether wrong. Waldstreicher said, "Capitalism is about extracting profit from others, and for that reason usually raises ethical issues."[32] How do you *extract* profit from others without being arrested for theft? Nobody extracts profit from anyone. Ordinarily one sets a price for the goods or services one wishes to sell. Customers either materialize and purchase those goods or services, or they don't. If they do, one earns a profit. If customers spurn your offering, then you fail to make a profit. Where does the *extract* come in? It doesn't, of course, but using the word betrays what the good professor really thinks of business.

This is a very strange double standard—zero tolerance for real or perceived financial wrongdoing, but infinite empathy for sexual wrongdoing. Again you can see that the American culture condones almost anything in pursuit of sex but tolerates very little in pursuit of money. The two appetites are looked at quite differently. Understanding why cruelty is excused in the pursuit of sex but not in the pursuit of money has been helpful historically to Jewish entrepreneurship, and it can help everyone today.

Journalist Michael Kinsley wrote, "The most significant political story of 1998 is not that the president had oral sex with a 22-year-old White House intern. The most significant political story of the year is that most citizens don't seem to think it's significant that the President had oral sex with a 22-year-old intern."[33] During the same period, journalists everywhere deemed Microsoft's monumental profits to be significant prima facie evidence of wrongdoing in the antitrust arena.

HUMANS ARE NOT JUST "SMART ANIMALS"

Applying principles of ancient Jewish wisdom to this double-standard conundrum yields the following explanation. On some subconscious level, humans find it convenient to view themselves not as very special beings touched by the finger of God, but rather as just a bunch of very smart animals. The smart-animal view of humanity is convenient because it liberates people from complex moral analyses of their lives: In the same way that no animal ever looks disapprovingly at itself, neither should I. As far as science knows, animals never experience the pain of shame. If humans view themselves as just smart animals, then they are freed from any discomfort at their own actions—they would never have to reflect on whether some thoughts they allow into their minds are indeed worthy. If humans are sophisticated animals, but animals nonetheless, everything they do is genetically predetermined, and they are less morally accountable.

Judaism argues that it would be hard to maintain the sort of society necessary for humans to live in comfort and security if nobody feels any moral self-accountability. There just would not be sufficient police. Even if there were, there wouldn't be enough police to monitor the police. Thus, humans cannot be animals in nature—they must be far more. The Jewish view allows that infidelity may indeed be genetic, particularly for males. There is truth in the frivolous old aphorism that claims that women tend to seek one man for their many needs while men tend to seek many women for their one need. Nonetheless, although men may be genetically predestined to want many women, Judaism insists that, unlike animals, men do not necessarily need to act on that call of nature. Overcoming nature is an essential element of Jewish faith. "It is natural" has never been an adequate defense for immoral behavior in the Jewish legal system.

Much of the sense of etiquette is derived from Jewish ritual protocol and is based on distinguishing humans from animals. For instance, people prefer not allowing their bodies to emit loud noises in public. Why not? What could be more *natural*? Although embarrassed by the recollection, I must confess that one of my mother's favorite phrases when I was a small boy was, "Stop sounding like an animal!" I was offending the vital human sense of being different from animals.

Similarly I was actively discouraged from combing my hair and scratching my underarm itch in public. "It makes you look like a baboon," denounced my long-suffering mother. "Well, what's wrong with looking like a baboon?" I would ask. "God made them, too." Yes, He did, but He made humans different and unique. That is fundamental not just to Jewish faith, but also to the structure of Jewish society, trust, business, and wealth creation. Why do people raise their food to their mouths instead of lowering their mouths to the plate? Judaism views the dining table as a contemporary replacement for the long-destroyed altar whose purpose was to raise the material to the level of the spiritual. The head represents a person's spiritually lofty component, while food is a material commodity. Seated at the dining table, either the material can be lifted to the spiritual or the spiritual can be lowerd to the material. As unique and special beings, people prefer doing the former rather than resembling animals in doing the latter.

It is this Godly view of human beings as spiritual entities that allows people to view that completely nonanimal activity of accumulating wealth as good. Wealth creation is partially how people express their spirituality. Of course, it is an *unnatural* act—no animals in nature ever do it—but overcoming nature, all nature, especially human nature, is what Judaism sees people as obligated to do. If people are nothing more than the rational animals that Aristotle considered them to be, then business may well be exploitative. It is certainly unnatural because no other creature on earth engages in behavior even remotely similar to business. To the Jews, however, most of life's little rituals are designed to help them *overcome* nature. Not relieving themselves whenever and wherever the urge overtakes them as animals do is part of that ritual. Humans overcome nature, as it were, by restraining themselves until they can enter an appropriately private place called a bathroom. But the popular culture prefers to view humans as nothing more than sophisticated animals. And, like all other animals, following their nature therefore is quite, well, natural.

Thus the popular culture looks at the sexual strayer not as a weak or wicked man or woman making a dreadful decision to betray the marriage vows and to inflict terrible pain on the family, but merely as an innocent victim swept up by the maelstroms of romance. Adultery is the altogether natural consequence of genetic conditions (hey, he's a man isn't he?) and intense hormonal activity (hey, she fell in love, didn't she?). This approach reassuringly confirms their animal origins.

However, financial straying, as it were, fails to confirm animal origins. On the contrary, it disturbingly hints at humanity's unique and spiritual origins. No animals have developed or have ever used a system of money. Animals merely seek their sustenance, whereas humans actively create theirs. The thirteenth-century Jewish transmitter, Rabeinu Bachya, explained that a man's active participation in the creation of his wealth is a mark of his spiritual greatness. Thus, according to the misleading popular culture view, even using money as a basis for much of human interaction becomes a suspect activity. It feeds the conceit that humans are actually far more than merely superintelligent animals. Owning money or property, again not done by animals, becomes questionable among those flaunting their moral vanity. They suggest that maybe using money is what causes humans so much unhappiness; after all, animals that spurn the use of money seem to live charming, natural lives.

This would help explain why the popular culture reserves the height of its criticism for those who make their livings in the most abstract monetary manner. While shopkeepers, particularly those in lower income neighborhoods, are often excoriated and, on occasion, even have their properties vandalized and torched, the voice of the culture does not play along. Very few endorse the destruction by announcing that the shopkeeper "had it coming." However, when the activity is more abstract than retail sales, when the activity is in finance or the creation of exotic new forms of investment instruments, for instance, the media are often quite unsympathetic. People tend to be more tolerant of activities that would fit a materialistic and animalistic worldview and less tolerant of activities that are uniquely human and spiritual.

It is almost as if the culture yearns to tear down anyone whose activities suggest that there is more to life than the material. Religious figures are particularly attractive targets. No figure is more eagerly and joyfully welcomed for front page prominence than the roaming rabbi, the prurient priest, or the concupiscent clergyman. In the same way, those who occupy themselves by making a living in business are also defying the materialistic stereotype and become unwitting enemies of naturalistic materialism and its spokespeople.

Who would ever have thought that part of business success is getting involved in the philosophical debate about the nature of man? You might say, "Spare me the heavy thoughts. I just want to get rich." Judaism's lesson is that it seldom works that way. Everything is linked through the magic of cause and effect. It may have been the butterfly flapping its tiny wings in Brazil that caused the storm in Boston, or maybe it wasn't. But it certainly was the conviction that humans are uniquely spiritual creatures touched by the finger of God that was partially responsible for astounding Jewish economic success.

EVEN BUSINESS PROFESSIONALS THEMSELVES HAVE GIVEN UP THE FIGHT

Even many M.B.A. students believe that capitalism is a tool of the devil, claims the dean of the business school at Arizona State University (ASU). One of his students recently wrote: "Capitalism is the source of all poverty." I can understand why that student hates commerce and the free market. If I were sure I had located the source of poverty, I would hate it, too. After all, Jewish scholarship[34] compares poverty to death, in that choices are dramatically limited in both those unenviable conditions. A professor of legal and ethical studies in the College of Business at ASU says about her students: "Many of my students are deeply offended by high levels of executive pay, deplore stock options, and believe that a company's gay-rights position is a litmus test for morality. . . . They believe that business spawned the homeless. They take it for granted that businesses cheat and are oddly resigned to it."[35]

I hope you don't feel that I am overdoing this, but it is almost impossible to overestimate the degree of cultural indoctrination. Just think about how easily people all accepted the label that the Internal Revenue Service (IRS) uses for interest, dividends, and capital gains—"unearned" income. Surely this label trivializes the productive and noble process of assuming risk and investing capital. It is precisely by taking control of language that ideas can gradually be changed. It is, of course, only a short step from calling investment income unearned income to the idea that there is something unwholesome about making money through investment. It is another even shorter step to the idea that people should not be entitled to the benefits of money they acquired through investment, because it is money they did not really earn. But I am less interested here in public policy than I am in how this subtle cultural indoctrination has handicapped your ability to really prosper.

Whenever a notable philanthropist makes a public gift, there is one phrase you can count on hearing. It is "giving back to society," as in "Isn't it wonderful that he is finally giving something back to society." Is referring to a charitable contribution as "giving back to society" implying that the for-profit activities that created that wealth in the first place are somehow "taking from society?"

Theodore Williams, chairman and CEO of Los Angeles–based Bell Industries, Inc., one of the nation's largest distributors of electronic components, has this to say: "Self-interest has its place, but we're going to extremes now. We've got all those people who have a great deal of wealth, like Bill Gates, but when you look at it, they give a pretty small portion of it to charity."[36] Poor Theodore fails to even consider the possibility that Bill Gates does quite a bit for the world even before making his very large charitable foundation bequests. After all, creating thousands of jobs and supplying magical software that allows millions to do their work and to communicate seamlessly with one another are in themselves rather large contributions. Theodore also fails to question entertainment and sports figures who undeniably "have a great deal of wealth" yet are notoriously stingy in their charitable giving. Apparently such criticism is reserved for people who earn their living through business.

HOW STARBUCKS DOES GOOD WORKS—EVERY DAY

Unfortunately, even business leaders themselves sometimes fail to see how people's respect for business can be subtly eroded by phrases like "giving back." Instead of emphasizing how much good it does for so many people during the daily conduct of its business, Starbucks Coffee Company recently published a twelve panel pamphlet entitled *Giving Back*. Beneath the headline banner *Giving Back*, this colorful booklet, available in every outlet, proudly announces: "A Guide to Starbucks in the Community." I don't mean to point a finger at a good, Northwest company that I admire. Countless corporations adopt the same public posture that disparages for-profit activities. Let me tell you what Starbucks wants you to know about how they "give back to the community."

- Its employees put in many hours of volunteer time for local nonprofit groups, such as AIDS walks and serving meals for the homeless.
- Each Starbucks store chooses a charity to receive its leftover pastries.
- Starbucks corporate contributions focus on literacy, AIDS outreach, environmental awareness, and the arts.
- Starbucks has Green Teams who continuously review ways to recycle.
- In some coffee-origin countries, Starbucks pays a premium above the purchase price of coffee to fund local education and health projects.

This is all very meritorious, but I would have preferred the pamphlet to have been called *Doing Good* rather than *Giving Back*. I would have welcomed a Starbucks pamphlet that also told of the tens of thousands of people who have fine jobs with many benefits because of Starbucks' success. I would have enjoyed reading about how retired Americans who own Starbucks stock enjoy a better old age because of the company's fine financial performance. How about mentioning that many Starbucks outlets have become little community gathering places? They function like warm oases because of the company's generous policy of not hurrying people away from the comfortable seating and pleasant atmosphere just to make room for the next round of customers. I am sure that the corporate public relations people could have found even more good things that Starbucks does through its regular day-to-day conduct of its business. It would have been nice to read of it.

I don't object to companies choosing to pay more for their raw material, choosing to recycle, or making corporate contributions. I don't even mind if they trumpet these high-minded actions from the rooftops. But I worry that people are already absorbing the essential message gleaned from the tone of these types of publications. Their tone is all too clear: The only good done in society today is done by government and by other non-profit organizations. They suggest that anything at all to do with profit is tainted and furthermore taints everything with which it comes into contact. The Starbucks brochure I refer to almost possesses a tone of moral redemption. It seems to be saying, "Look, we are sorry that we are a successful, large, multinational, highly profitable organization. But hold on, we aren't all bad. Read this and see how many really good things we do to make up for the fact that we earn large profits."

BAIN CONSULTANTS CAN TRANSFER TO "MORALLY UPLIFTING" WORK

Here's another example of a business not transmitting the message that running for-profit activities is inherently doing good for the world. Bain and Company is one of the country's preeminent strategic consulting firms. It has started a division that provides low-cost consulting services to U.S. nonprofit charities. Bain executives who do work for the nonprofit division have to take pay cuts that range from 20 percent to 80 percent of their customary salaries. This is because the fees that Bain and Company charges its nonprofit clients are typically about 20 percent of what it would charge for-profit corporate clients. So what does Bain get out of this? Thomas J. Tierney, Bain's worldwide managing director and father of the idea for the new division, explained to the *New York Times* that some Bain executives feel unworthy because they do no more than "helping condiment makers squeeze more profits out of their factories."[37] Rather than leave the organization, they can take a morally uplifting break and serve the new nonprofit division.

Apparently more than one-third of Bain's 2,400 full-time professionals have volunteered to work at the new division. Apparently over 800 men and women who are the top advisers to U.S. business are not convinced that there is something worthy and virtuous in helping a mustard manufacturer thrive. If such sophisticated professionals can fall victim to this sad mistake, I must assume that on some level everyone is being subtly indoctrinated.

MOST PEOPLE WORK "IN BUSINESS"—AND THERE'S NOTHING WRONG WITH THAT!

I want you to understand the extent to which people are subjected to a relentless barrage of negativity about how they earn their livings and why it is important to everyone. While you may think the way you make your living has little to do with how CEOs of major corporations make theirs, the fact is that with very few exceptions, most people develop revenue by doing or supplying things for others. That is called business. Unless you are a justice of the Supreme Court, a tenured professor, or a rabbi with a lifetime contract, you are probably in business. You may well be an employee; but like an independent business professional, you can find a new customer, which is to say, you are free to seek and find a better job. Just like an independent business owner, you too can find an *additional* customer—you can take a second job or develop a part-time home-based business. You undoubtedly have many products or services that could improve the lives of those around you. No matter what you do, the odds are that you are in business, and it is much tougher to succeed if, deep inside, you lack respect for the dignity and the morality of business. If the heads of Fortune 500 companies are being excoriated as immoral exploiters, so are you. The difference is only one of degree.

You can easily imagine what an enormous competitive advantage is acquired by the business professional who really believes—no really, *really*, believes—with every microscopic molecule of his or her being that doing business is one of the most moral and best things to do. Only if you understand the extent to which your chosen profession is vilified by so many of those among whom you live, do you stand any chance at all of expunging the subtle self-hatred from your own soul. Again, I assure you that if any lingering remnant of moral repugnance for business still lurks in your heart, you would best find another occupation. Once you realize how stealthily this notion that business is immoral insinuates itself into your mind, you can be ready for the crucial preparation for success: extirpating the false notion from your own heart.

The next step is discovering some of the virtues and aspects of morality in business.

YOUR PATH TO PROSPERITY

- *Begin embracing these two related notions: (1) You are in business, and (2) the occupation of business is moral, noble, and worthy.* If your life is bifurcated into the work arena and the social arena with the two never meeting, not even in your own mind, then remedying that gap is one of the first repair jobs you should undertake. To really succeed in whatever is the business of your choice, you have to come to understand and utterly absorb into your being the fundamentally true idea that your activities in your business are *virtuous* and *moral*, provided of course that you conduct your business affairs honestly and honorably.

- *Offer to write a short column or op-ed piece for your local newspaper that would forthrightly declare the profession of business to be noble and moral,* and explain why. When asked to deliver a short speech for any organization to which you belong, offer as a topic the morality and the nobility of business.

- *Read business nonfiction regularly.* Make sure that you are always in the middle of a pro-business biography. Use your local library, the Internet, and other resources to locate works by and about people who loved business. There are many gems from the late nineteenth and early twentieth centuries such as Russell H. Conwell's *Acres of Diamonds,*[38] as well as more contemporary books. Eventually you will come to find this enjoyable, and your soul will be infused with enthusiasm for the culture of business. Create your own small home library of this kind of material.

- *While reading, watching television, or seeing a movie, remain on high alert for subtle (and not-so-subtle) swipes at the dignity and the morality of business.* Identifying these gratuitous slurs helps to combat their subconscious impact on your being. Remember how you felt compelled to avenge insults when you were back in high school? You knew that you would feel compromised and unworthy if you stood by silently as the class thug made rude remarks about your mother. Speaking up, although difficult, would make you proud of yourself and make you feel closer to your mother. Here, too, your feelings about your work undergo a boost each time you defend your profession.

The Second Commandment

Extend the Network of Your Connectedness to Many People

Befriend many people who are a rung or two above and below your financial level, then find ways to help them achieve their desires. You will have discovered the secret of Partnership Power.

Stepping out of the Washington Hotel near the White House in Washington D.C., one frigid January evening, I felt so cold that it was all I could do to hold up my hand and hail a passing cab. I was on my way to deliver my first speech at the National Press Club, which I didn't know was just around the corner from my hotel. I felt an almost sensual pleasure sinking comfortably into the soft seat of the warm cab. Glancing out the window at the arctic wind blowing litter down the sidewalk, I smiled at my pleasant situation and instructed the driver, "National Press Club, please."

"Sir, that's just around the corner," he told me. I was crestfallen. Just around the corner may not be far to walk on a pleasant day or even on a reasonably unpleasant day, but it might as well have been a hundred miles across frozen tundra that evening. The prospect of exiting the comfortable cab was unwelcome, but I reached unenthusiastically for the door handle. "Please wait," the cabbie said, "I'll drive you there." I felt foolish but grateful. A few moments later the driver pulled up before the Press Club building, and I reached for my wallet. "Oh, no, sir, there will be no charge," he assured me. "I am happy just to do you a favor. I saw how cold you were; and anyhow, my grandmother always said that what goes around comes around."

I murmured a silent prayer for his grandmother and asked him for his card so I could try to employ him for other trips I would need to make across the city. I glanced at the Pakistani name on the card he had given me and marveled at this humble immigrant's grasp of what I call "Partnership Power." He had forged a relationship with me that absolutely compelled me to call him two days later for my long trip to Dulles Airport. I later came to know him quite well, and he drove me around on more than one subsequent visit to the nation's capital. Sayed's faith is Islam, but he obviously knew and practiced the second commandment by relating to other people as real people and doing things for them.

HOW TO BUILD RELATIONSHIPS? LEARN FROM YOUR PARENTS

Jewish tradition classifies the real Ten Commandments of Scripture into two categories: (1) those that dictate the relationship between man and God (the first through fifth commandments) and (2) those that dictate the conduct of humans toward one another (the sixth through tenth commandments). It is interesting that the fifth commandment reads, "Honor your father and your mother, as the Lord your God has commanded you so that your days will be lengthened, and it will be good for you"[1]—and this commandment therefore is the transition between the God section and the human section. In other words, according to Jewish tradition, you honor your parents not to please them, but to please God.

This Biblical commandment provides the original schematic for you to learn the principles of bonding with all the people around you, not just your parents. It also discourages you from viewing others as nothing more than instruments of your own desires. It all starts with your parents.

Who were the very first people you ever got to know? You won't actually remember the first time you saw those large faces beaming happily at you. It wouldn't be until much later that you would know that those proud people making cooing noises at you were your parents. Those strangers rapidly became the source of all your comfort and security, and they were the very first people with whom you developed a relationship. It is not surprising that to

Jewish culture, the relationship with your parents, captured in the fifth commandment, lays the foundation for the science of human relationships.

Ancient Jewish wisdom questioned[2] one aspect of this Biblical fifth commandment. In the sixth, seventh, and eighth commandments, only the bare directive is issued. The Israelites are warned not to steal, not to commit adultery, and not to murder; no reasons are given. The fifth commandment, however, gives a reason for its directive. God seems to be saying that you ought to honor your father and mother if you wish to enjoy a long life. Therefore, ancient Jewish sages asked the obvious question: Didn't God realize that sooner or later almost everyone would hear of a child who devotedly honored his parents and yet died prematurely in some tragic accident? Yes, many people who did honor their parents nonetheless died young. Why would He promise long life as a consequence of observing that commandment? Doing so could only serve to undermine faith.

The answer, explains Rabbi Moses Maimonides in his code of Jewish law,[3] is that this commandment is different. People who obey God and refrain from theft, adultery, and murder are unlikely to do so because of an ulterior motive. Nobody says, "Okay, I won't kill this irritating manager because I don't want to jeopardize my 'employee of the month' award from Human Resources." Or "Okay, I will not have an affair this week because I want my wife to bake my favorite cake." This is all quite improbable. However, you could easily find yourself obeying this fifth commandment, which is the root of all human relationships, with an ulterior motive in mind. You might be thinking, "Honor my parents so that they will give me what I want." From that, one might then extrapolate: "Be nice to other people in order to get what I want."

That some who honored their parents nonetheless died young is so obvious that the meaning must lie a little deeper. And sure enough, Jews have always understood the commandment of honoring parents as instruction to do so exclusively for the sheer joy and goodness of honoring parents. Only when performed with no shred of self-interest can the fifth commandment bring blessings of long life in its wake. Those blessings are bestowed in a statistical kind of way as if to say, any society that teaches its citizens to act benevolently toward one another without thought of ulterior motive will be a society that develops healthy longevity trends. The admonition and its consequence are best linked when viewed in the context of an entire community. Accidents will always occur; however, in general, if the citizens of any given society learn to honor parents and relate to other people for the sheer joy of doing so, then citizens of that society will enjoy longer lives that are actuarially verifiable. Actually verifiable? Yes, by examining the opposite.

STAY CONNECTED TO OTHERS: YOU'LL BE HAPPIER AND LIVE LONGER

Here's some evidence. According to a landmark study involving 222 cardiac patients and carried out by Nancy Frasure-Smith of the Montreal Heart Institute, patients who suffer heart attacks and are depressed are four times as likely to die in the following six months as those who are not depressed. Charles Nemeroff, professor of psychiatry at Emory University of School of Medicine in Atlanta, studied postcoronary patients and found that depression was the number-one factor in their deaths.[4]

And the number-one cause of depression? Dr. Gunnar Biorck examined 223 cardiac patients in the town of Malmo, Sweden, and found that the most serious medical problems were encountered by these patients *after* they left hospital. He wrote that a special problem in convalescence is the lack of contact with friends, neighbors, and family. Under those conditions, feelings of loneliness and then depression present themselves.[5] Health and human companionship do go hand in hand, says Dr. James Lynch in his book *The Broken Heart: The Medical Consequences of Loneliness.*[6]

FRIENDSHIPS LEADS TO WEALTH, RATHER THAN THE REVERSE

Health is not the only benefit that results from developing and maintaining a large circle of human relationships; wealth is another. Relationships can lead to transactions, and transactions can lead to wealth. Sitting around wishing for more money accomplishes nothing. Daydreaming or reciting self-affirmation mantras accomplishes even less. Only by actively and perhaps even joyously interacting with other people can the circumstances of wealth creation be set in place. In general, people prefer doing business and engaging in transactions with other people with whom they already have a relationship. It is too late to try to form a relationship with a potential transaction beckoning. Relationships need to already exist for the transaction to occur.

But remember the lesson of the Biblical fifth commandment: Honor your father and mother for the sheer joy of doing so, rather than to benefit yourself. Similarly, try to win friends not in order to influence people for your benefit, but for the sheer joy of forming and maintaining human relationships. Paradoxically, only in that way will you stand the best chance of enhancing your life.

I was always bothered by how Dale Carnegie titled Part One of his book *How to Win Friends and Influence People.*[7] He called it "Fundamental Techniques in Handling People." I know he didn't mean for it to sound so calculating, and I've found much value in his excellent book. But do you really want to be friends with someone who is figuring out how to *handle* you? Don't for a moment think you won't realize that someone is trying to manipulate you.

Everyone can sense when someone's interest is not sincere. For example, my only encounter with William Jefferson Clinton, the man who later became the 42nd president of the United States, was at a Los Angeles fundraiser for Clinton, the Democratic candidate, during 1992. He was conversing with me in an animated, intense, but somewhat mechanical fashion. Meanwhile, his eyes were constantly darting around the room. Although he feigned interest in me, it was clear that he was seeking a more rewarding guest on whom to lavish his attention. It wasn't long before he identified such a target and with perfunctory good wishes, he turned from me and made tracks across the room. I'm not criticizing a politician, but this encounter shows that people know when someone's interest in them is insincere. That is why this subject is so important—it simply cannot be faked. You are simply going to have to learn how to relate to strangers with the sincere warmth and interest that turns them into friends.

It is often said that the way to get all the things that you want is to give enough other people the things that they want. Although there is obviously considerable truth in that maxim, it is a terribly misleading maxim, and one that will not serve you well. Certainly the road to financial success is to come up with a product or a service that a lot of other people desire or need—and can afford. You might be producing or selling computer software or providing housecleaning services. You might also be selling your services as a sales professional to the highest bidding potential employer. The more people who are eager to purchase your software, the more homes that are desperate for your housecleaning services, or the more employers that bid for your skill in sales, the better paved is your road to success. It would appear that getting what you want can be achieved by giving enough other people what they want. However, remember the lesson of the Biblical fifth commandment. Trying to give other people what they want only to get what you want does not work very well in the long term. Somehow people sense the ulterior motive. Perhaps it is an air of desperation that you exude.

On the face of it, the Biblical fifth commandment advises building genuine and sincere relationships with as many people as possible with no thought of reward. Beneath the surface, it informs you that paradoxically, reward will follow in proportion to the lack of self-interest you projected while forming the relationships in the first place. The success everyone seeks is, in terms of this fifth commandment, only a reward for building those relationships that the Author of the Ten Commandments wanted His children to form anyway.

Consider this true story of success. January 2, 1924, was a bitterly cold day in New York, but Richard Simon had promised to visit his grandmother who still called him by his Hebrew name, Reuven. During his visit, he discovered that along with her neighbor, his grandmother loved doing crossword puzzles. The two elderly ladies kept one another company during the long winter evenings, working together on the crossword puzzle printed each Sunday in the *New York World*. The problem was that they usually completed the puzzle by Tuesday. Richard sat thinking for a while. His grandmother's eyes lit up when he asked her whether she would enjoy an entire book of crossword puzzles. "If only such a thing existed," she said. Richard persuaded his friend, a fellow he called Linc, to join him in creating and publishing a book of crossword puzzles. The subsequent *Crossword Puzzle Book* became the foundation of a publishing empire for Richard Simon and his pal, Lincoln Schuster, two young Jewish boys from New York.[8]

FIND OPPORTUNITIES TO MAKE MANY FRIENDS

If there is one lesson to be found in Jewish business success, it is this: Find opportunities to become friendly with many people. Jewish communal life undoubtedly offers a head start. Each day commences with a visit to a synagogue for a brief morning service. Traditional Jewish prayer rules call for a *minyan*, a quorum of 10 men present. Just think about it: 10 men may not sound like much, but the chances are surprisingly high that at least two of them share a birthday. You would need 366 men to guarantee that at least two share a birthday, so you'd expect the chances of a shared birthday among only 10 men to be pretty low. Instead, a short calculation shows the probability of a shared birthday in a *minyan* to be as high as 10 percent. Ten is a good number, not too many to be cumbersome, and not too small to be irrelevant.

Sharing a birthday is not the best basis for a relationship; but my point is that among 10 people, many more valuable commonalities will emerge than birthdays, especially if you were to meet those 10 individuals on a basis that was regular enough for friendship to result. If, on a business trip, you had just arrived in a strange city, on your very first morning there, you would go to the synagogue and meet at least nine other men. If each other person there had a circle of, say, 10 other business friends, then you would have suddenly acquired access to 180 potential new friends in a city in which you had just arrived the previous evening. In conversation after services, you would find something in common with at least one of the other people there. It might not be a shared birthday, but it would be something more important. Perhaps two of you are in similar or complementary businesses, or maybe someone there knows someone whom you need to meet.

You're probably saying that morning prayer service is not designed for making business contacts. Of course, it isn't, but remember that the idea is to make contacts specifically in an environment that does not shriek out your self-interest. This is why regular involvement in a civic service organization, such as Rotary International, does far more for your business than attending a professional breakfast whose only purpose is to allow attendees to exchange business cards. Rotary allows relationships to develop within an environment of *caring for others*; any subsequent business benefit is secondary to those friendships, which is just the way it works best. Those professional breakfasts do not build relationships; they are merely opportunities for self-interested and ambitious people to advertise their business. For the most part, those events tend to attract mostly people who, like Cassius in Shakespeare's *Julius Caesar*, have a "lean and hungry look."[9] It becomes apparent almost immediately to those who are enjoying some success, and they stay away from future events, in droves.

In contrast to those meetings intended only for business professionals to work the room distributing business cards, Rotary and similar organizations attract all kinds of people, including those who are already very successful. The reason these occasions work so well is simply that most people would rather spend time with professionals gathered for the purpose of helping others, not self-interested people advertising themselves. Prayer services are another perfect place to meet people without the stink of self-interest con-taminating the relationship building taking place. That is why attending morning *minyan*, although certainly not intended directly for this purpose, helps business in the Jewish community. (The identical dynamic serves singles seeking a mate. Hanging out at singles' events and bars telegraphs a message of pathetic desperation to every other single present. Far better to meet a suit-able person at work, at church, on an airplane, or at some social event where the subtle-as-scent process of relationship building won't be overwhelmed by the smell of the hunt.)

For the traditional Jewish community, however, morning minyan is just the start. There are services each Sabbath, both on Friday night and on Sat-urday morning. Very often, the Saturday morning service is highlighted by the celebration of a bar mitzvah, the coming of age of a young man. This attracts still more attendees, both friends and family members, many from out of town.

There are many happy events to attend in addition to bar mitzvahs. Jews go out of their way to attend circumcision parties whenever a baby boy is born, and they love to attend weddings. Is it gauche to conduct business while attending the wedding of your second cousin's daughter? Of course, it is. During the wedding you should be focused on nothing but adding to the joy of the celebrants with your presence. However, there is nothing wrong with calling someone with whom you would like to discuss a possible deal, and reminding him that you met him during one of the festive group dances at the wedding the previous weekend. Jews also join with one another for less happy events. They gather for funerals, and they subsequently gather at the home of the bereaved, each day for an entire week. These are all activities that cement human relationships in the most profound way.

Consider the story of young Aron Leifer, a Hassidic Jew who lived what most people would consider a fairly isolated life in Brooklyn, New York. As a typical Hassidic teenager, his day started with a before-dawn departure from his home for the synagogue. Early morning prayer services were followed by a day of study in a yeshiva, an academy of Jewish religious study. His day would end at the conclusion of his final lecture at 10 o'clock at night, where-upon he would return home and fall asleep. How did he win Fleet Bank's Youth Entrepreneur award and also become a millionaire by age 18? "Well, he's very comfortable dealing with everyone. It's very unusual," says Steve Kerner, a vice president at Fleet Bank. After his mom bought him a com-puter, Aron taught himself basic skills and then began helping others at his school and in his Borough Park neighborhood with their simple computer problems. Finally, his regular "clients" urged him to accept payment so that they would feel more comfortable calling on him. Two years later, he had hired 25 of his friends as freelance employees; he had a few hundred clients, and $1 million in annual revenue. He now works 14-hour days, six days a week and still studies at the yeshiva for two hours each day and never misses the morning prayer service.[10]

What if you are not Jewish? What if you are a woman and unlikely to be included in a traditional Jewish morning service? Well, I wrote this book to be of use to all readers, so fortunately the principles are readily transferable. I am explaining the principles behind the many day-to-day practices of Jews over the centuries that have contributed to their success. *Your* challenge is to seize these principles, massage them, analyze them, and find your own unique way to apply them to your life. You may not have regular weekday services to attend, but you could always join a synagogue or church or a sports or civic group in order to become friendly with more people.

There are many other ways to seek new friends. It is true that women are excluded from the business opportunities that surface during informal time at men-only venues. However, there are other venues that are women-only, such as many sports clubs and gyms, at which women will have excellent opportunities to form friendships. I think that, in general, women tend to be better than men at bonding with one another. Whatever your situation, I absolutely guarantee you that opportunities to meet others do exist in your life. You may never have contemplated them, but if you brainstorm, you will find them.

FORGE FRIENDSHIPS BY CREATING ONGOING OBLIGATIONS

Having located the many opportunities that exist in your life to extend your network of connectedness, how does one best establish contact? The clue is found within the Hebrew word for "friend," *chaver*. The etymological root of that word is *chav*, which means indebtedness or obligation. The idea is that friendship is forged and maintained by the dynamic creating and discharging of obligation on a continuous basis. Just do something for someone, and you are on the road to a relationship. This is one reason that on a dinner date, any man seeking a relationship will be eager to pay for the meal.

Everyone is familiar with the important little rituals of friendship. I invite you to dinner, after which you write me a thank you note. You give me a birthday gift, and I send over a bottle of your favorite wine. I help your daughter find a job, and you get me rare tickets for a popular ball game. While one party to the relationship creates an obligation by presenting a gift, the other reveals a vulnerability by accepting the gift and expressing gratitude.

The Hebrew word for "thank you," *hodeh*, is the same as the Hebrew word for "admission" or "confession"—expressing gratitude is equivalent to confessing subservience. By accepting your gift gratefully, I am telling you that when you bestowed that gift on me, you supplied something missing in me. By my acceptance of your gift and by my gratitude, I am confessing that I needed you. If, at any time, I need you, that makes me the subservient one at that moment. At another time, I may be the one creating the obligation by doing something for you, while you become vulnerable when you accept my offering. This ongoing dynamic forms and sustains relationships in the same way that two cities can be linked by cars hurtling to and fro along the connecting road and by electronic messages that fly back and forth along the telephone wires that run alongside the road.

Now some people may say, "Well, that is all very materialistic. My friendships are far too real and personal to require gifts and thank you notes. My friend knows that I care for him, and we don't need those little scraps of tangible evidence." This is a lot like the person who thinks he has discovered that one doesn't really need to water flowers. In fact, he thinks, one can even detach them from their plants and carry them indoors to brighten up a room. A little while later, when the flower has faded and died, the foolish horticulturist realizes that the water and the nurturing plant did serve a purpose after all. They provided sustenance and durability. Without them the flower eventually died. Similarly, friends who abandon these rituals that constantly form and discharge mutual obligation soon discover friendship fading. Constantly creating and discharging obligations nurtures and sustains a friendship.

There are two ways to create the obligation/vulnerability dynamic that forms friendship between two people: There are unilateral actions that either one can initiate and perform, such as one bestowing a gift on the other. Then there are also other activities that the two of them can share, such as experiencing a sunrise together. In this case the gift of the sunrise, if you will, is coming from outside the pair, while they both experience a vulnerability to the moment. Though both of these two types of activity work well in building and nourishing friendship, the second is more perilous. There are experiences that two can share that do very little for a relationship.

Suppose two people spend an evening in the same room watching television. We know that the time spent in this fashion does nothing for their relationship because they could just as well have been two travelers watching CNN news on the monitor in an airport waiting area. It is unlikely for them to establish any connection between them. Any woman inveigled into watching a football game on television with her boyfriend knows how little good the afternoon spent in this fashion did for their feelings for one another. Taking a hike together, one teaching the other a new skill, or one giving a gift to the other are all examples of activities that do enhance a relationship.

The key to knowing whether an activity or an experience will enhance a relationship is to measure how *active* or *passive* the roles of the people involved are. Are they subjects or objects in the sentence describing the activity? If both are utterly passive, the actual time spent in the activity has accomplished very little, although subsequently discussing the activity is an active process that does benefit a relationship. For instance, time spent in a movie theater does little for the relationship of the two people watching Hollywood's latest spectacle. However, eating dinner together after the show and discussing the movie does a great deal for their friendship. Use these principles in establishing relationships.

Remember, though, you are not trying to expand your business rolodex. You are trying to *warm your life* with new relationships. This one single point is both the hardest to absorb into your being and, at the same time, the most valuable clue to relationship building. You are trying to build relationships with other humans, not seeking new people to use. Succeeding in genuine relationship building will eventually increase your income. Just as important, it will immediately start improving your entire life.

MURDER AND THE CITY—HOW ONLY CROWDS OF PEOPLE CAN CREATE WEALTH

Jewish tradition has always encouraged its followers to view cities as places that offer them the most opportunities to do the most good for the most people. That is just another way of saying that cities offer the most opportunities for creating wealth. Far from merely a gruesome story of sibling rivalry, the Biblical account of Cain murdering Abel serves as a practical lesson in understanding cities. This story turns out to contain the seeds of history's first city. First we must find out the interpretation that Jewish tradition places on Cain's crime. What could have motivated him to wipe out about a quarter of the world's population?

The clue is in a name—his own name. Jewish tradition considers all names to be meaningful. Each Biblical name is linked to its readily identifiable root word. For instance, *Adam* means "earth," signifying that is where he came from, and *Eve* means "life," as she is to be the mother of all life. *Cain* means "acquisition" in order to signify that his entire essence is acquisitiveness. Apparently, acquiring wealth was the most important thing in the world to Cain. Aha! Here is a convincing motive for murder.

This answer provides a depressing but ultimately accurate view of human nature. The result of Adam and Eve having been banished from the Garden of Eden is that death exists in the world. Obviously that would leave Cain and his brother, Abel, as the eventual inheritors of their parents' legacy, the entire world. Jewish oral tradition focuses on an ambiguous sentence that appears at this point of the Biblical narrative: "And Cain spoke to Abel his brother, and this was while they were in the field, and Cain rose up against Abel, his brother, and killed him."[11] The glaring questions are what did Cain say to his brother in the field, and how did Abel's response precipitate history's first homicide? Recorded tradition fills in the gap, stating that Cain, realizing that acquiring the entire world was twice as good as owning only half the world, indicated his intent as older brother to seize everything. Abel rejected this idea, leading Cain to achieve his ends by killing his brother. This is followed by the well-known question "Am I my brother's keeper?"[12] spoken by Cain in response to the Lord charging Cain with murder.

Now here is where the lesson that Jews draw from this account becomes interesting. For Gilbert and Sullivan's famous opera *The Mikado*, Sir William Gilbert wrote that "A More Humane Mikado Never Did in Japan Exist." For him it was axiomatic that a great and just king would punish according to the crime. Gilbert had his humane Mikado sing:

> My object all sublime
> I shall achieve in time—
> To let the punishment fit the crime—
> The punishment fit the crime;
> And make each prisoner pent
> Unwillingly represent

> A source of innocent merriment!
> Of innocent merriment![13]

To Jews, it is axiomatic that when God punishes people, the punishment always fits the crime with Divine precision. In the case of Cain's act of murder then, what is the Divine response? Will Cain be sentenced to death? No, instead he is punished this way: "When you work the ground, it will no longer continue to yield its strength to you. A vagrant and a wanderer is what you will now become."[14] What? From now on, Cain can plow and plant, but he'll never harvest. How does this punishment fit the crime of murder? There is cosmic justice at work here. To the Jew, there have always been only two ways to grow wealthy from land: Cain's mistaken presumption was that the road to wealth lay in reducing the number of his competitors. God's message to humanity through Cain is that (1) you can plant wheat, or (2) you can build shopping centers. In other words, agriculture or development are the choices. However, the latter is only an option if there are many people around. Without a population, the only thing it makes sense to do with your land is plant food.

God seems to be saying to Cain, "You wanted the wealth that would have come from owning the entire world, right? Well, you've got yourself all the world now. Let's see what that limitless agricultural land will do for you once I command it not to yield to your farming." As if that is not enough, God continues with more punishment. Again one expects to hear God sentence Cain to some sort of punishment that is an appropriate quid pro quo for murder. Instead Cain is told that having wanted the entire world, he now is condemned to wander the vast lands he has inherited, never tarrying in one place long enough to make friends, let alone create relationships. Cain will never be in any one place long enough to build a building, let alone lots of buildings. And he'll never be in one place long enough to find tenants for his buildings even if he could build them. God now awaits Cain's response. Will he or won't he finally understand that wealth comes from interacting and cooperating with many other people, not killing them?

Does the text pored over by generations of devoted Jews reveal an answer? Cain appeals the severity of the sentence and wins some kind of reprieve that allows him to settle in the Land of Nod, east of Eden.[15] Now Cain commences the process of atonement, which is trying to make up for his hideous crime. The very next thing that the Bible reveals is that Cain conceives a child with his wife. This action of bringing a new life into the world is precisely the opposite of his earlier mistake of taking a life out of the world. Jews have understood that Cain is now committed to rebuilding the population from the fact that the Bible does not even mention his wife's name or even the information that he had married. When most people marry, they do so with a deep commitment to the person they are marrying; progeny is not the only motivation. That is why the news of weddings is usually broadcast before the good news of births. In this case, however, Cain is primarily interested in rebuilding the world's population. This is viewed as a good sign because it signifies that he understands the true nature of his earlier mistake.

Here comes the climax of the entire story: Cain's wife bore him a son called Enoch, and immediately Cain began building his legacy to his son. He built a city! Cain truly has learned the source of wealth. So profound was Cain's education that the name he gave his new son celebrated his education. The name *Enoch*, in Hebrew, means just that—"education." Cain even bestowed the same uplifting name on his new city, calling it Enoch—Education. From this Biblical chapter describing Cain's eventual education, Jewish children have grasped the essential message: Wealth is created in a populated city far more easily than in all the vast countryside with its silent loneliness. "Do you want wealth?" Cain seems to be asking? If so, locate yourself in the heart of large populations of people who share your values. Then begin making connections.

IMPROVING CONNECTIONS ENHANCES WEALTH CREATION

It is no accident that the graph depicting wealth creation in the United States has always spiked upward in concert with the adoption of technological developments that have aided humans in relating with one another. The invention and rapid adoption of the telegraph did for the Victorian era what the Internet has done for the present day. The telegraph ended what I call the Paul Revere era of communication. Up until the telegraph's arrival, the fastest way to convey information was by sending a man on a horse. By the time that folks in Baltimore could find out about low prices caused by a wheat surplus in Chicago, the information was no longer useful. The telegraph and the spread of railroads across the United States changed all that and helped in the creation of vast wealth.

The twentieth century was surely shaped by development in communication. It also became the greatest wealth-producing period in our history. As late as 1920, only 35 percent of U.S. households had a telephone. By the end of the century, penetration was complete, with many homes possessing more than one line. By 1930, only 39 percent of homes had a radio. By the end of the century, virtually every home had several radios and a color television, including those homes that the U.S. Census Bureau considers to be below the poverty line.[16] That communication accompanies wealth creation is not surprising. This is precisely the message that Jews extract from the Cain story. The contemporary significance of this message is best revealed by analyzing what economic life might look like for the last person on earth. Imagine some catastrophe that wipes out all human beings but one. Surely the survivor is the wealthiest human ever to inhabit the planet. The survivor owns not only Fort Knox but also all the gold beneath the offices of the Federal Reserve in New York City. He has access to every safe deposit box and owns every office building in the heart of every city. He owns more airplanes and yachts than have ever been owned by anyone in all of human history.

You might peer into the daily life of this unprecedented tycoon. What does he do once the sun goes down on his first day as ruler of the world? Why, read by candlelight, of course, because lights no longer go on at the touch of a switch. Nobody is left to operate the electricity utility. At first he will eat fairly well, at least until the grocery stores (all of which now belong to him) run out of produce. Sooner or later, even the canned foods will spoil. At that point he had better hope that his first harvest ripens successfully before he starves to death.

He may desire to travel. At first, he is free to choose any car on the road because they all belong to him. However, sooner or later they will all have empty gas tanks and will become quite useless to him. If he can catch a horse, he might be able to travel at a rate faster than he could walk, but that is his best hope. On his own, he could not operate a refinery to produce the petroleum that would so ease his life. It quickly becomes apparent that the "richest man in history" is enjoying a living standard slightly below that of a third-world subsistence farmer. In contrast, the more opportunities people have to interact and to convey information to one another, the more wealth is created for every participant.

Now you know why so many people play golf. It is not just because of the endless fascination and deep intrigue that accompanies chasing a ball around a big field, only to whack it again once you have located it. You may have picked up the subtle clues that I am not a golfer, but at least I know I should

be. You know why? Because golf allows people to experience long and intimate conversation with others, while self-interest is camouflaged by the game.
Ask people why they golf with business associates, and the answer is always
the same: It's a great way to build relationships.[17]

How does this knowledge help you? For a start it suggests that you need
to maximize your interaction with other people. Although it is certainly true
that modern advances in telecommuncations allow you to be in business
despite geographic isolation, moving to a small and remote community might
not be the best way to prepare for your new life of economic success. In
addition, if you happen to prefer spending your leisure time isolated with a
good book or glued to a television set, now might be a good time to start
using most of your available time for building new relationships. Is doing so
going to be comfortable for you? Initially, probably not, particularly if you
are the introverted sort. However, you are going to have to change if you are
serious about money. You must enlarge your Rolodex, and you must inten-
sify the relationships with the people represented by those Rolodex cards.

Never miss or ignore an opportunity to make new friends and to nurture
existing ones. You can always make a point of accepting invitations to others'
happy events; and, yes, you can always make a point of attending others' sad
events, too. In other words, engage in ongoing community-building activities. These days, everyone is busy; it is all too easy to casually dismiss invitations and other opportunities to spend time with others. This is a mistake.
How about if you have already been declining invitations for so long that
you now hardly receive any? Or what if you are relatively new in town? Two
of the ways in which channels of communication are built are receiving invitations and dispatching them.

A Jewish tradition links three seemingly separate pieces of information: It
is said (1) that Abraham built a close circle of friends numbering at least
20,000 souls, (2) that Abraham constantly invited guests into his home, and
(3) that his large tent had doorways facing each of the four approaching roads.
The historical aspects are irrelevant for our purposes, but the business lesson
is powerful. Even today's large department stores have absorbed the third of
Abraham's lessons, making it easy for guests to enter the premises. They all
possess multiple entrances facing different directions and opening onto different streets.

You too can make your home inviting to guests, and you can similarly
increase your circle of friends by inviting guests to enjoy your hospitality.
Bestowing your hospitality on someone is the very best way of establishing a

bond. Grabbing the bill at a restaurant is one way of doing this; another is inviting your new friend to join you for dinner at home. Not only is it considerably less expensive to entertain at home than at a restaurant, but it is also far more effective at creating bonds. For this reason, in long-ago days, when companies were contemplating hiring a particular executive, in addition to extensively interviewing the candidate, they would also interview his wife. Their concern was whether she would be an adequate hostess for those all-important home dinner parties. Today, life is considerably less simple, but the principles need to be recognized and applied to whatever realities surround your own life.

HELPING OTHERS IMPROVE THEIR LIVES HELPS YOU IMPROVE YOUR OWN LIFE

Finding genuine joy in friendship with others and cultivating many such friendships is essential. This alone, however, is not sufficient. One must be master of some way to help others live their lives. For example, suppose I have 90 minutes available this afternoon. Because time is the scarcest commodity, I want to decide very carefully how to invest that time. I could watch a game on television, but that would not be an investment of my time; instead, it would be a dissipation of my valuable hour and a half. I could mow my lawn with my hand-pushed lawn mower, which would at least have a health benefit for me. Or I could finish writing a manual for a car dealership owned by a friend of mine. The car dealership had provided me with details of its operation and desperately needed a flowchart-based operations manual.

Writing the car manual for my friend is the best use of my time. Here's why. Once I have completed writing the manual after about 90 minutes, I can drive over to the dealership, give my handiwork to the owner, and pick up a check for $350, the agreed-on price for the work. When I get home again, I find that the person I hired to mow the lawn has just about finished the job. I happily pay her the $60 we had negotiated and retire to my armchair to think about life. During the passage of the past two hours or so, instead of mowing the lawn, I had made two people happy—three if you count my wife who wanted the lawn mowed. On top of that, I still made myself a profit of $290. I could have mowed the lawn myself, but it would not have looked as good as it looked after being manicured by someone who really knew her job. Life is a miracle, provided you have many friends and provided everyone knows what everyone else does best. That, of course, is the value of advertising.

DON'T BE A "WAGE SLAVE"—BE IN BUSINESS FOR YOURSELF

One of the first questions that new acquaintances ask one another is "What do you do?" or "What field are you in?" You need to be able to answer that question with no more than about 20 seconds of description. What is more, you need to answer that question in a way that sounds absolutely fascinating and that almost compels your interlocutor to ask further questions. Now if your answer is nothing more than "Oh, I work for the Acme ball bearing company," you have squandered a potential wealth-producing opportunity. You have told me nothing really interesting about yourself. What do you do for Acme? Are you the chairman? Are you in sales, production, or accounting? Now had you smiled broadly and said, "Oh, I show manufacturers, chiefly the Acme company, how to produce the smoothest, shiniest, hardest little spheres in the whole universe," you might well have fascinated me. Apart from anything else, people with expressive faces who are really passionate about something are just more fun to interact with. If all you can tell me is that you work for someone else and are at his beck and call, frankly, I'd rather speak with him. He sounds more interesting than you. So, no matter how you serve your fellow humans, think of yourself as doing something fascinating; see yourself in business, rather than merely being something.

What if you have no passion for your work? Trying to earn money doing something you dislike is equivalent to boxing with one hand tied behind your back. You need to do everything in your power to cultivate an interest in what you do. If that is impossible, I would suggest finding a position you can be passionate about. Obviously, every job has its less stimulating moments; but you should feel an enthusiasm for what you do, be it flipping burgers or running a multi-million-dollar company.

Some people follow this logic to a false conclusion. They assume that the pay is irrelevant, so long as they are doing what they enjoy. I met quite a few destitutes on the Venice, California, beachfront where the synagogue I served was situated. They all assured me that they were writing the great American screenplay. Being a great writer was their dream; but they scoffed at the idea that because their work enjoyed no commercial success, they should consider alternative employment opportunities.

What should you do if the work you do and love is not remunerative? Unless you are one of the lucky few for whom money is not a concern, you might do one of two things. Perhaps your passion needs to be fulfilled in your leisure time as a hobby or through a volunteer situation. Meanwhile, grow an enthusiasm for a field you may never have earlier considered. Too many people fixate on a very small number of careers and remain unaware of the myriad of amazing opportunities the working world offers.

Sometimes, you can think in an unconventional way and channel your preferences into a more lucrative field. One of my daughters has loved teaching since she was five years old. While other girls set their dolls up at little tea parties, my daughter's dolls were lined up in a little classroom on her bed. She would spend hours instructing them while writing on her blackboard, which had been her favorite birthday present. She eventually grew up, left home, and became a teacher. The stark reality she encountered was that although she found her work immensely fulfilling, her paycheck did not reflect the many hours she invested in preparation, grading, and teaching.

Thinking creatively, she quit her position and pursued the less time consuming but far more lucrative field of tutoring students for their forthcoming Scholastic Aptitude Tests (SATs) and also creating for schools curricula that utilized many of the innovative techniques she had used in her classroom.

Traditional Jews understand the difference between being a wage slave and being in business, and so should you. You can be an employee without being a wage slave. There is the old tale of two friends who met up again 20 years after they both first began working for the railroad. The fellow wielding a pick while working on the roadbed was astounded to see his old friend looking prosperous as he stepped from his private railcar. In response, the second guy, now head of the railroad, explained: "Twenty years ago, you went to work for $3.75 an hour, whereas I went to work for the railroad. His point was that his unsuccessful friend always saw himself as a *wage slave* and focused on his meager salary. He, on the other hand, saw himself as being *in business for himself,* which allowed him to focus on his customer, in this case, his employer.

Just watch the owner of that shoe store eagerly greet every customer walking through the door. Does she feel surly and resentful toward them in the way that so many employees feel toward their bosses? No, she does not. That is because she thinks of herself as being in business, and these customers are not her employers, but her customers.

Even an employee can do exactly the same thing. He can and must consider himself to be in business. All he must do is view his employer as one of his customers. Consider the difference in success and happiness of two of my friends, Henry and Harvey. Henry is a dentist working for a large dental health group in town and doing very well, indeed. Harvey does something or other in the passenger cabin division of a large aircraft manufacturer; I think he is an engineer of sorts. Harvey is also a wage slave. Is there something about being an engineer that is inherently different from being a dentist? Not really, but the reason Harvey is a wage slave is also why I don't know exactly what Harvey does: Harvey never talks about his work, whereas Henry never misses an opportunity to talk about his work and always exploits the slightest opportunity to tell folks about the latest advances in dentistry that he is mastering. Admittedly, in the ordinary course of life, Henry will run into more people who need fillings than Harvey will run into who need large jet aircraft. However, Henry sees everyone he meets as someone he could potentially assist with a tooth problem.

Harvey misses countless opportunities, not to sell aircraft, but to sell *himself*. In the company of Harvey, I found myself at a social event one evening and met two people who could have done business with Harvey if they had only known what business he was in. I thought Harvey worked as an engineer for Boeing, because that's how he had introduced himself to these two people. Wrong! Harvey was really in the business of converting blueprints into finished products, but he didn't know it. His biggest current client, and admittedly at present his only client, was Boeing. He mistakenly saw Boeing as his employer rather than as his client. Who cares? I care about what you do for Boeing and what you might be able to do for others, like those two people.

Both people mentioned to me that they were each desperately in need of more production engineers for their factories. One was a national luggage manufacturer, and the other manufactured plastic vacuum-molding machinery. Either of them would have offered Harvey a compensation package worth effectively double what he was earning at Boeing. Either would also have offered him considerably more security than Boeing, which is constantly laying off workers, only to attempt rehiring them about four years later. Too bad Harvey was only an employee. Too bad Harvey was not on the lookout for new clients for Harvey, Inc.

BE PROUD OF AND LET PEOPLE KNOW WHAT YOU DO

This book's second commandment could be summarized thus: Make lots of new friends, try to help them, and make sure that they all know how you could help them and that you are eager to do so. Many people like Harvey hide their occupations. I think this sometimes is a lingering sense of British snobbery. In England it used to be "lower-class" to earn your money. Far better, they felt, to inherit and then dissipate it. One of the most snide pre–World War II British insults used to be, "Oh, he's just a merchant." Far wiser instead to be proud of how you earn your living, what you do, what you can do, and your eagerness to do it. That is what opens up doors.

Against all odds and in the face of cultural and regulatory difficulties, many Jews in Europe did very well financially. One way they got around some of the difficulties they faced was by announcing with their choice of names exactly how they could be helpful to other people. Jacob the Glazer was the village glass man. Isaac the Drucker was the printer, and Joseph Diamond was the jeweler. Weinberg produced and sold wine, while Feller owned the tannery. Schneider was the tailor, Cooper made barrels, and Wasserman brought the water. People weren't embarrassed to have their identity linked to a job or a way of earning a living.

The Talmud records the names of many great scholars and eminent sages who were known by their occupations, such as Rabbi Yochanan, the shoemaker. Jews were encouraged by these Talmudic heroes with their distinctive names to proudly declare their occupations, too. Jews also take the lesson to heart from Jonah, prophet of God, who was woken by the sailors terrified of the storm that threatened their ship. In an effort to identify the menace, the frightened men inquired of Jonah: "Tell us who caused this storm? (Was it you?) What is your occupation? Where are you from?"[19]

To this day, one of the first questions people tend to ask a new acquaintance is, "What do you do for a living?" It is a legitimate question because the inquirer really wants to know what the person does *for other people.* He or she is wondering how others find you useful. How you help your fellow humans is a proud part of your identity. The only person to be embarrassed by the question is one who has no answer. Traditionally, Jews have been quick to identify their occupations. This obviously makes it much simpler for others to make contact for business purposes, and it may be partially responsible for Jews acquiring the reputation of being forward and aggressive in business. Letting folks know your occupation benefits everyone and need not be obtrusive or obnoxious.

CHOOSE YOUR FRIENDS AND CUSTOMERS CAREFULLY

Anytime someone is about to tell you "the secret of life," you should interrupt and ask how long it will take to tell you this secret of life. If he or she answers anything under three years, don't waste your time. There is no way to communicate the secret of life in 30 seconds because there probably is not only one secret to life. One can easily fall into the trap of suggesting simple aphorisms to solve all of life's complex problems.

One obvious flaw in simple sayings is that many of them are countered by equally pithy sayings urging precisely the opposite course of action. *Absence makes the heart grow fonder* is unlikely to comfort the distant lover when he recalls the opposite *Out of sight, out of mind.* The timid soul happily hears *Look before you leap,* but his equanimity is shattered when someone reminds him *He who hesitates is lost.* People often procrastinate and reassure themselves with *Don't cross that bridge till you come to it;* but they must also remember *A stitch in time saves nine.* Life is far too complex for these one liners to serve as fail-safe guides and your business career should be too inextricably woven into the fabric of your life to allow it to be governed by just one proverb.

You have often heard the expression *The customer is always right.* Well, like all the other examples I just cited, this one is also unreliable. Have you never encountered a truly obnoxious customer who was clearly not in the right? Here's a painful thought: Have you ever been the sort of customer who was certainly not right? For example, Nordstrom is just one of several stores that discovered that not all customers are right. These stores find that their generous return policies are occasionally exploited by certain customers who take home dresses with the intention of wearing them for a special occasion and then returning them. Those customers are not always right, and up-to-date techniques are being used to screen for these customers and to try to encourage them to do their "shopping" elsewhere.

Another example is Paging Network, Inc., a paging services provider that for several years essentially gave away its pagers in a race to build market share. In 1998, the company began to chase away heavy users who receive a flurry of messages but often pay only a rock-bottom monthly fee. By the end of 1998 Paging Network, Inc., had cut loose nearly half a million unprofitable former customers.

Here's a third example: During 1997, FedEx began analyzing the returns on its business for about 30 large customers that generate about 10 percent of its total volume. It found that certain customers, including some requiring lots of residential deliveries, weren't bringing in as much revenue as they had promised when they first negotiated discounted rates. So FedEx went on the offensive, demanding that some customers pay higher rates and imposing double-digit increases in a handful of instances. A couple of big customers who refused to budge were told they could take their shipping business elsewhere.[19]

Finally, consider how several credit card companies have decided on the profile of the ideal customer with whom they wish to deal. If you fall into that category, when you phone them, you will reach a real live operator who will quickly and efficiently tend to your request. Perhaps you are the sort of customer who always pays your credit card balance in full and always on time, never incurring any finance charges or late fees. Or you may be the sort of customer who misses even the minimum monthly payment. In both these cases, when you call the credit card company's customer service line, caller ID software identifies you as, shall we say, a less desirable customer, the kind of customer who is not always right from their point of view. In this case, you will never reach a live operator. Instead you will be programmed to pick from an endless succession of choices and finally left to meander through the futile footpaths of voicemail until you finally surrender with a sigh and hang up.

Clearly, running the complexity of your business by the simplistic credo that the customer is always right is a recipe for failure. Instead, accustom yourself to first examine the transaction and the people involved. That way you can do what department stores and credit card companies do— determine whether the other party is indeed a customer. If this person is someone with whom you would like to conduct a transaction, then he or she is a customer.

Suppose you are in the plumbing business, and your business plan calls for you to develop relationships with owners of large apartment buildings. Your work is competent and quick; all you care about is stopping the leak and getting on to the next call. One day, you receive a call from the mansion of a temperamental dowager who expects a plumber to show up on her door-

step in gleaming white coveralls and color-coordinated, operating-room boo-
ties. You would be wise to decline the call—she is not your customer. Accepting her as a customer and following the rule that the customer is always
right will ruin your day, if not your week.

Having determined that someone is indeed a customer with whom you
would want to conduct business, how do you relate to that customer? Suppose that customer is being a bit difficult, as customers often are. One danger with saying that the customer is always right is that it generates feelings
of resentment in you when the customer is clearly not right. Instead of trying to inculcate within yourself and your employees the ethos that the customer is always right, try inculcating the idea of the principle of service. The
customer may be wrong, obnoxious, and ugly; but you have determined that
this is a customer you want to win, please, and retain. That means that whether
the customer is right or wrong is immaterial. What is very material, however,
is your attitude; and I don't believe you can modify your attitude effectively
enough to penetrate the customer's emotional radar by simply trying to psyche
yourself. Repeatedly invoking "the customer is always right" softly to yourself won't do it.

SERVICE DOESN'T MEAN SERVILITY

Remember that deference does not mean humiliation, and service does not
mean fawning obsequiousness. When I refer to *service*, I do not mean serving the customer, I mean instilling in ourselves a love of service. Without
intending to sound ethereal, I am advocating finding the kind of joy in serving another human that some of us find in long-distance running. Forcing
out each stride is hard and even painful for the first few miles, when all of a
sudden, the famous runner's high kicks in. You feel yourself to be almost
floating effortlessly as the miles slide by. Learning how to serve another human being lets you hit that same kind of high.

Everyone felt a little of it during the months following September 11, 2001.
All of a sudden everyone began to appreciate what real service meant. Americans' eyes misted over and a calm and faraway look crossed their faces whenever they spoke of the firefighters who raced into the burning towers on their
rescue missions to hell . . . brave men lugging 50 pounds of equipment on
their backs as they hurried up 60 flights of stairs. They must have suspected
that they might never return down those stairs. What did they do this for?

Six hundred bucks a week? No, they did it because they were servants to the public; that is what public service means. All of a sudden the word *service* had real meaning again.

This may seem a far cry from teaching yourself and your staff to serve your customers, but the difference is only a matter of degree. Either you believe that another human being is worth being served by you, or you don't. If you do, then you can risk your life to save his or hers, or you can go down on your knees to help your customer try on a new pair of shoes. If you don't think much of other human beings, well, then you are never going to be much good at customer service; and I think you will find other shortcomings in your life, too.

For example, ServiceMaster Corporation in Illinois was founded by an evangelical Baptist, Marion E. Wade, in 1947. Its primary mission was always "to honor God in all we do." Wade asserted that running a profitable business was not inconsistent with serving the Lord. He spelled out his notion of using the Bible as a guide to business in a book that for decades was given to every new manager. Yet in spite of and many would say because of its linking of God and profits, ServiceMaster quickly grew into a $6 billion Fortune 500 company that did well by doing good on everything from Merry Maids house cleaning to Terminix pest control and TruGreen lawn care. Early in 2000, ServiceMaster opened its web site on which customers could select, purchase, and schedule any of ServiceMaster's services directly.

During 2001, ServiceMaster brought in its first chief executive officer (CEO) from outside the evangelical fold. Nonetheless, new CEO Jonathan Ward was rightfully reluctant to modify the corporate culture that had worked so well for so long in this service-oriented company with its fleet of 23,000 vehicles. For instance, he retained the custom of calling corporate meetings to order by quoting from the Biblical book of Isaiah. That may seem irrelevant to modern business, but this company schedules thousands of visits to customers' homes. If ever a company needed to radiate a message of true commitment to service, this is that company. Even the company's motto is "We Serve"; and this, coupled with its unabashed embrace of Christianity with its own tradition of service, has certainly played a role in its success. ServiceMaster's very name proclaims its eagerness to serve.

In 1989, *Fortune* listed ServiceMaster among the country's top service companies, and in 1998, the *Financial Times* was quoted in the *New York Times* as calling ServiceMaster one of the world's most respected companies.[20] I hope it continues to prosper because it serves as a useful reminder that to truly excel at service, some form of inner belief is necessary. If you cannot wrap yourself around the notion that other humans are worthy of your committed service and that you are not diminished but are instead *elevated* by providing that service, you will never really excel at what you do.

A religious and educational nonprofit corporation called the Avodah Institute lists its address as ServiceMaster headquarters. This fascinated me because *avodah* is a Hebrew word meaning "service." The word is used both for serving as someone's servant and also for serving God, as in a prayer *service*. Even the English language retains that usage today. That is why both in Judaism and in Christianity, idiomatic usage has us attending "services" at synagogue or church. Nobody necessarily has to be a Christian, or for that matter a Jew, to become an expert at true service. However, everyone can derive a useful principle from this part of the Jewish tradition that teaches that there is nothing shameful in being servants, or people who serve. This is how traditional Jewish thought sees it.

Why does Hebrew use the same word for serving God and for serving our fellow humans? Because of all earth's creatures, only humans do both those activities—only humans worship God and only humans can choose to serve their fellow humans, not out of blind animal instinct but out of love, altruism, and a commitment to an idea, just like those firefighters. No animal ever "served" another animal; but service, giving of oneself to others, is at the core of what it means to be a human and at the core of the quest for career success.

LOVING OTHERS, NOT JUST YOURSELF

Yet another poignant insight into the importance of service is offered by the Hebrew word for *love*. That word, *Ahav*, literally means "I give." One of my teachers, the late sainted Rabbi Simcha Wasserman of blessed memory, used to gently tease his students by asking them, one by one, on Thanksgiving if they liked turkey. He was waiting for the one unwary student who would innocently respond, "Oh, I love turkey." Then Rabbi Wasserman with blue eyes twinkling, would pounce. "No," he'd say. "You don't *love* turkey—if you did, you wouldn't eat it. You actually love yourself." He would add that, many times, when a young man tells a young lady to whom he is not married, that he loves her, he means it just like that student who thinks he loves turkey.

The ancient Jewish model of love does not mean "I take from you," it means "I give to you." To love others does not mean simply to feel gushing emotions welling up in your heart; rather, and more important, it means to give to them—to serve them. God wants you to love other people. You do so through service. And He rewards you for it. If you have ever experienced the unpleasant ordeal of having your shoes shined by someone who clearly resents his own role even more than he resents his customer, you'll know what I mean by disservice. By contrast, an example of true service occurs in New York's JFK International airport at a shoe shine stand attended by a real professional. When changing flights at JFK, I happily walk half a mile out of my way to reach the terminal in which this person does business. It isn't only that he puts new life into my shoes, it is the free lesson he always teaches me about service. This man is not only an expert on shoes, he is also a wonderfully astute observer of humanity. I have sat in his chair while he pointed out which passersby were on their way to a business meeting and which were homeward bound. He was entirely comfortable at his job, and, as a result, he made me and all his other eager customers also feel quite comfortable.

Therefore, it didn't surprise me at all when I learned that he owned 14 shoe shine operations around the New York area, which an assortment of his relatives operated. He had also become a successful investor based partially, he claimed, on the tips and advice he received from grateful customers. He had no need to work, he explained to me. He just loved his job. Some might say that he only felt comfortable shining the shoes of travelers because he was quite a wealthy man. I would say that they would be confusing cause with effect. I believe that he only became a wealthy man because he felt comfortable serving others.

Here's another example of someone who derives joy from serving others. New York restaurateur and award winning chef Drew Nieporent has never had a single failure since opening his first restaurant, Montrachet, in 1985. He now owns seven restaurants, five in New York and one each in San Francisco and London. His secrets include service, which he explains to mean treating regular customers superbly, and new customers as if they were regulars. Cooking food for folks and serving it up to them is true service. Where did he learn this? Flipping burgers at McDonald's while in high school. If you have ever wondered about McDonald's success, it lies in its ability to thrill the hearts of minimum-wage youngsters at the prospect of wearing the uniform and serving people their food. And McDonald's drills into its workers service, quality, cleanliness, and pride.

Finally, consider the success story of George Zimmer, who hated buying clothes and realized that the only thing worse than a pushy salesman in a slick suit is a salesman pushing a slick suit. In 1973, he opened a men's clothing store in Houston and called it Men's Wearhouse. The store was based on his observation that "the average man enjoys shopping for clothes about as much as going to the dentist." So how do you build a company around customers who hate buying what you sell? By building a company that reinvents the shopping experience, says Zimmer. Getting down on your knees to measure some guy's inseam is not exactly the stuff of self-esteem, but any top-rate store that is succeeding has found a way to help its sales staff feel excited about serving a customer's clothing needs.

Men's Wearhouse now has about 6,000 employees in about 400 stores, and it went public in 1992. It has a market value of about $1 billion. I would say that George Zimmer's brilliance does not lie in his eye for color, fashion, and style, although he might well have those qualities, too. His brilliance was in designing and implementing a system in which participants absorbed a culture of service. Zimmer said, "When you get down to what really happens in the retail world, it's all about customers interacting with employees."[21] He is so right.

Learn to find joy and fulfillment in service to others, and you have removed one major obstacle on your road to success. How do you do so? That is easy, as long as you remember my warning you way back that you are going to have to become a new person. The secret to learning how to love serving others is to develop the character trait of humility. It will win you many new friends and delight all your old ones.

Humility does not mean persuading yourself that you are a worthless good-for-nothing. There are many worthless good-for-nothings in the world, but you are not one of them. I would like to say that holding this book in your hands proves that. No, trying to persuade yourself that you are nothing at all would be to make a lie of all the many years of hard work during which you became who you are today. Well, then, if you are really somebody rather impressive, how do you avoid becoming, well, . . . arrogant about it all? By recognizing how little credit you really deserve for your triumphs and achievements. You had the good fortune to be born and raised in a country that offered not only physical survival but also endless opportunity. Even the discipline that kept you at your studies or at your first job isn't something for which you can take total credit. You might have done fine in the genetic sweepstakes, and you might also have been the beneficiary of many helpful and generous people who gave you assistance along the way.

Find a little private quiet time each day to bow your head in recognition of all those who knowingly or unwittingly contributed to what you are and to what you have today. By performing this little exercise regularly, not only are you facing the truth, but you are also nudging yourself closer to possessing a more modest demeanor. With that process under way, you are ready to address the issue of service. Serving that other person no longer need irritate you or violate your sense of self-importance. He or she is just as good as you are, because most of what you are is reason to blow other people's horns rather than your own. Not only is this trait helpful for a businessperson, it is also enormously valuable for a spouse or a parent.

TO LEARN HOW TO SERVE, LEARN HOW TO *BE* SERVED

The corollary to learning to be comfortable and even happy while serving others is learning to be comfortable while being served by others. Restaurants, cabs, and clothing stores are just some of the places you experience service and where you can train yourself to appreciate top-rate service. Tipping is a practice that reveals a great deal about what people really feel about service. Hotel industry executives whom I have advised inform me that more than any other national group, Americans tend to leave a tip for the housekeeping staff in hotel rooms when they check out.

To deliver good service, it also helps to be able to recognize it. I have noticed that some diners are uncomfortable with the entire concept of tipping waiters in a restaurant. They actually prefer the dreadful system that is rapidly encroaching on the restaurant industry—"Gratuity Included." No, don't do that to me. I want to be able to personally acknowledge the good service I receive. It takes true professionalism to be a great waiter. The more modern, gender-free, term for *waiter*, "server," helps explain just what that professionalism is all about—service. It is interesting that since the War of Independence, Americans' sense of egalitarianism allows them to use the term "sir" in very few instances. One of the more common usages is to attract a waiter's attention by calling out "Sir!" What could more clearly make the point that Americans are comfortable respecting people who serve them?

The reason I am happy to be able to tip is that it forces me to be aware of the service and it encourages me to actively appreciate it. The habit is somewhat contagious; when I find myself in the company of people who administer service professionally, I am inspired to do the same.

THE POWER OF PREDICTABILITY IN MAINTAINING RELATIONSHIPS

Aim for predictability in your professional performance. It greatly enhances your value to others. Humans all prefer the familiar to the alien. One reason for the stunning success of the franchise concept during the second half of the twentieth century was that it offered the familiar and the predictable. Before franchises, business travelers could stop at any small-town hotel, but they could not predict the reception they would get—it depended on the mood of the proprietor. Needless to say the room and the amenities the hotel offered inevitably were a bit of a gamble. Then the Holiday Inn began to make its appearance in every town. Travelers flocked to patronize the Holiday Inn. Travelers would keep driving until they arrived in a town with a Holiday Inn. Why? Because it was standardized. As a traveler, you knew in advance how everything would be precisely the same as the Holiday Inn you lodged at the previous night in a town 300 miles away. The way you were greeted on checking in, the rates, and the amenities were exactly what you anticipated. You recognized the paintings on the walls, the strip of paper affixed to the toilet bowl, and even the location of the light switches. That kind of predictability and familiarity causes comfort. The unexpected and strange causes anxiety. Thus to benefit from this principle, you should endeavor to make everyone's interactions with you quite predictable and familiar. Everyone has had the experience of trying to work with an unpredictable and very temperamental associate. Never knowing just what reaction you will get to a request or a suggestion can be very trying.

All kinds of interaction between people depend on predictability. Provided a better one was available, nobody would subscribe to a telephone service that connected you to the right party only half the time. Driving in almost any U.S. city is quite different from driving in Rome or Rio. The main reason is predictability. Most U.S. drivers follow the rules of the road whose paramount purpose is to impose predictability. When passing through an intersection with a green light, I barely need slow down. In many other countries, a green light offers very little assurance that you won't be hit by a side-coming truck barreling through a red light.

In your professional work, you can benefit from similar predictability. For instance, any business that customers visit would experience real benefit from keeping the same associates for as long as possible. Banking and financial service firms in retirement communities near Palm Springs, California, or Broward County, Florida, have all learned the value of providing familiar faces and familiar surroundings to their walk-in clients. A patient trying to decide whether to undergo an expensive dental procedure would find the decision easier when surrounded by familiar and trusted faces.

Similarly, in whatever enterprise you find yourself, practice predictability. Never impose your mood swings on your associates and customers. They should never be able to discover how your life is going. This is called being professional. Given two alternatives, most customers and clients would prefer working with someone who does not display an entirely new personality on each occasion.

If there is one lesson to be extracted from this chapter it is this: Success in business means getting on with people. Now ask yourself what kind of people more easily makes friends—academic intellectuals of superhigh intelligence or more ordinary down-home-type people? Oh, yes, very intelligent people can be warm and friendly, but it is very rare. Superbly intelligent Warren E. Buffett, chairman of Berkshire Hathaway, manages to conceal his off-the-chart intelligence behind warm bonhomie and Midwest accessibility. He is both well liked and very intelligent. He is also very rich. I consider his annual "Chairman's Letter" (in the Berkshire annual report) to be indispensable reading for anyone wanting to do well in business. By and large, people may admire super intelligent people, but they neither like nor feel particularly comfortable with them. Think of expressions such as "too smart for his own good," "smarty-pants," and "wise guy." They are not fond endearments. You may be have been fortunate in the genetic sweepstakes and have the right parents; you may be blessed with very high IQ scores. If you really are to succeed in business, it won't be because people think you are smart; it will be because people like you. There is an old adage, "People don't care how much you know until they know how much you care." That raises the issue of how you show you care or, better yet, how you really care enough so that it shows. There is a subtle but important difference. Trying to show that you care is essentially devious, whereas trying to care enough that it shows is part of authentic human communication.

Realizing one important fact makes it far easier to develop and to radiate a genuine, almost palpable concern for others. That one important fact is that directly or not, your welfare is interlinked with that of everyone else in your extended order of social cooperation. Judaism teaches that God designed the system to reward people for not remaining isolated from one another. The Hebrew word for "human interaction that is economically profitable to both parties" possesses the same root as the Hebrew word for "shop" and for "encampment." It is the word that the Bible uses to describe ancient Israel camped at the foot of Mount Sinai in eager anticipation of receiving the Torah—*Vayichan*. Anyone familiar with Hebrew could not help noticing that the word appears in the singular. This is to suggest that all the vast number of individuals that made up ancient Israel were unified and single-minded. When large numbers of people are unified within a common system of values and are located in close proximity to one another, in a real encampment as it were, the best circumstances for economically productive interaction then exist.

In order to effectively play one's role in this vast, seamless web of human interaction, it helps to really get to know oneself. That is what you must do next.

YOUR PATH TO PROSPERITY

- *Learn to develop new relationships.* This will help you succeed not only in business but also in other aspects of your life. Try to win friends, not in order to influence people for your benefit, but for the sheer joy of forming and maintaining human relationships. Paradoxically, only in that way will you stand the best chance of enhancing your life.

- *Don't try to make connections in specific forums, such as job networking meetings.* Try to meet people in other ways—at church, at synagogue, or in your health club. Work to build these relationships. Talk to these people and make reasons to communicate, whether through notes or through e-mail.

- *Learn how to relate to strangers with the sincere warmth and interest that turns them into friends.* Everyone senses when someone's interest is not sincere. Trying to give other people what they want only to get what you want does not work very well in the long term. Somehow people sense the ulterior motive. Perhaps it is an air of desperation that you exude. On the face of it, this book's Second Commandment advises you to build genuine and sincere relationships with as many people as possible with no thought of reward. Beneath the surface, it informs you that, paradoxically, reward will follow in proportion to the lack of self-interest you projected while forming the relationships in the first place.

- *Make sure all your friends and contacts know that there are ways you could help them and that you are eager to help them.* Traditionally, Jews have been quick to identify their occupations. This obviously makes it much simpler for others to make contact for business purposes. It may be partially responsible for Jews acquiring the reputation of being forward and aggressive in business. Letting folks know your occupation benefits everyone and need not be obtrusive or obnoxious.

- *Choose carefully those with whom you do business.* "The customer is always right" is not true if you don't want to keep that particular customer. Don't feel obligated to meet the wishes of a demanding client if ultimately you don't want to be in business with that person.

- *Find joy in serving others.* Either you believe that another human being is worth being served by you, or you don't. If you do, then you can risk your life to save his, or you can go down on your knees to help him try on a new pair of shoes. If you don't think much of other human beings, then you are never going to be much good at customer service, and you will probably find other shortcomings in your life, too. The secret to learning how to love serving others is to develop the character trait of humility. It will win you many new friends and delight all your old ones.

- *Be predictable, and you'll be seen as a professional.* Everyone is moody on occasion, but you shouldn't let your emotions take control of your professionalism. Most customers and clients would prefer working with someone who does not display an entirely new personality on each occasion. Success in business means getting on with people. If you really are to succeed in business, it won't be because people think you are smart; it will be because people like you.

Get to Know Yourself

To change the way others see you, first you have to learn to see yourself as others see you.

Almost everyone is in business. You have your time, skills, experience, personality, and some other attributes to market. You have customers, clients, supervisors, employers, associates, bosses, or patients to please. You may not realize it, but you probably even have a board of directors. It consists of you as chairperson, perhaps your spouse, and maybe some of your trusted friends with whom you discuss your professional career. These people are also unpaid members of the board of You, Inc. You might include your accountant and maybe even your doctor. These people and many others all influence the progress of your company.

Did you say you were laid off? Not at all—you are merely going to be marketing your company's services elsewhere. Are you undergoing new skill training? Fine, you are merely finding new products to market to your customers. You're in business, all right!

Learning to view yourself as being in business rather than as merely an employee brings enormous benefits in its wake. You gain a tremendous sense of security. Also, you're no longer subject to the capricious whims of your employer. Finally, you come to see that improving your financial well-being is in your power and that you can do far more than await your next raise.

Of course, this also means that you have to seize responsibility for your life and for your new business career. This requires some attitude adjustment. You used to think that finding a job was the end goal and that from that point on the responsibility was all your employer's. He had to pay you, he had to tell you what to do, and he had to correct you when you made a mistake. Wrong! That is not how a business professional views his job. The responsibilities are mostly *yours*. *You* have to find ways to make sure that the wage paid to you is a bargain. *You* have to find out what most needs doing, and *you* have to do it. *You* have to know when you have made a mistake, and *you* must bring it to the attention of your boss or supervisor . . . oops! I mean, your customer. Finding a job is just the beginning. Now you must grow in that job, always seeking new areas to expand your responsibilities and continually seeking ways to enhance your usefulness. If your job truly provides no scope at all for these growth strategies, then, as scary as it may be, quit! Find a new job in which you see fewer limitations on your potential.

You need to recognize that no matter what you do, you are really in business to succeed. The raw material you bring with you into your career is not nearly as important to your success as how you run your business. Do you constantly try to deliver a little more to your customers than they expect? Do you always pay attention to advertising and marketing, which means, do you maintain your reputation in your company, and do you preserve your relationships? Regardless of whether you work in a supermarket or drive a bus, regardless of whether you have earned a lofty academic degree or didn't finish high school, the most important questions are: Are you in business, or do you just have a job?

Needless to say, the same principles apply to you as a manager of other people. Give them scope to grow. Teach them to see themselves as independent business professionals.

RECOGNIZE THE IMPORTANCE OF BUSINESS SKILLS IN EVERY PROFESSION

Did you ever wonder why some lawyers make a lot of money while others with similar academic degrees, from equally prestigious law schools, appear to be close to starvation? Successful lawyers have not memorized more case studies than unsuccessful lawyers have. They didn't necessarily get better grades in law school. Did you ever wonder why some doctors seem to do very well while others merely make a living? Successful doctors don't necessarily know more medicine than other doctors do. Indeed, most people probably don't know enough about medicine to begin to evaluate doctors on the basis of their medical skills. How likely are you to check into what your doctor's class ranking was back at medical school? I know that I have never done so, and I also know that my confidence in my medical adviser has nothing to do with how well he did as a medical student.

How do you choose the doctors, lawyers, plumbers, and car mechanics that you need in your life? You seldom select them on the basis of their technical knowledge or their academic qualifications. Here is the shocking truth: You actually choose them on the basis of their *business* skills. How they build their practices, how they market themselves, how they develop their reputations, and how they establish themselves in the communities of people in which they move, all of this determines their success, not how well they did in college 20 or 30 years earlier.

You can't do very much about how well you did in high school or in college years ago. You may not be able to do much about the job you have, but you *can* change your outlook. You can make this change devastatingly effective, and you can make it permanent. It is all about how you are going to interact with other people from this day forward. Your success depends on them, but most of it is totally within your control.

WHY YOU ARE SO IMPORTANT IN DETERMINING YOUR OWN SUCCESS

Suppose you want to operate a food processor or a drill press? No problem. I can quickly teach you which buttons to press. That's because any machine will always respond predictably to the same controls. Whether the button is pressed by a saint or by a sinner, by an insincere charlatan or by a noble hero, the machine, not knowing the difference, will do exactly the same thing each time.

However, in your business, you grow your wealth by interacting with *people*, not machinery. With humans, it does depend on what sort of person is pushing the button. Ever notice how people gladly comply with a request from one person but sullenly and subtly sabotage things when the identical request is made by someone else?

It helps to be the first kind of person. With people, it isn't *buttons*, it's *being*. You relate best to people with whom you feel spiritually compatible.

Learning how to radiate spiritual compatibility is not as easy as learning which buttons to press. Before signing any deal, say buying a car, don't you first want to feel comfortable with the salesperson as a *person*? The clever little selling strategies aren't sufficient: You can see right through them. Instead, you try to get to know the real person before committing to any transaction with him or her. Everyone with whom you deal, your employees and your clients, your customers and your supervisors, all try to get to know the real you, too. You should also try to get to know the real you. Only then will you be able to modify yourself and how you are perceived by others.

Modifying the real you for maximum effectiveness is what Jewish teaching advised its devotees. An entire body of ancient Jewish literature called *Mussar*, which means "redirecting," teaches how to *be* different, rather than merely how to *act* differently. It provides a kind of spiritual prism through which you can more clearly see yourself without being distracted by the glare of your own ego. Using this spiritual tool helps equip you to interact with all people more effectively and ultimately more profitably.

You Are Your Most Important Employee

Over the years, I have enjoyed exhilarating triumphs, but I have also endured bitter defeats. It was never difficult to identify and to thank the many people whose participation in my activities brought me to triumph and success. For that reason, my triumphs taught me magnanimity, but it was my defeats that taught me humility. Let me tell you why. It was initially difficult for me to identify those who contributed to my defeats, but I was finally able to do so. Of all the people who have ever worked with me and for me, there still serves in my organization one man more responsible than any other for every failure I have ever suffered. You have probably figured out his name—yours truly, Daniel Lapin.

Training forms an important part in the running of every organization. Whether it is a sales organization, a dentist's office, an oil change franchise, or anything else, the people there need training—except that in the practical application of the Jewish system, which I dubbed Ethical Capitalism, it is not called training, but teaching. The difference is that "training" is for animals and robots. One of the many advantages humans have over animals and robots is that humans can function creatively and productively after being taught only general principles and goals, whereas animals and robots must be programmed or trained in great detail to respond specifically to every anticipated situation. So, in spite of the fact that many organizations refer to their "training" programs, it is actually *teaching* that forms an important part in the running of all organizations.

People must first learn the basic competencies of communication. They must be able to read and write; they must be able to understand instructions and convey them intelligibly to others. They must then be taught the special skills pertaining to their roles in the organization.

In addition, somewhere along the line they must also have learned and absorbed the *moral* dimensions of their professions. This means that they must learn to show up at their jobs on time every day regardless of how they feel. They must learn how to accept not only direction but also criticism without responding resentfully or mutinously. They must learn to act responsibly and predictably, and they must learn to avoid the countless temptations in any occupation. It is the obligation of every boss and supervisor to ensure that all these lessons are taught to all their subordinates.

What if you don't have any employees? Are you exempt from the duty of teaching subordinates? Never! No matter what work you do and no matter where you work, you always have at least one subordinate: yourself. That special employee—you—is better situated than anyone else to either help or hinder you in the achievement of your goals. Nobody else can be blamed for your failures until your one most crucial and important employee—you—is operating at peak effectiveness. The one employee for whose education you must personally take responsibility is yourself.

You Are Your Most Important Student

Three times each day, fervent Jews recite the sentence, "You shall teach them (these vital principles of successful and good living) to your children."[1] Jewish tradition points out that one letter is omitted in the Torah text from the word *them* allowing the word to also be read as "you."[2] The verse now would read, "You shall teach (these vital principles of successful and good living) first to yourselves and then to your children." From this well-known sentence emerges the principle that if a father only has the tuition money to engage a teacher for himself or alternatively for his children, he is obliged to educate himself first.[3] The idea is that he will later be in a better position to then educate his children. Engaging the teacher for the children first and then having them educate their father is not a good idea because it distorts the basic idea of children learning from and revering their parents, rather than the other way around.

The lesson is clear. If you have employees, make sure that you remain ahead of them in all the material you are obliged to teach them. If you do not have employees yet, you fortunately have time to get a head start.

Regarding yourself as your most important employee in constant need of teaching and supervision seems a daunting task. How can you become accustomed to this view of yourself and your own reality? Again, Jewish tradition comes to the rescue: Begin viewing yourself as two separate entities. Do not worry about precipitating a fatal case of what is called Multiple Personality Disorder. Like so many other areas of life, degree is the key. For example, many substances, such as arsenic, that would be poisonous in large quantities are necessary in tiny quantities within a healthy human body. If those quantities are either reduced or exceeded, the consequences are unhealthy. Possessing no sense at all of being two entities is just as unhealthy as allowing that sense to become excessive and chronic.

The three diagnostic criteria for Multiple Personality Disorder are:

1. The existence within the individual of two or more distinct personalities, each of which is dominant at a particular time.
2. The personality that is dominant at any particular time determines the individual's behavior.
3. Each individual personality is complex and integrated with its own unique behavior patterns and social relationships.[4]

Like most people you can think of yourself as having two distinct personalities—call them two distinct impulses—only one of which is dominant at any particular moment. Furthermore, your behavior in any given situation can be pretty much predicted by knowing which of your two impulses is in charge. Furthermore, each individual impulse within you is complex and capable of making complex and persuasive arguments to you. Each is also integrated with its own unique behavior patterns. One may encourage you to go to the gym for a workout, whereas the other may try to drag you to the candy counter. Each individual impulse within you is integrated with its own social relationships. One is integrated with your spouse, children, and co-workers, whereas the other is integrated with the person sitting next to you on an airplane.

The technique that Jews would use to teach themselves this indispensable skill of viewing oneself honestly and from above, as it were, much as one might appear to an outside and objective observer, depends on using an image. The imagery is that of a donkey and its rider. Imagine a visitor from another galaxy coming on a man riding a donkey. The visitor might make an understandable error, and view the donkey and its rider as one, large, curiously shaped creature. Of course, another human would realize that the strange sight is really just an upper creature riding on and in command of a lower one.

In the same way, you can also make an understandable error. Like a recently arrived Martian sees a donkey and rider as one, you mistakenly view a person, specifically yourself, as only one creature. In reality, you can better understand yourself and others if you view yourself as an intelligent and spiritual creature in command of a more material creature—in other words, your soul riding on and in control of your body. At least, your soul is supposed to be in command, and that is the entire point.

HELPING YOUR WISE IMPULSE DOMINATE YOUR SELF-DESTRUCTIVE IMPULSE

You might be interested to see how the ability to dissect the complexities of personality into two constituent tugs, one conflicting with the other, embedded itself into the nature of the Jewish people, contributing to their success. The Bible relates a famous story about God telling Abraham to elevate his son in dedication to God.[5] (Most people mistakenly believe that God told Abraham to slaughter his beloved only son because the Hebrew word for "elevate" can also mean "make an offering of him." In fact, Abraham himself misunderstood, and later the Almighty had to dispatch an angel to prevent Abraham from making his own misunderstanding both fatal and permanent.)

Returning to the beginning of the story, the Bible recounts how, after receiving what he thought were instructions to kill his son, Abraham saddled his donkey. It is strange that there is no mention of anyone either riding or loading that donkey. The next time the animal is encountered is when Abraham instructed his two servants: "You wait here with the donkey while my son and I go further to worship."[6] Here I must point out that in Hebrew, when one Hebrew word means two things, say A and B, ancient Jewish wisdom regards A and B as closely related. This is not so for English where, for instance, the *sole* of my foot bears no relationship to the seafood I prefer to eat with chips—Dover *sole*. In Hebrew, the fact that one particular word means both "donkey" and "materialism" is highly significant. Jewish tradition explains that throughout scriptural nomenclature, the donkey represents the material body. If you have ever wondered why tradition has it that the Messiah will ultimately enter Jerusalem on a donkey rather than on a far more prepossessing stallion, or better yet, in a Lexus, you now have the answer: The Messianic arrival presages a period of mastering materialism. In Judaism's oral transmission, the donkey is a convenient and timeless metaphor for the completely material. Riding on a donkey or even firmly affixing a saddle to its back implies dominating the material—putting the head in charge of the body.

But, back to Abraham. Intending to kill his son according to his mistaken impression of Divine edict, scripture records that Abraham saddled his donkey. Now you can finally understand that the donkey is not included in the narrative to inform you about ancient modes of transport. Instead you understand that to obey God, Abraham had to force himself to follow his head rather than his heart—his intellect had to subjugate his emotions. In other words, he had to saddle his donkey. That is why you never read about the donkey serving any utilitarian transport function. As Abraham approaches Mount Moriah, where the putative sacrifice was to take place, he needed to further distance himself from his material longing to grow old with his son. What did he say? "You wait here with the donkey while my son and I go further to worship."

By informing the reader that Abraham and Isaac were going to go beyond the donkey, as it were, Scripture reveals that Abraham has successfully emancipated himself from the tyranny of the material. This essential ability to constantly teach oneself and improve oneself depends entirely on becoming accustomed to seeing oneself as made up of two separate beings: one tugging toward short-term gratification while the other is heard issuing warnings in the background. You can get a feeling for this central idea in the story of Pinocchio, whose conscience was indeed an entity external to himself, Jiminy Cricket. It becomes a little easier to follow your head rather than your heart when you become cognizant of the tug-of-war between the two impulses.

Constantly struggling to follow head rather than heart, as Abraham did, has been one of the keys to Jewish success. Contrary to many other faiths that do not condemn listening to one's heart, Judaism assists its followers by constantly insisting that they follow their heads and disregard the enticements of their hearts.[7] Knowing that your heart can tug you in destructive directions is rooted into the Jewish psyche, and you would do well to root it into yours, too. This concept is so important to Judaism that it is emphasized at the very beginning of the Bible: "and Lord God formed man out of the dust of the ground . . . ."[8] Later in the same chapter are the words: "and the Lord God formed all the animals of the field out of the dust of the ground . . . ."[9]

The fascinating detail lost in translation is that the word *formed* is spelled slightly differently when *man* is being formed from the way it is spelled in the verse referring to *animals* being formed. It contains an extra letter, which according to Jewish tradition[10] alludes to the two separate impulses that co-exist inside of every person but that are not found in animals. One impulse urges people to act wisely in accordance with what they know is in their best interests. Meanwhile, their other impulse seductively whispers suggestions about ignoring their diet and raiding the refrigerator or ignoring their marriage and making a move on the young intern down the hall.

You subconsciously acknowledge this duality within yourself every time you say "My head hurts" or "My body aches." Who is the "you" whose head hurts? Right there, you are recognizing that there is a "you" apart from your body. You can call it a soul; Judaism does. Rabbi Abraham Twerski recounted a tale of a paralyzed woman attending a wedding. "I danced along with everyone else. Of course, I could not move my feet, but I danced with my hands on the table. You see, when I became paralyzed I did not change. I am still the same person I was. It is just that this person is trapped in a body that is paralyzed." Twerski continued, "This woman's perception is that the body is but a container for the person, and the person need not be affected by changes to the body. Similarly, when one sets aside bodily demands, one is not depriving the 'person,' since the true person may not desire things which the body craves."[11]

In the quest for increased income, it is wise to improve one's tendency to act in accordance with what one's mind advises rather than to follow one's emotional tugs and the urgent summons from one's appetites. For one thing, doing so makes you more predictable and suggests that you possess what is commonly referred to as "good judgment." It follows that being perceived to be someone with good judgment increases your desirability as a transaction partner. It doesn't matter for now whether the transaction is a job interview or setting up a syndication deal for a skyscraper. Wealth is produced by transactions. You need to drastically increase the number of transactions in which you get involved. Everyone needs to do so, which means that you need to make yourself as attractive as possible as a potential transaction partner. Please understand that I am not doing the equivalent of the anxious mother telling her unmarried daughter to put on more makeup and don a flattering dress. I am not discussing cosmetic makeovers. I am not discussing external fixes. I am describing how to effect very real changes in who you are. These changes will lure you to embark on the exciting voyage along the countless winding rivers of financial flow that crisscross the economy rather than to live your life in a stagnant backwater.

Does this imply that Jews never make stupid mistakes that ruin their lives? No, it doesn't mean anything of the kind. Does understanding the medical principles of salmonella guarantee that you will never suffer from food poisoning? No, it just means that the likelihood of an unfortunate culinary accident is dramatically reduced. There are no guarantees in life, but your chances for success are dramatically increased the more you can shift the odds in your favor. Making it a habit to judge yourself and to sometimes criticize and even condemn yourself dispassionately—as painful as this process is—dramatically increases your chances for business success by making it far less likely that others will have to judge, criticize, and condemn you. In other words, you will be far more competent at working with other people as well as leading other people when they sense that you are evaluating yourself at least as harshly as you evaluate them.

Luckily, you have the ability to show those with whom you live and work that you can follow that small, internal voice of noble authority. Doing so consistently causes others to perceive you as a leader and eventually turn you into a true leader. Failing this challenge condemns you, sometimes fatally, at least as far as your economic aspirations are concerned.

LISTEN TO YOUR CONSCIENCE

Here's a case in point. Philip Potter was a successful, affluent, 25-year-old analyst at Wall Street powerhouse Morgan Stanley. Just a couple of weeks before the stock market's biggest drop in 10 years, the *New York Times* published an explicit account of this young man's luxurious lifestyle in the Money and Business section.[12] Describing himself as an "über-consumer," Potter lovingly listed his Park Avenue apartment, his 50-inch TV, his custom-made suits, and his expensive Rolex watch. The *Times* journalist must have enjoyed the interview. He described his subject as one of the Wall Street wizards who earn and spend prodigiously.

But with the market as jittery as it had been, investment banking houses were particularly sensitive to the old "But where are the *customers'* yachts?" joke. Along with most firms, Morgan Stanley's policy manual contained a Code of Conduct that all its employees were required to sign. It included warnings such as, "You should not be identified as a Morgan Stanley employee without first clearing it with Corporate Communications." The code also declared: "Morgan Stanley discourages its employees from participating in personal profiles or stories which focus in any way on 'lifestyle.' These stories could be perceived as self-aggrandizing and unprofessional, particularly by clients and others outside the Firm." Do customers whose stock portfolios are falling through the floor really want to read about their brokers' high life? Do competent and high-earning brokers really need to have this spelled out for them in a policy manual? Apparently some do.

You would suppose that the clearly worded policies that Morgan Stanley has in place would prevent reasonably intelligent employees from embarrassing their bosses. Yet Philip Potter, a Yale graduate, was apparently unable to restrain himself from participating in the *Times* interview in such delightfully unrestrained fashion. The day after he achieved fame, he "resigned" from Morgan Stanley and found himself unemployed.[13] However, the jokes proliferated, and chuckles echoed around Wall Street for days. For weeks, Morgan Stanley executives endured jibes about how well they paid their analysts who failed to predict the downturn.

Philip Potter was undeniably wealthy, intelligent, well-educated, and sophisticated. He was not confused about what sort of newspaper interviews he was permitted to conduct. One may safely assume that he knew his employer's policy manual and had understood the Code of Conduct. Yet like so many other well-educated and successful professionals, he acted self-destructively. He also seriously hurt his employer. The problem is that like so many people, Philip Potter lacked what is sometimes called the character strength to resist the appeal of doing the wrong thing. In other words, his positive impulse lacked the strength to dominate his negative impulse.

Self-destructive actions are usually enormously appealing in the short term. Part of character strength is being able to routinely postpone gratification— sometimes indefinitely. This might mean avoiding an impulse purchase, maintaining an exercise or diet regimen, or turning down a flattering but ultimately destructive proposition or any of the many other temptations—

yes, temptations—that present themselves throughout a typical work week. The phrase "resisting temptation" may have an old-fashioned ring to it, and that is exactly the point. If doing the wrong thing did not usually feel so good, you would act intelligently all the time. If negative impulses did not have good feelings working in tandem with them as allies, it would be a piece of cake for positive impulses to dominate.

What makes behaving wisely so difficult is the emotional tug everyone feels toward making the mistake. Perhaps Philip Potter deeply wanted to see his name in the *New York Times*, knowing that his relatives and friends would read of his success. The voice of his conscience probably objected, but its voice became weaker and weaker.

What makes the challenge even harder for you is that once your emotions have selected a preferred course of action, those emotions get to work on your brain. In no time at all, you become convinced that the desired action is not only wise but also noble. It helps to visualize this moral struggle as a debate between your two impulses.

How can you hope to succeed in this quest to make only wise decisions? Treat this quest as a war and, as in all wars, you must know the enemy and its goals. Then not only are you better equipped to defeat the enemy, but you also feel more courageously committed to doing so. Knowing everything about your enemy makes it suddenly appear far less formidable. Who is your enemy? Who thwarts your ambitions and obstructs the path to your dreams more than anyone else? That part of you I have been identifying as your negative impulse. Whatever you call it, the important thing is that you come to understand it.

You can be your own worst enemy, but you can also be your own best employee. Remember to see yourself as two people. One of you is all wise, all rational, and always dedicated to the long-term good. The other one of you tries to talk you into short-term delights. You are Pinocchio and Jiminy Cricket wrapped up in one human body. One part of you is encouraging you to act with self-restraint and courage. At exactly the same moment, the second part of your makeup is feverishly trying to persuade you to do what you really feel like doing. The only question is, "Who is going to lead?"

Philip Potter, like everyone, was the composite of two separate parts. One part was perversely devoted to bringing about his downfall, while the other was valiantly defending his future. In all the decisions people face dozens of times a day, these two internal antagonists furiously throw themselves on one another in fierce combat. One voice seductively urges, "Do it, you will feel great! It will all work out all right in the end anyway." The other warns of perilous consequences. Only one of them can win, and which it will be depends on the strength of your character. Each time you reject the destructive appeal and follow the voice of wisdom, your ability to do so again the next time is enhanced. Your system behaves just like a muscle that responds more effectively after it has been exercised. Conversely, each time you allow yourself to yield to the negative impulse, you subsequently find it harder to make the right decision the next time.

Long before you can hope to lead others, you must acquire the strength to lead yourself. You will be truly amazed at how quickly your associates perceive character strength or its absence. Just think how easily you recognize its presence or absence in others. People are far quicker to forgive your ignorance, particularly if you promptly confess it, than they are to forgive your weakness. Philip Potter, the Wall Street wizard, earned the contempt of his associates for his *weakness*, not for his ignorance of the rules. Conversely, you can earn the respect of those you hope to lead not by knowing everything but by demonstrating easily recognized character strength.

Once you understand all of this and, more important, practice using it, you can expect to dramatically increase your self-control and to vastly increase your earning power, and you can also confidently anticipate saving yourself thousands of dollars in therapy fees. Character strength is rare and can only come from within. More and more, information is in the hands of almost everyone—just think of the Internet—and information available to everyone isn't terribly valuable. The more common a commodity, the lower the market price. The more rare a commodity, the more valuable it is. Your value in business derives from possessing rare commodities. Strength of character is like gold, and there is nothing stopping you from acquiring it. Real gold often follows.

TO THINE OWN SELF BE TRUE

Judaism prohibits suicide under any and all circumstances. I was first told of this prohibition as a young boy horrified by the suicide of a neighbor. I recall immediately asking my father to show me which verse in the Torah prohibited suicide. In hindsight, I now recognize the expressions I remember seeing cross his face as he wondered how much of this I would be able to understand. I don't know how much of his explanation I did understand at the time, but at least I remembered it well. He walked me through what I have just explained to you. He spoke of how each person is really made up of two different entities and that each entity wants something different for the person. "It is like riding a donkey," he said, "the donkey wants to go one way, or perhaps the donkey prefers going nowhere. You, however, have a very definite destination in mind." Now you must decide who is going to win, you or the donkey? Who will command whom?

Once he had explained the duality of a human, he pointed to the Ten Commandments and highlighted, "Thou shall not murder." "The principle is clear," he said. "Whatever you are prohibited from doing to anyone else, you are also prohibited from doing to yourself. Remember, you really comprise two separate moral entities. An act of suicide is the negative impulse part of you attempting to do away with the rest of you. Similarly," he said with a gentle smile, "you may not lie to yourself. It is just as much of a prohibition or sin as lying to someone else. In fact, in a manner of speaking, it is lying to someone else."

Lying to yourself or misleading yourself causes double damage. You not only underestimate the challenge that makes it far harder to evaluate a situation accurately and to determine the correct course of action, but you also throw doubt about your judgment into the hearts of those around you. Being optimistic is one thing; being blind is something entirely different. Similarly, psyching yourself up for a challenge is a positive way to prepare for a formidable task. But using that ability you possess to self-persuade inhibits you from taking the necessary steps and merely blinds you to peril.

Seeing yourself as two people makes it easier to remember to treat yourself as honestly as you would like to think you treat others. It also makes it easier to resist your tendency to act self-destructively on occasion. By this, I don't mean necessarily cataclysmic actions, but just the damaging effect on your career that comes as the result of the gradual accumulation of many small mistakes. Should you wish to combat effectively the tendency of one part of your personality to drag you in damaging directions, try to understand motivations. As with any adversarial situation, it pays to know what is motivating the other side. In the same way that it is valuable for you to understand exactly what drives other people, it is even more useful to get to know what drives yourself. (See the matrix on page 103.) By understanding your own motivations, you can far more easily determine why you do things and how to change your conduct. After all, by remaining exactly the same today as you were yesterday, you are guaranteeing that tomorrow will be no better than today.

UNDERSTAND WHAT REALLY MOTIVATES PEOPLE

What motivates people? Why do you do the things you do? The answer is not as complex as you might imagine, and knowing it will be most helpful to you. First, you need to understand the difference between physical things and spiritual things. Now let me be very clear: When I use the word *spiritual*, I do not refer to anything necessarily to do with God, morality, heaven, or anything else that you may think of when you hear the word *religious*. I do not use *spiritual* as a synonym for *religious*; instead, I use it in a scientific sense. I use it to refer to things that cannot be measured in a laboratory. Physical or material things can easily be measured with standard laboratory instruments, whereas spiritual things cannot be.

When a band records a piece of music, you can easily measure the tune's volume, for example. You can even perform a frequency spectrum analysis to discover whether most of the tune is in treble or whether it is in bass. However, you cannot measure whether fans will consider the tune worth purchasing. There is no machine that can foretell whether a particular piece of music will make humans feel sad or glad. Volume and frequency are material, or *physical,* qualities of the music, whereas the value of the music and its emotional impact on the audience are *spiritual* in nature.

Spiritual and Physical Motivators

	WORLD delivers spiritually	WORLD delivers physically
My spiritual needs	1. Who is wise? Knowledge, skills, information	2. Who is powerful? Discretionary income, savings, emotionally satisfying possessions
My physical needs	4. Who wins esteem? Friends, affection, love, significance	3. Who is wealthy? Food, shelter, clothing, other basics of life

There are three rules that can help you distinguish between the physical and the spiritual:

Rule 1: Physical things can be destroyed, whereas spiritual things cannot. Computer hardware, for example, is physical, whereas software is mostly spiritual. If you drop your laptop into a lake, you will have destroyed it because it is the material part of the computer. You can get a replacement copy of whatever software program you were using at little or no cost. After being forced to pay for a new laptop, you might have expected also to have to pay for the software installed on the computer now lying at the bottom of the lake. But you will be pleasantly surprised when the software company explains to you that you did not really destroy any software. It is basically indestructible. You may be able to smash a guitar, for another example, but you cannot obliterate a tune.

Rule 2: Physical things can tolerate imperfection; spiritual things need to be precise. Think of a building and the blueprints from which it was constructed. One is the spiritual part of the building, and the other is the physical or material manifestation of the structure. Clearly the blueprints of a hotel's design are spiritual, whereas the actual bricks-and-mortar construction is physical. On the drawings, you can see that the floor-to-ceiling heights at the two opposite ends of the great ballroom are both exactly, say, 10 feet. If you visited the hotel and accurately measured the height of the ceiling in the ballroom, you wouldn't be surprised to find that it varies by as much as an inch or two when measurements are taken at different locations in the large room. This simply doesn't matter in the real world. Nobody will notice the two-inch discrepancy, but eliminating that little discrepancy would involve the contractor in prohibitive expenses. However, if the *blueprints* lacked accuracy, then the entire integrity of the structure would be threatened.

Another example of Rule 2 involves removing a small part of your computer's hardware. Imagine that a screen-adjustment knob or a keyboard key fell off and was lost. You could still use your computer. However, if you erased only one line of software code, say less than a millionth of an entire program, the odds are that the application software would not run at all. That is because things that are essentially *spiritual* must be complete and perfect.

Rule #3: The spiritual element of an event must precede its physical actualization. For example, a business plan (which is software) must precede the construction of a factory and the purchase of manufacturing equipment, all of which are hardware. A baby's conception must precede its birth. Conception is more of a spiritual moment, and I refer not to the romance of the instant but to the fact that virtually no mass is involved. An ovum becoming fertilized is an information event rather than a matter event. The matter component then begins happening with cell division culminating about nine months later with a birth—the arrival of some new matter into the world. Needless to say, accuracy and completeness are more important in the conception process than they are in the birth process. Even a tiny genetic irregularity can later become a birth tragedy. But equally tiny obstetric damage during birth, for example, a small scratch, will heal quickly. Perfection is more important during the *spiritual* process than it is during the *material* process, and the spiritual process must take place first.

RECOGNIZE THE DIFFERENCE BETWEEN PHYSICAL AND SPIRITUAL CHARACTERISTICS AND NEEDS

When someone hires you, is he or she mostly interested in your physical or your spiritual characteristics? If you are being hired as a model, then you are safe in assuming that you are being hired for your physical qualities. If you are being hired as the strong man at the circus, you are also probably being hired for your physical prowess. In most other occupations, including yours and mine, I dare say people are being hired for their spiritual qualities. That is even true for Navy recruiters considering volunteers for the notoriously demanding SEAL program, where one might have thought only outstanding physical fitness counts. Your employers are interested in how honest and loyal you are; and as an employer yourself, you wish a reliable instrument existed to test the spiritual integrity of potential new hires. Employers and transaction partners are interested in how effectively you communicate and how well you can sell their products or services. They are interested in your integrity and your persistence. They want to know that you won't give up until the job is done. They are far less interested in the color of your skin, whether you are male or female, or whether you are bald or possess a full head of hair.

Nowadays, there are or soon will be tests that can tell you not only the gender of your unborn baby, but also its height, body type, aptitude for athletics, and hair color. In other words, you can find out almost anything physical about a baby before it is born. However, in advance, you can find out almost *nothing* about that child's tendency to be persistent, loyal, of strong character, and honest or whether the child will grow up to be an optimistic person or a fluent communicator. These matters are *spiritual* in nature and also happen to be the characteristics that most critically shape your career. That is why you need to fully grasp the difference between physical and spiritual in understanding the area of motivation—why people choose to do certain things.

Many have tried to identify why people do specific things, why they act certain ways, and what motivates them. Anthropologist and playwright Robert Ardrey investigated the animal origins of humans' attachment to property and suggested that the "Territorial Imperative" explained much of human behavior.[14] Everything people do in their busy, multidimensioned lives is about increasing the number and the amount of things they own and expanding their boundaries. Ardrey reduces entire human lives, with all their richness and complexity, to the petty human equivalent of animals urinating on their boundaries to mark them for others.

Decades earlier, Sigmund Freud had ascribed most of people's motivations to human sexual natures. However, it soon became obvious that infinitely complicated human beings could hardly be explained in terms of just one determinant, even if that one determinant was as powerful as sex. Modern science still sought the secrets of why people do those things they do.

Then, during the 1950s, modern psychology took giant steps forward in trying to identify those things that truly motivated and drove humans along certain tracks. The famous Jewish psychologist Abraham Maslow (1908–1970), along with others, arrived at a blueprint that was necessarily a little more complicated but certainly more accurate than preceeding theories.[15] This blueprint reduced the vast complexity of human behavior down to five basics and then finally to only four: pertaining to (1) self, (2) relations with other people, (3) surroundings, and (4) the body. Simply put, Maslow explained that most people need to feel satisfaction in four areas of life:

1. A sense of *personal growth* and development of themselves in understanding how the world works.
2. A feeling of expanding *personal power,* which diminishes their sense of vulnerability and of being victims of capricious fate.

3. The *basic necessities* of life, including food, clothing, and shelter.
4. The *esteem* of other people.

In arriving at this blueprint of behavior, modern psychology converged with the stable and unchanging position taken by ancient Jewish scholarship on this subject for millennia. I do not know whether Abraham Maslow mined the 2000-year-old Jewish source for this wisdom, but I doubt it. What is not in doubt is that he, too, saw the relevance of understanding human motivation to business management. In 1962, Maslow wrote a business book entitled *Eupsychian Management* that was based on his research into human nature.

Jewish information on human nature is not based on recent research but on two ancient ideas:

1. That human nature has not undergone very much change during the past 5,000 years.
2. That nobody is likely to know more about the nature of His creatures than the Creator.

This is why certain human interaction problems that cause consternation in corporate boardrooms today are often the same ones discussed in Shakespeare's plays, such as *Macbeth* or *King Richard III* as well as in many Biblical stories such as the account of King David and his questionable seduction of Bathsheba.

Amid all the rapid change inherent in business, it is nonetheless important to be aware of those things that never change. One thing that has never changed is that Jews have always known that the mystery of what motivates humans boils down to, not three, and not five, but exactly four basic elements. Jews have known this from a traditional explanation of an otherwise puzzling verse: "A river flows out from Eden to water the Garden, and from there it is divided and becomes four headwaters."[16] Any atlas will quickly reveal that no such arrangement of waterways ever existed in the ancient world. This is *spiritual* data, not geographic. Another problem with a literal interpretation is that if the purpose of the river is to "water the Garden," it ought to flow *into* Eden rather than "out from Eden." No, the ancient sages knew better: The main river represents the human yearning to achieve the best life possible—a person's quest to find a way into his or her personal Eden. It is made up of four basic rivers, or elements, one of which encircles a land with gold—"And the gold of that land was good."[17] The inspiring message is that in order to find the way into Eden, each person needs to follow all four of the rivers, needs to fully develop and satisfy all four human drives—not just two of them, but all four.

The Jewish volume in which this advice is most succinctly presented is *Sayings of the Fathers.* Chapter 4 opens with an early sage known as Ben Zoma asking and answering four questions:

1. Who is wise?
2. Who is powerful?
3. Who is wealthy?
4. Who wins esteem?[18]

Later scholars ask why Ben Zoma contented himself with only these four questions. After all, he might also have asked, Who is humble? Perhaps he might even have asked, Who is virtuous? and Who is pious? The answer is that he was probing the *roots* of human motivation; and because Ben Zoma accurately understood the place of humans in the cosmos, he knew of the critical two-by-two matrix that yields four elements.

Why a two-by-two matrix? That's easy! Humans are physical, right? They possess characteristics like height, weight, eye color, and skin color. But wait! Humans are also *spiritual.* They can be more or less loyal, honest, compassionate, loving, courageous, and far seeing. People are known sometimes to act nobly and selflessly, against the interests of their own physical survival. When they do so, it is in response to the call of their *spiritual* nature. Because humans obviously have *physical* needs, such as food and water, it is hardly surprising to discover that humans also have *spiritual* needs. That means that as total human beings, people have two types of needs and are thus motivated to satisfy those two types of needs. There you have the first part, the "my needs" part, of the two-by-two matrix shown on page 103.

Now, the world in which you live can obviously supply you with physical goods such as apples, apartments, sunshine, and bread. However, this world outside of yourself also has the capacity to supply you with *nonphysical commodities,* such as friendship, information, money, and music. Thus, you can see how your physical and spiritual needs, which can be satisfied in both a physical and spiritual way by the cosmos around you, can also be taken altogether to yield a two-by-two matrix with the four cells that Ben Zoma supplied in Chapter 4 of *Sayings of the Fathers.*

I will discuss each of these four cells in turn and show that each cell corresponds to each of those four basic human needs. Failing to take into account all four of our basic needs is what often seriously handicaps people and makes them miserable as well.

The First Motivator: Wisdom

Referring again to the matrix on page 103, the top-left cell, cell 1, represents the intersection of the row that is about my spiritual needs and the column that is about a commodity that the world delivers spiritually. This cell is filled by some commodity that possesses two characteristics: (1) I depend on this commodity spiritually but not physically. This means that withholding that commodity from me will not cause me to die. (2) The world delivers this commodity to me spiritually. This means that an animal, unaware of the spiritual, watching will not see the commodity being delivered to me. The delivery of, say, a bottle of drinking water would be seen. What transfers itself from outside of my body into me invisibly and contributes only to my spiritual well-being? Only *wisdom* fits all the parameters. Without it, I will still live and nobody can witness little packets of wisdom enter my head.

What does this mean in practical terms? It means that people have a real need for keeping up with current events, learning new skills, maintaining professional knowledge, and staying abreast of developments in their field. It could include becoming knowledgeable in areas needed for your children's homework or simply setting out to know more about music or the geography and culture of China. Whatever it is, you should know that like most people you have a very real need for a sense of intellectual growth. Even if you don't feel it, you have it. Satisfy this need for intellectual growth, and you will better situate yourself at the crossroads of economic creativity in your community.

You probably do not feel your body's need for potassium or sodium chloride, but you try to eat intelligently and control your diet so that your body's need for these minerals is satisfied. Similarly, you should regulate your reading and your exposure to intellectual stimulation so that you don't subject yourself to just the mind candy found in popular entertainment. You also need the mind nutrition found in regular solid and substantial material that will provide deep and vital satisfaction. Without it, your being is off balance. Remember, you need to be supplied with commodities that correspond to all four cells. Apart from anything else, it also makes you a more interesting and attractive person, which is obviously good for business!

The Second Motivator: Power

So far, you have seen how all people yearn for a sense of growth in their understanding of themselves and their environment. I call that need for a sense of growth wisdom.

Now on to cell 2: This one is delivered very physically and once again your life does not depend on your getting it. Without this motivator, your life will be undeniably diminished, but you can remain alive. This motivator is *power*.

Most people would indignantly protest any suggestion that a lust for power motivates them. That is because they automatically associate the word *power* with negative stereotypes. However, that is not what the word really means, and what it does mean is not all negative. For example, to some small extent, the stark horror and abominable cruelty of September 11, 2001, shocked a sense of life's fragility into the hearts of millions of people. Americans had become spoiled by luxury, self-indulgence, and security. The way that even the least successful Americans live should not be confused with normality in other places and during other periods of history. As the fortunate beneficiaries of many decades of stable productivity on the part of the large U.S. population, Americans have become incapable of completely grasping what the basics of life really are. The basics of life can be reduced to the incredibly demanding task of extracting an adequate living from an often reluctant earth while expending the least amount of energy. Not everybody understands this, and losing sight of this reality can be a real handicap.

Jews have always retained a sense of reality from these words that God said to Adam and that regularly echo through their culture: "Cursed is the ground because of you; through suffering shall you eat from it all the days of your life. Thorns and thistles shall it sprout for you. . . . By the sweat of your brow shall you eat bread."[19]

Yes, that's right; life isn't easy. You can't eat video games, designer jeans, or a big-screen television. Those only become vital accoutrements to life *after* you have enough to eat and a way to be sheltered from physical harm. Once you are sheltered from harm, you can try to find shelter from pain, and eventually, even from discomfort. In other words, you can try to control your environment.

People attempt to adjust things in their immediate surroundings to suit their desires or what they perceive as their needs. To whatever extent you have the ability to control your environment, that is the extent to which you possess power. For instance, when you walk into a room and make a beeline for the thermostat on the wall, adjusting it to raise or lower the room temperature, you are exerting power. Here is another way in which you may try to control your environment: If you are lucky enough to be able to take a day off from work, you have power. Can you jump into your car anytime and go wherever you please in silent, heated comfort just by turning a key instead of waiting in the rain for a drafty bus that always runs late except when you too are late? If so, congratulations to you! You have succeeded in securing a measure of power. Could you afford to go hiking up a mountain last Sunday? If so, welcome to the ranks of the powerful. You are so successfully extracting a living from the planet that not only can you afford a day to hike instead of work, but you also own sufficient clothing to keep you warm at high altitudes. I'm impressed.

Power, therefore, is a measure of your ability to extend your influence and control into the world around you. If you are working all day, seven days a week, and merely surviving, you have zero power. On the other hand, if your professional occupation provides you with much of what you want by demanding only six days of work each week, you are pretty powerful. If, in addition to that, you own your home and have access to electricity, gas, and other utilities, you are really powerful. If you own a vacation cottage and some investments and don't have to worry about how you will live after you are too old to work, then you are almost indescribably powerful. If, in addition to that, your children obey you . . . well, what is there to say? Obviously, the fellow on top of the Forbes 400 list and the president of the United States are examples of people with rare power, but power is exactly what distinguishes them from you and me.

Now would you feel a little more comfortable in joining me in the quest for more power? I thought so. You see, without owning a boat and an investment portfolio, I will still be able to *survive*; millions of people do. However, don't denigrate the spiritual solace and value those extra things bring. Remember, they are things the world delivers physically. That fancy outfit does increase your power, and it did get delivered to you by FedEx in a completely material way that even an animal could observe. A person came to your door and handed you a package. That is a physical and visible transfer of something from the cosmos to you. Which leaves us with two more cells, motivations, to unwrap.

The Third Motivator: Wealth

Cell 3 represents the commodity without which I will not survive and that the world delivers physically. It can only refer to one thing: the basics of survival. It includes food, shelter, physical health, and so on. You may call it "wealth" as I do because Ben Zoma introduces it with the question, "Who is wealthy?" His answer helps you understand that when you think of wealth, you are often confusing it with power. Basically "wealth" means the ability to survive on this earth. Ben Zoma answers his own question by saying that the person is wealthy who is satisfied with his or her portion. That is true wealth. Obviously that is not power, only wealth—the means to have the basics that your body needs to continue functioning.

The Fourth Motivator: Esteem of Others

Cell 4 examines a commodity that enters a person *spiritually* but that is a *physical* need: Without this invisible substance, a person will literally die. What could this be? It is the *esteem* of other people.

This is not to be confused with self-esteem, which is a meaningless nostrum foisted on people by the feel-good movement. Of all groups in the United States, convicted murderers are said to have the highest levels of self-esteem. This makes sense when you think about it. To kill someone else, you must think quite a lot of yourself. Professor Roy Baumeister of Case Western Reserve University found that people with high self-esteem tend to have low self-control.[20] Indeed, why should anyone who thinks so very highly of himself bother himself with irksome self-control?

Those who want to succeed must concentrate on *self-respect* and the *esteem of others* rather than on self-esteem. Self-respect is the consequence of genuine achievement and cannot be conferred by others. To illustrate this idea, consider the findings of a landmark report published in 1993 by the

National Commission on Excellence in Education, called *A Nation At Risk*. It cited, among other problems, poor math performance by U.S. students. Along with an earlier 1989 international comparison of math skills, it showed U.S. students scoring at the bottom and South Korean students scoring at the top. Former Secretary of Education William J. Bennett said, "Ironically, when asked if they are good at math, 68 percent of U.S. students thought they were very good (the highest percentage of any country), compared to 23 percent of South Korean students (the lowest percentage of any country), which demonstrates that this country is a lot better at teaching self-esteem than it is at teaching math."[21]

Obviously, self-esteem is what you try to gain when you haven't achieved anything and thus don't deserve any self-respect. By achieving something, you earn the esteem of others and thus gain self-respect, too. Recent research establishes that while self-esteem among U.S. youth has been on the rise for the past 30 years, accomplishment and responsible decision making have been on the decline.[22]

Clearly the esteem of others is conveyed to me quite invisibly. It is a spiritual transmission that leaves me feeling unmistakably uplifted. Note that what is being discussed is cell number 4, which is in the "My physical needs" row. That means that without a regular and adequate dose of others' esteem, I will die. Is that true? If so, how does that work?

I think it is true, and here is how it works. It is a sad fact that the overwhelming majority of homeless people are single and alone. Most people who are connected to others through family, friendships, or associations such as churches do not end up on the street when disaster strikes. The need for the esteem of others is one of the mechanisms that motivates people to nurture and maintain those relationships.

Being without strong connections to others is potentially fatal. For example, when more than a dozen elderly people died during a Chicago heat wave a few years ago, their common denominator was not their age. After all, many thousands of other elderly Chicagoans survived the brutal heat. Only one common feature was shared by all those who died: They lived alone and were all out of touch with family and friends. Another sad example is that virtually all of those lying intoxicated in urban doorways and lounging in drug-induced stupors on city sidewalks are also alone. As hard as it may be to imagine, you are saved from the long irreversible slide down the slippery slope of self-neglect by your drive to preserve the good impression that your friends, business associates, and relatives have of you. When you lose the desire to retain others' esteem, you can deteriorate so far that death is brought on prematurely.

Sometimes after a divorce or the death of a spouse, especially when no children are present, a person (usually a man) begins tragically to lose contact with old friends and associates. Little by little his former acquaintances watch him deteriorate. His clothing begins to look frayed and less than immaculate. Personal hygiene and regular medical and dental attention are all neglected, and the slide downhill accelerates. Alcohol or other chemical dependencies sometimes develop, and death eventually follows. This is not an inevitable road map to depravity and destruction. Many avoid it, but without the esteem of people important to them, life does become more fragile. Suicide is almost always linked to a sudden void in the amount of esteem of others felt by the suffering individual. Yes, I do think that the esteem of others confers physical health and longer life.

BALANCING ALL FOUR MOTIVATORS TO ACHIEVE MAXIMUM SUCCESS IN ALL ASPECTS OF YOUR LIFE

All human desires and motivations spring from these four fundamental needs that grow out of humans being both physical and spiritual creatures operating in a world that can supply both physical and spiritual commodities. Some of the things people pursue satisfy more than one cell simultaneously. For instance, sex satisfies not only cell 4, in that it clearly enhances the ability to win esteem, but also cell 2, power. Earning money satisfies cell 3 because a part of a person's earnings does go toward providing him or her with the basics, even though the precise definition of basics is different for different people and, indeed, is different for any one person at different stages of life. However, earning money also satisfies cell 2, our pursuit of power. Having discretionary money, beyond that required for the basics of your life, means being able to influence what happens in your immediate vicinity. The more power you possess, the wider the area you can influence and perhaps control.

Spending real, scheduled time with my family is just as important as anything else I do. After an evening of playing a game together with some of my children, helping with homework, and talking on the phone with a disappointed daughter, I may feel rather noble and self-sacrificing; but this is a foolish sentiment. The fact is that I was the chief beneficiary of the evening's activities. When I dedicate time to the members of my family, I am satisfying at least two of the motivational cells, maybe more. At the very least, I am basking in the esteem of others and I am probably also winning new knowledge. Far from hindering my ability to launch myself at my fiscal challenges the next morning, having invested the evening in this manner actually helps my marketing abilities tomorrow.

One of the paramount gifts that this model of four types of motivators brings into your life is the ability to balance your existence. Ben Zoma's wisdom instructs you to constantly maintain balance in your own life and, as leaders, to also do whatever is in your ability to help others in your orbit to maintain balance in their lives. While focusing on cells 2 and 3, not only must I work at earning money, but my very capacity to do so will be diminished if I do not also work at gaining wisdom at the same time. My efforts at winning the esteem of others will be seen as buffoonish if I do not simultaneously work at clothing myself and my family adequately and increase my skills and knowledge. Think of it as a balanced diet.

Imagine a typical, underexercised "desk driver" who has enjoyed one too many good meals. Now see him embarking on a body-building regimen. If he were to spend the entire first year working only on his biceps, he would end up looking like a bizarre caricature of Popeye. Any professionally designed program would provide him with both cardiovascular exercise and body strength exercises. It would make him regularly work out every single muscle in his body. The same is true of the four motivators: If you focus exclusively on acquiring wealth, for example, and ignore the other three equally important parts of your life, the paradox is that you will end up being *less* effective at business over the long term.

Look at the example of Gerald Levin. In early December 2001, many years before he would have been expected to retire, Levin, the man who came out on top of the biggest merger in U.S. history, announced his departure from AOL Time Warner. A brilliant and effective executive, Levin had suffered a tragedy when his son was brutally murdered in New York in 1997. A shakeup like that can cause anyone to reevaluate his life. However, that had been nearly five years earlier, so other things could have also played a role. What could they be? Here is a clue: Levin, who is Jewish and who had at one time been a student of religion, told an interviewer, "I'm my own person. I have strong moral convictions." I certainly cannot explain his sudden decision to retire, but there are clues in various interviews he granted. "I want my identity back," he said on December 5, 2001. "I'm not just a suit; I want the poetry back in my life" was another clue. Levin seemed to be saying that he was retiring in order to devote time to developing other nonbusiness aspects of his life.

There is probably no single reason for Levin's decision, just as there is no single reason why any other relatively young executive might cap a lifetime of corporate success and boardroom triumphs with a premature retirement. Chief among the reasons, though, could be a nagging sense of neglecting an entire dimension of one's life and personality. By nurturing these areas consistently throughout life, the successful business professional will greatly increase the likelihood of deriving maximum fulfillment from his or her life. This may make him or her less susceptible to what, in Levin's case, sounds a lot like a search for meaning in life. Maintaining a Ben Zoma state of life-balance makes it much easier to resist the temptation of premature retirement. Instead of promising yourself that you will play golf, read good books, and enjoy time with the family when you retire, you should heed Ben Zoma's advice and take constant little slices of retirement as it were, each and every day of your life.

Jews have a word that captures this essential theme of constantly confronting multifront challenges. The word is *shalem,* from which is derived the far better known *shalom,* meaning "peace." The root meaning of the word is "totality" or "comprehensiveness." (Its "peace" connotation stems from the altogether reasonable principle that authentic and lasting peace is merely an illusion if both parties to the conflict do not feel they have been made whole and complete.) The word *shalem* is often used in the context of human development, implying that people must constantly work on all four zones of their humanity in order to try to achieve a totality. Does anyone really want to be rich and lonely? Does anyone really want to be wise but unhealthy? Of course not. So as appealing as it may be to block out all distractions and only focus your attentions on the one specialized area of your obsession, such is not the road to success. In this sense, Judaism frowns on specialization. I may have to specialize in my professional occupation, but I should not do so in the totality of my life.

Jews have always found inspiration in one particular Scriptural account that revolves around the word *shalem*. After Shekhem, a Hivvite prince, raped Jacob's daughter Dinah, he wished to marry her. Hoping to persuade his own people to accept Jacob's family, the about-to-be-formed Children of Israel, Shekhem uttered the following words: "These people are *shalem* with us; let them settle in our land and trade in it."[23]

Ancient Jewish tradition interprets Shekhem's words this way: "These people, Jacob's family, will make us *shalem*, or whole. Every nation lacks some resources that must be imported from elsewhere and can export its own products in exchange. In order for this to take place, every nation needs businessmen and traders. Jacob's family are natural traders and by importing our needs, they will make us *shalem*, or whole."[24]

Paradoxically, Jewish tradition teaches that only by not specializing, only by not excluding all the essence of life from your endeavors, will those endeavors be blessed. In other words, don't specialize.

A caveat is in order here. Achieving truly spectacular success and international prominence in any field does mean that you will have to sacrifice most other regions of your life. For example, if you wish to compete in the next Olympic games, you won't have much of a life for the next four years. Similarly, the late Golda Meir, former prime minister of Israel, once poignantly told a group of young women how her political aspirations and desire to lead the State of Israel penalized her marriage and her family. Are you driven to reach the very top of the heap in business? If so, you might give your family and friends ample warning and advise them to check back with you once a decade.

However, this book is not for those people. This book is for those of you who desire wealth, real but not mind-numbing wealth, along with a life. You face another paradox: If you spend all your time and vitality exclusively trying to make money, you will make less than if you had properly balanced your efforts in all four vital areas of human motivation.

This has always been one of the big secrets of the Jewish approach to money. Biblical figures are almost all larger-than-life, three-dimensional personalities. Although the Oral Torah describes many of them as fabulously wealthy, this does not usually emerge directly from the text. This is because wealth is considered to be the consequence of a life well lived, in the company and companionship of others doing the same, rather than a purpose of life in itself. These Biblical characters were, for the most part, exciting people, passionately involved in complex, multitiered relationships with others; so, not surprisingly, they became wealthy. Wealth was consequence and not a prime purpose.

Here is a tantalizing glimpse into the daily nineteenth-century life of the Seligmans, one of the wealthiest Jewish families ever in the United States.

Listen to this observation from Prince Andre Poniatowsky, a nephew of King Stanislaus of Poland, who visited the wealthy Seligman family of New York in 1892. After doing business with the Seligmans' bank and after visiting the family in both their town and summer homes, here is what the Prince wrote home:

> Money in itself, however, had no significance for them outside of business. Any observer listening to their talk during leisure hours would have taken them for good rentiers, given to sport, literature, art, and especially to music, who contributed generously to charity and still more to the finances of their political party, and, above all, were devoted to family life with an intensity to be met with today only in the French provinces.[25]

The enduring point revealed by the Seligman lifestyle is that certain things are best not pursued directly. Mountain peaks are almost never scaled by the direct approach. Successful climbers plot what usually turns out to be a long and circuitous assault. At times it probably even appears as if the climbing party is traveling away from rather than toward its summit destination. Nonetheless, that is the nature of mountain peaks.

Sometimes people find themselves in adversarial relationships. Nations find themselves at war, individuals find themselves in fights, both professionally and domestically. In these situations, it is usually a bad mistake to pursue peace directly. If peace is the only objective, then the means of achieving it are easy—merely surrender. A genuine peace with which both parties can live for the long term may only be achievable in the wake of conflict. Peace is just one of those things that is best pursued indirectly. Another is happiness. There are many things you can do to instill happiness in yourself. They include hard work and achievement, durable relationships, and, in fact, pretty much the four main motivators I presented a few pages earlier. However, desperate and determined attempts to pursue happiness directly often lead to spurious emotional substitutes and damaging excursions into the dark world of alcohol and other chemical abuse.

Prince Andre Poniatowsky learned from the Seligmans that money and wealth are exactly like mountain peaks, peace, and happiness. Attempts to pursue any one of them directly are seldom the most effective route.

ACKNOWLEDGE YOUR NEGATIVE ATTRIBUTES

Great athletic coaches have told me that when commencing work with a promising young athlete, their first task is to help him or her get rid of some accumulated bad habits. Only after that has been accomplished can the coach begin the task of teaching the right way to run, or to hit, throw, or kick a ball. This principle of banishing the bad habit before trying to adopt the good is one not unfamiliar to Jewish culture. King David famously wrote: "Turn away from doing evil, and then do good, seek and pursue total completion."[26] Jewish tradition has always seen this verse to be advising people not to attempt the difficult acquisition of good habits before getting rid of the bad. The recommended sequence is to first stop doing the destructive activity, then embark on making the good and desired activity part of your life. Finally, you can integrate it all into the new and complete you.

Imagine a man wanting to lose weight, for example. He knows that he must stop doing one bad thing: overeating. He also knows that he must start doing one good thing, such as physically exerting himself more. It wouldn't make sense for him to embark on a rigorous exercise routine while still indulging himself with too much of the wrong kinds of food. Perhaps he smokes cigarettes, too. In that case, he should surely wean himself from the two unhealthful habits while he gradually begins to ramp up his exercise program. In another example, a woman wanting to begin planning for her financial future should first eliminate unnecessary spending before setting out the details of her investment program.

How do you find the determination and the discipline to cease destructive behavior that has become deeply ingrained in your personality? Part of the answer is, as I mentioned earlier in this chapter, to recognize the two parts of your personality that vie for control. It is never as simple or as easy as just saying "no," but standing up to the seductive suggestions of your destructive side is a little easier when you know to whom you are talking. Here are just two of the destructive things that people do and that can be eliminated relatively easily from their behavioral repertoire.

Step 1: Admit Your Weaknesses. The first step is to acknowledge that you do dumb things. A question I force myself to confront regularly is this: Which of the actions I am currently taking or contemplating will, in the future, appear to be fully as stupid as those of last year, last month, and last week? With hindsight, I usually have a pretty good idea of what stupid mistakes I made last year, last month, or last week. I also know that at the time, my actions seemed prudent and rational to me. Frankly, they frequently even appeared brilliant for a while, until the full folly of my errors sank in. Therefore, contemplating that question will save me grief in the future.

Step 2: Don't Get Angry or Lose Control. Few of the stupid things you do are more stupid than allowing yourself to grow angry. When you're angry, you're out of control. Helen Gurley Brown, who ran *Cosmopolitan* magazine for more than 30 years, put it well: "Thou may not lose one's temper in an office, especially if thou art the boss. Out of control by you means in control by them—you've lost it."[27]

As I made clear at the beginning of this book, if who you are and what you do fail to bring the success you desire, it is not sufficient to merely do different things; you also need to become a different person. The best way (and perhaps the only way) to become a different person is by forcing yourself to do different things until they become second nature. In essence, when those things have become part of you, then you will have become different, and that is exactly what you need to do.

It will be devastating for your career if your colleagues cannot rely on you to keep on an even emotional keel. During my work advising corporate leaders, the issue of anger surfaces virtually every time I ask, "Do you have any executives in your company around whom people feel they must walk on eggshells for fear of setting off an out-of-control, emotional explosion?" There nearly always is such a person. Could it be you? You dramatically increase your value to others if you always maintain a calm and pleasant manner.

What is the reason that some folks seem to slide so easily over the edge of self-control and inflict their vicious tempers on all who are unfortunate enough to be in the vicinity? Do they not know the costs that their tempers impose on their careers? The answer is that anger is one of the most self-destructive of all human behaviors. It shatters romantic, social, and business relationships—and rightly so. Why should anyone have to endure the abuse regularly dished out by someone who can't control his temper? The twelfth-century scholar Rabbi Moses Maimonides can offer assistance. He pointed out that most human attributes have their purposes, with the exception of anger.

You see, his brilliant insight was that characteristics such as cruelty, compassion, truthfulness, and lying simply do not exist isolated and alone. Instead, each can only find meaning when placed at one extreme of a spectrum with its antonymic mate at the opposite extreme. Going to one extreme of the spectrum and delivering cold, heartless truth can often be as wrong as going to the other end of that spectrum and lying indiscriminately.

When a friend has just spent a lot of money on a nonreturnable purchase, he or she often asks your opinion. Here is where dishonesty becomes a virtue. This is really simple. Had the friend truly desired your opinion, he or she would have consulted you before the purchase. "Todd, do you like the BMW 545i I am considering buying?" or "Nancy, how do you think I'd look in a simple little black frock?" No, when you are asked for an opinion following the purchase, it is not callous honesty that is required but kindness and affirmation.

Someone who is constantly over at the cruel end of the spectrum is a tyrant. At the opposite extreme is the person who dwells way over at the compassion end of that spectrum. It is not pleasant to work for a cruel person who lacks all compassion. But it is also tiresome to work for a boss who lacks sufficient "cruelty" to sometimes discipline a malingering fellow worker or to deny an out-of-place request. One needs the ability to summon up the attribute of firmness, which can sometimes look like cruelty. Similarly, regarding compassion as the ultimate value and right guide for every circumstance means that you will never be able to negotiate with firmness and strength. It would be equally mistaken to negotiate harshly with complete disregard for the feelings of the other party. Ideal negotiation is transaction sculpting. It is designing a win-win outcome, which enhances the relationship between the parties. This desirable outcome is far easier to envisage while keeping one's focus on the midpoint of the characteristic spectrum.

Here is another circumstance in which I keep the midpoint rule in mind. When hiring executives, I usually ask "How would you go about firing someone whose performance in your department is inadequate?" While the interviewee thinks about my question and while he or she responds, I watch for body language as much as I listen to the reply. I want to hire people who will suffer real pain if they have to fire someone. I want someone who won't get a wink of sleep the night before he or she is to terminate a subordinate's employment. But I also want someone who nonetheless will unhesitatingly come in the next day and fire the underperforming employee and take whatever steps are necessary to preserve the safety and the integrity of corporate assets under the control of the departing associate.

Instead of simple-mindedly regarding some attributes, like kindness, as "good" and others, like miserliness, as "bad," it is better to move to and fro along the spectrum line as circumstances demand. Maimonides suggested usually hovering around the middle on all these spectrum lines, with the exception of anger.

Thus you can see that almost every human characteristic, both positive and negative, has its place, with the exception of anger. There is never any circumstance that demands that you become angry. Please note that I do not say, "Never *display* anger." Instead, I say, "Never *be* angry." In other words, there may well be many management situations, both at home and at work, where radiating an impression of being really upset, even angry, might be called for. But that is entirely different from really being angry. Being angry means you are out of control. What causes anger? Arrogance. Show me someone who readily loses his temper and showers those around him with angry yells and insults, and I'll show you a very arrogant man. Anger is the emotion you feel when you are not being treated with what you consider to be appropriate respect. When I erupt in obscene fury at a traffic jam that threatens to make me tardy for an appointment, what I am really saying is, "How dare they! How dare they make me late! Don't they know how important I am?" Were I to be as humble as I should be, almost nothing would make me feel anger. When my hammer hits my finger instead of the nail, my subsequent anger reflects not only the momentary surge of pain, but also the disparity I see between my importance and the trivial postponing of my picture-hanging goal.

The final fact I must tell you is that there is a common misperception about anger. I have heard so many folks tell one another, "If you feel that angry, tell him; it isn't healthy to bottle it up." Wrong! It is very healthy to bottle it up. In fact, the more you bottle it up, the less frequently will you find yourself feeling overwhelmed by anger. The best way of dramatically reducing your own stress as well as that of all those who must interact with you is simply to stop allowing yourself to react angrily to anyone. Take a deep breath, take a walk, or take an aspirin; but whenever you feel anger welling up inside you, do not allow it past your teeth. I know this sounds funny, but I guarantee it works. This advice is a staple of what has guided Jewish business professionals for generations, and I have watched it work repeatedly within companies that I have counseled on these anger management techniques. Stop showing your anger, and you will soon stop feeling it. In addition, watch that arrogance factor. If you frequently feel anger, it may be a useful arrogance barometer for you. The more you think of yourself, the less significant everyone else looks by comparison. And how dare such insignificant beings bother you!

Getting to know yourself is an ongoing part of the adventure of life. One of the perks of maturing is getting to know yourself a little better. One of the marks of sanity is seeing yourself pretty much as others see you. In your quest to increase the amount of money that flows toward you, getting to know yourself is vital. However it comes with some risk. Sometimes you do not much like the person you come to know. It is important that as you get to know yourself, and as this process stimulates the desire to improve certain characteristics, you evade the terrible trap of perfectionism. You can often find yourself paralyzed into total immobility by your reluctance to settle for anything less than perfection. This, and some of the other perils of perfectionism, will be seen in the next chapter.

YOUR PATH TO PROSPERITY

- *Set aside a short period each day during which your sole purpose is to become your own harshest critic.*   Rigorously maintain an utterly private record of each day's successes and failures in winning the struggle. Create a confidential file in your laptop computer, your personal digital assistant, or your paper organizer that you update without fail each weekday night before retiring.

  Briefly record each decision you confronted during the day that demanded a courageous or noble response. Detail whether or not you rose to the challenge. In the event that you did not, candidly examine the conflicting tugs you experienced, and write a few sentences describing what would have been the superior decision. Finally, analyze whether there is any corrective action for you to take in the near future.

  Do this at the end of every single weekday. It only takes about five minutes maximum, but the impact of this little exercise is impossible to overestimate. You will begin feeling the difference in no more than a week.

- *As difficult decisions are demanded of you during your working day, share the emotional conflict you are undergoing with your associates.*   Let your associates know and understand that you are not endowed with superhuman powers and that you feel the temptations of the unwise course of action. After laying out the alternatives, if you can then resolutely take the harder path, you not only strengthen yourself but you also encourage your employees and reinforce their perception of you as an effective leader.

- *Seek out small battles to win in your private life.* If you are committed to a diet regimen or to an exercise routine, you know only too well the compelling call of that destructive voice that earnestly reassures you that weight loss isn't terribly important. Winning that round will make you feel invincible and will endow you with additional spiritual resources for winning the next round.

- *Start drawing up an inventory of your skills.* No matter how irrelevant some skills might seem, write them down. Then, alongside each skill or aptitude, write down the kinds of people who might benefit from those skills. Now brainstorm all the possible environments in which other people might encounter or seek those specific skills. Be open to the possibility that you are not currently deploying your most marketable skills to best or exclusive effect.

    For instance, Linda in Los Angeles was an experienced editor. She had worked on editing manuscripts for publishers, and she had edited various newspapers and journals. Helping a friend apply to graduate school one day, she discovered an opportunity. In order to win precious seats in graduate school, candidates had to submit essays that described themselves and their life goals. She began to specialize in helping graduate students write winning essays to the schools of their choice. She now employs several ex-editors in her own thriving business, Accepted.com, which serves graduate school applicants nationwide.

- *Find out how you really spend your time.* Keep in mind the old adage "time is money." This is part of the secret of compound interest. Time is truly the only commodity of which you are genuinely in short supply. You must now start taking charge of your time, and you do this by finding out just how you are spending it.

First, chart how you use your time for a period of a week, two weeks, or even a month; it depends on what works best for you. The key is to emerge from this exercise knowing how you spend your time. Lay out the period's worth of days with enough space to detail how each hour went by either on a large sheet of paper placed on the wall in some private location, or on an electronic handheld digital assistant. At the end of the time period, ignore time legitimately spent on sleep, dining, exercise, and so on.

Then carefully tabulate the 8 to 10 hours that you have available each day for economic productivity. Find out whether your efforts were driven by your plans and your agenda or whether you were responding haphazardly to random stimuli. Determine the difference between important things that may not be urgent and urgent things that may not be important. For example, acquiring a new skill or searching for a better job may well be *important,* but each is not an urgent task. Job searching is easy to constantly postpone because your existing job is paying the bills. Reading the morning paper, surfing 11 news sites on the Internet, and opening your mail are all *urgent* because they convey timely data. However, they are not very important to your future wealth.

Discover how your time is being spent, and you may be surprised, even horrified. Now accustom yourself to seeing yourself as your own boss. As your boss, don't you want your employee (that is you) to put in a full day's work? Sure you do, so make sure that the hours set aside for wealth creation each day are dedicated to just that. Later on, you will see more clearly how to organize your time productively for the things that count. You will learn which activities are worth focusing on and which are expendable.

Do Not Pursue Perfection

Neither neglect the imperfect nor expend yourself on futile pursuit of perfection, while failing to make the most of less perfect circumstances.

You know that life isn't perfect. This awareness is rooted in your spiritual nature. It is only within the most abstract part of your being that you can conceive of an ultimate perfection for which part of us constantly yearns. There is nothing wrong with that yearning so long as you never allow it to paralyze you. Stay aware of perfection, but never allow it to sideline you to the spectator stands in the game of life and business. Which of the choices do you like less?

Life often boils down to being able to function within less-than-ideal circumstances. Take, for instance, the constant criticisms of business and of the entire socioeconomic system in which you operate. Does it function perfectly for all people all the time? No, of course, it does not. I would wager that there have been many times that you have felt that you did not receive the rewards you deserved. I know that I have felt this. Slightly less enthusiastically, I have also been compelled to acknowledge that on many occasions I have enjoyed rewards that I did not deserve. The system is not perfect; everyone agrees on that. Judaism has taught that people should operate as best they can within the imperfection because idealistic perfection is unattainable by human beings. Once I recognize that fallible human beings can never create a truly perfect economic system, I can also recognize that the present system in which I live and function is an amazingly successful one.

When something goes terribly wrong with an airplane in midair and it plunges into the ocean, countless investigators gather to probe the catastrophe and to find out why the airplane fell out of the sky. Without meaning to be flippant, I can provide the only accurate answer in one word: gravity.

The real question is not why the airplane fell; that is obvious. The natural condition is for everything to fall to earth. The real question is, "What kept the airplane up there in the first place?" It remained airborne because its engines converted much of the chemical energy stored in fuel into thrust. It had wings that could convert thrust into lift. Remove any one of these vital elements, and the natural effect of gravity will take its sad course.

The U.S. socioeconomic system is similar. Many well-intentioned people also constantly convene meetings to probe the root causes of poverty. They question what brought the plane down or why everyone isn't airborne and wealthy? The answer is simple, if unpopular: Poverty is normal, just as a plane on the ground is more normal than one in the air. This is true even though Americans are unaccustomed to real poverty. Smart people should really flock to conferences to probe the root causes of *wealth*. Just as it is normal for objects dropped off a roof to fall to earth, so it is perfectly normal for wealth to slide down the slope to poverty. It takes enormous energy to boost a 100-ton airplane off a runway and it takes enormous energy to create a society of wealth. A society of wealth is not made any less amazing by the fact that some or even many individuals in that society own less than many others.

When you examine almost any society that has succeeded in lifting many of its citizens above the level of day-to-day subsistence, you are likely to find some in that society who have considerably less than others. There is little reason to indict a society on account of those in it who have less. The miracle is that virtually nobody is struggling for actual survival. The condition of those who have less than others, even a lot less, is sad but normal. However, there is much reason to praise a society that has lifted the lives of most of its citizens well above the level of daily need and fear, even if it has not done so for everybody. Although society should do its best to make it possible for everyone to improve his or her lot and each citizen should be able to find a way to advance his or her economic interests, expecting the same results for all people is pursuing a perfection that does not exist anywhere in the real world.

For most people, life continues to be what it has always been: an attempt to wrestle the most comfortable life possible from an often reluctant earth. There is a view that has inspired Jewish efforts in this arena. It is seen from the entire structure of Scripture and emerges from 3,000 years of oral transmission. The view is that the entire Bible encapsulates the following pact that God made with humanity:

If you try to endure, each of you on your own, then your life will be hard and short. However if you learn how to cooperate with others and you structure a peace-loving society that follows certain basic rules, there is no limit to how comfortable you can become. Now you choose.

DON'T BLAME "BUSINESS" BECAUSE OF A FEW UNETHICAL BUSINESSPEOPLE

Conceding that many imperfections exist in the system that allows humans to cooperate economically is not the same as discrediting the entire enterprise of business, nor is it reason to do so. Yes, there have been many business professionals that have behaved scandalously. Business is a tool of human cooperation, and like any tool, it can be misused and abused. However, you should distinguish between judging certain conduct by business professionals as unethical and judging business itself. Only *humans* are capable of making moral decisions, and only *humans* can be judged and held accountable for those decisions and for the actions that flow from them. Like a sharp scalpel that can be used for healing in the hands of a dedicated surgeon or for assault in the hands of a thug, business can bring goodness and hope to all, or it can hurt.

Jewish tradition helps clarify one's view of the legal landscape by reminding that inanimate objects can never be blamed for causing distress of any kind. Only the people in charge of those objects can and ought to be held responsible. When a drunken driver slays a pedestrian, no sane person contemplates the moral deterioration of motorcars and impounds the offending vehicle. You could rightly throw the book at the driver, that human who made the decision to drink and drive. Of course, some business, philosophic, and political systems do exist that tend to provide incentive for immoral conduct and to reward misbehavior. I would argue that the system of Ethical Capitalism that has shaped commerce in the United States of America, one greatly influenced by a Judeo-Christian worldview, has for the most part been an honorable arrangement. When things go horribly wrong in a company or business (and from time to time they do), blaming business as an imperfect system merely obscures the identity of the real villain—the human in charge who made wrong and often illegal or immoral decisions.

WHY IS BUSINESS EXCORIATED WHEN OTHER PROFESSIONS ARE EXCUSED?

Other professions don't get blamed the same way that business does. For example, occasionally, a rogue doctor cold-bloodedly murders patients. Naturally, the sensational nature of the gruesome discovery guarantees extensive media coverage, yet no one suggests that the practice of medicine is inherently immoral. When, as occasionally happens, a teacher is discovered to be abusing students, people seldom blame the system of education. Horrible stories of rape and assault by professional athletes can often be found in newspapers, and the personal lives of entertainers reveal the full spectrum of human folly. Yet, there are few calls for government to step in and minutely examine and regulate the sports and entertainment industries. However, when those running businesses act wrongly and unethically, the media often suggest that their behavior is the norm and only to be expected by those in such a questionable occupation. The world of politics itself has more than its fair share of exploiters of women and practitioners of financial skullduggery. The public rightly condemns those elected representatives and frequently denies them reelection, but no one suggests abandoning the Constitution for another system entirely.

I don't deny that there are quite abominable people who earn their livings, often very good ones, in business. You have all met such people. They do exist and are not people with whom you'd want to spend a social evening. I myself have met many, and I make no effort to defend them. I consider them to be parasites. They indulge themselves in selfish, egotistical, and often cruel behavior—the kind of conduct that undermines and imperils the very system that lavishes its benefits on them. They are not the natural products of a system of free and virtuous economic interaction; they are destructive aberrations. Not only do these abominable businesspeople bring disgrace on a noble and honorable way of earning a living, they also demoralize everyone else engaged in honest business. Because of them people repeat sayings like, "Nice guys never win."

Decades of exemplary business conduct, during which time a company may have provided jobs for thousands of families and desirable goods for the entire world, can be obliterated by sensational news accounts of misconduct. For example, it seems likely that Monsanto Company discharged dangerous residue into creeks and landfills around the small town of Anniston, Alabama. Monsanto enjoyed a nearly 40-year virtual monopoly on producing a range of industrial coolants known as PCBs (polychlorinated biphenyls). Now known to be dangerous, PCBs were once hailed as miracle chemicals. They are nonflammable, and they conduct heat without conducting electricity. Many safety codes mandated their use as insulation in electrical equipment, such as transformers. Most people would probably consider it improper to excoriate Monsanto Company for manufacturing something in 1929 that, at the time, wasn't generally known to be dangerous. However, the company's internal memos that have come to light indicate actions taken by Monsanto executives that should indeed be condemned. The case is being made that senior people knew or at least suspected that they were harming the neighboring community. For example, internal memos emblazoned with warnings such as "CONFIDENTIAL: Read and Destroy" show that in 1966 Monsanto managers discovered that fish dunked into a creek poisoned with PCBs died within seconds. In September 1969, Monsanto appointed a committee to address the controversy. The minutes of one of the committee meetings reveal that two formal objectives were "Permit continued sales and profits" and "Protect the image of Monsanto." The idea was to maintain one of Monsanto's most profitable franchises as long as possible "while taking care to reduce our exposure in terms of liability."[1] In other words, it appears that Monsanto leaders did engage in truly reprehensible behavior.

Similarly, consider the Enron case. When Enron declared bankruptcy on December 2, 2001, it was the largest Chapter 11 filing in U.S. history. Everyone should perhaps be somewhat indignant. Every legitimate business professional has been hurt, not because he or she necessarily knows everything that took place or understands exactly how Enron's 3,000-plus partnerships were used to put some debt off the books. No, every business professional has been hurt because of the appearance of flagrant impropriety. Everyone heard news accounts of documents destroyed surreptitiously. Everyone heard accounts of how thousands of workers lost significant savings while senior executives had miraculously sold their stock, in some cases six months or more prior to the calamity. Everyone heard how, during summer 2001, Sherron Watkins, an Enron executive who had earlier worked for Enron's auditors, Arthur Andersen, expressed worries that Enron might turn out to be "an elaborate accounting hoax" in her seven-page letter to Enron chairman and chief executive, Kenneth Lay.

These accounts feed popular misconceptions about business in ways that would be almost impossible to counter effectively. The institution of business and the profession of business have been dreadfully harmed by the collapse of what had been regarded as the seventh largest U.S. company. During the fall of 2001, so much public outrage accumulated about these Enron stories that Congress convened more than eight hearings into the scandal. But focus on the real villains, urged the *Wall Street Journal*, rather than on the system. "All of which means that while the Enron pension story is tragic, it's more about specific corporate blunders and wrongdoing than it is about flaws in pension law or in 401(k)s. It's certainly no excuse for Congress to lobotomize a private pension system that has given millions of Americans a comfortable retirement."[2] Although some companies have destroyed evidence of wrongdoings and perpetrated cover-ups, the vast majority of commercial enterprises steadfastly refrain from anything even remotely approaching impropriety.

The astounding fact is not that wrongs have been committed by commerce and industry, but just how seldom these wrongs have taken place. It bears remembering that these events make the news precisely because they are relatively *uncommon*. This does not in any way excuse the conduct of the individuals, but it is a reminder that it would be wrong to indict the entire system. What is obscured by major scandals such as these is that these unethical individuals constitute a tiny but visible minority. Far more common are the ideal business professionals, the practitioners of what I term Ethical Capitalism, who through honor and virtue nourish and sustain the system while benefiting themselves and their families. It is surely a tribute to the inherent strength and goodness of the vast and wonderful network of human economic interaction that a few saboteurs are incapable of utterly destroying it for everyone.

THE "ROBBER BARONS" WEREN'T EVIL: THEY CREATED GOOD, TOO

Few people are all evil or all good. Each person is a complex amalgam of emotions, aspirations, and moral coordinates. Sometimes people do wonderfully noble things, and other times they can act in ways that leave them loathing themselves. Far more often though, people's actions themselves are complex. One reason that universal moral agreement can be so elusive is that most actions are combinations of good and bad. Suppose I bestow a lavish gift on my daughter. This is a good, selfless action that she will always remember fondly, but it may also have negative consequences such as causing jealousy in her siblings or postponing her achieving independence. Everyone must learn to identify and credit the good components in complex actions and complex people, and one group of notorious individuals provides us with an ideal laboratory.

During the nineteenth century, there arose business titans who strode across the landscape of the United States. Being human, none were saints, but neither were they all sinners. Were some of the moguls dreadfully unpleasant people? Of course. The legend of the "company store" and news stories of substandard company housing were often true. For example, the Pullman Company was found to have rented compulsory housing to its workers and required them to buy their food, fuel, and water through the company at above-market rates that were enormously profitable. It was not uncommon for workers' paychecks to be outweighed by their debts. There were ignoble and mean-spirited scoundrels among the wealthy industrialists. However, that was not the rule, neither should it have impugned an entire generation of builders. Among them were many admirable souls.

Here in his own words is Andrew Carnegie's reaction to receiving his first week's earnings at the age of 12 years old:

> I cannot tell you how proud I was when I received my first week's own earnings. One dollar and twenty cents made by myself and given to me because I had been of some use in the world! No longer entirely dependent on my parents, but at last admitted to the family partnership as a contributing member and able to help them! I think this makes a man out of a boy sooner than almost anything else, and a real man, too, if there be any germ of true manhood in him. It is everything to feel that you are useful.[3]

That may not be a saint speaking, but neither is it a robber speaking. Citizens of dozens of towns and cities around the United States still benefit from Carnegie's philanthropy every time they enter their local library. Parks, universities, and hospitals are some of the other benefits these generous entrepreneurs bestowed on their nation. Yet, Carnegie and his fellow tycoons were later dubbed "Robber Barons." During their lives, for the most part, they were viewed realistically—just as flawed as other people but having done more good than most.

Consider another, less well known example. James Jerome Hill was born in a log cabin in Ontario, Canada, in 1838. His father died while the boy was young, and he supported his mother by working in a grocery for $4 a month. Through great energy and hard work, Hill came to build a railroad across the Northwest. His concept was to build the line slowly and first develop the economy of the area before continuing on further. "To attract immigrants, Hill offered to bring them to the Northwest for a mere $10 each if they would farm near his railroad."[4] He organized farming instruction classes that taught the newly arrived farmers all about local conditions and such techniques as diversifying crops. He imported 7,000 head of cattle from England and handed them over free of charge to settlers near his line.

Hill told the immigrants who worked near his railroad that he and they were all in the same boat together. He explained to them that they would either all prosper together or all be poor together. To make sure that they prospered, he also set up experimental farms to test new seed, livestock, and equipment. He sponsored contests and awarded rich prizes to those farmers who most successfully produced meat and wheat in bounty.[5]

Was he doing all this out of selfless altruism? No, of course not. He did these things to build up the future customers of his railroad. By helping them prosper, he was ensuring that he would ultimately prosper, too, when his railroad would provide the only export facilities for the agricultural produce of these early settlers. He subsidized, assisted, and built infrastructure in order to become wealthy. However, you can be quite sure of one thing: Those pioneers who obtained $10 passages from overcrowded tenements to a promised land, those farmers who received gifts of 7,000 English cows and bulls, and all the others who built new lives alongside Hill's railroad felt only gratitude to this man.

This view changed during the Great Depression when a left-wing extremist named Matthew Josephson wrote a book called *The Robber Barons* that was published in 1934. Until that time, the nineteenth century had been seen as a period of unprecedented economic boom. Naturally, not everyone became rich, but most people began enjoying a standard of living of which their parents could only have dreamed. The economic prowess of those whom Josephson considered to be robbers definitely freed virtually everyone from drudgery. Whether it was availability of oil, train transport, or the limitless variety of new products, almost everyone lived better than had been the case only a few years earlier. Yet Josephson's nasty little book was rumored to be required reading among Washington's New Dealers, who saw Josephson's greedy tycoons as emblems of the corrupt economic system that had brought about the Great Depression. As Walter Donway put it,

> And as bank failures avalanched and the depression's misery set in, it was handy to have Josephson's gallery of villains and his taunting evocations of their riches to divert attention from the Federal Reserve System's role in the economic collapse and the protectionist folly of the Smoot-Hawley Act. With its damning portraits and Marxist analysis, *The Robber Barons* became a kind of instant classic and its epithet-title achieved a currency out of all proportion to the book's merit. . . . Like Josephson, today's moralists equate large profits with ill-gotten gain . . . as if such profits were, in themselves, proof of wrongdoing.[6]

WHEN YOU TAKE LUXURIES FOR GRANTED, THINGS MUST BE PRETTY GOOD

Much must be right about the economic system in the United States because it allows Americans to take so much luxury for granted. There is a sentiment often expressed that uses its high tone to obscure just how wonderful a well-running economic system is. Have you heard folks say things like, "Why not take the day off and spend it with the family?" or "Nobody ever dies regretting not having spent enough time at work"? Those are very pretty notions, but they can be said only by someone with no fear at all of having to put his children to bed that night, hungry and frightened. In some countries at this time and particularly in earlier times, many parents have been tormented not by not spending enough time with their children, but by not being able to prevent them from starving to death. Taking the day off, even for something as wonderful as spending time with your children, is a luxury; and being able to do so means that your worries do not revolve around food, shelter, and survival. Vast numbers of the inhabitants of the planet would be happy to change places with you in a heartbeat.

Now I know this might sound farfetched, but it is nonetheless true. For most of human history, and even in many countries now, large numbers of the earth's population have put their children to bed at night knowing that those children were still hungry. Imagine how painful it must be for a parent to know that he or she is failing in that most basic of parental responsibilities, feeding the children. No parents in that situation think they are doing something noble by staying home from work to watch a child's ball game. The price to be paid later by the parents who forfeited a day's wages for that little indulgence is too terrible to contemplate.

In today's amazing socioeconomic structure, however, it is quite different. It is hardly remarkable that in many companies, personnel policies encourage workers to occasionally take time off for family matters. Supervisors have proudly pointed to an empty desk while telling me, "Oh, Mike there is out on paternity leave." Paternity leave? I thought that it was only women who gave birth. Obviously, countries that have followed the broad outlines of Ethical Capitalism are so productive today that sometimes a worker can be allowed to stay at home for a few days with the mother of his new child. Do you have any idea of how utterly astounding this is?

HOW "ETHICAL CAPITALISM" DIFFERS FROM ORDINARY, EVERYDAY CAPITALISM

I use the term "Ethical Capitalism" to describe the elegant and durable system of human economic cooperation. Socialism advocates a governmental role of infinite size and limitless reach in a futile quest to bring equal prosperity to all. If many suffer and even die in this noble quest, so be it. In the heartless words of Vladimir Lenin, you can't make an omelet without breaking a few eggs. At the other extreme, laissez-faire capitalism advocates zero governmental involvement in the economy, enabling each individual to pursue his or her own self-interest with little or no interference. The first system denies its citizens even the most basic of rights, whereas the second offers its citizens perhaps too many rights. Both ultimately languish for ignoring the spiritual dimension of Godly gifts and Divine demands.

I suggest that when U.S. business is functioning at its best, employer and employee are each focused less on their individual rights and more on their obligations toward the other. For example, consider the "right" to a lunch hour. When I speak of Ethical Capitalism, I envision the way Jewish law deals with that hour. Although Jewish law mandates that one recite a grace after each meal, it specifies a specially abridged version for day-wage employees to use so they do not steal time from their employers. A moral obligation rests on the employee to deliver a full day's work for his or her pay.

Here's a splendid example of how some workers take seriously this moral obligation. One afternoon, as I was hurrying down the dock at Marina del Rey, California, to retrieve a book from my boat, "Paragon," I noticed a young man executing some flawless steel fabrication on a neighboring vessel. I stopped to converse with him, praised his workmanship, and tried to pick his brain about some similar improvement I planned for my boat. After a few minutes spent responding to my questions, Robert Dryer interrupted me by saying, "I'd be happy to answer more questions and even show you how to do this, but it would have to be after five o'clock this afternoon since I am paid by the day." I was astounded at his honesty and asked where his boss was. "In Hawaii until the end of the week," he replied.

I made it my business to be back on that dock at exactly five o'clock, and Robert Dryer, a former submariner in the U.S. Navy, was as good as his word. Soon after five o'clock, he packed up his tools and accompanied me to my boat where we opened a couple of beers and chatted for far longer than I had planned. He didn't see his diligence as anything special. It was just how he was raised. Without any hesitation, I promptly offered him a full-time job with me. He wanted to know what he'd be doing. I explained that I had not yet figured that out yet but that anyone with such a built-in awareness of how the system really works was someone I needed in my organization. Dryer subsequently worked for me for about six years, accompanied my family on our trans-Pacific sailing voyage, and became almost like part of our family. I know that Bob was far from unique. Many if not most Americans possess a similar ethic of fairness along with a sense of obligation. Judaism and, thus, Ethical Capitalism rest on a system of interlocking obligations rather than on one of rights. Whether you are my employer or my employee, it is not the right I have against you that is important, it is my obligation toward you.

It is of course, just as true that an obligation rests on each employer to pay employees in a timely fashion and not to burden them with meaningless work. For instance, regardless of how much compensation is offered, Jewish law mandates that no employer may direct a subordinate to dig a ditch one day and to fill it in the next, only to have him reexcavate it on the third day. Early years of experience in mass production and assembly lines during the twentieth century showed that treating workers like automatons and depriving them of meaning in their professional lives was not only immoral but also economically stupid. To the Jew who always viewed God as both be-nevolent and wise, this was no surprise. God wants economic enterprises to prosper because that would indicate that His Children are operating His system of Ethical Capitalism correctly.

Notwithstanding the breathtaking benevolence of a system that provides so much for so many, there is no shortage of naysayers who launch passion-ate moral crusades against U.S. Capitalism. Just take the next opportunity that comes your way to chat with a young university student. You might be surprised to hear what he or she believes about American business. From the Bible and its oral tradition, Jews constantly hear God expressing this refrain to humanity:

> I have created most of you with almost limitless yearnings and desires, but I have placed you in a world with apparently limited resources. It may seem that there is not enough for everyone. However, if you fol-low my rules of ongoing and constant cooperation, there will be more than enough for everyone. Should you decide to try it on your own, you will condemn yourself to a constant struggle for survival. I have set up the world in mysterious and counterintuitive ways. You are going to have to be generous and giving to one another. You are going to have to cooperate with one another, and you are going to have to under-stand that interpersonal economic interaction through Ethical Capital-ism is good and pleases me, while many of the other attempts to solve the problem of extracting a living from the world without voluntary cooperation are not only evil, but I have arranged for them ultimately to fail.

THERE'S ONLY ONE WAY THAT ETHICAL CAPITALISM WORKS

Only one way works? That goes against every human instinct. Let me ex-plain. What was then the world's third longest suspension bridge, the Tacoma Narrows Bridge in the state of Washington, was opened to traffic on July 1, 1940. A windstorm blew during the morning of November 7, 1940, and the deck of the bridge began undulating alarmingly. Soon thereafter, the road-way began collapsing into the cold waters of Puget Sound 200 feet below. Cables snapped, chunks of concrete plummeted down, girders buckled, and within an hour, the bridge was gone. Rebuilding it was delayed for 10 years because of World War II.

As you can imagine, commissions were convened to find out why the Tacoma Narrows Bridge failed. They concluded that certain fundamental engineering principles had been violated in the interests of both economy and aesthetics. One hundred years before the Tacoma Narrows Bridge was built, John Scott Russel, vice president of the Royal Scottish Society of the Arts, published a paper entitled, "On the Vibration of Suspension Bridges and Other Slender Structures." It contained much of the information needed to build a strong safe bridge. The replacement bridge was built taking all these sound engineering principles into consideration, and it has proven durable and safe.

Today, one can see many beautiful suspension bridges around the world, and each has its own unique appearance. Therefore, it would seem that there are countless ways to build a suspension bridge. The conclusion would be misleading. Although each bridge has its own shape, style, and color, these distinctions camouflage how similar they all are. Every single bridge ever built is designed to resist the same forces in the same way. Whether it is built of wood, to span the River Kwai in Asia, or steel, like the George Washington Bridge joining Manhattan and New Jersey, bridges are designed in a standard, well-tried way. You must consider the strength of the building material and its weight. You must take into account forces due to gravity, the planned-for load, and wind pressures. Complex calculations learned in the fields of physics and applied mathematics are the tools. As long as you operate within the broad parameters of the one reliable system of engineering constants, the bridges you build can each exhibit its own unique beauty and style.

This is how I was taught to apply the bridge-building lesson to other areas of human endeavor. As a child, I was encouraged to seek the moral message in almost everything. Being fond of dismantling old clocks and trying to repair them, I became the neighborhood repository for any old piece of junk that had ever ticked. Anyone with an old clock, kitchen timer, broken watch, or any non-functioning timekeeping device would drop by my home to present me with another treasure for my growing collection of such things. My father encouraged my attempts to resuscitate the deceased timepieces. And I happily dismantled the clocks and attempted to get them going again. Almost always, the process of reassembling was stymied by the five or six little cog wheels for which I could find no home. My efforts were not blessed with much success; I finally lost interest, as most people do with projects that yield none of the encouragement that comes from a sense of achievement.

Later, I wanted my father to explain why he had encouraged me to play with the clocks. His response was that he was waiting for me to discover the moral message of mechanical clocks. Moral message? I was only about 10 years old; surely this was a bit too early to be burdened with moral messages. But my father believed, and I have since learned, that for perceptive people there is a moral message in almost everything and the challenge to find it can't start too early. To this day I recall how my father applied that message: Although there are countless ways to reassemble a clock, it only runs when you do it *the one right way*. The face of the clock can be painted in any way you choose, and the case can be made of tin or pure gold; but the one system of basic principles must be retained.

Similarly, although there may appear to be countless ways for a society of people to structure a successful economy, that is not so. Although the old adage claims that there are many ways to skin a cat, a Jewish understanding of how the world really works insists that whether it is business or bridges, there is usually only one effective way that will achieve a goal and many other ways that will fail. Structuring the sytem within which citizens will interact economically with one another resembles building a bridge. Following the system of Ethical Capitalism provides the rigidly reliable framwork within which there is limitless room for individualism, choice, and personality.

In spite of its proven record, the system of rules, conventions, and protocols that govern human economic interaction in the United States comes under constant attack. Paradoxically, those assaulting its moral legitimacy are often among the most richly rewarded by the very system they besiege. All people need to feel a measure of moral confidence about the activity that not only absorbs many of their most productive hours, but also provides them with a living and often with part of their identity, too. It will be helpful to examine the four main charges leveled against the institution of business.

THE FOUR FAMOUS ALLEGATIONS AGAINST BUSINESS

I want to provide you with a practical prescription here. Humans are impacted by almost everything that happens to them. You may think you have forgotten something such as a tune or someone's name. However, as soon as a friend whistles the tune or reintroduces you to the person, you instantly recognize the tune and the individual's name. You had never really forgotten the tune or the name. Those pieces of information may have been in a less accessible place in your brain, but they were still there.

Anything residing in your brain becomes part of you and plays a role in the person you become, in the actions you perform, and in the things you say. You can use this fact by deliberately implanting in your mind those ideas and principles that you wish to retain and empower to impact you.

Viewing a movie or a theatrical production is a very powerful way of implanting themes in your mind. Reading something is another way of doing so. However, perhaps the ultimate method is reading something aloud. Somehow, when your ears hear your own mouth say something, you absorb it and believe it. I am sure you have watched how some liars eventually come to believe, literally, the lie they constantly repeat. I am not suggesting that you repeat lies; I am suggesting that you refute them. Whether during your professional life or during ordinary social intercourse, you frequently hear slurs against business. From now on, never miss an opportunity to refute those slurs. You will gain more power in business than you can possibly imagine when your own ears hear your own mouth telling the truth about your chosen way of contributing to the perfecting of the world—the practice of business.

Here are each of the four main charges against your chosen profession and ways of refuting them. Business is bad, immoral, fatally flawed, and/or unfair (take your pick) because:

1. Business causes inequality by giving some people more at the expense of others who are left with correspondingly less.
2. Business is driven by greed.
3. Business harms the environment.
4. Business dehumanizes people by turning them into consumers.

By examining these four myths you can come to see that, paradoxically, you can best pursue the perfection for which your soul yearns by practicing the very activity cited by its foes as the proof of imperfection. They claim that business is problematic because it is imperfect in these areas.

Myth #1: Business Is Inherently Unfair—It Causes Inequality by Giving Some People More at the Expense of Others Who Are Left with Less

As you examine this charge, ask yourself how the institution of business can possibly have potential for good when it is also the engine of disparity and inequality in society? Many people do see business as Robin Hood in reverse; taking from the poor to give to the rich.

Among those who think that some people just make too much money is Ben Cohen, the chairman of the specialty Vermont ice cream manufacturer, Ben and Jerry's Homemade, Inc. "One thing that we should consider is simply put a cap on how much income any one person can make. Ideally, no one should earn more than the president of the United States. I think it would be tough to argue that anyone else's job is harder or more valuable to society."[7] The owner of a premium ice cream company in rural Vermont might find it tough to argue that anyone else's job is harder or more valuable to society than the president's, but most ordinary people would find it a lot easier to make that argument. Many people might see the job of a teacher as more valuable and that of a firefighter as much harder. Nonetheless, many flaunt their moral vanity by voicing Ben's concerns in somber tones that show their underlying nobility.

It is funny that these people always seem more incensed about the income of business professionals than they are about the far larger payoffs made to sports and entertainment figures. I believe that this is because they feel that sports stars really do earn their massive incomes. National league players can do amazing things with a bat or a ball; and what is more, their careers end before middle age. This goes for musicians as well. Musicians have, well, real talent, unlike corporate chief executive officers (CEOs).

I think that most critics of business are even more comfortable with people hitting pay dirt through luck than they are with people earning it through market place profit. Nobody suggests that lottery winners receive too much income. I don't believe I have ever even heard anyone dourly remark that a lottery winner should give something back to society. Similarly, I think that many view the acting profession as a bit of a gamble. Some actors will win big, and that is fine. At least they are not taking it away from poor people.

But business, that is something else. Business professionals don't just luck out like the good-natured country bumpkin who won the three-state lottery jackpot. Business people plot and connive to accumulate more than other people. They are mean and selfish. They exploit people's simplicity with ruthless cunning. What is more, they have no particular skill and do nothing that anyone couldn't do just as well given the chance.

Those sentiments would unfortunately set too many heads nodding in agreement. Yes, business is bad, they say, largely because it widens the gap between the haves and the have nots. There is no question that many decent people are profoundly troubled by inequality. There are those who feel distress at seeing folks with so much more than they have. Then there are also those who have been blessed and feel emotions ranging from compassion all the way to guilt at seeing people with so much less than they themselves have. Virtually all decent people experience emotions of sadness at the sight of some poor soul struggling with so much less than those around him. These emotions can be felt particularly poignantly by those less favored themselves, and are not confined to the area of money.

Most teenage boys go through periods of intense envy of those in their class who are taller, better at football, or who seem to be magnets for the pretty girls in class. The feelings of teenage girls are not spared either. Some of them bemoan a world that so unfairly distributes physical charms. In a rare moment of self-disclosure, an actress once remarked to me that she felt genuinely sorry for ugly people. When I humorously thanked her personally for her sympathy, she seemed to feel that I had not fully grasped the depths of her sensitivity and compassion.

Oddly enough though, less indignation is felt about the unequal distribution of good looks than about the unequal distribution of money. Perhaps people feel that it is easier to do something about the latter than about the former. In reality that goal, desirable as it may be in theory, has never been achieved in practice, and its pursuit can be a dangerous illusion.

Sometimes people feel bad at how much less they have than others, but just as frequently, people feel bad at how much *more* they have than others. Naturally, with everyone exactly the same as one another in every possible way, these uncomfortable feelings would be alleviated. Thus the crusade to eliminate all differences between people mistakenly acquires moral prestige.

Jewish tradition taught that equality was neither realistic nor a goal. It would be fine and, perhaps, proper for a zookeeper to ensure that all elephants received equivalent amounts of hay each day for them to eat. All cows in the farmyard should probably be given the same relative quantity of food, proportionate to their body size. Needless to say, all cows should enjoy the same diet, the farmer does not offer an à la carte menu. However, there is an infinite variety of preferences and priorities among humans that makes it all but impossible for every one of them to live equivalent and similar lives.

The Jewish view accepts that for some people, enjoying a stress-free existence is more important than hard work and economic success. For some, marrying young, having many children, and living joyfully among a large and boisterous family is more important than having discretionary income for glamorous vacations. For others, that choice is unthinkable. There are those who defer marriage almost indefinitely while pursuing career success without distraction. Some lavish their income on exotic cars, whereas others develop passions for boats. Some live Spartan lives while saving and investing every earned penny. It is not unreasonable to suppose that such people are likely to have more comfortable retirements than those who spent all they earned. How can equality be assured to all amidst such a profusion of choices? Perhaps the only way people could avoid the discomfort of seeing poverty around them would be to prohibit choice and to enclose every member of society in one giant all-embracing cocoon of cradle-to-grave uniformity.

It is, of course, easy to become discouraged by the presence of poverty and easy to write off the entire social and civic structure that seems to tolerate poverty in its midst. In fact, it is easy to fall into the trap of considering such a social and civic system intrinsically evil. Thus people sometimes tend to drape a mantle of virtue over those who rampage and riot against global trade. They assume that because poverty is allowed to exist in this growing global marketplace, it must be intrinsically flawed, and they must find a better system.

Can Poverty Be Eliminated?

Do you recall the old riddle of three diners who eat together and have a restaurant check that comes to a total $2.50? Each man hands the waiter a dollar bill. On his way back with their change of 50 cents, the enterprising waiter decides that it would be needlessly difficult for the three patrons to divide up the 50 cents, so he pockets 20 cents and hands each man a dime. Now, each man paid a dollar and received back 10 cents in change. So each man really paid 90 cents. From all three, the total was $2.70. The waiter of course has 20 cents in his pocket for a total of $2.90. The riddle is that since they started with $3.00 but we have accounted only for $2.90, where is the missing dime?

The answer is that there is no such thing as a missing dime in this story. The reader is misled by the presumptive nature of the question. There is no reason why the amount paid by the three men, $2.70, should add up to $3.00 if you add it to the 20 cents the waiter put in his pocket. That 20 cents came out of the $2.70 they paid. So the correct calculation is that the bill of $2.50 plus the 20 cents taken by the waiter should add up to the $2.70 (3 x $0.90) that the men paid. Nothing is missing.

Similarly, asking the question of whether poverty can be eliminated is also misleading. Undeniably, there truly are poor people in the world. They are the dreadfully unfortunate people who, each morning, literally do not know where that evening's supper is coming from and, each evening, do not know where they will lay their heads that night. Given the welfare net and the availability of private and public shelters in the United States, most of those unhappy beings huddling on the streets are there largely because they are entirely outside of the system. About one-third of the homeless are mentally ill.[8] "Most of these are on the streets because of the astoundingly sentimental deinstitutionalization movement that swept through state mental hospitals during the mixed-up days of the 1960s."[9] Most of the homeless—three-fourths of all men in a Baltimore, Maryland, study conducted by clinicians from Johns Hopkins University—are substance abusers.[10] I do not describe this to diminish pity for those living under these circumstances; I do so merely to vigorously reject the blame for their predicament that is regularly heaped on the U.S. business system of wealth creation. When the term "poor" is used, it is usually used to describe people who have less than other people. In other words, outside of the truly destitute, "poor" is merely a relative term.

Jews have always derived their understanding of poverty from apparently contradictory Scriptures: "Surely there will be no destitute among you, God will bless you. . . . but only if you hearken to the voice of the Lord your God."[11] All right, I think I understand. Follow the rules, and there will be no poor people in your society. That sounds like a pretty good deal. Yet no more than seven verses later are the words: "Destitute people will never cease to exist in your society, so I command you to always open your hand to your brother the poor."[12]

Well, which is it? Either by following the rules there will never be poor among us, or there will never be an end to poor people. It cannot be both; or can it? Consider these facts from the U.S. Census Bureau's Annual Report on Income and Poverty in the United States (1998):

- About 30 million Americans are living in poverty.
- In contrast to poor people who are not fortunate enough to live in the United States, more than half of the U.S. poor own their own homes.
- Nearly 2 million of the U.S. poor own homes worth more than a quarter of a million dollars.
- Over 70 percent of the U.S. poor own their own car, and 30 percent own two cars.
- Of the U.S. poor, 98 percent own a color television, and over 50 percent own two.
- Of the U.S. poor, 75 percent own a video cassette recorder (VCR), and 20 percent own two.

Obviously most poor people in Asia or Africa would leap at the chance to become part of the U.S. poor in a heartbeat. Am I suggesting that these 30 million Americans are not really poor? Of course not.

Poverty Is Relative

But, again, Judaism teaches that poverty is *relative*. If one loses one's money and has to endure a dramatically reduced standard of living, one is poor according to Jewish definitions. What is more, such a person is a worthy charity recipient. If one owns one's own home with two color televisions, two VCRs, and a garage with two cars, but one lives among friends and associates all of whom live in far larger homes with many more amenities, then one is going to feel relatively poor. That is the point of the two seemingly contradictory verses I mentioned earlier.

The first Biblical verse I quoted on page 145 insists that there will be no poor among you: If you are fortunate enough to live within a large group of other people and you all maintain a culture in which you care for one another, trust one another to keep your word, and respect one another's property, there is no reason for you ever to consider yourself poor. Never accept the label of "poor." You may have less than you used to have, and you may have less than those around you, but you must view this as temporary. You have much more than many others; and what is more, you are on your way up to still more. Just find ways to interact with other people and find ways to be of use to them. Thinking of yourself as poor will handicap you in your quest. Although it is obviously true that you can look over one shoulder and see many who possess far more than you, this does not make you poor.

The second verse tells you that now that you know that you are not poor, look over your other shoulder and see all those unfortunate souls with far less than you. Now open your hands to them and give them some of what you have.

Why should you give away to others something that rightfully belongs to you? Is this because it helps them? No, helping those who have less is a side effect. The main reason is because it helps *you*. In this context, I recall, as a young student, encountering the Biblical admonition, "You shall not curse the deaf."[13] This is not because cursing a deaf person will hurt him. Clearly, the handicapped human will be quite oblivious to your curse. The reason not to do so is because of what the action does to you. Similarly, in ways that will become clear in Chapter 9, finding someone who has less than you and giving that person of your wealth is in your interest far more than it is in his or hers.

This credo is so strongly established that even people who depend on charity for their livelihood are obliged to give charity to those who have even less.[14] A charming scene in Disney's animated movie *Aladdin* shows the hero and his pet monkey settling down to eat the loaf of bread that he had just stolen. Aladdin's attention was seized by what appear to be two young orphans with large brown eyes, a little boy and perhaps his sister, obviously starving. Instead of saying "Let them steal their own," Aladdin, after a brief internal moral tussle, gives them the bread. The implication is that he is not a common street rat as his detractors charge. The roots of nobility are already implanted in him, and he is a suitable suitor for the princess.

The obligation to give of your own to those who have less is a firm one. There is no means test for the recipients of your largesse. The only requirement is that they should have less than you. That is sufficient for the recipients to be poor and deserving in your eyes but, of course, not in theirs. From their perspective, they are on their way up and they also seek those who have less than they do with whom to share what little they have.

The contradiction between the two Biblical verses is resolved. Let nobody consider himself to be poor. Forming that opinion of yourself erects an insurmountable obstacle to becoming rich. If nobody allows a self-image of being poor, then the first verse is correct, there will be no poor among you. However, there will always be some people with less than you. They must not consider themselves poor, but you are obliged to give something to those with less than you.

Inequality does exist, and it exists in so many different ways that it would be impossible and undesirable to redress it. Inequality is not an indictment of the world; it is testimony to human uniqueness.

For one person to increase his or her wealth, do a corresponding number of other people need to become poorer? Is my increase at the expense of others? If that is so, then it would be hard for me to argue against the morality of redistribution. In a world that has only so much wealth, it would be wrong not to constantly rearrange it so each person has the same amount. A quick glance at reality reveals that business *creates* wealth, it doesn't redistribute it. By contrast, governments have no capacity to create wealth, but they can and do redistribute it. Just ask yourself if you would benefit economically more by living among very wealthy people or among very poor people? Surely the former would spend more on your services or products, thus benefiting you, than could the latter. This is the magic of business. Through its alchemy, ordinary people interacting with one another increase everyone's financial opportunities. Needless to say, there is no guarantee that everyone will seize those opportunities in ways guaranteed to bring equal results. Sometimes the pursuit of perfection can blind people to beauty and obscure great opportunities that lie to hand. My life can be perfect, and I can be supremely satisfied with it even though to some outside observer I possess far less than others and perhaps even far less than the observer thinks I ought to have. In human affairs, perfection, like poverty, is relative.

Myth #2: Business Is Fatally Flawed Because It Is Driven by Greed

In a utopian world of ultimate spiritual perfection, not only would all your actions be perfect but so would all your motivations. Until then, however, in business, you would greatly benefit from recognizing that in the real world it is only possible to evaluate people's actions. Their motivations are hidden and often impenetrably complex. Your neighbors or your transaction partners are far more interested in how you *treat* them than they are in how you *intended* to treat them or in *why* you treated them the way you did. Detractors of business turn this simple principle on its head and discredit good actions by presuming to know the evil motivations that lie behind them.

This is the common moral error of discrediting goodness if the benefactor also receives benefits. I sometimes think of it as "the Mother Teresa syndrome." Meaning no disrespect to the Nobel prize–winning saint of Calcutta, greater business advances in India would eventually make her efforts less necessary. Although she undoubtedly mitigated the suffering of many unfortunates, business and industry have the capacity to eradicate many of the causes of that suffering. Surely, wiping out malnutrition and disease are as praiseworthy as catering to the victims of it? In the industrial world, to which legions of the less fortunate swarm, the benefits yearned for were produced and made available by business professionals who risked their time and their savings to do so. Did these entrepreneurs themselves benefit, too? Of course, they did, and so did those that invested in their ventures; but that does not negate the good they did. Somehow, people have uncritically bought into the notion that their acts of benevolence are negated if they benefit by those acts as much as, or more than, the beneficiaries do.

This is a mistake. Just put yourself in the position of a charity recipient. Suppose you are down on your luck and need a hand up. You have a choice: Either you may turn to Mr. Smith and accept his gift of $100, or you may favor Mr. Jones, who will give you $10. If you accept Smith's largesse, through some strange financial alchemy, you will trigger an avalanche of $500 into his bank account. When you accept Jones's much smaller gift of $10, Jones does not realize any benefit in any way from your acceptance of his gift. In fact it costs him exactly $10 to give you the gift. The way Smith looks at it, you and he are simply partners in a transaction that brings him a net of $400 and that brings you $100. From your point of view, which would you rather do? Surely you would prefer receiving the larger gift from Smith to getting the far smaller one from Jones. The fact that Smith will also benefit from helping you is only a good thing. It makes you feel less of a beggar; after all, you have helped him, too. Your dignity is preserved.

To be more precise, if instead of giving you $100, Mr. Smith gives you the opportunity to earn it for yourself, he is doing you an even greater favor. Possessing skills that can enhance his business allows you to earn the money as his employee while retaining your self-respect. One of the gigantic economic advantages that Judaism confers on its devotees is this deep, internalized conviction that making money is largely the consequence of a mutually beneficial interaction with other human beings.

I once had the opportunity to discuss this with the brilliant George Mason University professor of economics, Walter Williams. His definition of money remained with me and became part of my business seminars. "Take out a dollar bill and look at it," he said. "Now pat yourself on your back because you are looking at a certificate of performance. If you did not rob or steal from anyone to obtain that dollar, if you neither defrauded anyone nor persuaded your government to seize it from a fellow citizen and give it to you, then you could only have obtained that dollar in one other way—you must have pleased someone else." How true are those words. Whether you pleased a client, a customer, or your boss, that money is testament to your having pleased another human being. Having money is not shameful; *it is a certificate of good performance* granted to you by your grateful fellow citizens.

You Must Provide for Yourself First, so That You Can Help Others Later

Jewish tradition strongly establishes the principle that each person makes his or her own needs the primary concern, although not the only concern. One could say that Judaism declares it necessary but insufficient to focus on one's own needs first. As the Sabbath ebbs away each Saturday night, Jewish families prepare for the productive work week ahead by singing the joyful *Havdalah* service. This observance divides the Sabbath from the upcoming work week and asks God to increase both the families' offspring and their wealth. It also highlights their hands, as if to beseech blessing on the work of those very hands. The *Havdalah* service is recited over a cup of wine that runs over into the saucer beneath.

This overflowing cup symbolizes the intention to produce during the week ahead not only sufficient to fill one's own cup, but also an excess that will allow overflow for the benefit of others. In other words, I am obliged to first fill my cup and then continue pouring as it were, so that I will have sufficient to give away to others, thus helping to jump-start their own efforts. Judaism views attending to your own vineyard not as shameful, but as a moral obligation.

The Talmud[15] offers an imaginary case for your contemplation. Suppose you embarked on a journey across a remote and distant desert in company with an associate. Imagine that you brought a large water supply for yourself, whereas your associate neglected that elementary preparation. Halfway across the desert, it became apparent that there was insufficient water for two. You had two choices: You could either share your water with your companion, in which case you would both die of thirst; or you could hog it yourself, which would allow you to survive while he died. A horrible dilemma to be sure, but what would you do? The Jewish view of morality is that having brought the water, you must drink it and live.

You can see that it is only a short intellectual journey from there to a Jewish perspective on business and profit. No, business is not akin to theft, and profit is not plunder. I may be trying to sell you a product or my services chiefly in order to survive and thrive, but having the care of myself and of those who depend on me as my paramount concern is right and moral. Unlike the desert analogy, in business, taking care of my needs doesn't *condemn* you to suffer; it happens to *help* you. Surely there can be no reason to challenge the goodness of business just because the benefactor enjoys as much benefit at the recipient.

Gratitude Beats Churlishness

Finally, for the purpose of dealing with the allegation that business professionals only do what they do out of greed, you need to dispense with the silly notion that in human affairs, intention trumps action. People are mere mortals and often don't even understand their own real intentions. How can people possibly be so arrogant as to suppose they can determine someone else's true intentions? It is impossible to know what is in another's mind, so the only way for humans to judge one another is on their actions, not on their intentions.

Jewish law rules that if someone intended to harm you but he was such a bumbling incompetent that he ended up helping you, you are obliged to him and owe him gratitude for the good he did you. In the reverse situation, you also judge the outcome rather than trying to probe the perpetrator's intentions. It makes little difference to me if I am stabbed by someone who loves me or by someone who hates me. I may legitimately defend myself and retaliate in both cases.

Now for the next stage of the argument. Do I owe *gratitude* to a person who is utterly indifferent to my fate yet ends up unintentionally helping me? He only helped me because it was the inevitable accompaniment to helping himself, which was his chief motivation and intent, yet I owe him gratitude. It is right to thank someone who benefits you even if he wished you badly. It is even more right to thank someone who benefits you but is indifferent to you. It is still more right to thank someone who deliberately benefits you out of regard for your welfare.

When a businesswoman benefits me by providing me with a product, a service, or a job, I owe her gratitude. It is an immoral act of ingratitude to dismiss the benefit by claiming that she didn't do it out of the goodness of her heart. Therefore to the charge of greed being business's motivator, I say, "How do you know?" Are you a mind reader? And even if you are correct, and most times it might seem that you are indeed correct, it does not matter. Any person doing good for another deserves to receive gratitude rather than psychoanalysis of his or her motives.

Myth #3: Business Harms the Environment

Today, environmentalism has become an all powerful cultural motif. Responsible stewardship of natural resources is a good thing; turning environmentalism into an ultimate value, a religion in fact, allows it to be used repressively. If it is "right" and "good" to do whatever it takes to "protect the environment," then people's freedoms need to be sacrificed if necessary, as do their financial livelihoods. Before presenting an alternative viewpoint to this hoary old chestnut, I will tell you that I am passionate about the beauties of the natural environment. Within the anthology of Jewish blessings are found those to be recited on seeing beauties of nature. I find them particularly meaningful. I enjoy living and hiking among trees. I love clean air and much prefer crystal clear drinking water to any other kind. My favorite summer vacation is loading my family onto a power boat and slowly cruising the deserted bays and tree-clad islands that dot the calm blue waters between Vancouver Island and the British Columbia mainland. I do not enjoy seeing pollution, and I loathe littering.

Nonetheless, nature is not the paramount value of my life. To me it is not accidental that the Bible never describes God as creating "nature." Instead of lumping all the individual wonders of creation into one comprehensive entity called "nature," the Bible carefully catalogs all the detailed pieces of creation that the Lord engaged in during the six days of creation. That signifies to me that I ought to do the same. I enjoy a rainbow in a way that is different from how I enjoy a forest. When I laugh out loud in delight at the feel of warm rain, it is not as a tribute to nature but as an expression of my special relationship at that moment to the raindrops running down my face. I may marvel at the tree towering over my head during our picnic, but I also find myself astounded by the marvelous machinery of the wood mill that converts great logs into timber with which to build homes. I cherish the natural beauty available to me, but I do not think of myself as an environmentalist.

Although many people identify themselves as environmentalists (or perhaps because so many do), it is valuable to discuss two important features of environmentalism honestly and dispassionately.

First, environmentalism is not the ultimate value for everyone, and those for whom it is not are not thereby condemned to hell. Different people have different values and different beliefs and part of America's gift to her citizens is that she grants total freedom of belief to all. Environmentalism may be the ultimate value for some, including those who organized and were inspired by the first Earth Day in 1970. But although environmentalism is undoubtedly the ultimate value for some, many good and sincere people have other values they place ahead of environmentalism. That does not mean they don't care about the environment; it just means that, as important as it is, other things may be more important. In one way or another, people establish an informal list of ultimate priorities for themselves. For some, the ultimate priority is indeed environmentalism. For some, it is patriotism and love of country. For others it is God and faith. Still others will put family at the top of the list of those things for which they would be willing to make ultimate sacrifices.

Second, the strong emotions that environmentalism evokes are chiefly the consequence of beliefs rather than facts. My patriotism and my commitment to the faith of Judaism would fall into the same category. They may be debatable, but they are how I feel. For example, hardly anybody would suggest that global warming is as established a phenomenon as, say, the fact that the world is round and not flat. There is legitimate debate on both sides of global warming, and neither side has provided compelling evidence that would finally remove the issue from debate. It remains a belief. Some believe that global warming is a problem, and others believe it is not. Many other mainstay beliefs of the environmental movement, such as those made popular by Stanford University biologist and environmental doomsayer Paul Ehrlich, have proven unfounded. In Ehrlich's 1968 bestseller *The Population Bomb*, Ehrlich forecast global ecological collapse by 2000 and the imminent deaths of millions from starvation. And it turns out that the damage to human health caused by pesticides is far less than Rachel Carson feared it would be when she wrote *Silent Spring* in 1962.

Even False Beliefs about Environmentalism Must Be Taken Seriously

Still, even as only a belief system, environmentalism has to be taken seriously because business is blamed for the catastrophes, whether real or imagined. Let me explain why even false beliefs must be taken seriously, and I am not suggesting that environmental concerns are entirely without basis in fact. I am suggesting that those concerns, however, may not necessarily always outweigh all other concerns.

Consider this scenario. When one of my children was very young, she was regularly awakened by a recurring nightmare. Several nights a week, I would rush into her room to calm a wild-eyed little girl with a racing pulse. There, at two o'clock in the morning, I would sit on her bed while she pointed out half a dozen dogs sitting on the carpet waiting to munch on her toes. She would sit in my arms trembling while I futilely explained to her that there were really no dogs at all. After several weeks of interrupted nights had reduced me to a mere shadow of my usually robust self, I knew something drastic needed to be done. The next night when I awoke to my daughter's scream of terror, I strolled calmly in to her room and began rounding up the dogs. It didn't take me more than half a minute or so of arm waving and hissing to chase the six imaginary canines out of her room. I was rewarded with a sleepy smile and a "Thank you, Daddy" as I staggered back to my bed, there to once again find repose in the arms of Morpheus.

After two more nights of being chased out of the room, the dogs never returned. In my daughter's somnolent state, those dogs were a real problem. Trying to persuade her that the dogs did not exist merely frustrated her. She felt stuck with a handicapped parent who foolishly responded to dangerous dogs with discussion and debate. I had to enter her frame of reference, see the dogs, and get rid of them.

Environmentalism also possesses two frameworks of reality. According to one of these views, there is no real problem, just as there were really no dogs. This is obviously untrue. There are many very valid concerns. According to the other view, however, the problem is real, terrifying, and seemingly insoluble. According to this view, the world's original condition of natural perfection is being irreparably jeopardized by *business*. I think that intellectual honesty would compel people to concede that this view is also untrue.

This is not to say that there is no problem. There obviously is a problem. Seeing environmental problems is not the same as dealing with an unhappy child. It is to say, however, that the real problem may have more to do with beliefs and convictions than with objective and quantifiable peril. This in no way simplifies the problem because it is usually necessary to enter the framework in which the problem exists before one can effectively attempt a solution. In the bright light of sunrise, that little girl laughed at the nighttime intruders. At the time of the crisis, however, help only came from someone within the framework of her reality. If you really believe the dogs are there, the problem is not the dogs, it is the belief. The problem is nearly always the belief.

People Have Different Priorities, or Different Strokes for Different Folks

If you believe and are convinced that, for instance, no more important value exists than prolonging life span, you would be justified in prohibiting all activities that could abbreviate national life span averages. You would be doing the right thing by prohibiting sport parachuting and mountain climbing as immoral activities. But humans have always demonstrated that they are often motivated by other conflicting values. Soldiers often perform heroic acts that shorten their own lives. Patients often make "quality-of-life" decisions in which life span is not the paramount concern. Many individuals choose to smoke cigars, skydive, or mountain climb because of what these activities contribute to their lives, and they do so in full knowledge that they may be shortening their lives. Environmentalism places the preservation of nature in the forefront of moral consciousness, above and beyond most other values with which it may well be in conflict. In so doing, environmentalists may effectively censor out any calculation of relative benefits. They might also be making competing facts quite irrelevant.

My point is that you should not allow yourself to be automatically persuaded of business's culpability by well-intentioned environmentalists. Because environmentalism is as much a belief as almost any religious faith, trying to aggressively win converts is in bad taste. Rude evangelism is never excused by the fervor felt by the crusader for his or her cause. Furthermore, it is clear to almost everyone who is truly interested in facts rather than beliefs that modern industrialized countries are far more merciful toward the environment than other countries. One need only recall the condition of the environment within the old Soviet countries.

This section of my discussion is not intended to be a full-blown treatise on the large and complicated area of environmentalism. My hope here is to encourage you to reject the conventional wisdom and the cultural hysteria about environmental issues until you have conducted your own independent research. By this I don't mean for you to undertake complex experiments to determine average annual temperature changes since the eighteenth century. I merely recommend that you include within your reading list books and magazines that offer alternative viewpoints on this controversial issue. By doing so, you will provide yourself with the necessary data and statistics to serve as tools to fend off attack and thereby to become more confident within your own heart that business has less to do with environmental problems than it has to do with the solutions.

Myth #4: Business Dehumanizes People by Turning Them into Consumers

Some people's pursuit of ultimate perfection would have everyone else driven only by artistic aspiration. Any indication that people respond to what they consider lower and baser motivations is de facto evidence that such people are being manipulated by forces of evil. To their way of thinking there is no better candidate for the title of ultimate force of evil than business.

Their understanding of people may be poetic but it is unrealistic. Humans do not spend all their time writing poetry or painting masterpieces. Sometimes they just feel like eating an ice cream cone, buying a pretty dress, or even, yes, going to the bathroom. All human activities can be located somewhere on a spectrum anchored at one end by spirituality and at the other by physicality. Praying is near the spiritual end; reading and writing, composing music, and making tools are its neighbors. As the source of both great sensual pleasure and all new life, sex might be somewhere near midspectrum, while eating and all other bodily functions belong over toward the physical end. Where do commercial transactions fit? When a man exchanges coins in his pocket for the goods or services he desires, is he performing a physical act or a spiritual one?

Because animals, unlike people, are 100 percent material or physical, one way of identifying a spiritual act is by determining whether a chimpanzee would understand the action. When I return home from work and slump into a comfortable armchair with a drink, my pet primate undoubtedly sympathizes. As I move to the dinner table and begin eating, he certainly knows what is going on. When I open a newspaper, however, and hold it motionless before my face for 20 minutes, he becomes quite confused.

Another criterion for the spiritual is whether the action can be replicated by a machine. If a human soul is indispensable for a certain process, that process is at least partially spiritual. Only a human soul can compose music that inspires people to march to war or brings a lump to the throat. No machine exhibits loyalty or can even test whether an individual possesses that quality; therefore, loyalty is another spiritual characteristic.

These tests suggest that a business transaction is more *spiritual* than physical. A chimpanzee would not have the slightest idea of what is transpiring between proprietor and customer at the counter of a store. Existing machines can neither independently effect transactions nor predict whether a customer will buy something. Economic exchange takes place only after two thinking human beings will it. The process must be mostly spiritual.

It is important to analyze actions because human beings are always slightly uneasy about pursuits so physical that they have no spiritual overtones at all. When necessary, humans superimpose spirituality precisely to avoid being exclusively physical and thus animal-like. They apply ceremony and ritual to virtually all activities performed by both people and animals. On the one hand, only people read a book or listen to music, hence these activities require no associated ritual. On the other hand, all living creatures eat, engage in sexual activity, give birth, and die. If humans do not confer a unique ritual on these functions, they reduce the distinction between themselves and the animal kingdom. Therefore, humans celebrate the birth of a child, often by a naming ceremony; no animal does that.

Similarly, even if a person's hands are quite clean, he or she washes them *before* eating rather than after, like a cat. People prefer to serve food in dishes on a tablecloth rather than straight out of the can, although the physical, nutritional qualities of the food have not been enhanced. Many people even say a grace or a benediction before a meal. This is a human, spiritual way to eat; a dog is quite content to gobble his meal from the can.

The more physical the activity, the more awkwardness and subconscious embarrassment surround it. Any activity that humans do that animals do, seems to fill humans with subconscious discomfort. Nudism is practiced with a certain bravado in order to conceal the underlying tension. Famous photographer Richard Avedon shattered a barrier by capturing images of people as they ate. Frozen in the act of chewing, humans resemble apes rather than angels. The early English, and later the first Americans, raised within a Judeo-Christian moral framework, established certain cultural niceties such as never eating in public. For this reason, restaurants in their early incarnations had private rooms in which a group of people close to one another would eat together in private. The one large public eating room that is today's restaurant is a relatively recent phenomenon. Similarly, people express a normal and healthy reticence about bathroom activities, preferring to perform them in private.

Purely spiritual occupations, such as reading and art, evoke no discomfort. My point is that neither should buying and selling. Economic activity is another way in which humans satisfyingly distance themselves from the animal kingdom and draw closer to God.

Revealing his own brand of genius in *Paradise Lost*, John Milton etched the Bible's centrality in man's literary consciousness. He reflected everyone's subconscious awareness that the opening chapters of the Bible focus on the eternal tug-of-war for man's soul between the angels and the apes. There is a titanic struggle between the Divine aspirations of a person's nobility and his or her basest indulgences. Whom would Adam obey, God or the serpent, a symbolic personification of the animal kingdom? After thousands of years of human history, the lingering memory of that tussle still resonates in the human soul. Jewish tradition has always taught of the need for people to distinguish themselves from animals and to unequivocally demonstrate who won that primeval conflict. Seizing another's property by force is animalistic and a victory for the serpent; purchasing it voluntarily for the price set by the seller finds favor in God's eyes. That is how Jews have seen things. They have not seen business as dehumanizing, far from it. People have many needs, some are uplifting and have to do mostly with our souls while others are simpler, having mostly to do with our bodies. All can be legitimate and business is blessed for being the mechanism by means of which we obtain those many needs.

The Morality of the Marketplace

That relationship between currency and God's gift of economic creativity springs from the Bible and the Hebrew language itself. In the language that

William Bradford, second governor of the Plymouth Colony, described as "the holy tongue in which the Law and oracles of God were writ; and in which God and angels spake to the holy patriarchs of old time,"[16] the word for "God's gift of economic creativity" is *Cheyn*. This word is the etymological origin not only for the English words *coin* and *gain* but also for the Chinese word for coin, *Ch'ien,* and for similar words in many other languages.

That same word meaning God's gift of economic creativity is also used as the root of the Hebrew word for *store* or *shop* as well as for a *market-based economy.* A store or market is one of the few places in which people interact voluntarily leaving each party happier than he or she was before. Even Ayn Rand observed that when extracting specific performance from people, the only alternative to a gun is money.[17] No wonder then that God smiles on the marketplace. Freedom from tyranny is a necessary precondition for both worship and trade.

One of the Hebrew words for *businessman* is *Ohmein*, which means "man of faith" and shares the same root with the liturgical *Amen.* With no verifiable information that he will be successful selling his wares, the merchant nonetheless purchases inventory. He then delights in selling out his entire inventory, even vital commodities like food or clothing, in exchange for little metal discs. Instead of despair at how he will now feed and clothe his children, he has complete faith that whenever he wishes, there will be someone who will gladly sell him food or anything else he may need for those very metal discs. It is that faith that converts metal discs and printed paper into money. There is little actual value in the metal disc or the paper strip he holds. It cannot be used as food, medicine, clothing, or housing. It is really a spiritual representation of a magical combination of a promise and a claim. And without faith in the value of a promise, the promise itself is useless. Were he to trade on the basis of doubt and suspicion, he would contract no business at all. It is chiefly his faith that makes possible his profits. Does this sound like a dehumanizing activity? Not to Jewish tradition, and it shouldn't to you either.

It is therefore not surprising that economics used to be a field of study that belonged with religion and theology. Adam Smith and many other eighteenth-century economists were religious philosophers before they were economists. Smith wrote *Theory of Moral Sentiments* before he wrote *Wealth of Nations.* When the great universities moved the study of economics from their religious departments to their science departments, they were actually driving a wedge between the profoundly uplifting activity of business and the moral arguments and spiritual dimensions that underpin the validity of economics. Judaism always accepted that *faith* is the fuel that drives both commerce and religion.

Markets Are Very Human

Dehumanizing means "becoming disconnected from other human beings." It is difficult for a successful businessperson in the U.S. system to remain self-centered. It is precisely a preoccupation with the needs of others that characterizes the entrepreneur. Concern for customers is the hallmark of an American business professional. This is not so in other countries. Americans abroad are often shocked at the disrespect and insolence shown by proprietors of businesses in Europe and elsewhere, while one of the culture shocks foreigners face when visiting our country is the phrase "Have a nice day," accompanied by a smile as they shop.

In addition, successful businesspeople recognize their employees as a most valuable asset and understand the need to attend to their welfare. Recognizing employees as spiritual beings with their own Divine aspirations, the employer must endeavor not only to compensate them fairly, but also to help them find transcendent meaning in their work. The employer whose own selfish wants and needs constantly fill his or her mind is doomed. Thus, both business and religion discourage selfish and narcissistic behavior.

Jewish tradition tries to show that a close relationship exists between God and the marketplace because doing so helps us in three crucial areas.

1. Jewish tradition helps to explain why atheism and business are not natural allies. One would have supposed that a philosophy of secular socialism would have naturally succeeded in economic enterprise. One would have expected the old Soviet Union to excuse what it calls the "greed" of capitalism and to recognize it as nothing other than Darwinian law applied to the life of modern humanity. Yet, this is not possible: Something as truly spiritual as commerce simply cannot coexist with socialism. The avowed atheist recognizes that to be true to the credo, he or she must reject the free marketplace because of its great goodness and potential for advancing human growth.

2. Jewish tradition helps people integrate their careers into their life. Those daily 8 or 10 hours of toil should not be regarded as a faintly distasteful and isolated part of life. "Business is business" cannot serve as a convenient explanation for moral departures in the marketplace because business is really tied to life by overall spiritual awareness. Immorality in business is as repugnant as immorality in marriage. Business success is not the goal, but it is a natural outcome to widespread moral integrity.

3. Recognizing the congruence between work and spiritual reality, business professionals are all the better able to sell themselves and their products. Work is creative and therefore a legitimate way of emulating God's infinite creativity. Anyone with a sneaking suspicion that socialism has a point, that people and their abilities are finite, is forever handicapped as a businessperson. If the pie is of a fixed size, one creates nothing, merely taking from others. People do not throw themselves wholeheartedly into an endeavor they secretly consider demeaning and unworthy. The difference between the animal instinct of a squirrel gathering nuts and the inherent nobility of a human being earning a living becomes clear when you perceive economic enterprise in its correct position, at the spiritual end of the spectrum. Business dehumanizes? Hardly.

INSTEAD OF PERFECTION— THE NEXT BEST THING

I am not trying to make the case that business—and the Ethical Capitalism system within which it flourishes—constitutes the permanent redemptive solution for humankind's ultimate destiny. Like you, I have ultimate values, and business and money are not they. Still, you do need to ask yourself an important question: As a business professional, are you advancing an evil, exploitative, and destructive system; or are you promoting freedom from material want for yourself and for your neighbors within an ethical framework of noble endeavor? The real question is not whether the system whereby humans interact voluntarily with one another for economic gain is the perfect way to organize society, but whether there is a better way that business professionals are stubbornly resisting.

Here I come to yet another of the great advantages enjoyed by Jews who were inducted, consciously and voluntarily or not, into God's ancient worldview of Ethical Capitalism. One of the great gifts of Faith is that it makes it far easier for us mortals to live with imperfection. Religious Jews always accepted that only God was perfect and only He had the capacity to ultimately bring perfection to the world; but until He did so, it was just fine to take the best available option even if it wasn't perfect. It may not be ultimately perfect, but it was a far better way to function than in pursuing utopian dreams of perfection that would eventually prove to be futile and costly failures. In this way, the Jew thrived by coming to see Ethical Capitalism as the best available option. Did it solve all of humanity's problems, and did it alleviate all human suffering? No, of course, it didn't do that. But let me embark on more thought experiments that might disclose alternative options.

Warren E. Buffett, chairman of Berkshire Hathaway, Inc., frequently talks about how one might design an ideal society. He uses a clever example to demonstrate just how difficult it is to come up with a system superior to the one that has brought Americans the unprecedented freedom and prosperity we enjoy.

> Let's say it was 24 hours before you were born, and a genie appeared and said, "You look like a winner. I have enormous confidence in you, and what I'm going to do is let you set the rules of the society into which you will be born. You can set the economic rules and the social rules, and whatever rules you set will apply during your lifetime and your children's lifetimes."
>
> And you'll say, "Well, that's nice, but what's the catch?"
>
> And the Genie says, "Here's the catch. You don't know if you're going to be born rich or poor, white or black, male or female, able-bodied or infirm, intelligent or retarded." So all you know is that you're going to get one ball out of a barrel with, say, 5.8 billion balls in it. You're going to participate in what I call the ovarian lottery. It's the most important thing that will happen to you in your life, but you have no control over it. It's going to determine far more than your grades at school or anything else that happens to you. Now what rules do you want to have?"[18]

What sort of system for the extended order of human cooperation would you design? Buffett predicts that you're going to want a system that creates ever more *wealth*. The way he sees it, there are a lot of people out there, and they all need a lot of goods and services. The best thing to do is design a system, he says, that provides incentive for the most able and creative people to keep working long after they no longer need to work.

I have come to see how that system might look from the challenge that some in my audiences frequently fling at me: Why should only wealthy people enjoy so many of life's amenities? I do not consider it to be a really good question because everyone enjoys far more luxury and comfort than his or her ancestors ever did and far more than many, if not most, other inhabitants of the planet. Admittedly some people also enjoy less than some other people; but to say that only wealthy people enjoy so many of life's amenities is simply not accurate. However, it is sometimes better to answer the question than to appear to be dodging it.

Here is part of the answer that I provide to that question. I live with my family on Mercer Island in the state of Washington. It is a very beautiful island, and there is not a morning that I do not wake up profoundly grateful to live there. Around the rim of this small island are several hundred waterfront homes. I do not live in one, but I would like to do so. In this desire, I am not alone. I have discovered that literally thousands of people would like to live in a Mercer Island waterfront home. Suppose, just for argument's sake that 100,000 people want waterfront homes on Mercer Island of which there are only 500 available. The arithmetic means that 99,500 hopeful waterfront dwellers are going to be disappointed. How is it decided who will be disappointed and who the lucky 500 are to be? How does society decide on how best to allocate the 500 waterfront homes?

It seems to me that there are only five possible ways to determine to whom, out of 100,000 people, those 500 beautiful waterfront homes should be distributed. Here are the five possible ways to allocate them:

1. Hold a lottery. Issue 100,000 numbered tickets to all interested parties. Then hold a public drawing at which the Mercer Island homecoming queen draws the first 500 lucky numbers. Don't laugh at this option, because many states these days hold lotteries for all kinds of things. Why not also for waterfront property and all other desirable property for that matter?

2. Declare a free-for-all, stipulating the use of force. See a house you like? Grab weapons and sally out to dislodge the current resident. You should be able to move in before the end of the week. Oh, one little thing; before assaulting the current resident, make sure that he or she cannot outgun you. Furthermore, should your home acquisition campaign prove successful, be certain to maintain a full-time team of thugs, I mean mercenaries, to protect you from the next eager home acquirer. Finally, always pay your mercenaries on time, or they may help turn you into an ex-resident yourself. Don't laugh at this option either, because it is quite the popular means of property acquisition in many sad parts of the world today.

3. Form a committee to distribute the waterfront homes. This committee could comprise some politicians, some academics, and other assorted citizenry; and it would decide on whom to bestow the very limited number of waterfront homes. It may invite a measure of corruption, but please don't laugh at this option either, because quite a few societies during the past century have used variations of this approach.

4. Give the waterfront homes to everyone. Like most solutions that claim to act in the interests of "all the people," this one doesn't really give the property to all the people as much as it gives it to none of the people. You see, this option involves turning all the waterfront homes into a great big beautiful park ringing Mercer Island so all the people can enjoy these desirable locations. You may feel free to laugh at this option because it is no solution at all. It merely postpones the even thornier question of who is going to own the next tier of homes that overlook not only the water but also beautiful park land?

5. Create something called money. This abstract numbering system is a means of distilling the essence of a person's usefulness to his or her fellow human beings. It sums up this person's creativity, knowledge, experience, diligence, and ability to defer gratification. It even takes into account the circle of contacts the person has built and perhaps even allows him or her to benefit from similar numbers accumulated by his or her father. It then allows the person to bid the exact amount of personal resources that he or she is willing to sacrifice for the benefit of owning a waterfront home. Don't laugh at this option; it may not be perfect, but are any of the previous four preferable?

Do you know of a sixth way of deciding who gets the waterfront houses? If not, then this is it. Is the fifth option completely perfect and ultimately satisfying? Of course not. But it is clearly superior to the other four choices although it leaves 99,500 disappointed people who had hoped to obtain a fine waterfront home. But most of them accept this solution, partially because they don't see the current situation as permanent. They do not feel themselves permanently disenfranchised from ever owning waterfront property. They return to their businesses and endeavor to have more money to bring to the auction next time. In so doing, they will inevitably be helping others also improve their lot, because as you have seen, it is virtually impossible to profit without doing something of greater value for other people.

THE CIVILIZING EFFECT OF BUSINESS

Because many people assume that sentimentality plays so little role in business, they also assume that business professionals are likely to be heartless automatons fixated only on the bottom line and devoid of all feelings. They assume that they are far more likely to encounter generosity and altruism in remote regions of Africa, Asia, and South America where people live in small tribal groupings and hunt and fish for their livings. Anthropologists have conducted experiments to affirm the truth of these beliefs and found that they are not borne out by fact. The results were counterintuitive. The more involved people were in business activities—such as working for wages or buying and selling goods to others—the more generous they were. "The most altruistic and trusting societies are those that are the most market-oriented," says Jean Ensminger, an anthropologist at the Californian Institute of Technology, Pasadena.[19]

Seeking perfection in the extended order of human cooperation called the social and economic system entails considerable risk. The peril you face is that you devote your energies to resenting the system instead of participating wholeheartedly in it for your own benefit and also, most important, for the benefit of all those around you. Your prosperity is beneficial to your neighbors, friends, community, and society. People who resent the rules of the game seldom achieve distinction in that game. It may simply not be possible to achieve the perfection of human society for which so many people legitimately yearn. As I have shown, one area does exist in which the pursuit of perfection is not only legitimate but also somewhat achievable. The one entity that it is well worthwhile struggling to perfect morally, is yourself. Engagement in business provides a marvelous opportunity to do so, along with incentives for success. Taken with an understanding of how the quest for perfection can handicap your efforts, you are ready to observe just how you can spread the magic through the mechanism of what is often called leadership. I will show how to do this in the next chapter.

YOUR PATH TO PROSPERITY

* *Accustom yourself to questioning the conventional wisdom in all areas that seem to blame business.* You will often hear people making assertions with such self-assurance that you hesitate to question those frequently controversial positions. Learn how to do so politely but firmly with honest curiosity and openness. When encountering arguments on how business will run amok without additional governmental supervision, ask how the opposing viewpoint might respond. Similarly, when business is blamed for environmental problems, health problems, and any other social ills, consider the possibility that there may be real villains who are being ignored, and try to identify who they may be.

* *Rid yourself of all feelings of envy toward those who have much more than you do.* Replace envy with feelings of empathy and compassion for those with less. View your own condition as nonstatic. You are growing all the time, economically speaking. It may be a cliché to talk of whether your glass is half full or half empty; but one thing is for sure: The glass is a whole lot larger than it might have been. Focus on the good, the wonderful, and the miraculous. Think of how much you have to be grateful for. Your quest for wealth would be infinitely more daunting if you lived in a society less suited to wealth creation. Thinking, acting, and sounding positive, happy, and upbeat make you more pleasant company; and building many new friendships and relationships is crucial to your quest.

* *In both your business and your personal life, try to become comfortable with the second-best solution if the very best solution is unattainable.* In giving others advice, remember that you must first determine if they are able to follow your advice. If they are simply incapable of following the very best advice you can come up with, then the second-best advice now becomes the best advice.

Lead Consistently and Constantly

Learning to lead is important, but it may not be what you think it is.

Leadership is not a noun; it is a verb. It is not an identity; it is an action.

Don't try to become a leader, just do it. Just lead.

Serving as a rabbi to my beachfront community in Los Angeles during the 1980s, I saw it as my duty to teach the Torah. (*Rabbi*, of course, means "teacher" in Hebrew.) Most of the members I served were accomplished professionals in fields as diverse as business, entertainment, and medicine. What possible relevance could a 3,000-year-old document have to their busy and productive lives? I had been taught that the information in this remarkable book was indispensable to happy and successful living. But how would I go about demonstrating that to this impressive group?

My first step was to show that examining the Torah in its original Hebrew was an incomparably more profound experience than merely reading it in English translation. My next step was to show how even those familiar with the language in which it was written would still require a guide to probe the really useful principles contained in the Torah.

A useful model of this problem was provided by an original German version of the *Treatise on Thermodynamics* written by the great scientist Max Planck in Berlin during 1897. One fine California evening, I held the weighty *Treatise* aloft and explained to my audience that it contained truly useful information on how the world worked and that I wanted to read several pages to them. I hadn't read more than a paragraph in its almost incomprehensible German when I pretended to notice the baffled looks on the faces of almost everyone present. "What is the problem?" I asked. In tones usually reserved for addressing mental idiots, someone carefully explained to me that I was reading in German, a language few understood.

Apologizing profusely, I put away the intimidating book and replaced it with the English translation of the work, done by Alexander Ogg in Cape Town in 1926. I began reading. "*The energy of any body or system of bodies in any given state is equal to the algebraic sum of the mechanical equivalents of all the effects produced outside the system when it passes in any way from the given normal state. . . .*"[1] Again, I questioned the looks of bewilderment that I pretended to have only just noticed. Then, before my audience became too frustrated with me, I explained, "Just because you understand the language in which highly technical material is presented doesn't mean that you will understand the material." In connection with thermodynamics, you would need a guide to walk you through the introductory studies of physics and mathematics on which thermodynamics depended. Similarly, a full understanding of the Torah has always required a *guide,* a person known as a *rabbi,* who could explain the inner meaning as he was originally taught by someone who was his rabbi (and so on, until one establishes an unbroken line of verbal transmission back to Moses himself).

I tell you all of this only to explain that much of the business wisdom that financially successful Jews have extracted from the Torah is not easily apparent in translation. Because the Torah is a comprehensive theory on the totality of all existence, its principles and guidance encompass many facets of life, not just business. The Torah is not laid out along the lines of a conventional business book. One cannot, for instance, look up the chapter that discusses "leadership." Instead, as your guide, I have had to condense out the essence of leadership from the many places in which the principles are found. For this topic and others in this book, I have confined myself to the principles chiefly applicable to business interactions and the desire for money.

WHAT LEADERSHIP TRAINING IS NOT

You could easily find a teacher to instruct you in how to play tennis or chess, sail a boat, or operate a lathe. It would be far more difficult to learn how to be courageous, optimistic, and inspiring. Yet these are only some of the qualities necessary for leaders to possess. Is it possible to train people to become leaders? The short, if paradoxical, answer is that one can learn to lead, but one cannot really learn to become a leader.

Yet companies continue to try. For example, consider the following statistics:

- Of all U.S. companies with 100 or more employees, about 70 percent send managers to some form of leadership training.
- Penn State University estimated that about $15 billion is spent on executive training each year.
- Hundreds of organizations like the Center for Creative Leadership (CCL) in North Carolina attempt to turn managers into leaders by subjecting them to programs involving drinking green-colored buttermilk, leaping off high platforms while suspended from lines anchored by their classmates, and engaging in paintball games.
- The American Management Association prefers classroom situations for its course "Developing Executive Leadership" and promises instruction in such areas as "How to lead individuals," "How to communicate under pressure," and "How to handle difficult people."

These are certainly useful skills, but do they lead to the corner office? I don't mean to belittle the programs or the organizations. CCL, for instance, brings in revenues of nearly $40 million, and two of its programs topped a *Wall Street Journal* survey of the best leadership courses in 1993. The strikingly different approaches however, do raise this question: Why does everyone agree on how to produce top-rate doctors, car mechanics, and physicists, but nobody seems to agree on how to produce top-rate leaders? Medical education in Bombay does not differ substantially from medical training in Boston; but every single leadership training program claims to have its own unique system.

Part of the problem is that not everyone agrees on what *leadership* even means. Listen to two academics on the subject: Rosabeth Moss Kanter, a distinguished professor at Harvard Business School, said that leadership is "the art of mastering change," whereas Thomas P. Gerrity, the dean of the Wharton School at the University of Pennsylvania, said that it was "the ability to inspire and develop others." Here are the views on leadership of two chief executive officers (CEOs) of major companies: Michael Dell, chairman and CEO of Dell Computer, said that leadership is "the ability to quickly understand dynamism in the market." George Fisher, CEO of Eastman Kodak, once said it is "taking a group of people in a new direction or to a higher level of performance than they would have achieved without you." When asked to list what they considered the top ingredient for leadership, Moss Kanter responded, "Intelligence." Dell said, "Knowledge" of industry; Gerrity and Fisher said, "Character" and "Ability to inspire," respectively.[2]

Would Ernest Shackleton, who saved every last man on his ill-fated Antarctic expedition early in the twentieth century, have been considered a leader? I would say that he was a great leader, but only on his expedition. I doubt that he would have made it as a great leader had he subsequently embarked on a corporate career. Similarly, there is no reason to suppose that Michael Dell would necessarily emerge as a great leader of a mountain-climbing expedition.

Almost every poll about U.S. presidents shows that the presidents the public considers to have been great were those who served during wartime. Now there are only two possible explanations for this anomaly. The first depends on an incredible coincidence: The United States has been remarkably fortunate to have had great men lead the country on each occasion when its need was greatest. The second, more plausible, explanation is that the circumstances of wartime raise people to leadership and allow them to exhibit capabilities that were possibly also possessed by other leaders less favored by history.

BE READY TO STEP INTO LEADERSHIP

I am sure that stressful circumstances have created more leaders than have all the leadership training programs put together. Leadership is most needed precisely during moments of chaos, fear, and stress. When feeling fear and uncertainty, people turn gratefully to the man or the woman who seems fearless and who seems to know what is going on and the direction in which people or events should be going. For example, in the first hours after the terrorist attack of September 11, 2001, New York City's Mayor Rudolph W. Giuliani immediately demonstrated great leadership. Yet during the preceding couple of years, many people (including all those who discouraged him from seeking the U.S. Senate seat that Hillary Clinton later won) felt deep doubt about the mayor's leadership capacity. Professor Kenneth T. Jackson, a Columbia University historian, had ranked Mr. Giuliani behind Mayor Fiorello H. La Guardia, mayor of New York from 1934 to 1945, but he has reversed himself. "If not for September 11, he might have been almost even with La Guardia, but since then he [Guiliani] showed his best side—leadership."[3] For the weeks and months that followed, he was regarded as a great U.S. leader. Without the attack, he would have left office at the end of 2001, a well-regarded New York mayor, but without ever having achieved greatness. On Mayor Giuliani's last day in office, the *New York Times* ran a front-page story that claimed that there had "been a whiff of irrelevance" to the final years of the mayor's term; but due to his behavior on and after September 11, the article dubbed him "A Man Who Became More Than a Mayor."[4] One key to being a leader is to leap at the opportunity for leadership.

Consider another example from history. Hampton Sides, a journalist and author, described a critical moment in World War II when emaciated and tortured survivors of the infamous Bataan Death March were about to be executed in a prisoner-of-war camp. During their captivity, some prisoners had been removed from the camp and were thrown into the intolerably hot and crowded hold of a hell-ship where they began panicking, screaming, and suffocating. They were saved only because one of their number took charge:

> From the din, a single voice emerged. A man named Frank Bridget climbed high on the stairway and shouted down at the teeming masses in a clear, resolute voice. "Gentlemen," he said, "we're in this thing together, and if any of us want to live we're going to have to work as one." Bridget struck just the right cool note at just the right time, and the hysteria abated. "Keep your wits about you," he urged. "If we panic, we're only going to use up more precious breaths of oxygen. Now listen—we're all going to calm down, every one of us."
>
> Bridget was not a high-ranking officer, nor was he especially well liked or admired. Prior to this day, he had been known as a nervous, intense, overeager guy who wore jodhpurs and occasionally rubbed people the wrong way. But this day he rose to the occasion in a remarkable act of poise and resolve. Manny Lawton, who had positively hated Bridget

before, remembered his display of natural leadership with awesome gratitude. "Sometimes people rise to greatness," Lawton told an oral historian, "and you can never predict who will. Bridget was waiting in the wings, and he took responsibility. I don't know where he found the calmness. He saved us with his voice."[5]

Thus, you can see that leadership depends partially on circumstance. Consider Winston Churchill, who was a great wartime leader of the British people but who lost his first post–World War II election. One could diligently attend every single leadership training course offered in the United States without ever becoming a leader. I learned this from the Hebrew language, which doesn't even have a word for "leader." The next section explains how Jews have viewed leadership.

HOW JUDAISM DEFINES "LEADERSHIP"

Judaism has always been guided by the conviction that Hebrew is the Lord's language and that it possesses a word for every reality in the world. Conversely, when you encounter an idea for which no Hebrew word exists, you are led to question the reality of that idea. Obviously this does not apply to the natural sciences. The fact that no Hebrew word exists in the Torah for "nuclear reactor" casts no aspersions on the existence of atomic power. But for the basic areas of human life that have undergone little change through the eons of history, the absence of a word is grounds for suspicion.

Take the word *face*, for which no Hebrew word exists in the singular. The language only offers a word for the plural, *faces*, or in Hebrew *Panim*. Ancient Jewish wisdom regards this as a warning never to assume that any person only has one face. This means that every person is not only "two-faced" but even "three-faced" or "four-faced." This is not a derogatory accusation but a statement of fact. Your face changes as you age and mature, and it begins eventually to reflect aspects of your character. Relatives and friends who have known you for years have come to see those different faces. Furthermore different people in your life see different faces that you wear. Around the dinner table at home, your family sees one face, whereas an adversarial business acquaintance might well see quite a different face the next morning.

It is in this spirit that one must question why Hebrew possesses no word for "leadership." The language certainly has words for "king," for "ruler," and even for "director," but no word for "leader." Even Moses, surely the Old Testament figure who most readily leaps to mind when one thinks of leadership, was never thus described. One must distill the lesson from this absent word and see how it has influenced, perhaps subconsciously, the effectiveness of Jewish leaders throughout history.

In Hebrew, the word for "mother"—*aim*—is followed alphabetically by the word for "child"—*ben*. This Hebrew peculiarity would be duplicated in English were the word *child* to be spelled, not c-h-i-l-d, but n-p-n, following alphabetically, as it were, the word *mom*. This is of course not the case in English, but it is so in Hebrew. The "a" of *aim* is followed by the "b" of *ben* and likewise, the "m" of *aim* is followed alphabetically by the "n" of *ben*. This oddity, part of a kabalistic tradition, leads to the conclusion that no deep analysis is required to find out what a mother is. If a woman "is followed" by a child, that is to say she gives birth to or adopts a child, then she is a mother by definition. There is no way to become a mother other than by having a child.

Similarly, there is no need to analyze what a leader is. A leader is someone who has followers. There is no way to be a leader other than by having followers.

BECOMING A LEADER

How do you become a leader? The answer is, "Acquire followers." How do you acquire followers? First, acquire certain character traits, and then be willing to assume the responsibility of leadership by stepping into the role when circumstances bring that opportunity into your orbit of activities. Moses acquired the traits of leadership while living in the palace of Pharaoh. Later, God called him to leadership at the Burning Bush. At first he demurred, explaining to the Lord why he was not the right choice. Discovering that you don't say "No" to God, he went on to lead the ancient Israelites out of Egypt. He came with the character traits, he came with an attractive vision for the future, and he acquired followers.

There are no guarantees. Many people will acquire, or have already acquired, these character traits without ever becoming leaders. Others are thrust into leadership or appointed to leadership, without ever having acquired these traits, and they fail dismally. What are these character traits?

- Learn to follow if you want to learn to lead.
- Maintain a clear vision of your goal.
- Confrontation is often necessary.
- Leadership requires mastery of both faith and facts.

LEARN TO FOLLOW IF YOU WANT TO LEARN TO LEAD

"Learning to follow" is, of course, counterintuitive. I would have thought that to become an effective leader, I needed to appear powerful and invincible. That surely means conveying to my subordinates the impression that nobody tells their leader what to do. Oddly enough, precisely the reverse is what works. You stand more chance of making it to leadership if you never miss an opportunity to point out to those around you that your actions are not simply spur-of-the-moment impulses but the consequences of accountability to some external entity.

Before people will follow a specific leader, they must first become viscerally persuaded, on a subconscious level, of the system of hierarchy. A leader depends on his or her followers accepting a sense of hierarchy in order to validate his or her leadership. Without some feeling that hierarchy as such is legitimate, the leader's entire leadership is in jeopardy. This was part of Adolf Hitler's downfall. The Nazis inculcated the "Fuehrer Principle" throughout the Third Reich. *Fuehrer* means "leader," and the idea was that every loyal German was to have an immediate leader. To young teenagers, the Fuehrer Principle meant that they obeyed the orders of the leader of their local Hitler Youth chapter. To the German air force officer, it meant that he followed the word of Hermann Goering, chief air marshal of the Luftwaffe. It was easy to follow the chain of leadership upward until one reached the ultimate leader, Hitler himself.

The failure of the Fuehrer Principle was that the ultimate leader, Adolf Hitler, was not seen to have any leader himself. During the early stages of his leadership, he ruled by virtue of having pulled off breathtaking military successes. Later, as the tide turned against Germany, Hitler's leadership faltered because his decisions seemed to be capricious rather than in response to the orders of *his* ultimate authority.

In contrast, Moses was one of the great leaders of ancient Israel, and he was accepted as a leader regardless of whether things were going well or not.

This principle of a leader needing also to be a *follower* is even more important than technical leadership skills. For instance, everyone recognizes that a leader needs to be able to delegate. Yet Moses was evidently a rather inadequate delegator. The Bible records how shocked his father-in-law, Jethro, was by the sight of Moses doing all the judging on his own. "Moses' father-in-law said to him, 'The thing that you do is not good, you will surely become worn out, for this work is too hard for you. You will not be able to do it alone.'"[6] Moses took Jethro's advice and set up a management system of judges reporting to him.

Although Moses obviously was not knowledgeable in this area of leadership—delegation—he nonetheless succeeded because he did possess the far more important quality of appearing to be a good follower. There were occasional minor rebellions against his leadership, but whenever God stepped in to help quell the uprisings, Moses' authority was even more firmly entrenched. Part of the reason that he was accepted as leader by millions of Jewish slaves was that he was seen to be a follower just as much as a leader. He constantly made clear to his people that he was carrying out the words of God. The people themselves saw Moses punished whenever he deviated from such higher orders.

The U.S. institution that has perhaps the finest system of leadership training is the military. Again, the "leaders must be followers, too" principle is at work. Even the mostly lowly ranked soldier knows that his commanding officer has his own commanding officer and so on, all the way up to the president of the United States, who, in turn, owes allegiance to the Constitution of the United States. One secret behind each sergeant's leadership is that he is not merely an independent tyrant embittering the lives of the soldiers beneath him, but he is a representative of a higher authority and answerable to that authority.

A well-known directive found in the first chapter of *Sayings of the Fathers*, a well-loved volume of the Oral Torah, reminded Jews of the necessity of being a good follower. This section of the Mishna, which is still often read in synagogues on Sabbath afternoon, reads: "Yehoshua ben Perachya said identify a rabbi as your rabbinic authority."[7] This rule helped establish the idea that no Jew is an independent authority, but is instead bound to the traditions and rules of the past and only through following them acquires the power to rule others. To this day, it is not uncommon to find conspicuously successful Jewish business leaders who defer many major decisions to an aged parent who was the original founder of the business.

How to apply this "leaders must be followers, too" principle in your own career can best be seen from the Torah model of how Jews believe the Jewish family was designed to operate. One way in which the traditional Jewish family benefits from this principle is the greater tendency of children in these more traditional families to obey parents and to observe their parents' values. They tend to accept their parents' authority because they are made very aware of the many areas in which their own parents follow authority also. Obeying parents only makes sense if the fundamental principle of obeying anyone else at all in the first place is supported. If the family vehicle sported a bumper sticker such as those that were in vogue during the 1970s—"Question authority"—it would be difficult for parents to demand obedience from their children, without becoming figures of derision.

By contrast, children raised in traditional Jewish homes have ample opportunity to observe their parents upholding the principle of authority as they obey a wide swath of laws. The children are allowed to see how rules regulate how their mothers and fathers dress, eat, and even relate intimately. This evidence that parents follow a higher authority helps to validate the parents' authority with respect to their children. Parents are advised by Jewish tradition never to respond to the question "Why are you doing that?" with merely a "Because I want to" or "Because that's how it is." Instead, they commonly tell even their youngest children, "Because that is what God said I must do." In so doing, they are not weakening their parental authority, they are enhancing it.

In your career you can easily make use of this principle. You might not be in a situation in which you can claim to be obeying the authority of a board of directors. You might be an employee of a firm without a board of directors, or you might be the owner of a small private company. In neither case can you easily demonstrate that you are a follower because, to all appearances, as owner, you do whatever you wish. Fortunately, this principle works just as well when you declare yourself to be a follower of a set of principles, and this is something that anyone can do. Some organizations try to achieve this end with an honor code or a mission statement. It is important that these not be trite or even sound trite. Remember, you are trying to make it easier for people to follow your lead by showing that you subscribe to the leadership principle.

You must find ways to demonstrate that you do not operate capriciously on the basis of whatever you happen to feel like doing. Therefore, you should seek opportunities, in the presence of those you would lead, to say things like, "I would if I could, but my commitment (or the company's commitment) to this or that prevents me." In other words, do everything possible to avoid sounding like a big shot. For example, ambassadors derive considerable prestige and power by subordinating themselves to their governments. The ambassador's favorite phrase is, "I will have to check with my government." On the surface, this would seem to diminish the diplomat. After all, where is his or her independent authority? Strangely, it does precisely the reverse: It endows the ambassador with additional authority. So, whether you credibly claim to be under the authority of another person or a group of persons, like a boss or a board, or whether you claim to be under the authority of a set of principles or rules that you regard as rigid, your leadership capacity benefits either way.

MAINTAIN A CLEAR VISION OF YOUR GOAL

During the early 1990s, the wounded giant IBM nearly collapsed. From having nearly half a million employees and a market capitalization larger than the gross domestic product of half the countries on the United Nations roster, IBM appeared ready for demise. Then in early 1993, IBM's board appointed Lou Gerstner as CEO. His first public utterance as IBM chief was, "The last thing IBM needs right now is a vision." Since then, IBM went up fivefold while the Dow during the same period merely tripled. Gerstner has done well by his shareholders; but according to Rich Karlgaard, *Forbes* magazine's publisher, Gerstner lied. IBM *did* have a vision from 1993 to 2002.[8] It was to become a master of new technology. IBM led the nation's companies in recording patents. It developed blue-laser technology, speech recognition technology, optical microscopes, copper-wired microprocessors, and many other breakthroughs. People sometimes mock "the vision thing," but everyone needs a vision. Someone intending to lead when the opportunity presents itself needs one even more urgently.

You must have a vision of your goal. More important, you have to know when to focus on your goal and when to focus on the intermediate steps. Suppose your project is to build a house. Should you focus on the overall design and how it will integrate with surrounding scenery, or should you focus on finding a supplier for the bricks? In other words, vision or details? What would someone who aspires to leadership do?

Every Friday night, Jews sing a song welcoming the Sabbath by depicting the day as an approaching bride. One stanza concludes with these words about the creation of the Sabbath day: "Last in deed, first in thought." The idea is that although God only created the Sabbath after he had already concluded His work during the first six days of creation, the Sabbath had been in His mind from the outset. This is why Hebrew affixes no names to the days of the week, preferring instead to refer to them as day one, day two, and so on. The idea is that if named, each day could be said to have its own existence as a disconnected and independent entity. However, by being numbered, each day exists only as a link to the sequence of numbers that concludes with number seven—the Sabbath. In other words, the purpose of Sunday, Monday, and so on, is primarily to lead to Saturday, the Jewish Sabbath. In this way, God is not seen as having run out of steam on the sixth day and, having nothing else left to create, deciding to declare the next day a Sabbath. Instead the Sabbath is seen as an intrinsic part of the entire creation plan, although it was the last project in the creation. This tradition is kept alive by those words in the Sabbath welcome song, "Last in deed, first in thought."

More important, those words are also a guide as to the proper time for ultimate-vision, goal-oriented thinking. It should be last when you are engaged in deed, but first when you are engaged in thought. Do you remember that house? While designing it, think of its ultimate usage. Consider what it will look like up there on the hill. Should you include the existing trees in the final landscape? Now is the time to think about it. But soon the design phase will be complete and the blueprints drawn. Now it is time to begin grading the lot and digging foundations. At this deed phase of the project, contemplation of the final picture is merely daydreaming. Now there is work to be done, and that comes most easily when you focus on each step that lies ahead.

Thus the answer to the original question is that you should be able to focus on both the goal and on the intermediate steps. To begin a software design project or a business plan, you must focus on your ultimate goal. You must then break down that goal into intermediate phases, ensuring that each phase links seamlessly with those around it. Then, you need to break down each phase into specific tasks, each of which can be tackled without any distraction from the bigger picture. At regular intervals, you should glance up at the bigger picture to make certain that you are still on course. People are more liable to follow people who demonstrate that they know where they are headed as well as knowing how to skirt or overcome the obstacles on the way. I cannot tell you exactly how to apply this principle in your life and in your career, but I can assure you that no matter what your occupation may be, there are opportunities to do so.

CONFRONTATION IS OFTEN NECESSARY

If you aspire to leadership, you must have the courage to persuasively present your vision. Even if you fail to carry the day, you are still ahead, in leadership terms. Your vision may be a new marketing campaign, or it may be a vision of fairness and integrity. Naturally you know how to confront productively, but no leader fears confrontation.

I suspect that this important lesson crept into Jewish business culture from a famous Biblical account of an incident in the life of Judah. Out of all 12 of Jacob's sons, Judah was the one who passed royal leadership down to his descendants. (He was also the son whose name became the national identity of the Jews. This is more easily seen in the German word for a Jew, *Jude*, which was eventually contracted to Jew in English.) Ten of Judah's brothers plotted to kill Joseph, the dreamer. The eldest son, Reuben, suggested that instead of actually shedding blood themselves, they would do better to cast him into a pit where he would eventually die. Later, after they had done so, Judah approached his brothers with a plan to haul Joseph out of the pit and sell him to a passing band of merchants. It is believed that this was Judah's attempt to save his younger brother's life. A few verses later can be found the words: "And it was at that time that Judah descended from his brothers . . ."[9] Where did he descend to, and why use the word *descend*? Jewish tradition records the answer. Judah *descended* from his traditional position of *leader*. Deep inside their hearts, his brothers viewed him as having failed in leadership. Regretting the irreversible sale of Joseph, the brothers confronted Judah and blamed him for a failure of leadership: "Had you told us to return Joseph to his father rather than kill him or sell him we would have listened to you!" Judah felt himself diminished by their valid indictment, and the word *descended* accurately describes what happened to him.

Apparently Judah lacked the courage to confront his brothers with what he really wanted to say. "Look here, there is no way we can kill our brother. No matter how much we dislike him, we cannot hurt our father in this heartless fashion. I am not going along with this and neither are you. Now haul him out of the pit and send him home." Instead, he aimed for a halfway measure and lost the respect of his brothers. He literally descended from them.

Later Judah recovers his leadership when Joseph, as viceroy of Egypt, threatens to keep Benjamin incarcerated. At that point in the narrative,[10] it was Judah who stepped forward and explained to the feared Egyptian ruler that they simply could not go home without Benjamin. It was this display of courage, of fearless leadership, that moved Joseph deeply enough to reveal himself to his long-lost brothers. By facing confrontation, Judah recovered his leadership.

The Enron debacle of fall 2001 revealed several instances of willingness to confront. One person who displayed little fear of confrontation was Sherron Watkins, a senior employee at Enron, who, during summer 2001, told Enron chairman and CEO Kenneth Lay that accounting irregularities would bring the company down. In what appears to have been a high-flying, risk-taking atmosphere, her lonely cautionary voice would certainly not have been welcome. Nonetheless, she held her own and entered the pages of U.S. corporate history.

LEADERSHIP REQUIRES MASTERY OF BOTH FAITH AND FACTS

Some people master facts. If the facts they master pertain to the elasticity of polymers or the electrical resistance characteristics of semiconductors, those people tend to do well working as engineers. If the facts they master are legal precedents, they tend to succeed working for a law firm or for a law school. Other people who master the area of faith might find their niche as theologians.

Those destined to succeed in leadership when the circumstance presents itself are those who have mastered both faith and fact. The latter is the easier to dispense with. Clearly my confidence in my leader will be badly shaken if I find out that he or she is unaware of important and germane facts. This does not mean that my sergeant or my president must necessarily be an encyclopedia of facts. It does mean that the leader should be drawing on those who are in possession of the needed facts. He or she cannot risk appearing indifferent to facts relevant to the operation. For example, if an invasion is planned, I expect to be reassured by the leader's focus on intelligence. I want to see the leader assigning someone the job of finding out exactly what defensive capacity will be confronted. Similarly, if a new marketing campaign is being launched, I will more eagerly throw my efforts into the task if I know that the leader is aware of the competition. It is clear that your efforts to become a leader will be thwarted if you cannot master the relevant facts. Mastery of facts is an indispensable accompaniment to leadership, but it is only half the story. If facts are all you master, then you will always be valuable to the leaders, but you are not destined to become a leader yourself.

The other necessary element is that of faith. Does this mean only religious people can become leaders? No, of course not. When I use the word *Faith* with a capital "F," I mean a specific kind of faith, faith in Almighty God. However, when I use the word *faith*, I mean the ability to work as comfortably with something yet invisible as if it were already a present reality. Whether you are leading yourself or are already leading others, you are distinguished by something very important. You alone see the desired outcome in front of your very eyes, as plainly as if it were already a reality.

Abraham, the father of Judaism, effectively lived and taught this crucial point. As the first Jew and also as the first Jewish father, he set the pattern of leadership for a father. Later the Talmud codified it by saying: "A father is obligated to do five things for his children:"

1. He must first induct them into their socioreligious group so that they will never feel culturally disconnected.
2. He must then instruct them in what he expects from them.
3. He must also assist them to marry.
4. He must teach them an occupation by means of which they can become useful to humanity and thereby earn their living.
5. And finally, he must teach them to swim.[11]

These five obligations rest on business leaders, too. As a leader:

1. You must induct your employees into the culture of your organization. Without undergoing that acculturating experience, employees will never participate fully as members of a team. Without it, they will also fail to develop internal guidelines that will allow them to use their initiative in the absence of specific direction.
2. You must also be crystal clear on exactly what you expect from those who look to you for leadership.
3. You must also regard it as part of your mandate to ensure that no employee languishes in loneliness.
4. You must provide skill training that will allow each employee to contribute to the bottom line.

5. And finally, you must equip all your employees with the ability to remain afloat in turbulent waters.

Returning to the story of Abraham, he reached the point where he felt obliged to find his son Isaac a wife. He dispatched his trusted servant Eliezer with these words: "Swear to me that you will never select a wife for my son from the Canaanites among whom I live."[12]

When Eliezer traveled back to Abraham's hometown of Nachor and finally picked Rebecca, he recounted the incident to Rebecca's family in these slightly modified words: "And my master made me swear to him that I would not select a wife for his son from the daughters of the Canaanites in whose land I live."[13]

Tradition records that Eliezer subconsciously switched the words from "among whom I dwell" to "in whose land I live." That is the main difference between a leader and a follower. Abraham had been promised by God that the land was given to him. It was completely irrelevant that he was an isolated individual living among hoards of hostile Canaanites. To Abraham, they were now interlopers in *his* land. That was why he said that the Canaanites may be the people among whom he was living but he was living among them in his own land.

To Eliezer, the faithful follower, it was inconceivable that this was already Abraham's land. He lacked the *faith* to regard the invisible as an already existing reality. Eliezer felt that although God had promised the land to his master, it would become a reality when the transfer actually took place. To Abraham, the fact that God had promised him the land made it the present reality—he may be living among Canaanites, but he was doing so in his own land. But in recounting the story to Rebecca's family, Eliezer could not bring himself to utter the ridiculous words he had heard Abraham say, "among whom I live," thus implying to these strangers that he already regarded the land as belonging to his master.

Thus from the very start, Jews absorbed into their very beings the idea that you must *act* as if the desired outcome was already the *reality*. Before every single sales call, clearly see in your mind's eye the customer signing on the dotted line. In that way, you are magically transformed from a hopeful but apprehensive supplicant into someone merely formalizing something that is already a reality.

That is what I mean by saying that faith is more important than facts.

Obviously, you must know everything there is to know about your product and about how it will fill your customer's needs. That is necessary but hardly sufficient. You also have to see the not-yet completed transaction as clearly as if it were already a done deal.

You are best understood and appraised by others on the basis of the things you *believe* rather than on the basis of the things you *know*. For example, during the twentieth century, Jews again learned the importance of this principle. They learned that what the Germans of the Third Reich *believed* was far more important a guide to their actions than the things they *knew*. After all, Germany was a society whose universities had produced the world's most accomplished scientists, like Max Planck, and great philosophers, like George Hegel. Germany was a society that had produced writers like Heinrich Heine and musicians like Ludwig van Beethoven. Nonetheless, it was their beliefs about a superrace and the genetic inferiority of Jews—beliefs that had little to do with facts—that won the day and changed the course of history.

Most of the really important adventures on which you embark depend on belief and faith. For instance, when you marry, you seldom do so on the basis of incontrovertible facts: You don't walk down the aisle knowing for certain that you are going to live happily ever after in a state of permanently wedded bliss. And you don't enter the state of matrimony knowing everything there is to know about your spouse. You marry on on the basis of belief and faith.

Paradoxically, the more certainty you attempt to inject into the situation, the less successful is the outcome. For instance, living together on a trial basis prior to making the marriage commitment ought to confer advantage, but it appears not to. After all, who would purchase a car without trying it out first, goes the old adage. Wrong! Buying a car is an action that can and should be based on total mastery of facts. You would be foolish to make a car-buying decision on the basis of falling in love with a particular brand's effective advertising and its seductive brochure. Before driving that shiny new vehicle out of the showroom, you should know everything there is to know about the car and the deal. But marriage is different. Statistics concerning the durability of marriages show that couples who lived together before marriage suffer a far higher divorce rate than those who did not. This is not really counterintuitive once one realizes that marriage is a faith-based activity. For an entrepreneur, starting a business far more closely resembles marriage than it does buying a car. Faith is key.

USING THE POWER OF PRAYER TO ENHANCE YOUR FAITH AND TO IMPROVE YOUR BUSINESS SUCCESS

How do people most effectively develop their faith muscle, as it were? Obviously some are far better at this than others. However there is no reason to leave it behind. Human beings can improve their ability to memorize poetry, to hold their breath underwater, and to run five miles, and they can also increase their abilities in the faith arena. Your effectiveness as a leader will have much to do with how much faith you exude about desired outcomes, and you can increase your ability to both feel and exude faith.

An insight into how to increase your strength at faith can be gleaned from both religion and medicine. At Harvard Medical School, Dr. Herbert Benson, author of *The Relaxation Response*, found that psychological stress that impeded healing and that lowered immunity could be diminished by a simple prescription. Patients participating in the test were asked to utter a prayer, phrases, or other positive sounds repeatedly, while simultaneously shutting out other thoughts.[14] Isn't that a perfect description of prayer? When people pray, they repeatedly utter words and phrases that relate to a positive outlook about the future while they shut out opposing thoughts. It is not surprising that many investigations, such as the Dartmouth Medical School study of 1995, have linked recovery to prayer.

If you regularly participate in prayer, then you are already practiced in the technique. If not, then it will take just a little longer to overcome the self-consciousness that will tend to inhibit you. Dr. Benson at Harvard Medical School provided the clue. It simply is not adequate to merely *think* positive thoughts; instead, you must also actually *utter* them. I recognize that it isn't easy to speak out loud when nobody else is present. Initially, doing so will cause you to nervously glance at the door, perhaps expecting white-coated attendants to barge in at any moment to take you to the nearest mental hospital. After all, people tend to distrust those who wander city streets talking to themselves. That is why I would recommend that you practice this technique when alone. You will not necessarily find it easy. I don't think most people are comfortable following the talk-it-out-loud advice I am about to dispense. This is perhaps why prayer is most easily achieved in a congregation of many others doing exactly the same thing. You might feel a little less self-conscious praying in company. Through prayer, you have the capacity to bring about powerful consequences, but only if you actually utter the words loudly enough for your own ears to hear.

Here's another idea of how to expand the lessons of verbal prayer to the rest of your life. You might respond to this suggestion with incredulity, but I recommend that you try it for a few weeks, rather than allowing your skepticism to prevent you from undergoing a possibly exciting and profitable experience. My suggestion is quite simple: Early in each day, find a quiet opportunity to say out loud an affirmation of faith having to do with your business challenge. It need not be lengthy, but you should state it explicitly and it should reflect your conviction in what you intend to achieve. For example, if your professional goal is to increase revenue during the coming month, do not merely say out loud to yourself, "I know I can sign up more clients this month, and that is exactly what I am going to do." Instead, be more specific, and think about what has hitherto obstructed your path to greater revenue. Have you failed to line up sufficient meetings with prospects? Have you met with prospects but failed to persuade a sufficient number to give your services a try? Identify as precisely as possible the exact areas in which you intend to improve. Make certain that you are not being handicapped by any lack of technical skills or inadequate knowledge.

Once you are certain that you are equipped for success and that you know where you intend applying your energies, you are ready to commence your program. Dr. Benson might call it repeated uttering out loud of phrases and sentences that describe you succeeding, while simultaneously shutting out any negative thoughts. Now write down your specific goals. This is important. By writing them down, you will not be distracted by concerns over what to say next. Furthermore, you will benefit from using the same terminology repeatedly. That is why so much of prayer is formalized and standardized text.

This process should take about two or three minutes a day—don't rush it. Do it where you need not fear being overheard by someone. Say your affirmation loudly enough for your own ears to hear, and do it regularly for a period of at least two weeks before you dismiss it as ineffective. If you follow these instructions diligently, you will be pleasantly surprised.

Here's an analogy: Musical advertising jingles do not constitute great symphonic music, but they do add considerable value to radio and television advertising because the music makes the commercial more memorable and adds emotional wallop to the message. The simple tunes do not convey the lofty aspirations of the human soul that are found in a Beethoven symphony, but they effectively utilize some of the power of music. Only a cultural snob would frown on the commercial usage of music and its ability to penetrate the soul. Similarly, what I have just described to you borrows microscopic morsels from the infinite power of prayer and deploys those morsels to great effect. Obviously, this does not replace prayer or even resemble it in any meaningful way. Yet this process bears exactly the same relationship to prayer as advertising jingles do to Beethoven's symphony *Eroica*. Remember, advertising jingles work, and so does this.

Finally, consider this: What do you have to lose by trying? Skepticism is natural, and I would be surprised if you felt none. Everyone has been somewhat conditioned to think of humans as very little more than six dollars' worth of common chemicals. So how can talking to yourself possibly do anything for you other than getting you committed to a not particularly choosy asylum for the disturbed? If you are absolutely sure that this is the sum total of a human, then there is little more for me to say. But if you have come to suspect that humans are creatures whose domination of the world has more to do with their spiritual side than with the mass of their brains, then this idea should make some sense to you.

MAINTAINING BALANCE

One of the dilemmas of "leading" is finding the balance between two competing and often incompatible demands. Suppose a military leader has orders to take an objective regardless of casualties, and this military leader knows that part of what makes him a leader is his deep concern for each and every warrior under his command. For example, whenever he became aware of allied losses during World War II, Winston Churchill was unable to conceal from those around him the grief that welled up inside him. When touring bombed-out homes in London during the blitz, Churchill was met by brave homeowners standing astride the ruins of their former homes, and he wept openly. Similarly, any leader, whether military or corporate, needs to view those under her command simultaneously as both pieces in the overall puzzle and as unique and all-important human beings.

Jewish tradition is not baffled by an apparent indecisiveness that God has about Abraham's descendants. Sometimes He assures the Patriarch that his children will be as many "as the sand of the seashore,"[15] and at other times he predicts them to grow to be "As many as the stars of the heavens."[16] Why doesn't God stick with one metaphor? The traditional answer teaches a valuable business lesson in leadership. There is one key difference between grains of sand and stars. The former only have significance in concert with countless other similar grains of sand. Together they can form a dyke and hold back the seas, but alone each grain gets swept away. A star, on the other hand, stands alone in its brilliance and significance. God wants Abraham to learn to view his people in these two conflicting ways at the same time. Are you expected to cope with two conflicting ideas simultaneously? Yes. If you want to lead, you must.

This is where the Oral Torah teaches this lesson to Jews. A translation of the Bible's first chapter, Genesis, would quickly reveal that the first commodity created by God was light. The oral transmission asked the question, Why should light have been first? Why not water or people or air? It was the oral transmission that explained the answer in terms that would, much later, become familiar to twentieth-century theoretical physics.

The creation of the world was the original conversion of mind to matter. Things came into existence, apparently, not in a workshop but merely as the result of God thinking and speaking. No commodity more than light so obviously bridges that gap between ideas and reality. After all, light possesses an almost inexplicable duality. On the one hand, a light beam behaves with perfect predictability, as if it were a stream of tiny tennis balls called photons. The flashlight emitting the light beam even gives an immeasurably small recoil when one turns it on, just as would a tennis training machine as it commences firing its tennis balls at a waiting player on the tennis court.

On the other hand, light is nothing more than advancing wave fronts of intangible information with the capacity to interfere with one another. Well, which is it? Is light a stream of tiny particles with mass and presence, no matter how small, or is light intangible information and data? It cannot be both, yet it is both. Light is the interface of data and matter. It is the one thing that God would have had to start with if His mind was to bring matter into being from nothingness. Light is the original bridge from mere thought into real matter, and nothing else could serve this role any better.

As challenging as it may be, light serves as a reminder that for a leader to change a reality, he or she must nearly always cope with conflicting ideas and even conflicting demands. Not everyone can do it. Not everyone wants to make the effort to learn how. Leaders do.

Maintain Employee Individuality

Nowhere is the challenge of incompatible demands more difficult than in human relationships. Whether in dealing with employees, shareholders, family members, or even yourself, you frequently have to walk the line between two incompatible desires. Sometimes you have to choose one or the other alternative. At other times you can express your ambivalence in word and thought, even though in action only one course can be tolerated. You need to recognize that on an exquisitely spiritual plane, two apparently incompatible entities can usually be welded into one luminescent harmony. Just as particles and waves constitute light even though they should not be able to do so, viewing a person simultaneously as part of a larger mission and as an indispensable human like no other can constitute the highest form of leadership.

In ancient Israel, Jewish kings were prohibited from counting the people of Israel. Whenever a census was necessary, stratagems were contrived to avoid actual counting of the population. What lay behind this prejudice against counting? The whole point of counting a lot of objects is that in so doing, you are implying that they are all identical. You wouldn't count dollars, pesos, liras, and pounds and end up with one total currency figure. Were a king to count his people by conventional census, he would be accustoming himself to view them as a faceless crowd of anonymous and identical beings whose purpose is merely to serve him. No leader who becomes known for viewing his or her subjects or subordinates this way will survive for long.

It is true that on one level, the employees of an organization are there to fulfill the purpose of the organization. It is also true that cross-training is recommended and manuals are created in order to make the position indispensable, rather than making any one occupant of the position indispensable. Ideally, it would be wonderful to have an organization structured not to miss a beat if any one or even all of the employees walked out the door and were replaced the next day by new people. In reality, of course, that could never work. Even with the best operating manuals, organization charts, and management structure, any organization still depends on the subtle human network of accumulated knowledge, culture, and skills within all its people, which makes it behave more like a single interconnected organism than like a hotel filled with disconnected guests staying the night.

This is obviously true for a software development company in which virtually all its assets, namely its people, leave every evening to go home. Were an entirely different set of people to show up the next morning, the company would clearly be in turmoil. Any observer lacking the understanding that the commercial enterprise is at its heart a spiritual one would argue, "Wait a moment, these people look just like those who left last night. There is the same number of men and women, blacks and whites, and they all have the same backgrounds and training as your former employees. What do you mean the company can't operate?"

It is also true for a manufacturing enterprise in which most of the company's assets are its machinery and factory infrastructure. Still, the company depends on the relationships that its employees have built up between one another and on the trust between them. Replacing them all overnight would be a very perilous undertaking.

The wise leader recognizes this dichotomy between "nobody is indispensable" and "everybody is indispensable." Of course, businesses try to organize their enterprises around functions rather than around personalities. Whether you are setting up a workstation along a computer assembly line or a customer service phone desk, you know exactly what function needs to be performed at that point. You then ask the personality to adjust himself or herself to the needed function. However, you never lose sight of the personality. Wise leaders do their best not only to get to know the personality but also to make certain that the personality realizes that, to the leader, he or she is more than merely a function.

When Hitler assumed personal command of the German army on December 22, 1941, his words were selected to demonstrate how he, too, identified with the ordinary soldier: "Thus nothing that torments you, weighs upon you, and oppresses you is unknown to me. . . . My soldiers, you will therefore believe that my heart belongs solely to you, . . . What I can do for you, my soldiers . . . by way of care and leadership, will be done."

His actions did not match his words. Less than a year later, Albert Speer recalled an evening when he sat with Hitler in the dining car of his personal railway train stopped at a siding.

> The table was elegantly set with silver, glass, china, and flowers. As we began our meal, none of us at first saw that a freight train had stopped on the adjacent track. From the cattle car, bedraggled, starved, and, in some cases, wounded German soldiers, just returned from the east, stared

at the two diners. With a start Hitler noticed the somber scene just two yards from his window. Without as much as a gesture of greeting in their direction, he peremptorily ordered the servant to draw the shades.[17]

It is not surprising that while the German people were still infatuated with the Fuehrer, the German military machine was already becoming disenchanted. High echelon Wehrmacht officers formed more than one conspiracy to assassinate Hitler.

You must seek out opportunities to demonstrate your awareness of the person as an indispensable part of your commercial organism. Great loyalty is acquired by leaders who express concern about an ill spouse. Do you know anything about the children of your employees? Find out what hobbies and sports your employees pursue. These seem obvious features, but in my experience, many people fail at leadership because they fail to convince that they care. It is very difficult to find the balance between caring and effectiveness, but that is the challenge.

Maintain Balance between Short- and Long-Term Goals

Another area in which anyone wanting to lead must find balance is short-term versus long-term thinking. Every CEO of a public company knows the struggle between spending the morning trying to develop strategy for the next three years and then spending the afternoon with security analysts who care only about the next quarter's results. It is tough, which is why leading isn't for everyone. Parents have to do it constantly. They worry about their children doing their homework, but they are also concerned about long-term career choices. They worry about their children getting home on time from a date, but they also fret about their offspring's capacity to form long-term marital unions much later. Similarly, in your own money-making areas, you have short-term issues and you have long-term planning. Generally, you attend to the short-term fiscal urgencies while sometimes neglecting the longer-term planning. Whether as an executive, a parent, or a reader of this book trying to enhance your revenue-producing capacity, everyone needs to set aside scheduled time on a regular basis for longer-term planning. This is a function of smart time management, and it must be done.

Maintain Balance between Increasing Your Income and Cutting Your Costs

A final area in which balance must be maintained is the tension between increasing your revenue and containing your expenses. There is obviously a point of diminishing returns if you are spending much of your awake time and much of your energy on cost containment. It clearly needs to be done, but you must also remember that it carries a cost of its own. You need to make regular decisions concerning controlling expenses, but having done so, you must separate yourself from those anxieties in order to be able to focus on revenue growth. As a leader you must not only maintain this balance but show those who look to you for leadership that you are aware of both areas, aware of the tension between them, and are maintaining an effective balance.

USE BODY LANGUAGE TO *LOOK* LIKE A LEADER

I am about to explain something that fits into the category popularly known as body language. This is an almost imperceptible quality but an important one. Others use it to determine leadership potential but are often unable to put into words what it is. Often people feel they are in the presence of a leader; yet when asked what exactly it was that impressed them, most would shrug their shoulders and find it difficult to answer.

What I am about to describe to you should be applied to how you sit at meetings and how you deliver presentations in public. From the outside, it will make you *look* far more leaderlike and more important, from the inside, it will make you *feel* far more leaderlike. It is a behavior that will take you some weeks to learn. During that time, you will need to subject yourself to rigorous discipline. If you do, in due course, this valuable behavior will become second nature. I guarantee that it will play a role in changing your life for the better.

Let me first give you some background regarding why appearance is so important to great leadership. Have you ever wondered why popular Western culture depicts the lion as the king of the animals? The lion is neither the strongest nor the largest animal. Among animals, he neither lives the longest nor possesses the largest brain. As a rabbi, I turn to traditional Jewish sources for this answer. More than 2,000 years ago, the Talmud stated that the lion is the king of the beasts.[18] Through his fables taken from the Talmud, Aesop, who had been a Jewish slave by the name of Joseph (for which Aesop is merely the Greek equivalent), had probably carried this royal notion of the lion into Greek culture.

In the context of the Talmudic discussion, it becomes clear why Jewish tradition crowned the lion as king. Lions are more economical in movement than any other large animal. I had several opportunities to verify this Talmudic observation, because when I was in my early twenties, I rode a motorcycle and camped my way across much of Africa, which afforded me the opportunity of seeing many wonderful animals close-up. Even when exploding into action to pursue and kill its quarry, the lion's body seems to flow smoothly with no unnecessary movement. You would have to be fortunate even to see a lion in motion. Most of the time he will lie alert but almost motionless; only his open eyes and head occasionally moving slowly from side to side betray his wakeful state. In contrast, the elephant seems always to be eating, and he constantly flaps his ears or waves his trunk. So do most other animals. The lion's demeanor is regal because of his appearing to have total control over his body. That is impressive.

Similarly, as a 10-year-old boy in London, I saw the Queen's guards outside of Buckingham Palace for the first time. I can still recall my father drawing my attention to their ability to stand absolutely still, and I still recall my amazement as I stood and watched them for perhaps 15 minutes. During that August afternoon, I saw a fly crawl across one guard's forehead and he never budged. I saw sweat rolling down from beneath that large bearskin hat and the guard never budged. I saw tourists badgering him, and still the guard did not move an eyelash. It was a lesson in power that I have not forgotten.

Shakespeare puts these words into Hamlet's mouth:

> Rightly to be great
> Is not to stir without great argument,
> But greatly to find quarrel in a straw
> When honour's at the stake.[19]

This is exactly the same principle as demonstrated to me by the lion and the Queen's guard. Greatness in others is shown in part, by their careful deliberate movements that reveal an underlying control of themselves. Consider the opposite; for example I have always been impressed by Alfred

Hitchcock's classic thriller *The Birds*, based on Daphne Du Maurier's novel of the same name. If a studio had asked me to develop an unexpectedly terrifying scenario, I am certain that the brilliant idea would never have occurred to me of turning one of nature's most powerless creatures into the source of terror. What is it about birds that conveys their powerlessness? It is not only their relatively small size, but also the *jerkiness* of their land-based movements. Naturally they are far more graceful in flight, but as they walk, their heads dart here and there, and they progress by what seems to be a random progression of jumps and runs, a little sidestep here and a back step there.

CONTROL YOUR PHYSICAL MOVEMENTS TO SHOW SELF-ASSURANCE

You see where this is going, don't you? Stop fidgeting. Are you in a meeting? Stop playing with the pencil. Don't cross and then uncross your legs every five minutes. Place your feet on the floor. Find a comfortable place for your hands and keep them there. Talk when you must, sit as stationary as possible, and listen. Be lionlike. Don't allow your eyes to constantly wander around the room. Face whoever is speaking by turning as much of you as possible in the new direction. Instead of allowing your eyes to follow the speaker, rather turn your entire upper body to do so. Looking at someone out of the corner of your eye looks shifty. If you are sitting on a swivel chair, it would be better to swivel your chair smoothly until you are facing the speaker. Above all, avoid constant movement, and when you do move, make it for a good reason, as Shakespeare said. When you must move, make it a smooth, economical movement, moving just as much as necessary and not a millimeter more.

Are you giving a speech? Use your hands and arms to dramatize your points. However, be sure never to keep your elbows tucked into your sides while making fluttering gestures with your forearms. Gesture grandly with your entire arm. Move your arms from the shoulders and never from the elbows.

While speaking to a group, do not fix your body in a rigid forward-facing posture; instead, allow your upper body to swivel smoothly from the waist. Watch the inexperienced speaker's body remain locked into position while his or her eyes dart nervously around the room. This speaker looks nervous, weak, and shifty. You should keep your eyes in place. Sweep your gaze around the room by moving your entire upper body. And one more thing, do not grasp the podium. It will stand without your assistance. Gripping it will only convey the impression that it is you who are in danger of toppling without the podium's reassuring presence.

All of this is intended to make you look and ultimately feel regal. But of course, looking and feeling regal are only part of the technique. One must also *act* regally if one aspires to leadership. Again the metaphor of the lion is appropriate: Lions never appear to be petty, and neither should you. Nothing undermines your leadership more fatally than the appearance of pettiness.

The Talmud advises you to become the tail of a lion rather than the head of a fox.[20] One reason is that lions can often be observed walking with their tails erect, pointing straight up into the air, whereas foxes usually scurry around with their snouts almost on the ground as they follow a scent. The message is, don't associate with cunning and petty little people. Even though they may make you their head, in little time they will succeed in bringing you low. If, however, you succeed in associating yourself with people of stature and true greatness, even if you start off as their tail, they will encourage you, elevate you, and give you every opportunity for growth.

The practical lesson here is obvious. When faced with two alternative opportunities that involve different types of people, distinguished chiefly by the lionlike characteristics of one and the foxlike characteristics of the other, choose the lions. Being a lion means doing everything possible to elevate others. Once again, it is a paradox, but this makes you bigger, not smaller.

LEARN TO GIVE PRESENTATIONS WITHOUT NOTES

I was 14 years old when I received my first speaking engagement. A visiting group of minor dignitaries was attending a banquet at the synagogue my father served as rabbi. The powers that be had decided that there would be a seven-minute presentation by a representative of the synagogue youth, and because nobody else wanted to do it, the task fell to me. Make no mistake, I didn't want to do it, but Dad, who was a master orator, was impatient to launch my public speaking career and insisted that I prepare a speech.

On the way to the event several days later, he asked me if I had carefully prepared my remarks. Because I had watched him prepare hundreds of speeches over the years, I assured him that I had done so. He then asked me if I had written out the speech word for word. Again I assured him that I had done so. He asked me if I had brought my notes along with me. Assuming he wanted reassurance that I was not going to embarrass him, I reached into my jacket pocket and pulled out the sheaf of papers on which I had carefully constructed my speech. He reached over and took the papers from me. Then, with a sense of horror that I can recall today with all the emotional intensity of the moment, I watched him rip my notes into shreds and toss them from the car window. I will confess that protesting his littering was the furthest thing from my numbed mind reeling in anticipation of my impending mortification.

He slowly began talking to me. What he said was that I wouldn't understand this action for many years; but that in the meantime, he wanted me to believe that he acted in my best interests until the day it finally would become clear to me. He then pulled over the car and asked me to say my speech to him. At first I petulantly refused, saying there was no point because I had no intention of giving the speech anyway. But finally, I relented and tried to recall my speech word-for-word. It was horrendous.

Dad then laboriously began helping me to reformulate my speech in terms of its three classical components: (1) the introduction, (2) the body, and (3) the conclusion. He divided each component into three subsections and then helped me decide on the one key word by which I could remember the contents of each of my nine subsections. Finally, he helped me recall and memorize three key phrases until they could roll off my tongue with fluency. It was then I noticed that we were still in plenty of time for the banquet, and I suspected that we had departed from home so early because Dad had foreseen the entire scenario that had just unfolded.

He then told me that I was going to speak to the synagogue group with no notes in my hand or on the podium and that it was going to be a far more successful speech than the one I had originally anticipated delivering, or, to be more honest, reading. Nobody needs to come to an event to hear the keynote speaker read his speech. Everyone subconsciously realizes that it would have been far more economical had the sponsoring organization merely replicated the written speech and distributed it to attendees by mail. No, when one listens to a well-crafted and well-delivered speech, no matter how short it may be, one comes away with a sense of having been granted a glimpse into the speaker's soul. Furthermore, the speech reaches more deeply and more directly into the listener's soul than had he or she merely read the speech in printed form.

Abandoning my notes, knowing my subject matter, and being familiar with what I was going to describe next allowed me the luxury of eye contact with my audience. I could focus on gesture and modulation. Dad was right; my little maiden speech did receive more enthusiastic acclaim than a 14-year-old incipient delinquent was entitled to, only because of Dad's intervention. On the drive home, I churlishly failed to thank him for tearing up my notes, but I have done so a thousand times since. And I have almost never spoken from notes since that day.

I tell you all that only to be able to tell you this: Believe me when I say that I know just how hard it is to hurl the crutches into the fireplace and deliver that speech with free hands. That is what notes are to a speech—merely crutches. You do not need them. What is more, once you have given your first speech entirely without notes before you, you will never go back to notes. You will enjoy the experience more than you ever did while speaking from written notes. You will be far more effective, and your words will be more memorable. I will allow that if your work ever requires you to speak about many specific details and figures beyond your capacity to memorize reliably, use a TelePrompTer, if available. This device is virtually invisible in a large hall, and it allows you to look up at the audience rather than crouching over your notes. Still, try to avoid depending on the TelePrompTer. I could hardly provide you with more powerful and useful advice than to encourage you to accustom yourself to public speaking sans notes. It really is easier than you suspect; however, you do need a ready vocabulary and an ease of public communication. It is hard to think of any effective leader, whether political, military, or business, who has not been an effective orator.

My advice on how to increase your vocabulary and ease of public speaking is deceptively simple. It appears to be so simple that only some of those leaders who have paid me substantial fees for training them in the art of public speaking have actually followed through with the program. It seems too simple to be worth doing. I hope you don't make this mistake. Reading about it and thinking about it are not the same as doing it. You will astound yourself and everyone else if you follow this regimen for six to eight weeks.

Read aloud. Yes, that's right, all you need to do is read aloud. It is much easier to do this effectively with an audience; so if you have a friend, a spouse, or a child who will listen to you reading aloud, so much the better. Pick a good book; that is important. Pick a book written in a style that you would like to emulate. George Washington and Abraham Lincoln used the Bible. I myself use the works of Winston Churchill. Again, I must emphasize that it is your own ears that must hear your own mouth shaping itself around the words, so you must read aloud with full intonation and expression.

Do this for 20 to 30 minutes a day. I am recommending quite a tough discipline here, I know it. However, the results will themselves soon begin to urge you on. You won't believe the powerful effect this regimen will have on your ability to communicate with others. And without a strong ability to communicate, you can forget about leading anyone.

ADOPT A "MASK OF COMMAND"

Throughout this chapter, I have repeatedly emphasized that not only must you *act* in accordance with the principles of leadership, but you must always be sure to *be seen* doing so. It is often even more important to be seen that way than to actually feel that way. For instance, necessary qualities for leading are optimism and courage. It is far more important for, say, a platoon leader to exhibit optimism and courage than it is for him to reflect how he honestly feels. His choices are either to radiate to his frightened and demoralized men an optimism and courage he doesn't feel or to openly and candidly reveal his own uncertainties and fears. Should he select the latter course of action, he is no leader. Should he select the former, well, won't he feel like a fraud?

Leading does mean not always revealing one's inner feelings of doubt. Greater store is set by sincerity than it deserves. For instance, would you rather have your neighbor act generously and graciously toward you, although deep down in his heart he doesn't much care for you, or would you rather have him scratch your car and kick your cat as sincere expressions of his feelings? Of course, everyone would rather have associates and neighbors act in accordance with a common code of decency than in accordance with whatever their emotional condition of the moment dictated.

Similarly, there are times in leading that it is simply inappropriate and counterproductive to reveal doubts, because doing so would undoubtedly cause ripples of morale-sapping fear to spread throughout the organization. How does one develop the vital qualities of optimism and courage?

The key principle employed here is one that lies within the heart of ancient Jewish wisdom. It concerns the relationship between how one feels and how one acts. You might mistakenly assume that you act in accordance with your feelings, but the ancient sages teach that in reality, you just as frequently come to feel in accordance with how you act. The principle is clear: If you don't like the way you feel about something or about someone, start acting the way you would act if you already felt the way you wished you would feel, and you will soon come to feel that way. Did you get that? Just read it again.

Here is an example. Suppose you had an argument with someone important in your life. You spent all day seething in anger at the unreasonable position taken by this person earlier that morning. When you meet the individual again, the argument probably picks up where it left off, or, at best, a glacial iciness envelops the two of you. Here is a better way. If you really did feel wonderful about that person, wouldn't you show it? Well, do the same thing now. Bring a gift to the other person who probably was at least as angry with you as you were with him or her. Is the gift going to make that person forget the argument and start loving or even liking you? Probably not, although it will probably mystify him or her. What it *will* do is far more important. Giving the gift will reduce *your* hostility and bring you to a different frame of mind. Your actions can change your feelings. That is not the same thing as saying that your actions can change someone else's feelings. That is far less likely, although they certainly can do so. It is your feelings that your own actions can certainly change.

In the same way, if you act the way you would act if you really were filled with optimism and courage, then pretty soon you actually will start feeling more courageous and optimistic. This may seem as if you are pulling on a mask to wear among the people with whom you work and live. Well, yes, that is true, and if you really want to become more effective, not only in the area of economic productivity but in all of life, then you need to develop a comfort in yourself about leading and a comfort in others about being led by you. That sometimes does entail wearing a mask. I cannot say it better than the great military historian John Keegan:

Heroic leadership—any leadership—is, like priesthood, statesmanship, even genius, a matter of externals almost as much as of internalities. The exceptional are both shown to and hidden from the mass of humankind, revealed by artifice, presented by theatre. The theatrical impulse will be strong in the successful politician, teacher, entrepreneur, athlete, or divine, and will be both expected and reinforced by the audiences to which they perform.[21]

One of the most exciting aspects of a life in business is that no day is just like the day before. Constant change is both the stimulus and the challenge. Learning how to relate to change is an obvious characteristic possessed by successful leaders and, indeed, by all successful business professionals. That is where I lead you next.

YOUR PATH TO PROSPERITY

- *Learn to follow if you want to learn to lead.*   Leaders depend on their followers accepting a sense of hierarchy in order to validate their leadership. You stand more chance of making it to leadership if you never miss an opportunity to point out to those around you that your actions are not simply spur-of-the-moment impulses, but are the consequences of accountability to some external entity. For example, it is not uncommon to find conspicuously successful Jewish business leaders who defer many major decisions to an aged parent who was the original founder of the business.

- *Have the courage to persuasively present your vision.*   Your vision might be a new marketing campaign, or it may be a vision of fairness and integrity. Naturally, you must know how to confront productively, but no leader fears confrontation.

- *Induct your employees into the culture of your organization.*   Without this, your employees will never participate fully as members of a team, and they will fail to develop internal guidelines that will allow them to use their initiative in the absence of specific direction. Be crystal clear on exactly what you expect from those who look to you for leadership. Ensure that no employee languishes in loneliness. Provide skill training that will allow each employee to contribute to the bottom line. Finally, make sure all your employees have the ability to remain afloat when things get turbulent.

- *Adapt the power of prayer to your business goals.*   Early each day, find a quiet opportunity to say out loud an affirmation of faith having to do with some business challenge. It need not be lengthy, but it should be stated explicitly, and it should reflect your conviction in what you intend to achieve. Identify as precisely as possible the exact areas in which you intend improving. Then, write down your specific goals. Say your affirmation loudly enough for your own ears to hear, and do this regularly for a period of at least two weeks before you dismiss it as ineffective. If you follow these instructions diligently, you will be pleasantly surprised.

- *Make sure you balance short- and long-term business goals.* In your own money-making areas, you have short-term issues and you have long-term planning. Generally, people attend to the short-term fiscal urgencies while sometimes neglecting the longer-term planning. Whether as an executive, a parent, or a reader of this book trying to enhance your revenue-producing capacity, everyone needs to set aside scheduled time on a regular basis for longer-term planning. This is a function of smart time management, and it must be done.

- *Make sure not only that you have a long-term plan but also that those whom you lead are well aware of your long-term views.* When addressing immediate urgencies, find ways to express what needs to be done right now in terms of how it advances your entire organization along the track of its longer-term plans.

- *Carry yourself like a leader.* Don't fidget during meetings. Look people directly in the eye when speaking to them. Speak authoritatively, and be able to give presentations without notes. Improve the quality of your speaking voice so that you sound like a leader. Don't let others know you have doubts; instead, project confidence, optimism, and courage.

Constantly Change the Changeable While Steadfastly Clinging to the Unchangeable

Convert change from enemy to ally by understanding when to enjoy the exhilaration of change and when to fight it and steadfastly defend the unchangeable.

Cultural customs and popular habits seem to swing, pendulum-like, from one extreme to another. At times, people seek adventure for their leisure and high-risk challenges in their work. They revel in swift changes, swooping exuberantly from one trend to the next. Then at other times, as a society, people swing back to the stable and predictable. People cocoon at home instead of roaming, they vacation at nearby instead of exotic destinations, and they invest conservatively instead of riskily. You can almost hear them crying out, "No more change."

Then times change again—the pendulum swings back, and the giddy excitement returns. People abandon stable jobs for the exhilaration of joining a start-up company, and they travel the world on their vacations lusting for the latest thrill.

Are human beings creatures of habit, preferring the reassurance of the familiar, or do humans love the spice that variety brings to life? It is not surprising, considering the complexity of the human race that the answer is that both are true. One of the most important distinctions you need to learn to make is between those things in your life that should be constant and unchangeable and the kind of change you should welcome. Sometimes you can control the change you experience; and occasionally you can only react as a canoeist does caught in the rapids—coping with the wild ride of change by lunging with your paddles to avoid the largest boulders and prevent the canoe from capsizing. Other than that, you try to hang on until the ride calms down and your ability to make meaningful changes to your course increases.

One of the most distinctive aspects of the traditional worldview that has always assisted Jews to cope with change is the view that humans aren't merely smart animals but are qualitatively distinct and unique beings. You may recall the old childhood guessing game of "animal, vegetable, or mineral." Well, the view that has informed Jewish wisdom is that there is a fourth category to add to those three—human.

Minerals undergo almost no change through the ages. Marble, for example, is cut from a quarry in Italy and shipped to New York City where it will form the façade of a bank. The years go by, and the marble remains virtually the same as it was. Finally, the building may be demolished, but the marble is preserved to be reused in another building.

Vegetables don't last anywhere near as long as minerals. During the existence of, say, a radish, the vegetable changes more than a mineral does, but its changes are minor. It may grow larger, it may become redder, but it is still just a radish. There is only a small quantitative difference between a ripe radish and one that still needs a few more weeks in the ground.

Animals change far more than vegetables. A newborn puppy dog can be almost irresistibly appealing; yet the same animal a few years later might be a mangy cur, the scourge of the neighborhood. A newborn calf must be nurtured by the farsighted farmer until it can take its useful place in the herd. That mature cow is very different from the calf it started out as; but once it is mature, it will change very little in appearance or even in milk production.

According to this schematic, Judaism makes the claim that humans are indeed unique. Not only does the appearance of a person continue to change throughout his or her life, but so do experience, character traits, and skills. Few people would like to be judged by the way they were 20 years ago. People change; and for the most part, they would like to think they change for the better.

If you are having a bad time, you can rest assured with the knowledge that things will be different a few months later. Very few people would have described their present lives accurately had they been asked to predict the course of events a year or two earlier. People's lives are constantly changing—that is part of what it means to be human. The other part is the yearning for complete stability with no changes at all to shake up the predictability of existence. The trick is to recognize that yearning as your radish part or your cow part and to resist granting it control over your emotional and psychic state. The upper-level human part of your being revels in change: You constantly find within change all kinds of unexpected opportunities to grow and prosper.

THE JEWISH STAR SHOWS HOW TO BALANCE CHANGE WITH A FIXED FRAME OF REFERENCE

Paradoxically, the freedom to grasp change eagerly and to squeeze it until it yields its seeds of new opportunity depends entirely on your not being swept away down the river of change yourself. The only way to prevent change from utterly dominating your life until you are driven to distraction by the absence of any fixed framework of reference is to make sure that your life does possess a fixed and unchangeable framework of reference. Your ability to embrace some changes and to profit from them depends on your ability to staunchly resist other changes. Confusing, isn't it? No, not really. A valuable clue exists.

The clue to this dichotomy can be found in the Jewish star, otherwise known as the Star of David. Only a few Americans know the significance of the Star of David above the eagle's head on the reverse side of the one-dollar bill. It is made up of 13 stars that represent not only the 13 founding colonies, but also the 13 sons of Jacob once Father Jacob had replaced his son Joseph with Joseph's two sons Ephraim and Menashe. This often-used Star of David symbol actually represents the Jewish goal of maintaining an exquisite balance between eagerly embracing the new and, at the same time, remaining anchored to those things that don't change. This balance lies at the heart of effectively utilizing change as an ally in your quest for wealth.

In geometric terms, the Jewish star is nothing but one equilateral triangle superimposed upon another just like it but displaced by 180 degrees. In other words, draw a triangle with three sides of equal length. Draw another just like it, but turn it upside down. Place it directly upon the first triangle. Within that simple shape lies a clue to the way humans should function.

A triangle is one of the strongest of engineering shapes. That is why the triangle is used as the preferred shape within trusses and girders. Next time you drive over a girder-style bridge, look for triangles. To understand why the triangle is so strong, first look at a rectangle. Imagine constructing a rectangle and then setting it up vertically on one of its sides. Suppose you placed a large weight on its horizontal upper beam and asked a child to push its finger against one of the two vertical arms. The rectangle would easily collapse and fold down flat onto the ground, as can be attested to by anyone who has attempted to sit on a cardboard box and found themselves ignominiously sitting on the floor instead.

You could conduct the same experiment with a triangle, standing so it rested on its base with an apex pointing upward. If you brought a weight down to bear upon that apex and pushed against one of the sides, the triangle would not fold. It would only fail when the weight you placed upon it exceeded its load-carrying capacity.

The triangle is thus an immensely durable way of linking three elements, which is to say, its three sides. By way of contrast the weakest way of linking three elements is in the form of a "Z" with a vertical middle element. As you can surmise, a weight placed on the horizontal upper beam, or element, will fold it down, first into a regular "Z" and then flat to the ground even more quickly than a rectangle would have collapsed.

Although the Star of David is made up of two identical shapes, each comprising three straight lines superimposed on one another and rotated, there is actually another shape that also fits that description exactly—the swastika. Once again, three lines are attached to one another, but this time in the weakest imaginable configuration. If you duplicate the result, rotate it 90 degrees, and lay it on the first three-line shape you made, presto—you have made a swastika. Amazingly, what emerges is that a Star of David and a swastika are identically described conceptual opposites.

You might understand this a bit better if you compare it to hearing the sound of someone laughing or crying. All parents have had the experience of racing, heart pounding wildly, into a room where they hear their child hysterically shrieking, only to find the child shrieking with laughter rather than tears. The two sounds are remarkably similar if you have no visible clues as to the emotional state of the person wailing, although in reality they are polar opposites. Similarly, if I just describe a shape made up of two superimposed

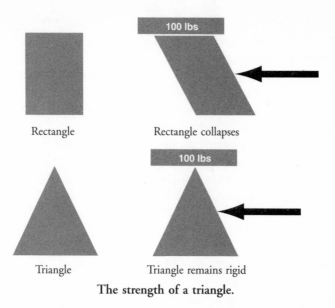

The strength of a triangle.

and rotated identical arrangements of three straight lines, some will draw a Star of David, while others will draw a swastika. Both symbols are intrinsically powerful and accurately represent a worldview.

In describing the reaction to the introduction of the swastika in 1925, Konrad Heiden, perhaps the best of Hitler's biographers, said, "The effect was so inflammatory that Hitler himself was surprised and pleased." He continued,

> In the swastika, historical accident gave Hitler one of his mightiest magic weapons. It was a lucky find. The old German Workers Party had not come across it; Italian Fascism was denied a symbol of such strength. One of its strongest qualities became apparent only in the course of time: Every child could draw it, and its expressive form encouraged people to draw it—even those who did not know what it meant. An uncanny power emanated from the mysterious sign: Hitler could point at it and calmly say: "It is not knowledge that helps us, but Faith."[1]

Similarly, an uncanny (if opposite) power emanates from the swastika's moral mirror image, the Star of David. Its shape describes a fundamental truth of reality, with each side representing a rugged and unbreakable bond between three aspects of life. The three lines, in turn, represent the three fundamental entities of existence: God, human beings, and the tangible, material world. Thus it is as if each triangle were telling Jews that strength lies in unifying these three fundamental elements. One's effectiveness as a human being is diminished if one tries to function on a straight line linking any two of those fundamental elements; instead all three are needed.

If you mistakenly assume that life can revolve about forging a link between God and human beings but ignoring the *material* world of forests and factories, swamps and skyscrapers, your life and your effectiveness at living it is drastically diminished. Suppose you try to enjoy this wonderful world by eliminating the *spiritual* dimension entirely and focusing only on the relationship between yourself, a human being, and the material tangible world. Well, think again, illustrates the Star of David; that also won't work very well. Finally, perhaps you find human beings to be a blight on creation, and you visualize a perfect world of spiritual and material existence blended into a people-free perfection. Forget it. Without human beings, life is all morally impotent and meaningless. Never can only two of the three sides of totality form an effective and durable union; all three sides are needed. Therein lies the power of the Star of David and the effectiveness of its spiritual message for the Jewish people.

Now why does this powerful symbol, the Star of David, require two triangles? Surely one alone makes a sufficiently eloquent case of this three-way link. The answer is that one triangle represents a God-Human Beings-World matrix that *never* changes, whereas the other triangle depicts another God-Human Beings-World that must always *be open* to change. The reason the two superimposed triangles are angularly displaced is because that way they resemble two graphs. The first triangle, standing firmly on its base, represents the core aspects of life that do not change and on which you can depend while everything else around you may shift and take on new and unfamiliar forms. These core aspects include the need for a relationship with your Creator, your family, and your friends, which doesn't change whether you are living in the 1200s or the current year. Neither do basic human motivations and satisfactions vary much. In the Jewish view, God laid out these truths when on Mount Sinai He gave humanity His Biblical blueprint, and each passing year finds humanity further away from connection to that moment. This is signified by the narrowing of the triangle as you move up toward its apex. The second triangle, upside down and balanced precariously on its point, signifies the natural and technological world, in which each passing year adds to the store of knowledge and control.

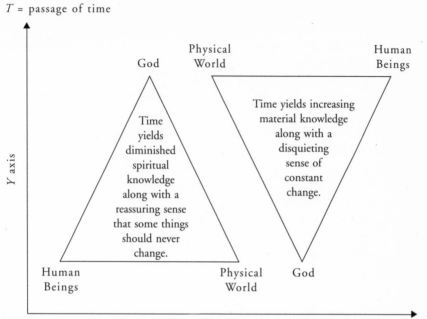

Spiritual knowledge can shrink as material knowledge expands.

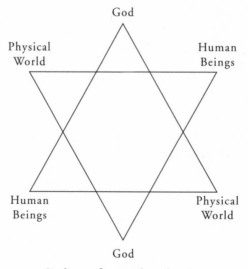

Six lines of strength and unity.

You can doom yourselves in two contrasting ways: (1) You can blind yourself to the things that never change, and (2) you can blind yourself to those things that must change. Either you can pretend that everything changes constantly with no fixed reference points, telling yourself that a new high-tech business paradigm exists that regards eyeballs on websites as more important than profits, or you can refuse to acknowledge that the material aspects of existence in the world are constantly changing, remaining rooted in the past, distrusting modernity and spurning its comforts with Luddite-like intensity.

In contrast, the unspoken message of the swastika was that there were no absolutes in the world, other than those that emanated from its one connecting point, the Fuehrer in the center. Everything was open to reinterpretation. Just when you thought that you were on a line that led somewhere, it abruptly changed direction and then terminated in nothingness. Not surprisingly the "Thousand-year Reich" only lasted 12 years and 4 months.

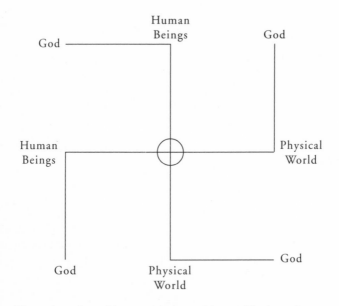

⊕ — The only point of intersection provides an illusion of superman in a world where nothing else meets, unites, or makes sense.

Six lines of fragility and fragmentation.

INNOVATION AND CHANGE ARE
A NECESSARY EVOLUTION

How can you use this knowledge in your business life? Examine two different scenarios. In the first, technology moves unrelentingly forward. You may
have heard of the possibly apocryphal tale of the Detroit manufacturer of
buggy whips early in the twentieth century. Although he heard rumors of a
newfangled horseless carriage that some chap called Henry Ford was building down the road, he made no changes to his profitable business. Needless
to say, he was soon out of business.

Similarly, when steel eventually was discovered in the nineteenth century
and began to replace cast iron, a vast part of U.S. and British wealth that lay
in the many old-fashioned foundries and iron-casting operations was tossed
aside as these now obsolete operations were destroyed and replaced with early
forms of steel-making furnaces. Then Englishman Henry Bessemer invented
the Bessemer converter and made possible the economical manufacture of
steel, which quickly replaced cast iron as the building material of choice for
bridges and other constructions. All the earlier furnaces were scrapped and
replaced with the faster and more efficient system.

Later, the Bessemer converter itself was replaced with the Siemens Open
Hearth Furnace, which in turn was replaced in the middle of the twentieth
century with the Electric Arc Furnace. Innovation, even in the mature steel
industry, is not over. Minimills are encroaching on larger and less flexible
operations. This phenomenon is not limited to the steel industry. Many
technology firms of the 1990s experienced similar demises as their specialized products and complex patents were leapfrogged by rapidly developing
new technologies.

In each case of innovation, in any industry, millions of dollars' worth of
equipment is scrapped. Amazingly, that apparently destructive and wasteful
behavior is exactly what leads to greater wealth and to increased standards of
living for millions of people. The downside is that people lose money they
had invested and, even more wrenching, workers lose jobs during those regular
upheavals. Some of the laid-off workers quickly find new and sometimes better
employment. Many do not. This is a tough and tragic reality. The choice is
either to accept innovation along with the pain of some or to reject it
and assure poverty and pain for almost everyone all the time. But the reality
is that there is no way to hold back this progress. As the Jewish Star of

David shows, technical knowledge of the world and its practical application expand constantly.

The only way for a company to survive over time, whether it is a buggy-whip maker or a company like Cisco building complex Internet switches, is for it to adapt to change by destroying creatively on a large scale. Corning did this as it moved away from cookware and glass consumer products and into fiber optics. Judaism has taught me that waving a defiant fist at an uncooperative Deity is a waste of time. Sometimes there is a choice between two undesirable alternatives. For instance, Corning had to choose between the painful alternatives of closing some plants and retooling others to manufacture glass fiber instead of glass bowls or making no changes and dying a lingering and inevitable death as a great company. It is a mark of maturity to be able to recognize that although both choices are terrible, one is worse than the other.

In my own family, it has been fascinating to watch that stage of maturity arrive at different ages for different children. During their early teen years, most of them would retreat into semiparalysis when confronted by two undesirable choices. For instance, a while back, one of my daughters had to make a choice between two difficult and undesirable choices: (1) She could go away to a school that offered enormous benefits, both socially and academically, but entailed living in a dorm and coming home only every few months, or (2) staying home but losing the advantages of the distant school. She hated both ideas and wasted valuable weeks insisting that there must be a better third way. Often a better third way can be found; but sometimes, including this occasion, no third alternative exists.

My daughter simply could not wrap herself around the idea that she would have to do something she really dreaded because she dreaded the alternative as well. Although my wife and I were gratified that she saw being at home with us and her siblings in such a positive light, we realized that the most important lesson of the choice was for her to mature and realize that sometimes you must go with the "least bad" of the available choices.

In business, constant innovation along with creative destruction is often the "least bad" of the choices. Whether it is firing employees, pulling the plug on a project, or leaving behind a safety net to try a new field, we must be comfortable with the idea that even positive change will most times have negative components.

This trend, whereby the market spits out older companies that don't adapt to change, has been an ever-accelerating phenomenon. For example, consider these statistics:

- Of the 500 companies that made up the Standard & Poor's (S&P) 500 in 1957, only 74 remained on the list through 1997.
- In 1926, the S&P 500 had a turnover rate of about 1.5 percent. That meant that a company stayed on the list for an average of 67 years. In those days, three generations of a family could have worked for the same company their entire working lives.
- By 2000, the turnover on the S&P 500 was about 10 percent, meaning that the average company life cycle on the S&P index is more like 12 years. Not only couldn't your parents and your children work for the same company all their working lives, but you couldn't either.

The German economist Joseph Schumpeter, who later became a respected teacher at Harvard, explained this process of what he called "creative destruction" in 1942. The way he put it was that the constant march forward to ever-newer ways of doing things was not just a lamentable side effect of commerce, but was an *essential* element of wealth creation. The task of creating wealth absolutely depends on change. The old Soviet Union was a marvelously preserved museum of nineteenth-century industrialism. This was not because it lacked capital. One need only recall the vast sums it pumped into its side of the arms race. The Soviet Union was the first to launch a space satellite, the famous Sputnik in 1957, and it even had access to new technology. However, the one thing it would not do was to close old-fashioned and unprofitable factories. Here's how economist Edward Luttwak so clearly put it:

A brand new automobile plant would be imported from Italy, complete with assembly lines, hand tools, and training. But right alongside that plant where modern cars came off efficient production lines, other plants employing 10 times as many employees turned out ancient models. There was innovation aplenty, but there was no way for it to spread, because the up-to-date plant lacked the power to invest more capital and hire more workers; both had been preassigned. With no competition, obsolete factories just stayed in business forever. There was no junked machinery and no unemployment. But the overall result was to leave the population in poverty, squandering the world's largest store of natural resources along with immense amounts of capital and the skills and talents of a vast labor force.[2]

This does not mean that individuals need to blindly invest in or convert to the latest technology. Although the successes become famous, they are often built on the debris of earlier failure. Eventually, much money will be made via the Internet. It won't only be eBay or Amazon, but countless other companies as well. When this does happen, you must remember that the success would never have come had the earlier attempts not been launched and then allowed to fail. No, investors certainly do not need to always lurch from one new thing to another even newer thing.

Success does require keeping an eye on the world at large, regardless of your own particular field of endeavor. Especially in this time of universal communication, no one can afford to say, "I'm a physician, so what is going on in the computer industry is irrelevant to me," or "I run a dress store. Why do I need to know about the latest medical breakthrough?" Just as the buggy-whip maker was affected by the arrival of the car, as was every citizen of the world, you are going to be affected by the implementation of plans that you may not even be able to picture today. You need the ability to let go of the old in these cases and to embrace the new. Not being taken by surprise is a great benefit. You ought to cling to the firm pilings of the unchangeable and resist being swept away by the maelstroms that swirl around your very foundations. Change can be frightening and painful.

INCREMENTAL CHANGE IS EASIER TO ACCEPT

Jewish tradition calls for a bride and groom to celebrate their wedding for seven days. This is because it is plainly unreasonable to expect a young couple to experience this life-changing event and then, on the very next day, simply return to normality. Whereas Western culture presents the couple with a honeymoon, the Jewish system sees an isolated vacation in the Bahamas as a pleasurable but false picture of married life. Instead, while settling into their new apartment and getting accustomed to being seen in public together, a new husband and wife enjoy small parties hosted by friends and relatives for a full week following their marriage. A marriage is so profound, and, it is to be hoped, so permanent, that it requires seven days for the human organism to return to normal.

Another life-changing event is losing a close relative. Obviously, the death of a family member is both profound and permanent. That makes it stressful; and once again, Jewish tradition believes that the human organism is not constructed to go safely from, say, a father's funeral directly to a shopping mall or to a corporate staff meeting. Once again, the process is seen to require seven days; and so, following the funeral, Jewish mourners commence a full week of stay-at-home recovery, being visited by friends of theirs and the deceased. This way, they are able to follow a gradual slope from change and emotional turbulence back to normality.

This concept that the human body and psyche need time to adjust to drastic change is an example of an unchanging truth represented by one of the triangles in the Star of David. Is is not surprising that modern science bears out this reality. In 1986, *Science Magazine* reported that heart attacks tended to occur in the morning, clustering at about 9 A.M. This discovery came about by accident. In the spring of 1984, James Muller of Harvard Medical School was presenting data from a clinical trial on heart disease. Someone in the audience commented that from Muller's data it looked as though heart attacks were more likely in the winter than in summer. Muller thought that plausible—it certainly fit the image of the middle-aged man who has a heart attack while shoveling snow. Muller decided to review the data to see if the observation was correct. It wasn't. Heart attacks were equally likely to occur at all times of the year.

But there was something peculiar about the timing of the heart attacks. He found that they tended to occur around 9 A.M.[3] Why 9 A.M? Because that is when most people are either fighting traffic on their way to work or just starting to fight the challenges of work at their workplaces. Yet people fight traffic and need to face the challenges at home in the evening as well. Therefore, shouldn't there be *two* clusters corresponding roughly to morning and evening rush hours? No, because there is one major distinction between the two times of day. For most people, the period leading up to 9 A.M. is only minutes rather than hours since they were horizontal and resting. The human was not designed for instantaneous change. Many people in the morning move from bedroom repose to racing for the train to work within less than half an hour. That is plainly not healthful.

The change between dream-filled sleep and the harried reality of work is so violent that it must be made gradually. And indeed, Jews have the perfect buffer zone—a brief prayer service of about 45 minutes each morning—right between the two contrasting conditions of restful sleep and combating traffic on the commute to work. You may not be interested in morning prayer, but there are other effective ways for you to place a buffer between waking and working. How about setting aside 20 minutes each morning to do nothing but contemplate all that is good in your life and for which you owe gratitude? This should happen even before working out and breakfast.

My son supplied me with yet another example of the body's intolerance for the step-function change. As an ardent scuba diver, he knows that as one descends deeper under water, the air supplied by the scuba (self-contained underwater breathing apparatus) gear increases in pressure to combat the increased pressure on one's chest and lungs from the weight of the water. This increased pressure allows air to dissolve into the blood just as it does at the surface under normal conditions. A problem, often fatal, develops when a diver ascends too rapidly without pausing for decompression stops. In just the same way that the dissolved carbon dioxide bubbles out of soda as you suddenly yank off the bottle cap, air starts bubbling out of the diver's blood as he surfaces. This painful and dangerous condition is called "the bends" and is only avoided by a slow and gradual ascent. People can handle almost anything as long as it comes on gradually enough.

MAKE CHANGES GRADUALLY WHENEVER POSSIBLE

Understanding this concept allows me, as both an employee and an employer, to handle change in the workplace more effectively. Clearly, change can make people most uncomfortable—even unhealthy. Equally clearly, there are better and worse ways to cope with change. So be intensely aware of when you are inflicting stress-inducing, rapid change on others. On occasion, you will elicit an entirely unexpected response from a person to whom you merely made an innocent announcement or to whom you issued a routine instruction. Often, it will be because you underestimated or even ignored entirely the major change your announcement or directive caused in that person's life. For example, you may not think that minimally changing working hours or even putting in a new computer system is a big deal, but it may be a very big deal for an employee. There is a much greater chance of positive cooperation if you can present the information in a gradual manner rather than as a terse notice.

Needless to say, making things as gradual as possible is advice that does not apply when surgery is taking place. In the same way that surgery necessary for the amputation of a limb is not drawn out over several months to minimize shock to the system, so it is that the termination of one or several people is best handled decisively. People often sense approaching threats; and in such circumstances, not only is a lengthy period of uncertainty cruel, but it can also be perilous for the organization.

React to Sudden Change Slowly, Too

When you are on the receiving end of a sudden change, you are seldom under any obligation to respond while your soul is still coping with the initial stress and still trying to adjust. For example, suppose your boss has just informed you that your position is terminated or that the company is going under. Or imagine that your daughter has just told you, with an exaggerated air of calmness and normality, that she is abandoning her college studies to elope. Perhaps your banker has just told you that because of a recently announced law suit against your company, the bank is closing your firm's $5 million line of credit. In each of these situations, even if you do not instantly feel stressed, recognize that you are stressed. The best response is not to respond. Instead, you could just say something like this: "Well, you have obviously had a few days (or hours, if appropriate) to think about how you were going to tell me this. I must now take the same period to consider my response to what you have just told me."

More than one person, I can assure you, has consulted with me after responding impetuously to these types of situations. Family relationships can be irreparably ruined. You can walk away from a job termination with far less than you could have obtained with a more judicious response; and you can end up negotiating from a position of more serious weakness than was necessary. Don't have responses to sudden change forced on you if you can possibly avoid it.

Being alert can keep change from being a sudden surprise as well. Workers at Kmart had years to contemplate the company's declining fortunes in the face of the superretailers like Wal-Mart. Those who lost their jobs during early 2002 were not nearly as shocked as were the Enron workers who lost their jobs three or four months earlier when the energy giant imploded. In the case of Enron, it was almost overnight that the company went from high-flying, high-spending, high-profile Texas darling to doomed and disgraced skeleton.

It is extremely rare for there not to be clues that major upheaval is coming. Many people prefer to put their heads in the sand, rather than to have to begin to cope with something they would hope would just disappear. However, a far more effective strategy is to deal with these cataclysms on your own timetable, rather than that of someone else's choosing.

Discomfort with Change Makes the Familiar Welcome

People love the familiar because it reassures them that nothing is changing. Cartoons of Mickey Mouse are perennial favorites—Mickey doesn't change; he remains impervious to the ravages of time. Harvard Professor Stephen Jay Gould has pointed out that from Mickey's original debut in *Steamboat Willie* in 1928, Mickey's appearance had actually changed, though in a way that made him more familiar.[4] Disney must have realized that most people tend to be sentimental about children and fond of them, so he found ways to make Mickey appear more childlike. The anatomical distinctiveness of infants comes from a head that is disproportionately large for their bodies and also from large eyes. These features tend to produce a response of disarming tenderness in most adults. So Disney artists removed all sharp angularity from Mickey Mouse, giving him a disproportionately large head along with his large eyes; and his ears became more rounded and moved further back on his head. Not only was Mickey not going to change, but he was also going to look more and more familiar by looking more childlike. Discomfiting change was avoided, and people flocked to animated films.

Sometimes suffering terrible changes through one's early years can teach how much people yearn for stability and predictability. For example, Frank Lowy was a 15-year-old Czechoslovakian Holocaust survivor when World War II ended. The war had robbed him of his childhood and of his innocence. He turned his back on his shattered past and haunting memories of horror and joined the Jewish underground, fighting for independence in what would soon become the State of Israel. Understanding that nothing remains the same and that eventually the fighting would end, he prepared for whatever the future would bring. He studied accounting at night; and, after emigrating to Australia in 1951, he began delivering sandwiches for a deli in Sydney while saving his money and buying vacant suburban lots and subdividing them. In 1955, he visited California and saw his first shopping mall, so he returned to Australia, determined to bring this new change in the way people shop to his adopted country.

By 1974, he had become Australia's dominant owner of shopping malls. Today he is among the wealthiest men in Australia and is a confidant of politicians, including former Prime Minister Bob Hawke. He is also a member of Australia's central bank board.[5] With Australia conquered, Frank turned to the United States. He bought and built shopping centers until he owned eight in San Diego, eight in Los Angeles, four in Northern California, and five in St. Louis, Missouri, where he was the city's biggest landlord. In 1998 he began branding all his malls, renaming them all Westfield Shoppingtowns. Each mall was to have the same signage and the same red, white, and blue uniforms for security guards, information booth attendants, and other personnel. Why the branding? Says Frank Lowy: "For the same reason that McDonald's brands its hamburgers. A customer in San Diego can expect the same product as one in Washington, D.C." He wants his malls worldwide to be known for the same high quality of service. He thinks this consistency of experience will play well in a country where people are always on the move, constantly changing jobs and homes.[6]

This concept is clearly applicable to your life, both business and personal. Especially when great change is happening in one area, you should try your hardest to focus on familiarity and consistency elsewhere.

IN CONTRAST TO OTHER CULTURES, JUDAISM *EMBRACES* CHANGE

The problem with change is, of course, that life is seldom accommodating enough to telegraph us adequate advance warning of impending change. When the travail caused by that change arrives suddenly, you find yourself ill-equipped to cope, experience energy-sapping stress, and make mistakes. Therefore, a worldview that recognizes the benefits of change, as does Judaism, is of great value. While clinging relentlessly to those areas where change mustn't be accepted, Jews have tended to view the concept of change in a fundamentally healthful way.

The cities of Athens and Jerusalem represented the cultural differences between Jewish philosophy and Hellenism, the other dominant culture of the second century B.C.E. In contrast to Athens, which denied change by glorifying eternal youth, Jerusalem venerated age and the wisdom that often accompanies it. The Greek philosophy of Athens depicted a changeless world that was always here. In contrast, Judaism, through the Bible, depicted a world that instantaneously came into being through a primeval cataclysmic big bang—the original giant change that made all else possible. Greece expressed an aristocratic disdain for work, whereas Judaism viewed work as human beings' partnership with God in the ongoing *process* of creation.

It is almost impossible to overestimate the effect that that transcendent conviction can have on a culture or, indeed, on an individual. It can surely be no accident that approximately 80 percent of all the scientific and medical advances of the past thousand years have taken place in Christian societies. It may seem strange to hear an Orthodox rabbi identifying Christendom as the source of most of the technological developments that have so improved life. However, in reality, the source is not Christianity per se, but a transcendent conviction that Judaism and Christianity both share. Unlike many faiths that have mysterious and colorful accounts of the origins of the world or those philosophies that utterly ignore the question of how humanity came to occupy this spot in the cosmos, both Judaism and Christianity depend for an answer on the eight words that open all of Scripture: "*In the beginning God created Heaven and Earth.*"

Why was it Isaac Newton, a devout Christian, who laid the foundations of modern physics rather than, say, a thinker from some other culture? It is simply because Newton, who wrote extensive religious treatises well before he published *Principia Mathematica* in 1687, possessed a crucial transcendent conviction—that if, indeed, an omnipotent and benevolent God created the universe, then it would be natural for Him to have created it according to a recognizable pattern and according to fixed rules. Those rules are merely the materialistic equivalent of the spiritual rules disclosed in His Book. That means, therefore, that searching for those patterns and rules should yield results. Unlike a member of a culture who supposes creation to have been random and capricious, Newton was motivated to launch his investigations by a conviction that what he sought did indeed exist. In similar ways, transcendent convictions about the nature of money and how it relates to change would also endow those who hold those convictions with superior chances of success.

In his poem *Ode on a Grecian Urn*, the poet John Keats expressed adoration for the painted lovers on the urn because, unlike their real-life counterparts, these wouldn't age. Thinking of the consistent contrasts between the worldviews symbolized by Athens and Jerusalem, respectively, I am always amused by one outstanding example of that contrast. Judaism appreciates gray hair as a symbol of experience, character, and wisdom whereas the commercially available preparation that conceals gray hair and returns it to its original characterless color is sold under a brand name that alludes to the *Grecian* origin of the never-mature philosophy. My father always spoke of his love for each of his gray hairs. Each served as an eloquent reminder coming at him from his mirror each morning, he said, of how important it was to make every present moment count.

INTEGRATING CHANGE AND THE UNCHANGEABLE INTO YOUR LIFE

You can prosper by integrating into your life the things that must never change along with an openness to the things that can and should change. Turning change into an ally helps companies adjust to technological advances, and failing to do so hurts them. Likewise, using change correctly can help you, and failing to do so can hurt you. Change produces opportunity for business professionals.

Think of the fashion industry, for example. You may not think it makes sense for men and women to discard perfectly good clothing just because it is no longer "in fashion." Their doing so nonetheless stimulates fabric manufacture, photographers, designers, fashion magazine publishers, and many other workers in supporting industries. And the desire for those new clothes stimulates customers to spur themselves on to greater efforts of productivity to everyone else's benefit. That is how they can afford those new clothes. In any event, as you shall see later, for humans, clothing has always been far more than merely utilitarian.

The ancient Jewish source for learning about how economic productivity always depends on change is the blessing that Moses gave to Zevulun: "Rejoice, Oh Zevulun, in your breaking-out, and Issachar, in your tents."[7] Traditionally, Zevulun is understood to have been the entrepreneurial representative of commerce and business among the 12 sons of Jacob. "Breaking-out" means escaping conventional ways of thinking and common ways of doing things. Moses blessed Zevulun by telling him that he was preordained to lead the Children of Israel in the areas of business and commerce and that, as such, he would need to know how to always break out of his present comfort zone.

The lesson there is to always prepare for change. Expect the unexpected, plan on it, and profit from it. In areas having to do with wealth creation, never, never expect the status quo to be maintained. Your job next year will not resemble your job this year. If it does, either your employer is not thriving or your position in the company is not secure. Either way, your days are numbered. If things are going well, you will be doing different things or more things. Perhaps you will be using tools and machinery that don't yet exist. Maybe you should prepare yourself for that.

It is interesting that the closing phrase of the blessing Zevulun received prior to the aged leader's death is: ". . . by the riches of the sea will they be nourished, and by the treasures concealed in sand."[8] I recall being taught by one of my elderly rabbinic relatives during the 1960s that "the sea" is a metaphor for travel and trade. He added that the mysterious reference to "treasures concealed in sand" alluded to a future time when people would derive enormous wealth from very complex products made with sand. He explained that God was guiding humanity to a lesser dependence on matter and a greater dependence on mind. Thus, He intended to show humanity that wealth did not lie merely in rare and expensive gold but also in plentiful and cheap sand, provided that sand was leveraged by human creativity. In 1962, what would you have thought if you had been told that before the end of the century, a great company called Intel would arise and produce incalculable wealth from products called chips made almost entirely from sand? Or that one of the wealthiest spots on the planet would be nicknamed Silicon Valley, where sand is mostly composed of the element silicon?

THE MORE THINGS CHANGE, THE MORE YOU MUST DEPEND ON THINGS THAT NEVER CHANGE

If Zevulun is linked to wealth creation, what is the meaning of the partnership with his brother Issachar, which is suggested by their linkage in the blessing? The blueprint is found in the verse just discussed: "Rejoice, Oh Zevulun, in your breaking-out, and Issachar, in your tents."[9] Jewish tradition describes a special relationship between the two brothers, Zevulun and Issachar. Theirs was to be a mutually dependent relationship. As always, everything God does has to do with enhancing human ability to interact peacefully and productively. One mechanism for achieving His purpose is, of course, money. The brothers' mutually interdependent relationship started off with Zevulun providing the economic wherewithal to support his brother Issachar.[10] This left Issachar free of monetary concerns so he could dedicate himself to his own vital purpose. Issachar's reciprocal role was to become a repository and to provide access to the moral and philosophical framework without which Zevulun's efforts would be ultimately doomed.

In other words, business success depends on change and on readiness to embrace change. However, and this is a great big, gigantic "however," one can only feel truly free to embrace change and one will only succeed in dealing with change if one is solidly anchored to a set of almost Cartesian-like coordinates that *never* change.

James Collins, author of *Built to Last*, puts it this way.[11] He asked readers to imagine the president of the United States holding a memo in his hands that reads: "We no longer hold these truths to be self-evident. We can no longer afford to hold the belief that all men are created equal." Glancing down at his memo, the commander-in-chief says: "We need to take a hard look at the Bill of Rights. We certainly can't let those outdated values get in our way. We cannot allow obsolete notions such as freedom of religion, freedom of the press, and the right to trial by jury to inhibit our drive toward progress. We must change and adapt to changing times."

Collins pointed out how many of the most successful companies have conducted massive changes and adaptations, while never abandoning *their core values*. For example, Disney almost religiously preserves its core value of wholesome entertainment. When it did decide to produce material that didn't fit its pattern, it created or purchased another production company like Miramax, through which to market controversial entertainment without tainting the Disney brand. To what extent this strategy has entirely succeeded, I am not quite sure yet; but Disney certainly understood the danger of ignoring this principle.

Boeing is another example: It recently moved its headquarters from Washington State to Chicago without modifying its unchangeable value of leading-edge aviation technology and product integrity. Its core value system even underpinned a more dramatic change back in the 1950s. Then, Boeing depended for 80 percent of its business on military acquisition and focused almost single-mindedly on fighters and bombers. By remaining anchored to its core values, Boeing was able to bet the company on commercial jets. You will remember the debut of commercial jet aviation with the arrival of Boeing's famous "707." During 2001, Boeing supplied 527 commercial jets to the airlines of the world, which figure constituted 62 percent of all airplanes sold in the world that year. Boeing broke out of the confines of its box quite dramatically but retained fealty to its unchangeables.

SOME THINGS SHOULD NEVER CHANGE: PROFIT IS A CORE VALUE

Temporarily forgotten was another area in which some things never change—the role of profit in a business. Just when things were changing at a dizzying pace during the 1980s and 1990s, business ought to have depended more certainly than ever on the unchanging role of profit.

Consider this case study—the Gniwisch family. In the 1970s, a Holocaust survivor named Isaac Gniwisch and his wife, Leah, started a jewelry business in Montreal. They began by buying pearl necklaces from Asia and selling them to department stores for $100 when their competitors were charging $800. They were profitable from day one. In the summer of 1999 their four sons, who were all rabbis as well as "old economy" entrepreneurs, decided to join the new economy by starting an Internet jewelry store they called Buyjewel.com.

Back then, a gold-fever atmosphere surrounded any enterprise with "dot-com" after its name, so you won't be surprised to hear that Goldman Sachs soon offered the brothers $10 million in seed funding for the fledgling company. They turned that offer down; but in November 1999, they met with e-commerce guru Bill Gross; his brother, Larry; and other Idealab executives in Pasadena, California. (Idealab was a high-tech incubating firm.) The day of that meeting, the share price of one Idealab company, eToys, reached an all-time high of $52.50. The next day, another Idealab company, Tickets.com, went public, and its shares closed $7.50 above the initial offering price. Breathing the very air around Idealab was intoxicating. Bill Gross and his Idealab were flying high, and they acquired a majority of Buyjewel.com for several million dollars.

By April 2000, the Gniwisches had moved to Los Angeles; and the company, now renamed Ice.com, was ensconced in the flamboyant Idealab office, which was decorated in a style meant to emulate the solar system, with Bill Gross managing from the sun's position in the center.

From their parents, the Gniwisch brothers had learned to infuse their work with equal parts business acumen and spiritual values. They felt that the office was as good a place as the synagogue for a spiritual lesson. Mayer Gniwisch's wife, Naomi, put it this way: "For us, business and religion are one thing." This may be what helped insulate them from all the dot-com mania. For instance, when America Online offered the brothers advertising banner space for the bargain price of $70 million, they didn't bite. "How the hell do people have the chutzpah to ask for so much?" asked Mayer Gniwisch. "De Beers[12] doesn't spend $70 million on advertising and they do billions of dollars in sales." Nonetheless, the brothers were spending, or "burning," as Internet start-up nomenclature would have it, nearly half a million dollars a month in exchange for monthly sales of under $100,000. Because they understood the principle of those things that never change, they knew something was wrong and were particularly chagrined to have spent $40,000 to photograph some unknown models with the company's jewels for the web site illustrations.

During the second half of 2000, the free-spending culture of Idealab and that of the conservative and religious Gniwisches collided. "We need to make money!" Shmuel Gniwisch recalls saying repeatedly. "We were hoarse from repeating ourselves. We need to make money!" Monthly sales were up to $200,000, but Ice.com was still losing money. By fall 2000, Ice.com competitors like Miadora.com and Jewelry.com had failed, taking nearly $50 million of venture capital with them. They were obviously less obsessed with profit. In fact, almost nobody spoke of profit in those heady days. It was considered a little gauche to mention profit; market share was king. But the Gniwisches with their spiritual roots knew the difference between things that change and things that don't.

So the brothers relocated their families and their business away from the heady atmosphere of Los Angeles back to their parents' home in Montreal. Moving the office into an old building their parents owned and replacing Californian programmers with Canadian tech experts, they cut their "burn rate" down to about $100,000; and two months later they turned their first profit.[13] Having been steeped in the ancient Jewish wisdom of the Torah, the Gniwisches saved their company by remembering that "limitless capital raised from investors" does not mean the same thing as "profit from customers." They knew that some things never change. Businesses that don't do something valuable for others do not survive and should not survive. Profit is a way to measure how useful a business is. That doesn't ever change.

EVALUATING WHEN CHANGE IS NECESSARY BECAUSE OF NEW CIRCUMSTANCES

Some things change and others do not. By the evening of that terrible Tuesday, September 11, 2001, most Americans were shaking their heads saying that nothing would ever be the same again. They were wrong, of course—understandably wrong, but still wrong to think that the attack changed everything in life. It changed a lot of things, but not everything. The sheer magnitude of that appalling act of cruelty certainly overwhelmed the immediate ability of Americans to analyze its effects. Much time would elapse before it became plain that some things like air travel would change indefinitely, whereas other things like grocery sales would remain exactly the same. People always need to buy food—that does not change. On September 12, airline executives threw themselves into redesigning air travel and restructuring their companies, and they were quite right to do so. Supermarket chains, lawn service firms, and pest exterminators would have been wrong to count on any major changes to their industries. Business must learn to be deliberate about change.

Understanding what is essential and what isn't allows one to more effectively cope when unexpectedly assaulted by change. Consider the case of the Pacific Coast Biscuit Company in the early years of the nineteenth century. Pesach, or Passover, is one of the most widely observed Jewish holidays. Its most famous symbol is the food staple utterly unique to this holiday, a dry and somewhat indigestible cracker called matzo. Today, many food companies manufacture reliably kosher matzo for the Passover holiday, but back in 1916 far fewer matzo manufacturers existed. One of the best was the Pacific Coast Biscuit Company in Portland, Oregon. Each year, as spring approached, successive issues of the *Jewish Tribune* of Portland would carry advertisements for Pacific Coast Biscuit Company's matzo. Beneath a large conspicuous swastika was the headline:

This Trademark Stands for Supreme Quality.

Beneath that, the advertisement read:

> Wherever you see the famous Swastika sign, just remember its significance to The Fathers and its present meaning. Then it meant brightness and prosperity—today it is a symbol of Purity and Quality.

MATZOS

> When sealed in a carton with this trademark, [a small swastika] is pure, clean, and wholesome beyond compare. . . .

> When buying Matzos, . . . this trademark is your surety of Purity.

> Pacific Coast Biscuit Co., Portland, Oregon.

Talk of change being thrown at you! Imagine being the proprietor of the Pacific Coast Biscuit Company and its prized swastika trademark in 1921, only five years after this advertisement appeared. It was in that year that Hitler's new red banner was unfurled for the first time. Yet, in reality, although changing a logo is expensive, it doesn't truly change the *values* that a company has. It is a cosmetic, rather than a core, change.

For instance, soon after Andersen Consulting broke away from Arthur Andersen in August 2000, it changed its name to Accenture. Although this was merely cosmetic at the time, the change turned out to be fortuitous, allowing the international consulting firm to escape name association with Arthur Andersen's death throes during the Enron scandal!

Companies and individuals that attempt to ignore unchangeable truths end up losing in the long run. Certainly, honesty in business falls into this category, as the 2001 debacle at Enron illustrates.

Some people mistakenly assume that a transaction can only take place if one side withholds information from the other. They assume that a transaction constitutes one party outsmarting another. This is a failure to understand that when two parties sculpt a true transaction, it is not one party taking away something from the other, but two parties cooperating to create entirely new wealth.

The transaction is more likely to take place if both parties understand that nothing needs to be hidden. Furthermore, the transaction is more likely to be successful if each party trusts the other and feels confident that no material facts are being withheld. This might be one reason for the success enjoyed by retailer Wal-Mart. Says Chris Ohlinger, chief executive of Service Industry Research Systems, Inc., "When trust is an issue, Wal-mart always wins. Trust is probably their largest merchandising weapon."[14] Another unchangeable truth is that although human beings will often put their home lives aside and work 18-hour days, seven days a week, for a limited amount of time, sooner or later the most dedicated employee will want a life. In the early entrepreneurial phases of a company, the almost palpable excitement and atmosphere of limitless promise can intoxicate employees. They will work long hours, often for little more than a promise. In the long run (and all wise business management takes the long run into account), encouraging employees toward full balance between personal and business lives will help to ensure low turnover.

Sometimes these unchangeable truths don't mesh with the conventional wisdom of the day. Although we have all gone to great trouble during past decades to decree that male and female employees should be treated as if they were all gender neutral, Jewish wisdom would suggest that this idea, carried to an extreme, can be perilous. Talmudic wisdom suggests that because of the unmistakable power of human sexuality, men and women should never allow themselves to be secluded alone with a fellow worker of the opposite gender. This seemingly quaint worldview would suggest leaving the door to one's office ajar when meeting a co-worker and, if on a business trip, getting together at a coffee shop rather than one's hotel suite.

This caution serves a dual purpose. First, it provides protection against unwarranted sexual harassment charges, as well as not providing opportunity for actual misconduct. Second, it serves as a reminder that company policies against office romances are by definition limited. Whereas one company may ban such relationships entirely and another allows them with certain restrictions, the reality of the world is such that I need to be aware of the temptations both for myself and, if I am the boss, for my employees. Pretending that personal relationships in the workplace can simply be ruled out of existence may lead to crises.

Remember how casual clothing overtook much of U.S. business during the 1990s? "Things are so different now," chortled junior associates as they ambled into work in their dungarees and sandals. Well, after a 10-year excursion into clothing styles that hurt corporate image, encouraged slacking off, and fostered an environment ripe for sexual harassment, companies are asking workers to dress up rather than down. For the first time in 10 years, the year 2000 saw the number of companies permitting casual attire dropping. In 1998, 97 percent of companies in a Society for Human Resource Management poll allowed staffers to dress casually once a week. By 2000 that number had shrunk to 87 percent.

In a survey of 1,000 firms conducted by Jackson Lewis, employers were asked whether they had noticed an increase in absenteeism and tardiness after instituting a casual dress policy. Nearly half said yes, and 30 percent reported a rise in flirtatious behavior.[15] At Federated Investors in Pittsburgh, a traditional dress code requires women to wear skirts, nylons, and dress shoes. Men must wear suits and ties. The Chicago Board of Trade requires men on the floor to wear shirts with a collar and a tie. After experimenting in 1999 with casual dress, executive search firm Korn/Ferry International returned to business attire with a memo that spelled out the firm's return to a suit-and-tie dress code "in response to a more traditional business environment."[16]

Clothing styles do change. Elizabethan gentlemen looked nothing like their contemporary brethren do today. Casual clothing becomes acceptable and even chic. However, a few years go by and once again things revert to basics. It may have had something to do with the White House of President George W. Bush, which has a dress code dictating jackets and ties, and no jeans, even on weekends. This was in marked contrast to the Clinton administration's laid-back attitude. But certain principles do not change; and remaining aware of these principles, even anchored by them, grants a certain amount of freedom.

Why should a man presenting himself for a potentially career-enhancing interview dress in a suit and tie rather than in shorts and a tee shirt? The would-be employer wants to see how willing the candidate will be to subordinate his own comfort to the discipline and demands of the job. Appearing in a suit that is obviously less comfortable than casual clothing and one that certainly took more effort to don than a one-piece mechanic's overalls would have done, sends a clear although perhaps subconscious message—"I can take it." Furthermore, Jewish tradition explains that for society to function safely, men must lose some of their adolescent individualism. Wearing clothing similar to that worn by all other men on the train into the office is a little like soldiers in an army all wearing the same uniform. The system just works better if men see themselves as team players rather than as unique chest-beaters bellowing out the sounds of their special importance. Even women's clothing in the workplace loses a little of the individuality it ordinarily displays in a social context.

Can change be frightening? It certainly can, but it can also be exhilarating. It allows business to create wealth as changing conditions create new opportunities. Above all, clinging resolutely to the unchanging fundamentals allows the freedom to innovate without limit.

THE IMPORTANCE OF MEMORY IN MAKING CHANGE MEANINGFUL

Judaism places much value on memory. Blessings during the holidays always mention memory; and Rosh HaShana, the Jewish New Year, is also called the Day of Memory. Why is memory so important? Without memory, the passage of time becomes meaningless. Without memory, even music can no longer be heard. Don't forget, you can actually hear only one note at a time. You are capable only of hearing exactly what is being played at the instant. For a tune to be heard in your brain, you have to employ memory, just as you need memory to make sense of a novel you may be reading.

It is memories that make change meaningful. Just think about it . . . without memory, there would be no change in your life just as there would be no music. Each moment would stand alone, with no relationship to any preceding instant or to any successive event. You need to understand the seamless interconnectivity of time in order to allow the past to guide your present actions and so to give you the future you seek. Therein lies the secret to living with change.

It is sometimes difficult to remember how little does change. Part of the reason for the confusion is technology. Many more and far greater technological advances have occurred since World War II than occurred during the previous thousand years. It is easy to suppose that technology is totally changing everything. Of course, present-day human beings are far less dependent on the harsh whims of nature. It is wonderful to be able to have my dentist drill my tooth painlessly while I am on Novocain. It is wonderful to be able to talk to people on the other side of the world and to cross the United States in five hours. I love air-conditioning, and I love my car that starts up every time I turn the key and can travel 20,000 miles between tune-ups. But is my life really that different from that of my great-grandparents?

In certain ways, technology doesn't change things as much as it camouflages just how little things have changed. Just think about it. I travel for business, as did my great-grandfather. True, I travel in a comfortable leather seat in a jet airliner while he traveled in a wagon. It is also true that I travel enormous distances relatively quickly and in comparative comfort while he endured grueling travel between neighboring towns. Yet, I spend roughly the same number of days away from my home and family each month as he did. While traveling, he missed his loved ones and the little comforts of home just as much as I do while on the road. I hope that my travel will result in revenue to my family just as longingly as did my great-grandfather. And while sleeping in a strange bed in a distant Sheraton is certainly far more pleasant than on a pile of straw in the corner of the loft of a rural German inn, my traveling life is not that different from the one my great-grandfather experienced.

Today, most people work for about a third of every 24-hour period. They sleep for approximately another third of the day, and the remaining third goes by in taking care of the auxiliary aspects of living. That is almost exactly how people a century ago divided up their days. Is sitting before a computer monitor so very different from the work they did back then? Well, yes and no. It is far more pleasant than working in a claustrophobic and unhealthy factory, but work is work. It means doing what you must do instead of what you might prefer to be doing. Were your great-grandparents to return to witness your life, they might well be surprised at how little things have changed. If they are surprised at all, they might well be more surprised by social changes than by technology. It is easy to mistake change for more than it really is. Change is reality, but what kind of reality?

THE REALITY OF CHANGE IS DEPICTED MORE ACCURATELY BY A VIDEO THAN BY A SNAPSHOT

The old Greek philosopher Zeno confounded all his contemporaries by presenting this conundrum: An audacious tortoise once challenged the famous runner Achilles to a race. The tortoise demanded a head start of 100 yards. *Photograph the scene showing the tortoise ahead of Achilles by 100 yards.*

At the starter's signal, Achilles, who runs 10 times faster than the tortoise, sets off and quickly covers 100 yards, reaching the point from which the tortoise began. By that time the tortoise, running at one-tenth of Achilles' speed, has run another 10 yards. *Photograph the scene again, showing that this time the tortoise is still ahead but by ten yards.*

By the time Achilles covers that additional 10 yards, which is to say reaches the 110-yard point, the tortoise is now one yard ahead of Achilles, since he still runs one-tenth as fast as the human. *Photograph the scene again, memorializing the fact that the tortoise is still in the lead.*

By the time the human runner has covered that additional one yard, the tortoise is now one-tenth of a yard ahead of Achilles. *Time for another snap shot.*

No matter how many "snapshots" are taken, they will always show Achilles lagging behind the tortoise. While it is true that the lead enjoyed by the tortoise in each successive photo is a diminishing one, he does seem to remain the leader and thus, eventually, the winner.

Obviously Zeno and his wily friends knew that Achilles would eventually win a race against a tortoise. What bothered them about this paradox was that they could not find the catch. The catch is that real life is not reflected accurately by a series of snapshots; it is correctly depicted only by a smooth and continuously running video. Watching a video of the race between Achilles and the tortoise would quickly have shown the runner outpacing the tortoise at a little more than 111 yards from the start. It is easy to be confused or even misled when trying to interpret reality with a sequence of snapshots.

In the same way, you could examine a snapshot of 10 workers struggling to get by on minimum wage. It is not a pretty picture. However, if you revisited these workers six months later, if they had kept their jobs and worked on improving their skills, you would find that most would be earning somewhat more for their work. Government statisticians would have to locate another 10 workers to produce a snapshot showing 10 Americans that are still on minimum wage. Although it is true that there are still 10 workers on minimum wage, it is surely not irrelevant that they are a different set of 10 people and that the first 10 are now moving up the economic escalator.

There are only three job skills necessary to find and keep an entry-level job. First, show up regularly and on time. Second, obey instructions. Third, speak and act respectfully. These are character attributes rather than real work skills, and they can be acquired from parents or from an employer who really cares far more easily than they can be acquired from any "job-training program." Almost anybody obeying these three rules in the United States can find an entry-level job and keep it. By keeping the position, one quickly becomes trained and worth more to an employer.

An employee who has learned his way around the job and acquired the job-specific skills cannot be replaced by a new entry-level person. The experienced employee is worth more to his employer than any newcomer; and most intelligent employers, recognizing this obvious fact, will pay him more in order to keep him. The employer has something invested in the employee and certainly does not want him leaving for the competitor down the road who would also offer him the minimum wage. Thus the fortunate newcomer to the job market finds himself on the economic escalator. The snapshot of him from six months earlier is now meaningless.

Similarly, a snapshot of a successful lawyer photographed a year before she graduates law school may well show someone apparently in need of government assistance. The snapshot will show a young woman working (well, okay, studying) all day without being paid a penny. She may live in one little room that she shares with another student. She may subsist on macaroni and cheese. The snapshot demands a compassionate response from anyone seeing it, but it fails to show that this woman is only months away from earning an enviable income and in absolutely no need of help from anyone. Least of all should she extract assistance from middle-income families whose total income is considerably less than she will earn in her first year with a prestigious law firm.

People often view misleading snapshots such as these and become convinced that higher taxes are necessary to help the poor. There may be poor, but it is a dynamic group, just as there are children but they are not the same people who were children 10 years ago. It is not surprising that, as reported in *Forbes* magazine on May 4, 1998, shelters for the poor compete for homeless people in order to justify their budgets. Grand Central Neighborhood Social Services Corporation in New York City even ran a marketing special during November 1997 to engage new clients by offering a free breakfast and $5 in cash. What better way to get good people to agree to higher taxes than to play on their natural and Biblically inspired compassion for the poor? All that's needed for this scam to work are lots of warm bodies labeled "The Poor" who can be paraded before the well-intentioned and gullible, who then nobly open their wallets.

Are there people who have far less than many other people? Of course, there are. Is this a fatal flaw in the entire U.S. socioeconomic system? No, it isn't, because many of them are only poor when viewed with a snapshot rather than a video of reality. Snapshots conceal reality, they don't reveal it.

Jews have traditionally benefited economically by their intuitive rejection
of the snapshot view of the world and the mass manipulation it allows. Religious Jews were always more likely to view life through a video rather than
through a dishonest sequence of snapshots. Their familiarity with the Bible's
approach to recounting events accustomed them to seeing the *moving timeline*
of history and to the ever-repeating Biblical laws of cause and effect.

Jewish faith educated its devotees to distrust superficial appearances. Show
them a snapshot depicting an attractive-looking couple strolling hand in hand,
and they instinctively ask themselves questions. They wonder whether this is
a devoted married couple anticipating many happy years in one another's
loving company or an extramarital couple caught in a moment of adulterous
bliss. They just do not know from the photograph and are not prepared to
celebrate their evident joy until they see the video. Jews want to see what led
to this moment and what follows from it. They never take a snapshot at its
face value.

Through always thinking video and not snapshot in this way, genuinely
compassionate and charitable religious Jews are far less vulnerable to the
politics of poverty. They recognize that not a single person has everything he
or she needs or wants, and therefore poverty is more a state of mind than a
state of pocket. Jews also recognize that self-discipline and Biblical principles
of Ethical Capitalism are the stepping-stones to a family's economic growth.

Another key to how Jews view the role of past and future and how they
impact their experience of the present is provided by the total absence of any
present verb *to be* in Hebrew. Anyone speaking a grammatically and Biblically correct Hebrew can say, "*I will be* here tomorrow." He or she can also
say, "*I was* here yesterday." Although there are phrases that are accepted to
mean "*I am* here now," in actuality the verb *to be* doesn't exist in a usable
form. While Israelis work around this dilemma, allowing the conventions of
everyday speech to be maintained, Jews, as well as many others who consider
Hebrew to be the Lord's language, recognize that He in His wisdom decreed
that there is effectively no such thing as the present.

That present moment, rather than a true moment of reality right now, is
instead a mathematical creation of Isaac Newton and Gottfried Leibnitz.
When each separately perceived the bright truth of the calculus, he was giving birth to a way of quantifying and relating to that *now* that is subjectively
felt to be the present. In reality, the present is no more than an experiential
mechanism by means of which humans can convert the future into the past.
That's right; the present is not so much a *time* as it is an *action*. The present

is the activity I am currently engaged in during every instant, with the purpose of turning the infinitely malleable future into a better past.

Correctly understanding how the present instant is less real than the past or the future can also help people deal with fear. As important as it is to be "future-focused, it is also important to remember that fear only exists in the future. Although it is unhealthy and impractical to live only in and for the present instant, it is not hard to see that those who do live this way experience very little fear. If all that counts is the present instant, there can be nothing approaching from the future to hurt you. This is a psychological defense mechanism that humans evoke during moments of extreme physical peril. Soldiers in action often speak of reaching an exultant phase of activity in which all fear abandons them. The present crisis in which they find themselves obscures all thought of the future; and along with that it obscures all fear.

You obviously cannot eliminate all thoughts of the future, neither should you try. On the contrary, your success to some extent depends on your ability to accurately read the future. However, in dealing with fear, shifting your focus just a little from the future to the present helps deflect the paralyzing effects of fear.

Recognizing this truth about the present makes change easier to deal with and easier to manipulate to your benefit. Remember the mantra, "Everything is constantly in motion, and change is perpetual." For some approaching changes, as for a fast-approaching and difficult ball in baseball, I must step backward to give myself more room to swing at it. For other approaching changes, as for a sweet, slow lob, I must step forward to embrace and exploit it as quickly as possible. The trick, of course, is telling the difference between the two. For that trick, two useful props exist: (1) recognizing and remaining anchored to those things that never change, and (2) improving your ability to see future trends that so influence just how you should best modify the present instant. The next chapter shows how you can more accurately foretell the future.

YOUR PATH TO PROSPERITY

- *Understand that the Star of David represents a strong life view that helps deal with change.* The first triangle, standing firmly on its base, represents the core aspects of life that do not change and on which you can depend while everything else around you may shift and take on new and unfamiliar forms. The second triangle, upside down and balanced precariously on its point, signifies the natural and technological world, in which each passing year adds to your store of knowledge and control.

- *Accept innovation and embrace change.* The choice is either to accept innovation along with the pain it may cause some people or to reject it and ensure poverty and pain for almost everyone. You should cling to the firm pilings of the unchangeable and resist being swept away by the maelstroms that swirl around your very foundations. Change can be frightening and painful, but there is no way to hold back this progress. You need the ability to let go of the old and embrace the new. Not being taken by surprise is a great benefit.

- *Try to absorb and make changes gradually.* Set aside some time each morning, say 20 minutes or so, as a "stress equalization" period. Read something not directly work related, ruminate over your longer-term goals, or merely meditate spiritually. Thereafter, proceed with your workout at the gym or your breakfast or whatever else comes next as you prepare for the day's work. This will help you ease into the day, instead of abruptly embarking on the day's work.

- *Do your best to avoid two or more simultaneous stress-inducing changes in your life.* If you are planning on a major move, say, to another city, don't schedule your wedding for the same week. If you unexpectedly lose your job, postpone the surgery you had planned for the same period until you have had a chance to absorb and adjust to the career change.

- *Create a file in your computer or on a dedicated page in your organizer on which you make, modify, and maintain a list of those things that never change for you.* Those constitute the anchor that will hold your ship steady regardless of how violently the gale howls or how high the waves threaten to hurl you. You can reach me at the address at the end of this book if you would like free work sheets that will help you compile this list.

- *Keep in mind your core values—as an individual and in your business.* These should never change, regardless of the technological developments or market changes that are occurring around you.

The Seventh Commandment

Learn to Foretell the Future

Who is wise? One who can tell what will be hatched from the egg that has been laid. Not he who can see the future—that is a prophet. Wisdom is seeing tomorrow's consequences of today's events.
—Babylonian Talmud, tractate Tamid

During the year immediately preceding my worst business failure, all I saw was sunshine and good times ahead. Many investors eagerly clambered aboard my swiftly growing enterprise. Potential partners sought participation. Things could hardly have looked more promising. Our company's growth rate was so heady that, with no hesitation, I violated the rule of diversification by placing virtually all my eggs into one basket. I invested all my assets into my own business on the assumption that no one else would look after it all as diligently as I would.

Then, an exciting acquisition opportunity came up, and I consulted a man who was the name partner of a professional firm, a person whom I considered to be perhaps the wisest businessman in California. He listened to my presentation and spent about five minutes paging through my spreadsheets. Then he passed all my material back across his desk to me, leaned back in his chair, and began to speak. I had such confidence in his judgment that, on hearing his words, I felt as if I had been hit by an express train. "Your company will be out of business soon," he said. He must have seen the look of shock on my face for he continued, "I cannot help you with the strategy you propose; it would be futile. But when you need me to help you wind everything down tidily, I'll be available."

I thanked him a little coolly and walked out of his office more resolute than ever to complete successfully the acquisition I had planned. A few months later, California began to experience one of its worst real estate downturns ever, its economy languished and hundreds of businesses, both large and small, failed—including mine. That I had not seen the faintest hint of the gloomy future was mortifying enough. What made it so much harder to bear was a man that I respected had seen my impending doom with complete clarity long before that time. While trying to emerge from the wreckage of my hopes, I resolved to ruthlessly examine why I had so fatally failed to see the future.

Some people can see the future more clearly than others. Let me hasten to add that this wise and far-seeing business professional was accomplished at seeing only the future of a business. He was entirely without prescience, for instance, when it came to the disastrous marriage of his son, which he had originally encouraged ardently. No one can see the future clearly when one's emotions are involved. Therefore, one of the clues to becoming accomplished at seeing the future is to learn how to disengage one's own emotions. This is very difficult and is surely one of the reasons that most medical professionals do not attend to their own close relatives. Wise doctors recognize how difficult it would be to disengage their emotional involvement with their spouse or their children. Consequently they correctly doubt their own vision of a problem's future course and the proposed treatment. They would rather that a trusted colleague, to whom the relative is merely a patient, performs the diagnosis and treatment.

Different people really do possess different abilities at seeing the future, just as different people possess different abilities at playing the piano or making omelets. But as with cooking or music, it is relatively easy to greatly enhance one's ability in any field through training and practice. You may never become a concert pianist or a great chef, but you will become far more capable than you had been prior to training yourself.

RECOGNIZE WHEN EXTERNAL EVENTS WILL AFFECT *YOUR* BUSINESS OR LIFE

Further into this chapter I will show you how to improve your ability at forecasting the future impact of current events. For now, it is sufficient that you understand two facts: First—some coming events can cause real change that will impact your business yet leave other kinds of businesses immune, whereas other future events will not affect your activities but might well disrupt those of someone else. Second, you should never procrastinate in the face of the former, and you should refuse to be stampeded by the latter.

Newt Gingrich, for example, failed to see this difference. Gingrich was a professor in Georgia before he entered politics and became the speaker of the house in 1994; and he was passionately interested in educational problems in the United States. In 1996, as the Internet began to enter the national consciousness, Gingrich told me that he thought the Internet would totally end America's educational crisis. He was, of course, wrong. The Internet has not contributed to any improvement in the academic performance of U.S. high school students, and it is unlikely to do so. He would have been correct if he had predicted that the Internet would bring about as much *change to the economy* as did the railroads back in the 1850s when two-thirds of all public offerings were railroad stocks. The Internet dramatically impacted the U.S. economy and continues to do so, but it has had almost no effect on teenage literacy.

In other words, if you work for a tech company or own one or if you sell investments or advise on them, the Internet causes change that should concern you. If you drive a taxi, you don't need to be equally concerned. If you are in the dry cleaning business or the auto repair business, you should watch pending environmental regulations very carefully. If you sell software, you can afford to be much less vigilant monitoring enrironmental regulations.

INTERPRET EVENTS WITHOUT EMOTION

Seeing the future has little to do with native skills or intelligence. Many highly educated individuals are conspicuously unsuccessful at predicting the future. Other people with no apparent educational advantage possess what seem to be almost supernatural abilities to see the future. Two statesmen who presented a marvelous contrast in prescience were Winston Churchill and Neville Chamberlain. Here is what Churchill wrote about Chamberlain:

> He had formed decided judgments about all the political figures of the day, both at home and abroad, and felt himself capable of dealing with them. His all-pervading hope was to go down in history as the Great

Peacemaker; and for this he was prepared to strive continually in the teeth of facts, and face great risks for himself and his country. Unhappily, he ran into tides the force of which he could not measure, and met hurricanes from which he did not flinch, but with which he could not cope.[1]

In September 1938, Neville Chamberlain had visited with the dictator he obsequiously referred to as the honorable Herr Hitler in Munich. On returning to England, Chamberlain exited his airplane at Heston Aerodrome, waved his infamous umbrella triumphantly, and held up the joint declaration he had gotten Hitler to sign. From the windows of his office at Downing Street, he again waved the paper at a crowd fearful of war and used these words: "This is the second time there has come back from Germany to Downing Street peace with honor. I believe it is peace in our time." Within only one short year, England was engaged in a mortal struggle for her very survival.

Chamberlain had turned out to be a very poor prophet, whereas all that Churchill had warned of came to pass with uncanny accuracy. One of the secrets to Churchill's ability to see the future was that *he kept his emotions at bay*. Unlike Chamberlain, whose own sense of ego was notoriously wrapped up within his political persona, and unlike Hitler whose frequent public ranting testified to his emotionalism, Churchill was disarmingly *indifferent* to his public image. Many dignitaries recall midmorning meetings conducted in Winston Churchill's bedroom, with the great man himself propped up on his pillows while wearing his yellow pajamas. Few ever saw the pajamas of Chamberlain or Hitler.

Ego is one enemy of effective futurism. Learn to overcome it, and you will be well on the way to seeing the future far more clearly.

Let me assure you that I doubt it is within one's power to become prophetic across the board and to see the future of everything. It is, however, completely possible to train oneself to become adept at seeing the future in one or two areas. Because in this book I am discussing wealth creation, it would be advantageous to focus on foresight in the area of business. Being personally and emotionally involved can definitely obstruct attempts to peer into the future, but that is not all that makes the task difficult. When glimpses of the future are dark and dim, as they usually are, brilliant peripheral light can also obscure a clear picture of what you strain to make out. When driving at night, you try to block out the blinding glare from headlights of oncoming cars; and when squinting into the future, you must do the same.

George Shaheen, for example, was a wise business professional. He had been a professional "fortune-teller" for 32 years, advising businesses about what lay ahead of them and what they should do about it. He headed the legendary Andersen Consulting company, which, during the 1990s, was earning revenues of close to $10 billion a year. If anyone should have been able to see the future, it was Shaheen.

But less than a year before his lavish retirement package would have triggered, Shaheen left Andersen Consulting and joined Internet grocery start-up Webvan in September 1999. He obtained options to purchase over 10 million shares of Webvan before its initial public offering, along with other generous compensation and equity inducements. Unfortunately, Webvan had lost $35 million in just the first six months of 1999 and announced its expectation to have operating losses for the foreseeable future, just like many other Web firms.

What was shocking was the speed with which Webvan collapsed. By spring 2001, Shaheen stepped down from his position as chief executive officer (CEO) and was left without a job; with a pile of underwater, valueless options; and even without the lifetime annual payments that had been promised him regardless of his stay at Webvan. By that summer, Webvan had filed for Chapter 11 bankruptcy protection. "I can only tell you that we did the best we could," Shaheen told CNET's Greg Sandoval. "Look around; this whole space got clobbered. No one foresaw what was going to happen."[2]

Wrong! Although most people certainly did not foresee what was going to happen, some did see exactly what was going to happen. Those who did sold Webvan short. They were people who had no emotional connection to Webvan. To them, it was just another stock. They were not in love with the Internet; they were in love with accurate investment analysis. They were also people who blocked out the bright lights of lavish capitalization that would have spoiled their "night vision." And that is what seeing the future is most like—peering out at the nighttime gloom from inside a well-lighted room. It is hard, but not impossible. Naturally, looking backward in time is most similar to looking through the window into a well-lit room while standing outside in the dark night. That is easy; anyone can do it.

Ever since Aristotle, people have thought that you can see stars at midday from the bottom of a well. In reality, descending down a shaft will not allow you to see stars during the daylight hours, but the theory wasn't crazy. The idea was that by blocking out all the bright extraneous daylight, the faint speck of starlight would become visible. Fortunately, in attempting to glimpse the faint flecks that indicate the future, the principle of blocking out bright extraneous light works very well.

How could the crystal ball of the oracle to whom so many had turned for a glimpse into the future have gone so dark? George Shaheen was far from the only smart and experienced business professional to have been blinded by the incandescent flashes bursting from the Internet. Any excessively bright lighting makes it difficult, if not impossible, to make out details in the dark corners of the room.

LEARN TO SEE CLUES IN THE PRESENT THAT FORESHADOW THE FUTURE

Time is fascinating—the instinctive desire to seize the present instant and keep it alive, the way people cherish memories and seek to preserve them with the aid of millions of photographic images and miles of videotape, and that staple of science fiction, fantasies of time travel. Experiencing the present and recalling the past are all good, but not nearly as intriguing as seeing the future. People are drawn to those who call the future accurately, whether they successfully predict the rise or the fall of stock prices or coming events. It is unfortunate that because people are accustomed to dismissing the carnival clairvoyant as a charlatan, they tend also to dismiss every aspect of seeing the future. They feel that anything less than complete rejection of futurism would cast aspersions on their rationality. In reality, a full understanding of time and its role in life requires nothing less than full rationality.

Intuition may work with quantities such as length and weight that are used to define the physical environment. Regardless of the activity in which I am engaged and regardless of my age, I can pretty much guesstimate the length of a table or even of a bridge. Like almost everyone else, I can also come up with a fairly good estimate of the dimensions of a box and, after picking it up, a weight that will be close enough for many purposes. However, estimating how much time has elapsed since a particular event or a particular moment is far more difficult.

To a child, a year is almost endless, but to his middle-aged parent, a year flies by with frightening speed. You might explain this by saying that, well, time is relative. Relative to a child's life experience of perhaps only 10 years, a passing year is a full 10 percent of her experience. To the adult, however, the same year is a far smaller fragment of her life experience, thus it feels far shorter. This may be a true and convincing explanation, but no similar explanation is even needed for quantities like weight and volume. When I'm working on an aggravating business or financial problem, time drags. The same period spent enjoying a long-awaited vacation can vanish with bewildering rapidity. This is not the only strange thing about time. For instance, I can experience an entire table, bridge, or box at the same time but only a fleeting instant of any event. For the remainder of the event, I must depend on memory and on a matching faculty, sensing the future.

I do this all the time without even thinking of it. I have learned to interpret the clues of the present in order to predict the approaching future. Suppose I take a short cut across a golf course one fine day when I hear the clear crack of a club connecting with a ball. I then hear someone yelling "fore." I immediately throw myself to the ground in the hope of avoiding concussion. My deaf friend is astonished to see a small white projectile come whizzing through the space that, until an instant earlier, had been occupied by my head. Using sign language, I explain to him that although completely capable in so many areas, he is unable to pick up the clues on a golf course that suggest the imminent arrival of a fast-moving golf ball. Because his handicapped reality is normal for him and is all he has ever known, he looks at me as some kind of prophet.

Now imagine a family picnicking on the banks of a large pond one very misty day. One little boy detaches himself from the group and wanders a few feet down to the water's edge. Suddenly he calls out to his family, "Quick! Look! In a few moments you are going to see ripples on the water." Sure enough, after a few seconds, ripples appear out of the mist and roll in toward where the amazed family sits. "How did you know?" they ask. By wandering down to the water, he had isolated himself from the hubbub of noise generated by the happy picnic, and that allowed him to hear a faint splash. He correctly interpreted it as someone on the far side of the pond, hidden by the mist, tossing a pebble into the pond. He reasoned that if he was right, the ripples from the pebble should soon arrive. Had the boy not provided the simple explanation for his apparent prescience, he would have looked like a prophet.

Cicero said, "It was ordained at the beginning of the world that certain signs should prefigure certain events."[3] Whether you perceive those signs as listening for the faint footsteps of approaching events or whether you prefer to think of them as looking out for the shadows that coming events cast before them matters not at all. What matters is only that you realize two facts: (1)

Within obvious limitations, seeing the future is quite possible, and (2) you can improve your ability to see it.

LOOK BACKWARD TO SEE FORWARD

Isaac Newton's first law of motion also serves very well as the first law of seeing the future. In 1686, Newton specified that any object will tend to continue doing whatever it is then doing unless it is acted on by some external force. If a stationary vehicle is parked at the curb, it is going to "want" to remain there unless a driver starts the engine and engages the gears or unless someone gives it a mighty shove. Likewise, if the car is traveling smoothly down the freeway at 60 miles an hour, it will "want" to continue doing so unless air resistance and other frictions slow it down or unless the driver stomps on the brake or the accelerator. In the absence of any of these outside forces, and in the real world they are never quite absent, the car would indeed continue traveling at 60 miles an hour indefinitely.

By the way, when a driver does stomp on the brakes of a fast-moving car, the car changes its state from motion to rest because of the external force of the driver's foot on the brakes. However, the passengers inside that suddenly stopped car will tend to keep moving forward because nothing is interfering with their state of rapid forward motion, that is, until the windshield or dashboard arrests their forward motion, which is why wearing seat belts improves one's safety in most situations. Away from friction and gravity, objects in space can be seen to behave exactly in accordance with Newton's first law of motion.

You can apply this law to your attempts at improving your ability to see what lies ahead. If things are stable and steady, they will continue to be stable and steady unless acted on by some force. How likely is it for some force to materialize? If things are changing rapidly, they are already being acted on by some force. Find it, recognize it, and determine how that force is likely to behave. Will it continue? Will it strengthen or weaken? In other words, before looking forward, look backward. Examine the trend of the matter concerning you. What has it been doing up to the present? Once you have discovered the trend, you must ask yourself whether it has been behaving in this way because nothing has made it behave differently or whether it is behaving this way only because something is preventing it from behaving differently.

For instance, there was recently a period during which the price of gold remained remarkably steady. Ordinarily, the gold price has tended to rise during times when people perceive problems such as inflation or unrest. Gold's price might have remained steady because indeed there was little inflation and almost no civic unrest. Alternatively, gold's price may have stayed steady in spite of inflation and unrest because some other activity was counteracting the expected price rise. A little research showed that Russia was busily engaged in raising foreign currency by selling off some of their vast reserves of gold. All this new gold coming onto the market was forcing down the price that would otherwise have been driven upward by real inflation.

Recognizing that it was the application of an *external force* that was maintaining an illusion of stability, wise investors figured out that eventually the Russians would have sold off enough to satisfy their needs. Having seen the future, the investors bought gold-related investments and prospered. Indeed inflation was not beaten, and the Russians did stop selling off their gold. When that happened, the price of gold began to rise.

Or consider this famous historical example. In his famous "Give me liberty or give me death" speech to the Virginia convention on March 23, 1775, Patrick Henry said: "I have but one lamp by which my feet are guided, and that is the lamp of experience. I know of no way of judging of the future but by the past. And judging by the past, I wish to know what there has been in the conduct of the British ministry for the last ten years to justify those hopes with which gentlemen have been pleased to solace themselves and the House." All he was saying was that Britain could be counted on to do more of what it had been doing unless some force materialized that would change its approach. Unless anyone could inform Henry as to what that force might be, he was for fighting then rather than later.

Paul Reichmann, the Canadian business professional whose sphere of influence spans the entire globe, is someone who understands how important recalling the past is while trying to see the future. Whether it is changing the skyline of Toronto, Mexico City, or London, his almost prophetic forward vision is based on his ability to recall the past:

> Then he looks back in time to see what the ancients would have done, and forward to see how his actions might affect succeeding generations of Reichmanns. His vision is a quality he developed early in life and still hones by studying the Talmud, a collection of Jewish thought more than 2,000 years old. "I'm still studying, but I wouldn't call myself a

scholar," he says. "There's a lot of wisdom to be taken from ancient cultures. I have found that Chinese businessmen will still apply philosophy that is thousands of years old to today's events. Among Westerners you find it less because of a certain blindness that comes from being captivated by modern science and technology. You forget you can find knowledge in other teachings, especially if you want to develop your mind. If you want to know tomorrow, you must know yesterday."[4]

Finally, here's an example from my own experience. On more than one occasion while sailing with my family, I have had to fall back on a rough-and-ready form of navigation called "dead-reckoning." Imagine that fog closes in and obscures landmarks. One quickly identifies one's last known position on the chart. Then one tries to steer a steady compass course while maintaining a steady known speed. It now becomes an easy matter to draw a line on the chart extending from one's last-known position in the direction of one's course. By taking into account currents and by extrapolating one's speed onto that line, it is possible to predict one's exact position for any time in the future. This is another example of how one can see the future.

This principle that explains how examining the past can provide a beacon into the future is what lies at the root of one of Judaism's best known aphorisms: "Whatever has been is what will be and whatever has been done is what will be done. There is nothing new beneath the sun."[5] There are remarkable rabbinic predictions from the nineteenth century that describe the future founding of the State of Israel in 1948. There is a Biblical prediction that 10 anti-Semites will be hanged in one day during the year 1946. Few rabbinic scholars were surprised when the Nuremberg tribunal hanged 10 of the Nazi defendants on one day, October 16, 1946.[6] By clearly understanding that things change only with a cause and that coincidences can mostly be ruled out, the task of sensing the course of future events becomes a lot more manageable.

KEEP IN MIND THE PATTERNS OF TIME

Although no reliable accounts exist as to how the calendar came into being, some presumptions can be safely made. Mine is that some early humans watched the progression of shadows from day to day as the earth moved further in its orbit around the sun. They quickly concluded that a sort of cosmic pattern existed—one that lasted for about 365 days. They also spotted the 30-day cycle of the moon and thus were able to construct a mathematical model of time that is called a calendar. It depicted the passage of time in the form of 12 of the shorter periods fitting into one of the longer ones, and it made time far easier to grasp than it had been.

The use of a calendar also granted the fortunate discoverers enormous advantages in agriculture, construction, and navigation. By thinking of the seasons as being part of a 365-day cycle, they were able to predict roughly when the rain would start falling and when the stormy weather would give way to reliable winds. To other humans who lacked insights into time, the calendar users might have appeared to be magicians. Yet all they did was identify *patterns*. Identifying patterns has much to do with what is thought of as intelligence. Most IQ tests routinely measure an individual's ability to identify patterns. They might ask the subject to recognize which shape does not belong in a group or what the next number in a given sequence of numbers should be.

Some people invest on the basis of having identified what they thought were patterns in the historic movements of a stock or a group of stocks. This is not a very good idea because it imputes some form of intelligence to price levels that are, after all, merely a system of measuring how desirable the stock is to many people. Although drawing meaningful conclusions from perceived patterns in stock prices is likely to prove reckless, drawing meaningful conclusions from larger social trends is intelligent. These larger trend patterns may very well also shape stock prices, but it is always better to understand underlying causes.

Clothing fashions seem to swing pendulum-like from one extreme to another, but people who have made themselves intimately familiar with the fashion industry are able to see the future of next year's styles with some accuracy. They recognize the recurring trends and the repeating patterns that emerge whenever trends are studied. Statistically, men and women are marrying far later today than their parents did. Will this last? Probably not. At some point, the average age of marrying will start inching down again. Those who spot the turning point in advance will know how to cater to it and thereby help themselves.

The Bible lists the 10 generations that separated Adam from Noah.[7] Many people have wondered why the name of only one representative for each generation is listed. The answer is that epochs tend to follow predictable trends. For instance, three of the sequential generations mentioned are Kenan,

Mehalalel, and Jared. Their names, like all names in the Torah, translate to specific meanings. "Kenan" implies material acquisitiveness, "Mehalalel" suggests spiritual quest, and "Jared" explicitly means cultural decline. It is not too fanciful for anyone with a longer time perspective to examine the second half of the twentieth century in terms of these three cultural trends.

A Period of Material Acquisitiveness

The generation that lived and fought through World War II returned to normality with hopes of making up for the years of sacrifice. Many still harbored painful recollections of the depression years that preceded the war. For whatever reason, the years immediately following World War II were certainly the years that launched American's love affair with material acquisition. The size of homes skyrocketed during that time, and the number of square feet dedicated to the bathroom grew at an even faster pace. Two cars began to become common for many American families. Appliances filled the kitchens, and savings accounts started swelling. Material acquisition began to become a value in and of itself. It could truly have been called the epoch of material acquisition. As so often happens, this period sowed the seeds for the next.

A Period of Spiritual Quest

Somewhere during the 1960s came the birth of the so-called hippie movement. A full-scale sociological survey isn't necessary in order to see the basic pattern. Whether it was the way the hippies adopted clothing their parents would have donated to a charity or the way they rejected the conventional progression of study leading to job and career, the hippies were clearly intent on replacing what they saw as their parents' materialism with some form of spiritual quest. Their music gradually switched from the Beatles' "I Want to Hold Your Hand" of the early 1960s to music that reflected obsession with exotic eastern cults that promised spiritual nirvana.

I suspect that growing drug use among the children of the generation of material acquisition was part of the same spiritual quest. First look at alcohol and then draw conclusions perhaps valid for mind-altering chemicals. For the most part, when you enjoy an alcoholic drink, it is not in quite the same way you enjoy a plate of delicious food. The food can be said to be satisfying a very physical need, but until addiction sets in, your body has no physical need for alcohol as it does for food. No, when you drink, you are satisfying a *spiritual* need. I was led to this view by my own faith, and indeed by others, too, which sacrimentalizes the drinking of wine. There is clearly a strong link between alcohol and the human spirit—people turn to alcohol because of a spiritual need. For some unfortunate people, alcohol becomes a spiritual anesthetic to dull the emotional pain of their existence. Many suffer this condition while living in great comfort and physical sufficiency.

In January 1961, the great psychiatrist Carl Jung wrote a letter from Switzerland, where he lived, to Bill Wilson, the founder of Alcoholics Anonymous. In this letter Jung referred to a patient called Rowland H. "His craving for alcohol was the equivalent on a low level of the spiritual thirst of our being for wholeness, expressed in medieval language: the union with God." Jung worried about referring to God in a scientific and therapeutic context and next said, "How could one formulate such an insight in a language that is not misunderstood in our days?" Then, explaining why it is not possible to discuss alcohol without recognizing its relationship to humans' subconscious desire for spiritual harmony, he concluded: "Alcohol in Latin is *spiritus*, and you use the same word for the highest religious experience as well as for the most depraving poison. . . . I remain yours sincerely, C G. Jung."[8] Of course, the old Latin usage is retained to this day by calling strong alcohol *spirits*.

Beyond the compelling call of addiction, I don't think that anyone deliberately absorbs mind-changing drugs into his or her system for anything other than to quiet a gnawing spiritual dissatisfaction with life. It would certainly seem odd that the first U.S. generation to have been raised with almost limitless material possession was the generation to have turned for relief to a substance that up till then was usually found in the sordid waterfront dives of the downtrodden. By its notable naming of the generations, the Bible identifies a common and recurring trend. Generations raised with very little in the way of material possession often focus so single-mindedly on providing their children with everything they didn't have that they neglect to provide their children with some of the things they *did* have. Through this invisible mechanism, the generation of material acquisitiveness often gives way to the generation of spiritual searching. Unfortunately, this spiritual searching is not in itself valuable, and it often leads to a widespread cultural decline reflected in the Bible's name for the successive generation—Jared.

A Period of Cultural Decline

This can hardly be considered a comprehensive sociological analysis, and I do not intend to dismiss a complex field of study with a couple of sentences; but certain forms of cultural decline could certainly be identified between the hippie period and the end of the twentieth century. Whether it was the rising crime figures during this period or the dramatic increase in children born to unmarried mothers, something disturbing was happening, and it would have been hard to characterize it all as anything but cultural decline. The period was marked by lengthy lines at gas stations and by double-digit interest rates; and it was marked by an increase in public vulgarity. Although many sectors of the economy were thriving, the culture as an essential part of the civilization was not.

In general, one can always count on the three epochs of materialism, spiritual quest, and cultural decline to follow one another. Beyond that, there are always patterns and trends to watch and to try to understand. As business professionals, you should remain on high alert for these trends, and you should try to understand the underlying causes driving them.

HOW TO USE THE CYCLES OF LIFE TO DETERMINE OTHER TRENDS

During the 1920s, a Russian economist called Nikolas Kondratieff studied the economic, cultural, and social life of the nineteenth century[9] and concluded that the Biblical rule of the 50-year-cycle did indeed hold up.[10] This Biblically identified cycle occurs naturally within any reasonably free society and is called *yobel*. There is a well-known J/Y transliteration revealed by the English translation of the Hebrew name of the prophet and reluctant sailor who got swallowed by the whale—*Yonah*. With the same J/Y shift that made *Yoneh* into *Jonah*, *yobel* became jubilee in English, the word for a 50-year celebration of any major event.

Kondratieff noticed a 50-year pattern to everything, even war, that is even clearer today. Although it is obviously far from mathematically precise, the approximate periodicity was nonetheless eye-catching to Kondratieff and to his later devotees. Many amateur historians are entranced by the apparent tendency for wars to be fought approximately every 25 years, with a longer superimposed 50-year cycle of popular versus unpopular wars. I am using the terms "popular" and "unpopular" to describe popular *sentiment* about the war in question. These sentiments are usually retrospective, so that a "popular war" is one seen to have had a positive outcome and about which people tend to look back with some degree of nostalgia. For example, consider these wars over the past 150 years:

1990	(Popular)	Gulf War
1965	(Unpopular)	Vietnam War
1940	(Popular)	World War II
1915	(Unpopular)	World War I
1890	(Popular)	Spanish American War (Actually 1898; however, the first Pan-American Conference was held in October 1889 that laid out U.S. commercial interests in Latin America that were later threatened in Cuba by Spain.)
1865	(Unpopular)	Civil War

Students of international political economy are interested in the relationship between various wars and what they call the Kondratieff Wave. Although Joseph Schumpeter endorsed the concept during the 1930s, many scholars are profoundly disturbed by the implication that, among human beings, there may be an inexorable inevitability about war. Needless to say, the Kondratieff Wave theory, like many other wave theories, is considered quite controversial. Although much less disturbing than war itself, the apparent inevitability to *economic* cycles is no less interesting.

Again, although it is not mathematically exact to the year, there does indeed appear to be some reliable correlation from 1800 to 2000 between U.S. wholesale prices and an idealized, perfect 50-year Kondratieff Wave. Eras of great economic growth also appear to be separated by either 25 or 50 years, depending on what you examine. For instance, these are the approximate years in which various scientific and industrial developments entered popular usage and began contributing to wealth creation:

2000	Internet
1975	Computers
1950	Plastics
1925	Broadcasting
1900	Auto industry
1875	Telephone
1850	Telegraph

Many people find the notion of regular cycles appearing to "govern" human affairs to be eerie, even sinister. Unfortunately for Nikolas Kondratieff, his boss, Joseph Stalin, was one of those who did not much appreciate the idea that a 3,000-year-old Bible contains an insight that might help explain the economic development of enlightened Russians. In 1938, he executed Kondratieff, but the Kondratieff Wave continues to entrance generations of observers.

You may find yourself intrigued by the Kondratieff Wave or by other similar wave theories. Alternately, you might find yourself repulsed by them. As a business professional, you should embrace neither extreme. No wave theory is a brilliant beam of light illuminating both past and future of all there is to know. However, neither ought you to entirely discredit the notion of cycles and periods in human affairs. They are present and do play something of a role. For example, consider these patterns:

- The earth rotates on its axis approximately once every 24 hours, causing the sun to appear fairly predictably on the eastern horizon every morning.
- The moon revolves around the earth roughly every $29^{1}/_{2}$ days, and the earth revolves around the sun about once in $365^{1}/_{4}$ days.
- Once every 28 years, the sun and the moon return to the same points relative to one another.
- Once every 93,408 years, the entire solar system completes one full cycle, with all the planets in the same relative configuration.
- Ocean tides rise and fall about once every $12^{1}/_{2}$ hours.

Weather cycles are influenced by longer-term solar and lunar cycles:

- The sun's temperature rises and falls every 11 years, as does its electro-magnetic activity as indicted by sunspots.

- The moon's gravity seems to vary on an 18.6-year cycle, and the earth's temperature and pressure averages seem to vary according to a 20-year cycle.

Finally, consider these patterns in nature:

- Every 3.86 years, Norwegian lemmings leap from cliffs into the sea below.
- Every 9.7 months, on Ascension Island in the South Atlantic, terns swarm in to hatch their eggs.
- In Canada, the lynx population has risen and fallen regularly every 9.6 years since at least 1735, when records began to be kept.[11]

Some of these things are known because of the work of Edward Dewey, an economist at the U.S. Department of Commerce during the 1920s and 1930s. Intrigued by the obvious cycles in business, banking, labor, and the production of goods, he assembled an enormous collection of more than 3,000 documented cycles and the associated data. There are cycles in water levels in U.S. lakes, in numbers of U.S. marriages, in the abundance of grasshoppers (9.2 years, in case you wanted to know), and in the rate of residential home construction. There are well-established cycles for industrial bond yields, auto sales, and cheese consumption. The periodicity of aluminum production, airplane traffic, and mental health are fact. No one really knows whether any of these cycles are related to one another.[12] It seems bizarre to think of a link between grasshopper fecundity and sales figures at the Fortune 500 companies. However, from the point of view of a statistician, it is out of the question to explain this all by coincidence. The correspondence of similar cycles is far too pervasive to be explained by mere chance.

Therefore, you should be open to the possibility of cycles and trends; but you should never allow yourself to become blinded by them. They should be a factor in your assessments of what the future will bring, but only one factor; and they should be given appropriate weight—neither too low nor too high. Perhaps you are considering buying a rental property, investing in a preschool program for working mothers, or simply trying to select a good stock in which to invest. In each of these cases, the wise course of action would be to try to see the future.

Part of developing an effective understanding of how the world really works includes accustoming yourself to analyzing cause and effect. With a little concentration, it eventually becomes a useful habit. Few events are totally isolated. Instead, you ought to try to see events as links in a chain. Even modern meteorology depends on analysts wondering how the distant hurricane will effect local weather. The person who habitually asks, "What caused this thing to happen?" and then asks, "What in turn will be caused by this thing?" is well on the way to becoming a wise person.

Smart investors do this each time they open their morning paper or watch the television news programs. What's that? A pipeline explosion in some far-off place? Could that cause a shortage of whatever commodity was being piped? A new type of miniaturized liquid crystal display with built in magnification was just invented? Now who could benefit from a product that is ideal for workers requiring access to a computer while also operating other machinery? A new president who is more favorably disposed to the military than his outgoing predecessor might be interested in increasing military spending, some of which would benefit those companies making the kind of weaponry that a modern army needs. Is my town growing? What is causing the growth, and in which direction is it growing? Should I perhaps buy some property in the part of town into which people seem to be moving?

In each case, information is already available; Jewish culture calls this "the laid egg." How and when that egg will hatch and what sort of creature will crawl out of it is up to you to determine. That is why learning to think in terms of understanding the future is so important.

CONSECRATING TIME FOR FORECASTING

Have you ever lain awake late at night and just listened to the sounds in your home? You will hear slight creaking sounds as beams, roofs, or even window frames expand or contract with changing temperatures. You may hear the whistle of a distant locomotive or tug boat. If you listen carefully, you will hear the refrigerator in your kitchen cycling on and off. Now when did you last hear your refrigerator cycling during the day time? It does so during daylight just as surely as it does at night. Did you ever hear your home's creaking sounds during the day? You seldom hear them, yet all those noises are taking place then, too.

My point is that when your sensory input mechanisms—i.e., your eyes and ears—are being bombarded with a large number of powerful stimuli, you become less sensitive to the soft, subtle sounds and sights. You may marvel at the almost imperceptible scent worn by the woman with whom you are dining or at the fragrance from the flowers on the table in the restaurant. Now walk into the restaurant's smelly kitchen with your companion while carrying those flowers, and I can assure you that you will smell nothing but the odor from the chef's deep fryer in the corner.

Coming events do indeed send soft and subtle signals. The reason almost everyone disregards them is that few set aside the necessary quiet time to take note of them. If it is truly important to you to hear your refrigerator cycle on and off, then you must send the party revelers home and turn off the radio and television. Block out all the noise, and then you will clearly hear the almost silent compressor motor turning on and off. If it is truly important to you to hear the soft footsteps of approaching trends, then you have to do the same thing. You need to set aside time when other more compelling stimuli are absent. Only then will you be accessible to these tiny signals.

One person who capitalized on his observation of trends was an entrepreneur named Morris Shepard. He was a high school dropout from rural Ohio who joined the Air Force, where he discovered a love and a knack for cryptography. He finally earned a university degree and became a teacher at a succession of colleges. He taught at Penn State, Northeastern, Bridgewater, and other schools. Morris loved the classroom, but he wasn't too skilled at the political games played for promotion and tenure in the academic community. He was adored by his students, for whom he enhanced the courses with his boxes filled with news clippings, articles, and stories he collected. Whenever he changed jobs, he would lug along his file folders and crates of material with which he supplemented what he felt were the highly inadequate textbooks foisted upon his students. He was 58 years old and without a job in 1995 as he sadly contemplated his future of moving from one short-lived teaching assignment to another.

One summer morning, he sat himself down under a shady tree for some quiet dedicated thinking time. Away from all distractions, he paged idly through a copy of the *New York Times*. In the business section, he saw a description of a new Xerox copier capable of churning out short runs of entire books. Because he was not inundated with noise and interference, the future became clear to him. He saw textbooks becoming more expensive. He saw college bookstores becoming less competent at getting students their books before the opening of class. He saw emerging technology allowing him to create custom books for specific classes. He saw that his background was far more suited to creating these specialized teaching materials than it was to actual teaching.

So Shepard mortgaged his home, sucked his credit cards dry, and purchased the necessary photocopying equipment. Establishing relationships with professors at various colleges and universities, Morris Shepard was in business. He obtained copyright permission for each component and printed bound volumes containing all the collateral materials that each professor required for his course. Within three years, he had produced more than 2,500 course packs (as he calls them), and his business had grown to 38 employees. No longer does he have to endure the stuffy academic environment he detested, and no longer does he have to endure the employment uncertainty of the teaching profession. Shepard peered into the future, and because he did so in circumstances that allowed the soft signals to reach him, he saw it clearly, acted, and prospered.[13]

Almost anyone can use the model for seeing the future that is rooted in Jewish tradition. This model is based on the fourth of the Ten Commandments, observing the Sabbath day. Although many view the Sabbath as appearing to be governed by an incongruously primitive set of rules, the effect is to create a tranquil oasis in time and space from which the future can be effectively contemplated. For 25 hours each week, Jews are required to put aside all work-related objects and activities. They are to abstain from activating any form of technological machinery, such as cars, televisions, computers, and phones. In fact, all devices that assist Jews in reaching out of themselves into the outer world and impacting it are off limits.

By restricting themselves from the usual acts of creativity and impacting the world, Jews are restraining themselves from being the *subjects* of creation, those who do the acts. Instead they become *objects,* those upon whom the world works its magic. They are prohibited from imposing their creative drives on their environment because, by not doing so, they are better placed to absorb what the environment has to offer them. This slice of time, one-seventh of each week, becomes not only a tremendous luxury but also an indispensable aid to creative thinking during the rest of the week. It is a regular weekly period of time during which their beings are set on "receive mode" rather than "transmit mode."

Whatever time you determine to set aside for stoking up your creativity and enhancing your future vision should be governed by three rules:

1. It is far more important that it be a *regular* time than that it be a *lengthy* period of time. In other words, rather make this time short but regular than long but random. Set aside an hour every Monday and every Thursday or perhaps one morning every two weeks. Block it out in your calendar as if it were an appointment with your doctor or lawyer.
2. You should be doing nothing else at the same time. You should not be exercising, not listening to music, and not eating a snack. In this way, you place yourself in "receive mode."
3. You should alternate between keeping your mind quite clear and focusing your thoughts on the specific agenda you had earlier prepared. This will help prevent undisciplined mental meandering.

Suppose, for example, that you are trying to determine the future significance of a new fact or of a set of numbers that has just come into your possession. Relax and try to put yourself into a receptive mode. Feel the sun warming your arms; perhaps you hear the buzzing of a nearby bee or the rustling of some leaves in the tree overhead. Don't think; just look, smell, see, and feel. Then jerk yourself into thought mode and reflect on the fact or figures that you suspect contain a germ of an idea for you. Wind the facts and figures around your mind. Wrap your consciousness about the data, and try to visualize seeing it from every direction—from above and from below and even from within the data themselves. When your brain shrieks for a break, get back into thoughtless receptive mode, and just feel and absorb. Repeat the cycle several times. Don't be discouraged if you do not emerge from this "Sabbath session" without a breakthrough. That may come a few hours later or even a day or two later.

Many people are often inspired while in the shower. The reason for this is that taking a shower is almost like doing nothing, because for most people, it has become an almost mindless, automatic activity. They wash all the same parts in the same sequence in the same way. Meanwhile, the white noise of rushing water effectively blocks out all other sounds and distractions. No wonder then that people are most sensitive to small, silent little thoughts that creep into their consciousness while taking a shower. Creating a "virtual shower" by regular "Sabbath sessions" is one way of enhancing your ability to see the future for your financial benefit.

HOW TO DERIVE THE MOST BENEFIT FROM YOUR QUIET FORECASTING TIME

One more caution is in order. This may be hard to swallow, but I recommend that for a period of at least 24 hours, and preferably double that, before you embark on your regular "absorb the sounds of the future" sessions, you abstain from entertainment in the form of either movies or television programs. I realize that the usage of television is so ubiquitous that it is hard to imagine doing without it for any period of time. But watching television tends to make one lethargic, noncommunicative, inactive, and sleepy. And the effects of almost any activity linger. If one eats some disagreeable food or ingests some toxic substance, it can take quite a while for the body to become completely free of the deleterious effects.

The problem is that screen images are so seductive that it is almost impossible to escape their impact for some considerable period of time after exposure. The powerful pictures send emotional shock waves ricocheting around your brain. As the result of an hour or two in front of either a large or a small screen, you become desensitized to the delicate. What is more, you are rendered more passive by the nature of this form of entertainment. Lloyd Billingsley pointed out that the very word *amuse* conveys a clue.[14] The word *muse* means "to think or ponder." The "a" in front of a word implies the opposite of the root word just as it does in words like *atheist*—the opposite of a theist. In other words, amusement is used to prevent thought or deep pondering.

There are three main reasons that explain why amusing yourself through the medium of either television or cinema is damaging to your ability to foretell the future.

Reason 1: Light shining into your eyes possesses a mesmerizing quality. One recalls the phrase, "She stood immobilized, just like a deer caught in the headlights of a car." When you view a real-life scene, your eyes are converting into neural impulses the light they received by reflection from the scene. You do not look into the sun, the source of the light. Instead, the sunlight shines on to the scene, illuminating it; and the light is then reflected from the scene into your eyes.

When watching television, however, the cathode ray gun, powered by about 25,000 volts of electricity, is aimed right at your face. It is beaming electrons directly toward your eyes. These strike the phosphor-coated glass screen located between the cathode ray gun and your eyes; and in turn, this screen emits the light that strikes your eyes. The light from images seen this way is propelled directly at your eyes in a way not found in nature. In fact, people are wisely cautioned as children never to look directly into a light. The images seen in this way tend to be powerfully implanted in memory and tend to affect thoughts more than they would have had they been absorbed, say, by reflected light.

In contrast, reading about ideas or things grants you the most freedom to absorb or to reject. Pictures impact your emotions in a way that can cause temporary emotional imbalance. For this reason, shopping networks use television but never radio. By dangling a glittering necklace before your eyes, the marketer stands a better chance of getting you to pick up the phone and place an order than if she had merely described it on the radio. Direct-mail catalogs tend to be heavy on brightly colored pictures rather than on descriptive text. Thus, when you need all your faculties of discernment working at maximum efficiency, you certainly do not need powerful images thrust into your brain and overwhelming your subtle thought processes.

Reason 2: Television images are very fast moving. The average television scene lasts no more than 25 seconds. This rapid-fire delivery of images accustoms your mind to immediate gratification. In reality, your most constructive thought processes do not work that quickly, and seeing the future requires you to patiently absorb the information at more real-life speeds. In a sense, television tends to produce in you an impatience quite antithetical to picking up and analyzing future trends. Here the far slower process of assimilating data by reading works to your great advantage.

Reason 3: Television dulls your imaginative powers, whereas reading or listening to the spoken word develops these vital powers. Imagination is a crucial faculty in the process of trying to foresee the future. The methodology is quite simple. You start off by carefully examining the past and fully comprehending both the internal as well as the external factors that have brought you to the present. You then contemplate the current conditions along with the resources you are able to bring to bear. Finally, you allow your imagination free reign to come up with a variety of scenarios for the future. Some of these you will wisely reject out of hand. Among those remaining, you will find some that amaze you and some that terrify you. Some will attract you, whereas others will repel you.

The key is to ensure a healthy imagination in order to summon up a *range* of possibilities for you to consider. Reading an account of some event or hearing it retold exercises your imagination. That is why watching a movie made of a book that you have read usually disappoints. At the very least, you recognize the movie to be quite different from what you had imagined from reading the book. Reading that book stimulated you to fill in the blanks. You develop a notion of what the characters look like and what the setting is. Later, while watching the picture, you note how very different it is. That picture up there on the screen deprives you of the freedom to create within your mind.

GOAL SETTING IS SEEING THE FUTURE

As a motorcycle enthusiast, I once had the privilege of experiencing a few days of training at the hands of one of the experts who trains motorcycle officers for the California Highway Patrol. Although I had been riding for a long time and, in fact, had ridden my old motorcycle across much of Africa many years ago, I was a self-taught rider. The very first day of real training I experienced drove home to me just how little I really knew. I was struck by how close to a miracle it was that I had survived my earlier two-wheeled adventures while so ignorant of basic riding techniques. I was also struck by how closely many aspects of motorcycling resembled running one's business life. For instance, under certain circumstances, one "counter-steers" by momentarily turning the handlebars *away* from the direction in which one really wishes to travel. Likewise in business, it is frequently necessary to temporarily steer *away* from one's objective precisely in order to reach it in the quickest way possible.

Even more useful is the lesson in riding safely through a long sweeping curve on a motorcycle. Contrary to my earlier self-taught practice, I learned how much more effective it is if one twists one's head enough to keep the end of the turn in one's field of vision. I can still hear that instructor yelling the directive that has since saved my hide more than once: "No, don't look where you *are* going; look where you *want* to go!" With great insight, he further explained that your body will subconsciously try to take the bike where you are looking. Knowing that, one may as well benefit from it by looking clearly at the goal. Watch tight-rope artists at the circus; they know the same lesson. They do not look down at the rope; instead they fix their focus clearly on the little platform that marks the end of the perilous traverse.

In your business life, although the same principle still applies, it is a little more complex because the goal is usually not in sight. That is where the ability to see the future becomes quite crucial. The constantly recurring Biblical injunction to "fear the Lord your God" is a reminder of how important it is to be able to "see" the invisible, because the Hebrew verb used for the phrase "fear the Lord" is actually the Hebrew word for "seeing." In other words, the Bible is informing its devotees that if you can bring yourself to actually "see" God, then you will automatically come also to "fear" him.

Most people will never fear what they cannot see. For example, during the early years of the twentieth century, it was close to impossible to persuade people of the peril of radioactivity. As a matter of fact, many sought out dubious "cures" by spending extended periods in radium mines. Years later, these patients developed horrifying symptoms of radioactivity burns; but at the time they were reluctant to believe that they could be harmed by something invisible. Whether you intend it in a religious context with an upper case "F" or in a business context with a lowercase "f", the definition of possessing "faith" is having the ability to see the yet invisible as clearly as if it were present in material form right before your eyes.

Whether you are contemplating an investment or planning on opening a new business, faith is paramount. If you are unable to clearly visualize what it will all look like were it to go well, you would be better off deferring the action until you can see it. If you are about to pick up the phone to make a sales call or to propose a transaction, the ability to see the future is necessary. Your chances of success are vastly enhanced if you spend a few moments first *actively visualizing* the conversation with your prospect culminating triumphantly.

Here is why I am asking you to expend the energy necessary to force your brain to think positive thoughts. As the decoding of the human genome project progressed, few of the many attendant discoveries thrilled me as much as this one did: According to psychologist David Moore of Pitzer College in Claremont, California, thoughts can cause the release of hormones that can bind to DNA, turning genes "on" or "off." The difference between human brains and chimpanzee brains is not which genes each brain has, but which genes are turned on and which are switched off.

Apparently the discovery sprang from a science researcher who had to spend periods of several weeks at a time on a remote island in comparative isolation. He noticed that a day or two before his scheduled return to civilization and his family, his beard grew noticeably. The scientist was puzzled. He shared the information with his colleagues, all of whom knew that sexual activity releases a flood of testosterone. This hormone affects beards the way that a bag of grass food affects your front lawn. The astonishing aspect of this story is that the researchers realized that not only does the aforementioned activity stimulate beard growth, but merely anticipating female companionship also did the trick. Imagine that! Your thoughts can tweak your genetic expression.[15] By spending a little preparation time actively anticipating a successful outcome to your efforts, by dwelling on that outcome, and by savoring the success with a smile on your face, you will actually be impacting your body and mind. You will be preparing yourself to bring about the success you crave.

Suppose, for example, that you are about to enter a meeting during which you hope to persuade another party or parties of something; it could be anything. First, spend a few moments using your imagination to clearly visualize the ideal conclusion. Are you about to deliver a speech to your Rotary Club or to a large group of Wall Street analysts? First take some quiet private time just prior to the event during which you clearly visualize a triumphant presentation. Include the smallest details; imagine the audience applauding. Remember my motorcycle instructor's warning that one tends to go where one is looking. Seeing the desirable outcome is one of the most useful aspects of developing an ability to see the future.

Accustom yourself to analyzing today's events in the light of yesterday's history for the purpose of making necessary changes for tomorrow. As you read the newspaper or watch the news, always ask yourself, "What is the underlying principle?" If the news describes fanfare surrounding the invention of an improbable urban scooter that will completely revolutionize city planning, as happened in late 2001, think of the basic human need that is being catered to. During one of your quiet contemplation sessions, you will come to see that it is the desire of people to overcome the frustrating human limitations of time and space. "Nobody can occupy two separate spaces simultaneously" is how science might express it. People have always distinguished themselves from vegetables and from animals by the desire to travel, and to travel quickly, thereby coming as close as possible to overcoming the frustrating limitations of not being able to be in two places at once. This principle would have enabled people to predict the gradual replacing of luxurious ocean liners by fast and uncomfortable jetliners. The human desire to not be restricted in any way at all is a spiritual desire and is thus found in the Torah.

In the same way that the Torah has always been seen by Jews to contain a blueprint of reality in the realm of morality, it has also been seen to contain a blueprint of reality in the realms of ultimate physics and, of course, in ultimate economics. As I have shown, some things change during human history, whereas others hardly change at all. For example, whether humans make war with bows and arrows or with tactical nuclear devices, the one unchangeable is that humans make war, and the Torah discusses war as an ultimate reality. Whether humans travel by camel, canoe, Cadillac, or the Concorde supersonic airliner, the one unchangeable is that humans have a deep desire to be able to travel, and the Torah discusses the ultimate principles of travel.

When a young Fairchild Semiconductor scientist named Gordon Moore formulated what has come to be known as Moore's Law in 1965, he quickly came to be seen as a prophet. He predicted that the power and the complexity of the silicon chip would double every 18 months. When you double something 20 times every 1.5 years for 30 years, it increases by a factor of more than one-million-to-one. By 1995 Moore's Law was still going strong. The 1995 four-megabit chip was four million times more powerful than its predecessor, the transistor. In 1968 Moore, along with another Fairchild alumnus, Robert Noyce, started Intel, which became a more-than-$20 billion company in less than 35 years. A prophet? No, Gordon Moore learned to read the future in his field.

The only son of poor Russian Jewish immigrants, Al Lerner grew up living behind his parents' candy store in Queens, New York. He served in the Marine Corps and then became a furniture salesman. But Al Lerner understood what money was. He eventually became the country's leading specialist in affinity credit cards through his finance company, MBNA. Since its founding in 1982, MBNA's strategy has been to sign up endorsing organizations who would help market Al's credit cards to their members in exchange for a small percentage of every transaction. Quite an odyssey: Child of candy store owners to furniture salesman to billionaire credit card banker. Only someone with a deep and almost intuitive sense of what money really is could do it. Al Lerner possessed that insight.

Whether humans interact with one another through bits of gold or with credit card transactions communicated through bits of electronic data, the one unchangeable is that money has always served as a means of human interaction. Knowing exactly what money is, how it comes into being, and how it vanishes grants one a wisdom that can easily be confused with prophecy. The next chapter looks at money.

YOUR PATH TO PROSPERITY

- *Recognize which external events will affect your business or your life and which will have no effect at all.*   Some coming events can cause real change that will impact your business yet leave other kinds of businesses immune, whereas other future events will not affect your activities but might well disrupt those of someone else. Never procrastinate in the face of the former, but refuse to be stampeded by the latter.

- *Interpret events without emotion.*   Seeing the future has little to do with native skills or intelligence. Some highly educated individuals are conspicuously unsuccessful at predicting the future. Ego is one enemy of effective futurism. Learn to overcome it, and you are well on the way to seeing the future far more clearly.

- *Before looking forward, look backward.*   If things are stable and steady, they will continue to be stable and steady unless acted on by some force. How likely is it for some force to materialize? If things are changing rapidly, they are already being acted on by some force. Find it, recognize it, and determine how that force is likely to behave. Will it continue? Will it strengthen or weaken? Examine the trend of the matter concerning you. What has it been doing up to the present? Once you have discovered the trend, you must ask yourself whether it has been behaving in this way because nothing has made it behave differently, or is it behaving this way only because something is preventing it from behaving differently.

- *Watch for patterns.*   There are always larger patterns and trends to watch and to try to understand. As business professionals, you should remain on high alert for these trends, and you should try to understand the underlying causes driving them.

- *Be open to the possibility of cycles and trends, but never allow yourself to become blinded by them.*   Cycles and trends should be a factor in your assessments of what the future will bring, but only one factor; and they should be given appropriate weight—neither too low nor too high.

- *To hear the soft footsteps of approaching trends, block out all the external "noise."* Set aside time when other, more compelling stimuli are absent. Only then will you be accessible to these tiny signals. Make sure you set aside a *regular* time, even if it is only a short amount of time. *Do nothing else* at the same time. In this way, you place yourself in what I call "receive mode." Finally, alternate between keeping your mind quite clear and focusing your thoughts on the specific agenda you had earlier prepared. This will help prevent undisciplined mental meandering.

- *Visualize your future.* Whether you are contemplating an investment or planning on opening a new business, faith is paramount. If you are unable to clearly visualize what it will all look like were it to go well, you would be better off deferring the action until you can see it. Your chances of success are vastly enhanced if you spend a few moments first *actively visualizing* the conversation with your prospect as culminating triumphantly.

- *Practice memorizing.* To the extent that seeing the future is the flip side of remembering the past, our ability to recall becomes even more valuable. Although you probably haven't done this since elementary school, you should recover your ability to memorize. The best way to achieve this is by selecting poetry or prose you enjoy. Then set yourself a schedule to memorize something in its entirety.

- *Select reading material that will help you recognize trends.* There are magazines available, such as *American Demographics*, whose entire content is devoted to demographic trends. There are volumes published by the U.S. government, such as the Statistical Abstract of the United States. Initially you will find much of this material unappealing and alien. Don't feel you must read these books and magazines cover to cover. In each, you will find at least something of interest. As time goes by, you will become increasingly familiar with the technology of analyzing trends, and you will come to enjoy both your mastery of the field and your growing arsenal of facts.

Know Your Money

Your money is a quantifiable analog for your life force—the aggregate of your time, skills, experience, persistence, and relationships.

Fishing for salmon one summer in the spectacular Saanitch Inlet of Vancouver Island, British Columbia, taught me a useful lesson. After hooking what appeared to be a magnificent, large salmon, I began licking my lips in anticipation of a barbecued salmon dinner with my family that evening. My elderly guide interrupted my reverie by calmly saying, "You have lost him." Because I could feel the fish fighting my attempts to reel him in, I hastily assured my well-intentioned mentor that he was wrong.

With a jerk of his head, the guide indicated a large eagle sitting atop a tree on the shoreline about 20 or 30 yards away. "He's seen your fish," was all he said, as the eagle lazily spread his wings to their eight-foot wingspan and launched himself into the air. Within under a minute, during which time I was frantically winding in my line trying to outrace the eagle, the raptor effortlessly swooped down on my doomed salmon and with a lightening strike of his talons, scooped up the fish, ripped it off my hook, and returned to his perch on the tree to enjoy his dinner. Perhaps I imagined the mocking look he gave me every few minutes.

What did I learn? I absorbed a practical lesson, one that I had only known in theory up till that moment. I had always learned how important it was to have as much information as possible about your quarry. Now, I understood what that meant. I needed a guide not only to tell me exactly where in the vastness of the ocean to find salmon and what sort of bait would attract a salmon, but also to tell me exactly who was my competition for that salmon. In other words, if I was serious about catching salmon, I needed to know all there was to know about them.

During my 20 years as a congregational rabbi, I have counseled many single people who, in theory, wanted to be married, although they claimed not to know how to bring this about. The salmon experience helped me advise my friends. To convince a particular woman to marry you, I explained to men, it is not enough merely to desire her. You must also understand her. Perhaps she seeks assurance that in various areas—be they emotional, sexual, social, physical, or economic—you are capable of taking care of her and protecting her. If so, you need to beam her pictures, not only of who you are and who you have been, but also of who you could ultimately become with her help. Trying to really understand the woman is the only way to win her.

To women, I said much the same thing. You have to understand as much as possible about men in general and the man in whom you're interested, in particular. You need to know not only what he has to offer you, but also what he needs you to offer him. You should know what is going through his mind, even if his thoughts are wrong. That was just a start. There was much more I would tell single men and women seeking marriage, but you get the idea. If you are trying to attract and acquire something, you need to know as much as possible about that thing first.

Trying to learn how to increase your income by studying those who have done so instead of first understanding the true nature of money would be a little like an aspiring actor studying Clint Eastwood instead of first studying the craft of acting. This eager thespian is not Clint Eastwood and will never be Clint Eastwood. His only hope of success on the stage lies in becoming himself.

Similarly, you could study how Alan (Ace) Greenberg, who became the legendary head of the financial firm Bear Stearns, started off as a $32.50-a-week clerk before he pestered the head of the risk-arbitrage department into giving him a position with responsibility. Or you could examine the rise and fall of Gary Winnick, who wouldn't spend the $25 that his immigrant grandfather, a former pushcart peddler on New York's Lower East Side, once gave him to invest. Winnick later built Global Crossing, the fiber optic cable giant and then watched his creation sink into demise under too much debt.

You could watch how cosmetic tycoon Leonard Lauder, who learned from his mother Estee that business is all about relationships, handwrites a personal, intimate note within 24 hours or so of meeting a new potential transaction partner. It would also be fun to learn about the founder of the Neiman Marcus stores, Stanley Marcus, who learned from his father that when you sell, you are not really selling soap, fur coats, or perfume, you are selling satisfaction. But you and I are not Ace, Gary, Leonard, or Stanley. You and I are just you and I. Their lessons are interesting and instructive, but we will do better by understanding the fundamentals from first principles that will allow us to develop our own unique abilities to attract money.

If you want to attract and acquire more money, then you need to start by understanding it as deeply as you can. Exactly what is money?

WHAT IS MONEY?

Open your wallet and take a look at the currency inside it. Try to see it for what it really is: a collection of grimy strips of green paper and metallic discs of varying sizes. Is that what money is? Wait! What's that other folded piece of paper? Oh, yes, that's a check for $40 that someone gave you. That must be money, too. That's not all. What about those colored plastic cards with a narrow brown line on the back? Aren't they money, too? Does that mean that money is really a particular orientation of iron oxide molecules in a magnetic strip?

Reading your monthly bank statement might suggest that money is nothing more than a succession of ones and zeros on some financial institution's computer hard drive.

Perhaps you own some impressive-looking stock certificates? They attest to your ownership of part of a company; but if the company fails, you would find that your pretty certificates grant you partial ownership of a few used desks and an old soda machine. Not a pretty picture.

All right then, colored paper, iron oxide molecules, and stock certificates are not actually money; perhaps they merely *represent* money. That still leaves unanswered the question of what money is.

As oversimplified as this may sound, my money is really *me* and your money is really *you*. You may say that there is more to your life than your money, but there is truly nothing more to your money than your lives. Your bank balances are inseparable from the rest of your lives and are a function of those lives. Here is how pioneering psychologist William James put it:

In its widest possible sense, however, a man's Self is the sum total of all that he can call his, not only his body and his psychic powers, but his clothes and his house, his wife and children, his ancestors and friends, his reputation and works, his lands and horses, and yacht and bank account. All these things give him the same emotions. If they wax and prosper, he feels triumphant; if they dwindle and die away, he feels cast down—not necessarily in the same degree for each thing, but in much the same way for all.[1]

THE JEWISH PERCEPTION OF MONEY

This idea—that your money is you—and what it means has long been known to Jews and is alluded to in the Talmud's expansion of the story of the Biblical patriarch Jacob's desperate wrestling match with a mysterious being.[2] Jacob was on his way to a reconciliation with his estranged brother, Esau, when he inexplicably returned across a river. It was there that he battled a formidable foe until the dawn, incurring a permanent injury. Jacob risked the encounter, says the Talmud,[3] because he wished to recover some assets he had left behind. The rule is, ancient sages say, that a wise person values his money more than his body.

This seemingly bizarre statement is actually the foundation of a healthy relationship to money, and one that has stood generations of successful Jewish business professionals in good stead. Money is the most effective way ever invented for men and women to quantify their creative energy—a most convenient measure of our time, dignity, skills, health, experience, and persistence.

The Talmud means to say that human beings at work are more than just bodies. They are bodies plus the sum of their creative energy, part of which is distilled in money. More than the gross matter of hands and feet, eyes and ears, a wise person cherishes the totality of his or her own creativity. Indeed, more important than merely my body is the totality of what William James calls the Self. There is more to me than my money, but there is nothing more to my money than my entire Self.

THE USE OF MONEY INVOLVES *TRUST*

Money can be created by almost anyone, not just governments. When you write someone a check in exchange for having repaired your roof, you just created your own money. Before accepting your check and driving off in his truck, did the roof man know that you had sufficient funds in your bank account to cover the check or even whether such a bank existed in the first place? No, he didn't know any of this for sure. The roof man accepted your check only because he felt certain that you were not the sort of person who would write him a bad check. He *trusted* you.

Similarly, the roof man may assign your check as tuition to his child's piano teacher by endorsing the back of the check. She could subsequently pay it to a third party before someone finally deposits it into a bank and the funds to cover it are removed from your account. During this time, the check has been in circulation just like ordinary currency. But each party that accepted the check had to feel confident about the trustworthiness of the person behind the check, the "I" in the "IOU," if you will, which is what both a check and a dollar bill really are.

People have good reason to spurn currency from countries that renege on debt payments. In late 2001, Argentina notified its creditors that it was not going to pay over $130 billion in debt. It will be a long time before banks, companies, or individuals will again accept currency issued by the government of Argentina. The same thing happens to someone who writes bad checks to stores in his or her neighborhood. Pretty soon, the cashiers at local businesses place the check writer's name alongside their cash registers as a reminder that his or her word is no longer reliable and the checks must not be accepted.

The U.S. dollar has become the currency of choice for day-to-day transactions in many countries whose citizens lack confidence in their own currency. In Argentina, once the peso became shaky, virtually all real estate loans and other long-term commercial contracts were written in U.S. dollars. This means that Argentineans lacked confidence in those who minted and controlled the value of their currency.

The very word *dollar* is a reminder of the role of ethics in currency. The word evolved from the German word *Thal*, meaning "valley." In the sixteenth century a wealthy count known for his high ethical standards began minting silver coins near an old silver mine in the valley where he lived. The coins were known as "valley coins," or "Thalers." Because the German aristocrat maintained very strict tolerances on the weight and the purity of silver in each coin, his money's reputation grew; and it became a widely accepted and trusted medium of exchange. As Thalers spread across Europe, each country pronounced the word slightly differently; and when people such as the Dutch began minting their own coins, they called them *daalders* and later *dallers*.[4] The lesson of the Thaler is still true; anyone with a reputation for reliability can create money. Its nature is to serve as a medium of exchange between people and it should never be adulterated.

Two Jewish business professionals who clearly understood the nature of money were Robert Levitan and Charles Cohen, the chief executives of Flooz.com and Beenz.com, respectively. These two companies, until their demises in mid-2001, each attempted to create a version of Internet-based currency. You could buy Flooz.com's currency called "flooz" with a regular credit card payment and then redeem it for goods at the web sites of retailers that accepted flooz. Beenz, also redeemable at certain sites, were earned by spending money or time on certain other sites, such as MP3.com. (You could even buy flooz with your beenz.)

Although these two companies eventually failed, the prospects for some form of Internet currency are probably still good, although the vehicle may turn out to be the more conventional financial institutions who already possess the know-how, the infrastructure, and, above all, the trust. Money can be created by almost anyone, as long as a system of trust exists. Without it, people will not accept your flooz, beenz, or checks; and, ultimately, they won't even accept your dollars.

The problem with all private currencies, whether flooz, beenz, or your check, is obtaining information on the *reliability* of the issuer. Suppose you were selling an asset to, say, Mr. Jones, a man with vast financial resources and limitless integrity. He could write you a check drawn on an obscure bank in Albania, he could scrawl an IOU on the cocktail napkin, or he could just tell you that he'll messenger over the money in the morning. Each of these three choices would be acceptable to you and is an example of private currency. You would find that you could use each of these three forms of payment; each would be acceptable to your creditor as long as he knew of Mr. Jones by reputation. The problem is trust and reputation.

How do people discover the integrity of the issuer of the promise? The Internet has evolved a fascinating means for discovering the integrity of traders. Whether you purchase a used book from a private seller on Amazon.com or a brand new treadmill exerciser from a vendor on eBay.com, you will be asked to rate your vendor and the quality of the transaction. That rating becomes part of the trader's permanent record on the Internet and is instrumental in his or her ability to further conduct business. This is just the electronic equivalent of developing a reputation for honest business in a small-town environment, and it is just as effective.

MONEY IS INTANGIBLE: IT DEPENDS ON REPUTATION

Another reminder that money is really quite intangible, a mere symbol for something else, is the $9 billion that then-head of Ford Motor Company, Jacques Nasser, paid for two utter intangibles, the names "Jaguar" and "Volvo." Two brand names are worth $9 billion? That is correct. No factories were moved from England or Sweden to Detroit. No accumulated inventory of cars was shipped across the Atlantic. The owners of those two brands, Jaguar and Volvo, simply said the magic words, "The brand is now yours; send the check to my office." If three-quarters of the world's population were afflicted with amnesia on the day before the transaction closed, would the transaction have gone through? No, because the value of the brand name lies in the *reputation* built up over the years. If most customers have forgotten that Jaguar means "performance" and Volvo means "safety," then the names have lost their value.

Consider another example. Why do stocks like Coca-Cola sometimes sell for more than 40 times earnings and a huge premium to book value? Because people have come to understand that money is spiritual rather than tangible. Coca-Cola's value is not just in its factories and bottling plants. It is also in the company's management integrity and brand recognition, which are so much harder to quantify. That is why money is so often misunderstood.

Here's another case in point. In December 1994, after some political intrigue, the board of directors of the advertising agency Saatchi & Saatchi fired the founder of the company, Maurice Saatchi.[5] According to standard accounting rules, the dismissal of one of the Saatchi brothers was irrelevant to the balance sheet. Nevertheless, the stock, which had been trading on the New York Stock Exchange at about $9, immediately fell to $4. The market realized that without the brilliant mind and the compelling business connections of Maurice Saatchi, all that Saatchi & Saatchi shareholders owned were desks, chairs, and a soda machine.

These examples are intended to help you understand that money does not exist without a framework of intangible connectivity.

Let me warn you that any pithy definition of *money* is likely to be misleading. You see, although I can point at a long, tasty, yellow fruit and say "banana," it is simply not possible to provide intercultural definitions for abstract ideas. For instance, try to define the word *love* to an abused child. Under the best of circumstances and over time, the sad child could learn what *love* means; but nobody could define it meaningfully for her at the outset. Pointing at money and saying "paper" or "metallic discs" is missing the point.

Part of the reason you hold this book in your hands right now is to enable you to wrap your being around the idea of a powerful abstract—money. Money is a numeric analog for how you run your life and what you have done for others. Money is a *metaphor* for the strength of your human relationships. Unlike a swamp or a forest, money ceases to exist in the absence of people. Money is a combination of a claim and a promise. Money is intangible. It is only as good as the invisible network of trust that links vast numbers of humans into a loose kind of unity. It is a claim against other people for the goods and services you need, and it is a promise on their part to supply those goods and services to you.

A WIDESPREAD SYSTEM OF COMMON VALUES PRODUCES WEALTH

In 1991, Salomon, Inc., the parent of the large bond-trading firm Salomon Brothers, was rocked by charges of having used fraudulent bids in government bond auctions. Salomon was threatened with the loss of its right to participate in Treasury bond auctions, a crucial area of activity for the firm. Not only were the disclosures of wrongdoing embarrassing, but they were imperiling the very survival of the company. Key personnel were becoming convinced that their futures lay elsewhere, and lawsuits against Salomon were mounting. The general feeling was that of sharks circling.

During that summer, Warren Buffett, who owned a 16 percent equity stake in Salomon, arrived on the scene. By agreeing to step in himself as interim chairman and by agreeing to replace most of senior management, Buffett was able to persuade then U.S. Treasury Secretary Nicholas Brady not to exclude Salomon from the government's bond auctions. Buffett was also able to persuade many key Salomon people to remain, and he helped people regain confidence in the survival of the company. This scenario of one person saving a company happens often enough to demonstrate the spiritual roots of wealth. It was not just anyone who could have turned Salomon around. It had to be Warren Buffett—or at least it had to be some unusual person capable of instilling the same feelings of confidence and hope in the hearts of employees, government officials, and creditors that Buffett was able to generate. Saving Salomon required far more than just working one's way down a checklist of fiscal repair. It required spiritual energy. That may be the best term to use for what lies at the root of wealth—*spiritual energy*, a term that sounds wispy and weak but at the same time hints at power and potency.

A claim of money owed doesn't sound very substantial either, but that is deceiving. When you think of bank runs or when you think of dreadful inflation, such as that suffered by the Germans in the 1920s when they would have to drag pillowcases full of currency to the store in order to buy a loaf of bread, you see that a claim and a promise are only valuable if one very important feature exists: trust. The entire monetary system exists only because people have faith that the symbol of money that they carry in their wallets, be it in the form of credit card or cash, will be honored when they wish it to be. Without trust, the system collapses. Not for nothing does history's greatest engine of economic prosperity print on its currency, In God We Trust.

During a Senate committee hearing in 1912, crusading lawyer Samuel Untermeyer was trying to make the point that only the rich have access to capital, and he insisted to banker J. Pierpont Morgan that commercial credit is based on property and money. Morgan explained that the lawyer was wrong; that instead, *character* came first. Said Morgan, "A man I do not trust could not get money from me on all the bonds in Christendom."[6]

Imagine a society evolving so you can watch trust exerting its influence in the group's development. Ideally, you would need to conduct a 3,000-year experiment. Because it might be difficult to obtain grant financing for this kind of research, you can do exactly what Albert Einstein used to do when he lectured on relativity at the Max Planck Institute in Berlin. I learned of Einstein's practice during a long hike through the hills behind Pasadena, California, when the late Max Delbruck (who was a professor at the California Institute of Technology, a Nobel prize winner, and a DNA pioneer) recalled to my wife and me his times with Einstein in prewar Berlin. He related that Einstein explained that what he really wanted to do was cut the wires supporting the institute's elevators in order to measure the effect of the fall on the elevator's occupants. To his shocked audience, Einstein then explained that regulations prohibited this experiment, but they did not prohibit him from conducting exactly the same experiment in his mind. He then proceeded to do so, calling it a thought experiment. By conducting a thought experiment, you can imagine what trust does, and without expending capital and resources.

In the thought experiment regarding how trust is requisite in any money system, you place a baby boy and a baby girl on an utterly isolated desert island and stipulate a benign environment in which the babies not only survive, but also grow and thrive. You install sophisticated clandestine surveillance equipment so that, over the years, you can easily check in on how they are doing on that island paradise. I think that it is safe to assume that they will discover one another and that the island's population will increase to three, and then eventually to an entire tribe.

Further imagine that the tribespeople appear to be evolving into a fairly peaceful and productive group. As the years turn into centuries, they will, in all probability, develop agricultural skills and grow all manner of crops and will begin to use fire, eventually smelting iron and copper and slowly entering their steam age. By that time, they have probably split up into several tribes and groups. Obviously, in real life, not all cultures on the planet mastered the natural sciences and built a technological and industrialized future, but you can assume that this island society does so.

At some point, instead of them all practicing Spartan self-sufficiency, they will discover the advantages of specialization and trading. One farmer will become adept at raising sheep. Through trial and error plus diligence and care, he will succeed in producing wonderful wool. Another islander will similarly thrive as a dairy farmer. Yet a third produces the finest wheat. Each finds himself better off by exchanging his own product for those he needs. In other words, a barter system will naturally spring up. It has the natural advantage that both the quality of the commodities as well as the available quantities are far greater than they had been while each farmer had independently tried to provide for all his needs.

At some point the natural deficiencies in the barter system will become evident. Perhaps the shepherd will knock on the door of the dairyman, offering to trade the fleece of a sheep for a quantity of cheese and milk. The following discussion might ensue.

SHEPHERD: Good morning. I've come to trade this fluffy, warm wool for some of your cheese and milk. This is the finest wool you'll see in these parts, and I could really use some nice cool milk and a few pounds of cheese.

DAIRY FARMER: It's so hot out that my cows are producing steamed milk! The last thing I need is wool. Come back when the weather turns cold.

This impasse is suddenly broken when the shepherd has a brilliant idea.

SHEPHERD: Eureka! I will give you some little metallic discs, and you give me all the butter and cheese I need. When the weather turns, you bring the discs to me, and I'll hand over the wool that you will then need.

The money inventor presented his proposal so enthusiastically that he utterly failed to sense the growing skepticism in his audience.

DAIRY FARMER: You want me to hand over my creamy milk and tasty cheese in exchange for these metal discs? How do I know you'll accept them back? And, what if I need carrots this week? I'll have given you my milk, and I'll be left with less to trade to the vegetable farmer. He certainly won't accept these pretty little discs from me. And what if you die before I redeem my discs for your wool?

SHEPHERD: No, wait, let me explain. It is so much easier to store metallic discs than it is to store butter and cheese. You must give my system a try.

But the dairy farmer and his family were dubious, even if the glib shepherd assured them that his system would solve all sorts of problems. They could hardly feed their children metallic discs, could they? Of course, if everyone in the village bought into the system simultaneously, it might have worked. The problem is that most people are far too careful with their hard-earned harvest to let it out the door on just a promise.

Not only does barter dramatically limit commercial exchange, as you saw in the shepherd/farmer thought experiment, but without money there can be only limited wealth accumulation. I cannot store cheese indefinitely, but I can store your promise. What is more, storing your promise need not cost me expensive warehouse capacity. I can store it by means of strips of colored paper that symbolize your promise and my claim; or I could store it by a particular arrangement of iron oxide molecules. If our trust system was in really good shape, I could store it merely by your word.

It is clear, however, that without some sort of invisible network of trust throughout the communal system, there can be no money. The trust system has to precede the money. It would be hard to imagine money becoming popular without trust in place first. Money developing before a broad web of community trust is difficult to imagine in this thought experiment or in any other one.

Assuming a monetary system is working, how do you decide the value of each object or service? How many discs of metal should be exchanged for each pound of cheese or bale of wool? Who should decide whether a pair of shoes should be the equivalent of 4, 40, or 400 dollars?

VALUE: HOW MUCH SOMETHING IS WORTH

What is the value of a current model Volvo S80 sedan? Well, I know that on the Volvo's window sticker on the showroom floor of a Chicago dealer, the manufacturer's suggested retail price is shown to be $42,150. But is that the vehicle's value? If, after much bargaining, the dealer allows one customer to drive it away for $39,850, is that its real value? If the dealer then sells another identical vehicle to a less argumentative individual for the full $42,150, has the value of a new Volvo S80 increased?

Objective Value

It is very difficult to state an *objective* value for any object. It tends to depend on where and for whom. For the first customer, the car's value was obviously more than $39,850, because were it not so, she would hardly have yielded that much money for it. Had its value to her been exactly $39,850, she would have been in no rush to purchase because the exchange would have been economically neutral to her. As it is, the car was worth $39,850 plus some additional dollar figure that represented her need for the car and the emotional attraction she felt toward the car. The price of the things you purchase is usually less than the total value you place on those things. Were it not so, why would you go to the trouble of the exchange?

Now the value of the Volvo may be difficult to establish, but fortunately its weight is not. The weight of the Volvo is pretty much the same whether it is weighed in Chicago or in a jungle. That is also true for its length and its color, but it is not true for its value. For example, what is the current value of an identical model Volvo if it were parachuted into the mountainous jungles of Borneo, 1,000 miles east of Singapore? There, in a land with no roads and no gasoline, the 3,600 pounds of metal is of no great value. The primitive tribesman who encountered this gift from the sky could best utilize it as a sort of home or fort that offered welcome protection from the arrows of his enemies. What might persuade him to exchange the car? I am not he, so I don't know exactly; maybe seven yams.

Similarly, a large iceberg in the North Atlantic doesn't have very much value, but the same growler towed to the Persian Gulf and placed in a dry dock in Bahrain to melt could have considerable worth. The many millions of gallons of fresh water that it would yield are worth far more there than they would be worth in Greenland.

How Hebrew Defines Value

From my studies, I know that the Hebrew language appears, almost magically, to convey the deeper meaning of words through the structure of its vocabulary and syntax. This ability of Hebrew to shine a light onto the real meaning of words can be helpful. This insight to value can be seen in one of ancient Hebrew's words for "money"—*kesef.* This word contains within it the word *kaf,* meaning "sole of the foot" or "palm of the hand." The traditional explanation is that those are the two ways to add value to a commodity or product. You may work on it, a process symbolized by the hands, or you may transport it somewhere else, the movement being symbolized by the feet.

I remember once standing on the banks of the River Rhine and noticing two almost identical, fully loaded coal barges traveling in opposite directions. I asked my father, an esteemed rabbi, why each barge couldn't have simply remained where it originally was. He explained that each of the separate barge journeys was the result of two people striking a deal for the supply and purchase of coal. The two sets of traders did not know one another. Neither did either of them know of the local availability of a bargeful of coal. It was an anomaly resulting from inadequate communication.

There just wasn't sufficient human interaction. When that is rectified, my father told me, all the traders will talk to one another, and the local price of coal would drop, reflecting the absence of a transport cost in its price. That will be good for consumers, who will pay less for their energy; and it will be good for the traders who will probably sell more coal, he explained. It might appear to be worse for the bargemen, but that is not so either. Their coal and all the other commodities they buy will cost them less, too, so things will work out. In any event, they will be busy enough shipping the products for which no local source exists.

You could say that increased communication saves everybody money, which adds to their wealth. That day, I began to understand how knowledge can add value. Furthermore, I began to see that there was no infallible encyclopedia in which one could look up the value of anything. The value number always depends on at least two humans and on what else is happening at that place and at that time.

TO CREATE VALUE, YOU MUST UNDERSTAND VALUE

You may be wondering why you need to know all this information when all you really want is to increase your revenue. Remember, it is not enough to merely *know* things; you are going to need to absorb them into your being.

Value is not like any other measurement. I could look at an old glass jar and easily determine its weight. To do so, all I would need is an accurate scale. With a ruler, I could tell you its height, and it wouldn't take very advanced mathematics for me to calculate its volume. The figures that I would arrive at are true regardless of where I would move that jar, and they remain true regardless of where on earth (or even in space, as long as I speak of its mass rather than its weight) I place it.

The value of that glass jar, however, is quite different. There is no instrument to measure its value other than a very special human construct called a "marketplace." Even if the jar happened to be created by an innovative Pacific Northwest glass artist, the famous Dale Chihuly, its value would be rather low were it in the hands of someone ignorant of its artistic value and to whom it only had utilitarian value as a water carrier. Such a person might even toss it away when he or she finds a larger or more robust jar. However, to an art collector, it might have significant value; and to an art collector who received it as a token of affection from a loved one, it might have still more value. Unlike an object's physical parameters such as length, height, or volume, its value is more of an intangible or *spiritual* parameter, which can only be determined in the context of other human beings.

What is often mystifying is how an object's value can increase without any corresponding increase in its physically observable measurements. If a barge of grain increased in value because another 50 tons of wheat was loaded onto the now topped-up barge, you would understand that it now is worth more. No mystery there. However, when the barge of wheat seems to increase in value simply because the trader who purchased it happens to have knowledge about a certain place where grain is badly needed, the transaction reeks of sorcery or cheating.

This may be partially why the trader is viewed so often with a mixture of envy and loathing. For example, in England, right up to World War II, describing someone as a "merchant" was to dismiss him with disdain and contempt. Somehow, this upstart was presuming to hobnob with the aristocracy on the basis of having amassed vast quantities of money in a mystical fashion that nobody understood. Friedrich Hayek, the twentieth-century Austrian economist who was a professor at the London School of Economics, put it this way: "Value is not an attribute or physical property possessed by things themselves, irrespective of their relations to men, but solely an aspect of these relations that enables men to take account, in their decisions about the use of such things, of the better opportunities others might have for their use."[7]

Get it? You only know the value of that thing you own after finding out what other people would give you *in exchange* for it. That is why there is profit to be made by roaming the isolated countryside and purchasing old furniture for resale in your antique store in the city. The farmer would rather sell it to you than truck all his pieces into the city himself without even knowing what he will succeed in selling and what he will have to transport back home again.

A hundred years before Hayek, an economics professor at the University of Vienna, Carl Menger, said that value "is a judgment economizing men make about the importance of goods at their disposal for the maintenance of their lives and well being."[8]

Yes, that's right, value is a *judgment* made by men; but not all men will always agree on the value of something. If they did, there could be no trade, because there would be no reason to trade. Any object or commodity would be worth to you exactly what it is worth to me. Why would either of us conduct a trade? The entire point is that different people at different times and different places evaluate things differently.

This link between economic creativity and human uniqueness was well

established in Jewish culture. A millennium before the FBI started identifying miscreants by employing the principle of fingerprint uniqueness, revered
Jewish sages were asking this question: Why would God choose to place the
mark of human uniqueness upon the fingertips? That each and every human
being should possess a mark of uniqueness was no problem. God declared
that He would create man in His image. What does "in His image" mean?
Talk about unattainable goals! To Jewish scholarship, this meant that humans
would resemble God in two important ways: (1) Alone among the creatures
of the world, they would possess the ability to create things, just like the Deity
Himself did. (2) Each human would be as unique as God is. What better
way to link these twin Divine similarities found in humans than by placing
the mark of uniqueness, the fingerprint, on that organ with which humans
create—the fingers.[9]

In 1570, a renowned Jewish scholar explained that although the value
of all things depends on their relationships with human beings, those values
also depend on place and time. In other words, the value that humans place
on things also depends on the point in the space-time continuum that
those things occupy. The great Rabbi Yehuda Loew of sixteenth-century
Prague put it this way: Time and space are best understood when linked
together into one concept.[10] He wrote this exactly 300 years before Einstein
submitted his paper on the special theory of relativity, and Herman Minkowski
pointed out that Einstein's new view of the universe only made sense if one
viewed time and space as a kind of joined reality. "Henceforth, space by itself, and time by itself, are doomed to fade away into mere shadows, and
only a kind of union of the two will preserve an independent reality."[11] This
bond between space and time is embedded in Jewish culture and thus was
always available to Jews, who, not surprisingly, based their commercial strategies on it. Jews understood that value could be added not only by catering
to human uniqueness, but also by other forms of creative endeavor.

Physical work is not the only way to manipulate space and time creatively.
It is not necessary for everyone to be engaged in shaping, molding, mining,
growing, or constructing an object. It is not necessary for everyone to be
occupied by transporting the object and neither is it necessary for everyone to be storing things while time passes. One can also effectively manipulate space and time with information and with transactions. It then
follows that one can add value simply by conducting transactions with
other people.

FINANCIAL RECORD KEEPING ON WHICH EVERYONE CAN AGREE

What do the Harlem Globetrotters and the late comedian-pianist Victor Borge have in common? They both prove the principle that if you want to explore the unconventional, it helps to first have a firm grip on the conventional. The basketball showteam are first and foremost expert basketball players. The entertainer who referred to himself as a Great Dane was an accomplished classical pianist before he discovered that making people laugh paid him better.

Similarly, looking at money in an unusual way becomes easier once you are well rooted in the generally accepted perspectives. In other words, understanding conventional bookkeeping is very useful. If you are already able to read and understand financial statements, you are ahead of the game. If you are one of those people whose terrified eyes routinely skip past any columns of numbers you may encounter, my advice is going to be tough to take but necessary. Like the advice to those with, say, a fear of elevators, the best antidote is simply to keep riding the elevator until the phobia is driven away. The following advice is the only way to lose your fear of numbers.

You need to develop comfort and fluency with numbers. This will bring you three benefits:

1. *You will become accustomed to thinking and talking with precision.* You will become comfortable asking for exact numbers instead of accepting terms like "a living wage," "affordable housing," and "suitable compensation." You will start sounding crisp and knowledgeable and stop waffling with such phrases as "to tell you the truth," and "well, candidly."

2. *You will develop confidence in your judgment* about a particular transaction instead of going with your "gut" and hoping for the best. A wise supermarket shopper can almost instantaneously reduce the per-jar price of mayonnaise to a per-ounce price so brand and package comparisons will have validity. Similarly, with numeric literacy you will be able to competently compare deals and investments yourself.

3. *You will feel more alive because you will feel more related to the world around you.* I know that accountancy is not usually thought of as the most exciting of professions, but I am not suggesting you become an accountant. I am advising you to grow to love numbers, not in themselves, but as a language of communication that can bring intimacy with the inanimate.

Sometimes the earliest warning signs of declining fiscal health at your place of employment can be found in the annual report. I want you to become familiar enough with the world of financial statements that you look at everything and assimilate all the data. Don't look only at balance sheets, which note a company's assets and liabilities. You should also study all other parts of a financial report, like the cash flow statement, which can alert the knowledgeable observer to dangerous conditions such as inventories rising faster than sales.

Normally, companies record the revenue that plays a role in the stated earnings when merchandise is delivered to customers, even though the customers may not pay for that merchandise for say, 60 days. The cash flow statement tells how much cash is actually received. If you notice that the revenue of a company climbs and, thus, its earnings soar while cash received lags far behind, you may be watching the incipient stages of a bad debt crisis.

I don't mean to immerse you in the technicalities of financial accounting, but I do want to recommend it as a vital tool in your quest for greater prosperity. Not only will it bring the three benefits I enumerated, but it will equip you for one more task: Once you have achieved numerical literacy, you will be ready to *compile and maintain your own accurate set of financial records*. Of course, sophisticated software tools exist today that will enable even the numerical illiterate to keep their records, but you want more than that, don't you? There is nothing wrong with using one of those software packages, but you will increase your ability to make on-the-spot, intuitive judgments if you really understand what the numbers mean instead of just knowing which buttons to press on your laptop computer.

Now that I have told you a little about becoming competent at the conventional systems of keeping track of money, you must consider less conventional, but no less reliable and no less useful, ways of understanding money and value.

HUMAN INTERACTION = WEALTH

Imagine a young man strolling through a modern suburban shopping mall. He has exactly $20 in his pocket, and every fiber of his being yearns for a pair of those sneakers with little lights in the heels that flash with each step you take. All he can think of is how cool he will look if only he could find an affordable pair of those shoes he so ardently covets. He enters a shoe store to be graciously greeted by a total stranger, the proprietor. After hearing her customer's request, the owner retreats to her stockroom and returns with a box. She kneels before the young man and quickly slips the fancy footwear on the customer's foot. The young man is delighted with the elegant effect and happily hands over the required price, which just happens to be the $20 he had in his pocket.

What does the emotional balance sheet look like? The storekeeper is ecstatic as she places the $20 bill in her till. Perhaps this sale helped her reach her sales target for the day. Someone unaccustomed to commerce might assume that for her to be so happy, she must have exploited the customer. Is the young buyer suffering from buyer's remorse? No, he is a jubilant male exuding happy confidence because he knows he walks in truly enviable shoes. (Stalin would have found this little scene strange, because this transaction made two people happy instead of making one happy and one sad, as he would have expected from an exploitation.)

How does the financial balance sheet look? Suppose this little transaction is viewed as a minisystem. Assume the young man has only $20 to his name—all the wealth he possesses is $20. For simplicity's sake, ignore the entire inventory in the shoe store, and assume that this pair of illuminating sneakers was the only stock in the store. In this model then, how much wealth does the storekeeper own? Well, she owns one pair of electric sneakers that she bought from the manufacturer for $10. What is that box containing the shoes worth to her? Well, more than the $10 she paid the maker, otherwise she wouldn't have paid it. She assumes she will sell the shoes for more than she paid for them. Although she is hoping for more, she is willing to part with them for $15. If she were preparing a financial statement, she would list her net worth as:

Inventory: One pair of shoes valued @ $15

Conventional bookkeeping conducted under the generally accepted accounting principles (GAAP)[12] would prefer her to list her net worth as merely the $10 she paid for the inventory or perhaps even only $5, being the amount for which she could quickly dispose of them at a flea market. However, as long as she has faith that customers will continue to flock into the mall, and as long as she is confident in her ability to predict fashion trends, it makes more sense to calculate her net worth on the basis of the amount she expects the sale of the shoes to yield.

Although it is obvious that GAAP rules have their place in the wide scheme of accounting, these rules can also mislead in certain circumstances by forcing one to undervalue real assets. For instance, during the mid-1990s, America Online (AOL) sustained very large customer-acquisition costs. You may remember multiple free copies of AOL software discs tumbling out whenever you opened your mailbox. They were so ubiquitous that bars were using AOL software disks as drink coasters.

In its accounting, AOL made the case that the money spent on sending out millions of copies of free software was *invested*, not spent. The company claimed that it invested the money to acquire a valuable asset, namely, a massive pool of AOL users, each of whom was going to pay AOL about $20 a month. Thus AOL felt justified in capitalizing those acquisition costs. Auditors and analysts were outraged, claiming that by capitalizing those costs, AOL was just trying to artificially inflate its earnings figures. The clamor forced AOL to restate its financials, this time classifying about $400 million as expenses instead of as capital expenduture. This naturally meant that AOL's reported earnings had to be reduced by that amount.

Who was right? Well, by the end of the decade, AOL's market value was about $150 billion, so the contested item in AOL's financial statement represented about one-quarter of one percent of the company's market value. The analysts were not wrong, but I would imagine that, based on their own figures, few of them invested in AOL; so they were not right either. It is sometimes hard to figure out the value of an asset because of intangible factors.

One of those intangible factors is faith in tomorrow. How much would your assets be worth right now if the world were coming to an end in one hour after being hit by an unstoppable meteorite? The correct answer is probably "zero." How much would your assets be worth if you and everyone around you were going to live forever? The correct answer is "probably a great deal," if for no other reason than the magic of compound interest. For normal people in normal times, however, life spans are presumed to be somewhere between the next hour and forever. Thus, few people truly value their assets in their minds to be no more than what they would fetch in a distress fire-sale tomorrow morning. People tend to presume that normality will continue and will allow them to liquidate at advantageous prices and in an orderly fashion without even alerting anyone else of the need to sell.

CALCULATING TOTAL VALUE OF GOODS IN THE TOTAL ECONOMY

Look again at the young customer. His balance sheet when he wandered into the mall might look like this:

Cash in hand (or pocket, to be precise) = $20

The total value found within this minieconomy would be the sum of the wealth of the storeowner, $15, and the young man's wealth, $20, for a total of $35.

Now you must create a posttransaction balance sheet. Again, ignoring all other assets, after the friendly transaction, the wealth of the shoe-store proprietor consists of a $20 bill in her cash register. How about the young man? How much wealth does he have? Well, that would be the value of the shoes in his eyes. One way of finding out that value would be to find out how much he might be able to sell those shoes for at a garage sale. Although an accountant might prefer that method, the young man has no intention of selling his shoes; so the garage-sale price would not be an accurate picture of his financial well-being.

Actually, using the conventional form of appraisal would mean that virtually every purchase makes one poorer, and the logical approach would be never to purchase anything at all. Of course, you know that driving a newly purchased car out of the dealer's lot means that you cannot get your exact purchase price back. If just then you needed to convert the car back into money, you would find that you have lost many dollars by owning a new car for an hour. In this scenario, your wealth has been drastically diminished by purchase of an automobile. Your balance sheet will show that you are poorer for your purchase. However, the only reasons for having to immediately sell your new car are that you planned very badly and bought a vehicle you couldn't afford or that the economy took a downturn and you needed the value found within your new car for food.

Remember the role of faith. You don't invest, purchase, or even marry on the basis of the world coming to an end. While putting away savings for the inevitable rainy day, you operate on the presumption that tomorrow will be better than today. Rain may fall, but it will be a sprinkle, not a Noah's flood. Therefore, there is no reason to value your new car on the basis of what some mean used-car dealer might give you were you in dire straights. Instead, you can safely value it at the figure it deserves in your life.

Ancient Jewish wisdom teaches that this is one very valid way to evaluate your wealth. Most people do not sell their cars shortly after buying them. Instead, they enjoy driving them; they lavish care on their vehicles, taking great pride in owning them. This style of bookkeeping shows that the manner of calculating your wealth is to ask yourself how much you would accept in return for parting with your new car.[13]

Similarly, you can now evaluate the young man's wealth by means of another little thought experiment. Imagine walking up to him as he exits the mall. "Would you please sell us those scintillating shoes for $20?" you ask him. He refuses. Why should he sell them? He wants such a pair of shoes and would only have to return to the store to buy another pair. So you up the ante. "Would you please sell your shoes for $25?" Not worth it, he thinks. Five dollars isn't enough to cover the time and trouble of returning to the store. Perhaps that vendor won't have any more pairs in his size. Forget it.

However, you persist. "How about selling them for $30?" Now he hesitates. He can make a profit of $10, and most likely the store only a few yards away will have another pair in stock. But, he thinks to himself, if these people are so eager for my shoes, perhaps they'll be willing to pay even more? "All right, I'll sell them to you" he might say, "but for $35." You probably don't want them for $35. Truth be told, you don't want them at all. Remember that you are simply conducting an experiment, which you have just successfully concluded. You have discovered that the value for those shoes on his balance sheet is $35.

Now you must calculate the total posttransaction value found within this minieconomy. That would be the sum of the wealth of the store owner, which is the $20 in her cash register, and the young man's wealth, composed of a pair of shoes he values at $35, giving a total of $55.

Here is a table showing the wealth of the minisystem both before and after the transaction:

	Customer has:	Store Owner has:	Together, they have:
Before transaction:	$20	$15	$35
After transaction:	$35	$20	$55

The customer has gained $15 by the transaction, whereas the storekeeper has gained $5. The aggregate increase in wealth in the minisystem is $20. Remember that emotional satisfaction has value, too. The customer possesses an emotional attachment to his new shoes, whereas to the storekeeper that same pair of shoes was merely part of her trading inventory. For this reason, goods are often worth even more to the customer than they are to the supplier who sold them in the first place. However, the trading incentive is diminished if the dealer falls in love with her inventory and becomes reluctant to part with it.

HOW JEWISH TRADITION ASSESSES THE VALUE OF POSSESSIONS

The importance of distinguishing between your personal possessions and your trading inventory was emphasized to Jews more than 2,000 years ago when Rabbi Isaac admonished: "A person should always keep his money in three parts; one-third in real estate, one-third in merchandise, and one-third in readily available cash."[14] This remains good advice today. First, owning some real estate is viewed not only as a wise economic step, but also as helpful for personal growth. The good Lord makes more people, but He doesn't make more land. The resulting rise in the value of real estate owned helps to impart a sense of purposeful destiny to its owner.

Second, Rabbi Isaac's advice is obvious for those who own stores or who are active in other businesses requiring investment in inventory. However, even people holding down regular office jobs, for instance, can also benefit from this wisdom. For example, investing part of one's assets in moveable property that can be sold and traded is sound conduct. Today, vast armies of people augment their income by developing an expertise in Victorian porcelain figurines, old firearms, antique furniture, or almost anything else. They purchase these items at estate sales and garage sales and then sell them at a

profit on the Internet or at fairs and flea markets. Quite apart from the potential for gain in having some of your assets in this kind of tradable merchandise is the benefit you realize from being constantly reminded that you
are a business professional. This kind of leisure-time trading activity that starts
off as a hobby for many folks often ends up causing wonderful changes in
people's fortunes.

Third, keeping part of one's assets in cash allows one to be prepared for
emergencies. It also allows one to exploit unexpected opportunities.

Remember that shoe store? Now imagine that several young men crowded
into it at the same time, all lusting for the last remaining pair of psychedelic
sneakers. The storekeeper might well decide that the best way to determine
who gets the shoes is to see who wants them most. One way to measure desire
is to find out who will bid the most money for them. In all probability, the
price would have been driven higher than $20. Now, let's imagine the store-
keeper postponing the conclusion of the auction till the next day. With
grumbles, the footwear fetishists leave the store and promise to be back in
the morning. Overnight, the proprietor evaluates her wealth and feels certain that the mere demand for her merchandise has increased the bottom line
of her balance sheet.

This example is not that different from all those stock market investors
who gleefully estimated their high net worth based on what they saw as
high demand for the shares they owned. Even such important numbers as
the market capitalization of public companies depends on the feelings that
a large number of people have about the stock of those companies. Were
large numbers of people to suddenly vanish off the face of the earth,
one certain consequence would be a substantial drop in the value of those
shares. As you can see, human interaction can produce wealth, once you get
accustomed to seeing things through the eyes of cosmic truth, even if it is a
little unconventional.

One of the great Internet success stories has been eBay.com, whose business plan called for it to become, quite simply, an electronic peddler. It has
done so and thrived. Consider the role of the old-fashioned peddler coming
through the village. From one family, he purchases an old table that has sat
unused in their basement for years. To them it is junk, so they happily accept the $10 the peddler offers them. He later sells that piece of furniture to
another family, who needs just that size table and doesn't mind the scars from
years of usage. Instead of spending $60 on a new table, they consider them-
selves fortunate to acquire this one for $20.

Again, compute the value brought to the village by the passage of this one peddler. The first family is now $10 richer than they had been. The second family has $40 in their bank account that they no longer need to spend on a new table. The peddler has $10 he didn't have before. By simply facilitating one transaction, the peddler has added to the aggregate wealth of the community by a total of $60. Now multiply this effect by the vast number of transactions facilitated by eBay, and you can easily see how the company is succeeding by creating value.

JEWISH TRADITION ESPOUSES THE MOVEMENT OF MONEY

Money helps to create additional wealth by moving from person to person. If, as a result of economic anxiety, people place all their money in their mattresses and keep it there, the system begins to wind down and experiences a recession, or worse. One of the terms used for money in Hebrew is *zuz*, which actually means "to move." Money must be kept moving. I must trade, which means allowing someone else to do those things for me that I do not do effectively myself. In this way, I can increase value for everyone.

The late leader of the Lubavitch Hassidic movement based in Brooklyn, New York, Rabbi Menachem Mendel Schneerson, well understood the secrets of money. (I was privileged to meet with him privately in 1974 and we discussed some of these matters. I gained much understanding from him.) As part of his blessing to people, he was accustomed to distribute one-dollar bills. More than one spectacularly successful entrepreneur attributes his success largely to the Lubavitcher Rebbe and his dollar bill.

During the Rebbe's lecture delivered during the Jewish holiday of Tabernacles in 1983, he said: "People are different—differently endowed with talents, resources and opportunities. Money can deepen these differences when it is used to hoard wealth, reward privilege, and exploit the needy. But money is far more suited to unite and equalize. It is the ultimate abstractor—converting goods, talent, and toil into a commodity that can easily be traded and shared. It is a medium of generosity and cooperation between men and between nations, a consolidator of resources to a common end."

Here's another, real-world example of the importance of keeping money in motion. In December 1995, when fire destroyed the Massachusetts plant where he manufactured the Polartec fabric used in outdoor clothing, 70-year-old Aaron Feuerstein did not pocket the $300 million insurance payout and call it quits. Instead, he kept all the idled employees on payroll and set about rebuilding his factory. At the dedication of the new plant, Feuerstein, an Orthodox Jew, offered this Hebrew prayer: "I thank you majestic God of the universe for restoring to Malden Mills and its employees our life and soul." A rebuilt factory is their "life and soul"? Yes, Aaron Feuerstein got it right. Earning one's living is inextricably bound up with a human's life and soul. Money is the key. To succeed in this noble endeavor of creating wealth, you must know money in general and also specifically come to know your own.

Paradoxically, like love, money is best won by renouncing a need to totally possess. The more fixated people are upon both money and love, the more trouble they seem to have finding them. For money, at least, an easy remedy exists. Ceremonially release your grip on your money through regular acts of charity. If the concept of charity did not exist, those who seek wealth would need to invent it. Philanthropy is as necessary for creating wealth as sunshine is for growing flowers. The next chapter will explore this fascinating relationship and how to use it in your quest.

YOUR PATH TO PROSPERITY

- *Regardless of your past performance in this area, turn over a new leaf and start developing your trustworthiness.* Trust is essential to any monetary system and to successful wealth creation. Promise less than you deliver is the advice of Rabbi Hillel in *Sayings of the Fathers*, and it is good advice for us all. In other words, always do more for other people than they expect. Not only will you surprise and delight them, but you will be setting the stage for enhancing your business effectiveness.

  For example, establish an almost inviolable rule for yourself that you always return calls within 24 hours. Respond carefully and specifically to questions and requests from family members and associates. Some people hope to postpone unpleasant confrontation by responding vaguely and ambiguously to a request, instead of simply saying "no." Their family members or associates misinterpret the verbal waffling to have meant the agreement or the concession they sought. When you later attempt clarification, you come across as evasive and untrustworthy. It is just as important for you to appear trustworthy in your own eyes as it is to appear so in the eyes of others. You must think of yourself as an upright kind of person, which you can do only if you really are trustworthy.

- *Learn a specific and very valuable new skill: namely, how to read financial statements.* At the very least, become more familiar with them. Please don't dismiss this important component to the Ten Commandments program. On your time management plan, dedicate some serious time over the next few months to mastering this important skill.

    You should be able to achieve this goal on your own with the help of a good book such as John Tracy's *How to Read a Financial Report.*[15] You might be tempted to neglect this step, thinking that you are not about to become an accountant. That would be a mistake. Mastering this vital skill starts you on the road to visualizing yourself as a successful business professional.

    Once you have studied the material and practiced the exercises in the book you choose, send away for the annual reports of several public companies. It does not really matter which companies, although it would be more interesting if they were companies active in industries that interest you. Make sure that you receive and understand the cash-flow statement; public companies are required to release them once each quarter. Work your way through them slowly, making certain at every step that you understand what is being conveyed. It is not hard to do; it's just basic arithmetic once you have caught on to the concepts. If you have trouble, find a friendly accountant; or, if necessary, enroll in an evening accounting course at a local college.

- *Prepare and maintain your own personal financial statements.* Your statements don't have to be of major accounting firm quality. You might already have prepared your annual and monthly budgets and cash-flow statements, as well as your balance sheet. If not, you should now do so. Either of the two major personal accounting packages, "Quicken" by Intuit or "Money" by Microsoft, will help you develop an accurate financial picture. You need to know your money, and this is how to know it. You need to know your exact financial situation because that is what you are intending to improve. You can hardly measure improvement if you have no way of keeping score. Finally, examine your figures monthly.

- *Search for your own "tropical island" on which to successfully market your goods and services.*   A dentist I once knew sold his practice to sail around the world for a couple of years. He had hoped to augment his income en route by practicing his craft. Unfortunately, most of the remote islands he visited lacked electricity to operate his high-tech tools and instruments. Furthermore, their inhabitants had little interest in the cosmetic dentistry that had been his specialty. He quickly discovered, however, that he possessed another skill that was far more valuable in the palm-tree-encircled boat anchorages he frequented. His hobby of scuba diving allowed him to do underwater repairs and lost-anchor retrievals for his fellow yachtsmen. Back home in Seattle, scuba diving would not have earned him anything at all. Among the South Sea Islands, his dental diploma was worthless. You, too, possess skills, aptitudes, and experience in which lie real value, provided you locate the people to whom your "merchandise" would be most valuable.

Act Rich: Give Away 10 Percent of Your After-Tax Income

Through the mystical alchemy of money, giving charity jump-starts wealth creation.

Hanna Bandes worked as a professional storyteller, using her dramatic skills to excite both children and adults about Jewish history and traditions. To drum up business, she developed a mailing list of synagogues and religious schools to which she sent regular advertising mailings. Her very first paid job was for a local synagogue. She describes it as having been such an embarrassing disaster that she removed that institution's address from her future mailings, knowing that it would never hire her again. Hanna said, "The life of an artist can be precarious, and besides telling stories I did temporary work to make ends meet. Every month I paid my bills, but sometimes it was a real struggle. I knew of the Torah rule about tithing from my earnings, but in my financial position I didn't see how I could possibly give ten percent. I rationalized that since I was performing for Jewish charitable organizations, I was giving time instead of money."

Then one evening, she found herself inspired by a speaker who explained the value of tithing from one's income. On the spot, she decided she would donate to charity 10 percent of the fees from her very next storytelling job, which is exactly what she did. A few days later, Hanna received a phone call from the synagogue where she had given that first miserable performance. "We've built a new sanctuary and will be dedicating it. Will you tell stories at our dedication? I'm afraid all we can offer is $xxx," the lady on the phone told Hanna, mentioning a fee far higher than she would have asked.

A coincidence, perhaps, but Hanna believes not. "That wasn't the only job that came in unexpectedly. Within weeks of deciding to give away ten percent of my storytelling income, that income doubled. And the principle has proven to be true in the ensuing years. As long as I tithe, my freelance income is reliable. If I forget, it dries up."[1]

All religious traditions stress the importance of giving to charity; however, Judaism's impact on its followers is augmented by its unique approach to charity. The Midrash on the Book of Proverbs for instance insists that "if you see someone donating to charity, be assured that his wealth is increasing." The almost impenetrable textbook of Jewish mysticism, the esoteric *Zohar*, states, "He who donates much to charity becomes richer because of it inasmuch as he opens up a channel for God's blessing to reach him."[2] What is the value of these ancient statements of faith to a modern, and perhaps even secularized, business professional? Just this: They have survived as part of a living culture of oral transmission. That means something. It means they have passed the test of credibility. Let me explain.

Watch people walking down a sidewalk on which a ladder has been set to lean against the second story of the adjacent building. The easiest passage is directly along the sidewalk and under the ladder. Yet as you watch, you will observe most pedestrians avoiding that route, preferring the narrow and congested passage outside the foot of the ladder. Is this because everyone is superstitious and recalls that walking under a ladder brings bad luck? I don't think this adequately explains everyday behavior. The real reason that most of us avoid walking beneath a ladder is not superstition but common sense. The superstition followed reality—it did not cause it. Over the years, enough people walking beneath a ladder were struck by a tool dropped by a careless workman aloft. Large enough numbers of people who ignored their grandmothers' admonitions not to walk beneath a ladder collected a dollop of paint on their heads. Little by little, over perhaps hundreds of years, the culture absorbed the lesson—it is indeed bad luck to walk beneath a ladder.

Far fewer people avoid black cats. This is because no cause and effect has been observed by rational people over the years between black cats and bad luck. Only a small number of loopy and superstitious cranks worry about black cats, but nearly everybody worries about walking under ladders, for very good reason.

Similarly, over hundreds of years—well, actually thousands—the connection between giving charity and increased wealth has been observed. Ancient Jewish wisdom is not prescribing a behavior as much as it is describing a reality. Giving money away increases the wealth of the donor. People who are part of an orally transmitted culture know this to be true. Too much anecdotal evidence keeps popping up. Many Jews are still raised today knowing that giving charity is not only a good thing to do but is also a rather smart thing for ambitious people to do. If you seek out philanthropic friends, you too will hear accounts that appear to mysteriously link effect to cause, the effect of wealth caused by giving charity.

WHY PEOPLE GIVE TO CHARITY— EVEN WHEN IT'S NOT RATIONAL

Steven Landsburg, an immensely readable professor of economics at the University of Rochester, has written on charitable giving.[3] Surveys show that about two-thirds of U.S. households give to charity and that they tend to spread their giving among a number of different causes. On the surface, this seems a little irrational because in giving, unlike investing, diversifying makes little sense. Donors could increase the impact for the cause in which they most believe by channeling all of their giving to that one cause. Yet as irrational as it may be, most people continue giving of their income to a number of different causes. The reason is that they don't always base their decisions (particularly economic decisions) on purely rational grounds. The same person who yesterday drove across town to purchase a dress at a sale might well pay away yesterday's savings today in the fee at a parking lot instead of parking at a metered space three or four blocks away.

Rationality is a poor tool to use in trying to understand how people interact with money. Imagine a chef trying to determine whether his oven is working by using a thermometer taken from a steel manufacturing plant. Because it only registers temperatures from 1,000 degrees to 2,500 degrees, it won't budge when placed in the cook's 400-degree oven, misleading him into believing that his oven is faulty. Of course, his oven is fine; he was simply using the wrong instrument.

Or consider the case of an engineer trying to determine whether any radio waves are penetrating into a shielded room. He could carry an ordinary portable AM radio into his sanctuary and determine that no radio signals in the frequency range of about 500 kilohertz to 1600 kilohertz are present, but that particular instrument would fail to inform him of whether other kinds of radio waves were present.

Rationality is an excellent instrument for solving puzzles and paradoxes, but it is rather less effective when used to explain human behavior. Even Professor Landsburg once told *Forbes* columnist Dan Seligman, who had asked him whether he gave to charity, "Yes, I do, and I can't figure out why."[4]

It is interesting that the study of economics used to be undertaken in the *religious studies* departments of universities, rather than in their science departments. I see this as more appropriate because religion probably provides more insight into human behavior than science does. Human beings are not robots; they are entirely unpredictable people. Nowadays, economics is treated as if it were a science, although to be sure, it is called the dismal science. What the study of economics does is make scientists dismal at their inability to plumb the unpredictable ways that people behave with their money.

Take just one of many studies that highlight human irrationality when it comes to money. A study published in the French *Annales d'Economie et de Statistique* is called "Are People Willing to Pay to Reduce Other's Incomes?"[5] The experiment involved grouping subjects into clusters of four people each, who were all given equal sums of money. The four had to gamble in random, computerized games that were arranged so that two of the four always came out ahead while the other two lost money in each round. Richer or poorer, each subject was then given the opportunity to spend some of his or her money to reduce the take of the fellow subjects. Doing so would not only fail to make the individual subject richer, but it would actually cost between two and 25 cents for every dollar of his or her fellow players' money that was destroyed.

The researchers were certain that no rational person would spend money merely to impoverish others. They were shocked to find that even at the top price of 25 cents for every dollar burnt, 62 percent of the participants paid for the privilege of making their peers poorer. One obvious conclusion of this study is that wealth is relative. Within the closed system of that game, burning your friend's wealth is making you richer—relatively richer. At a cost of only 25 cents, destroying a dollar of your friend is almost a bargain.

The other and more important conclusion is that people do seem to behave unpredictably and often irrationally about money. They behave the same way about matters of love, too. That is because attraction and love are so subjective. They depend on human uniqueness, and money does, too. Being far more of a spiritual than a physical commodity, each person relates to money in his or her own special and unique way. In certain ways, we act similarly to one another. Few of us literally burn cash by tossing it into the fire, but many people spend it in ways that others consider little improvement over burning it.

JEWISH TRADITION TEACHES THAT CHARITABLE GIVING BENEFITS THE GIVER

Jewish tradition teaches its adherents that many of its required actions are for reflexive reasons. For instance, the Bible is emphatic about prohibiting cruelty to animals. Urging kindness to animals is not because Judaism views animals as independent beings with rights not to be molested or subjected to any cruel treatment. Instead, Judaism warns that inflicting cruelty on animals brings about a coarsening of the human personality. You must be kind to animals because doing so turns you into a more sensitive and more vital person.

Jews are even instructed in how they ought to behave toward certain inanimate objects. Again, this is not because the inanimate object cares about how it is treated. It is because someone who is careful about how she interacts with even inanimate objects is someone who will become supersensitive about how she interacts with people.

Finally, there is the example in which the Bible prohibits cursing a deaf man. Although the disabled victim does not hear the invective being hurled in his direction, it is still forbidden behavior because cursing anyone does more harm to the curser than to the recipient.

In similar fashion, Jews give money away regardless of how much the government is doing to solve a problem. They give money away regardless of whether they actually would be doing more social good by investing those funds in a profit-seeking venture capital fund. They also give money away regardless of the fact that sometimes people who actually make use of the supported facilities could easily foot the bill. They give money away because on some deep level, they recognize that doing so does more for the giver than it does for the recipient.

Jews do not give money away because it is always rational to do so, but in spite of the fact that it is often irrational. Jews give money away not because it is rational but because it is right. It is part of the traditional way of life in the United States. People often confuse cause and effect. The err in believing that Americans give so much more away to charity than do the citizens of other countries because U.S. tax laws make gifts nontaxable. On the contrary, U.S. tax law was constructed in this fashion precisely because it reflected a fundamental belief already held by many citizens. This belief was that religious charities—and in the early days all charities were religious—were not to be taxed.

Nevertheless today, about half of all U.S. charitable dollars go to religious causes.[7] The devoutly Christian founders of the United States based their views on the Biblical verses describing Joseph taking charge of Egyptian economic affairs during the seven years of plenty and the subsequent seven years of famine. To stimulate economic productivity, Joseph not only lowered the tax rate to 20 percent, but he also exempted the priests from all taxation.[8]

Another error in confusing cause and effect is the mistaken belief that having wealth enables charitable giving. Many really do believe that the United States is the most charitable nation in the world because it is also the wealthiest. In reality, charitable giving contributes to *wealth creation*. It is far more likely that the United States evolved into history's greatest wealth-creating machine because of its deeply ingrained cultural habit of giving. This is true not only on a national scale but also on a personal level. One of the most important habits that anyone interested in increasing wealth should acquire is giving away money. This appears to be paradoxical. Accumulating money would appear to be easier if you held on to every dollar you receive rather than following this irrational advice. Yet it is good advice. It may be irrational and it may even be counterintuitive. but it is good advice. Here's how it actually works.

DON'T LIVE BEYOND YOUR MEANS; INSTEAD *GIVE* BEYOND YOUR MEANS

Suppose you have begun viewing yourself as a business professional. Suppose you have identified the fields in which you would like to contribute to the well-being of your fellow citizens. Suppose you have effectively proclaimed what these fields are so that people can find you when they need you. Suppose you have started finding ways to make yourself twice as valuable and useful to your employer. Suppose you believe in the intrinsic morality of business, you yearn to lead, and you are sensitive to the future. It would be hard to deny that you have absorbed the lessons of this volume. Just as you thought you had it all down, just as you expected a Niagara-like cascade of increased income, you now hear that you ought to separate a proportion of your newfound revenue and give it away. Could anything sound more counterproductive?

GIVING MONEY AWAY MAKES MORE COME BACK TO YOU

People are suspicious of doing business with desperate people. I am sure that, on occasion, you have found yourself at the hands of a salesperson who is painfully and transparently desperate to make the sale. Unless you were equally desperate to acquire the product or service, I am sure you did not buy from that salesperson. Desperate people make others uncomfortable. Apart from anything else, their pathetic eagerness makes others doubt the value of the prospective purchase. One of the invaluable services performed by professional realtors who sell houses is that they insulate the buyer from the seller's visible eagerness to sell. The buyer feels far more comfortable with someone who seems less emotionally invested in the sale. Sales professionals who do nothing but sell every day are far better at camouflaging that eagerness to close the deal than the ordinary individual who only very occasionally sells his or her house or car.

People are also uneasy about others who appear overeager to become friendly. Premature use of first names or other very informal salutations, like using someone's nickname before having been invited to do so, can have the same effect. There may well be someone with whom you could do some deal. Perhaps it might be the opportunity to moonlight for him and bring some of your work skills to bear on some problem he is encountering. Perhaps it might be a possible deal whereby you become partners in an enterprise, where he invests some of his capital and you invest your knowledge and effort. Whatever it is, your chances of establishing the link that allows the other person to comfortably say to himself "Maybe I can profit from some interaction with this person," will be improved if you do not come across as desperately needy.

One of the very best ways of overcoming that appearance of desperate eagerness is to make yourself feel rich. If you were rich, then another deal would be *nice* but not crucial. That is exactly the perception the other party should have of you. That way she will say to herself, "What can he do for me?" However, if you come across as needy and desperate, she is saying to herself, "I wonder what he wants from me?"

This is why one of the most used sales techniques is to suggest an urgency. For instance, "This sale ends at midnight tonight!" or "This is the very last suit in this color that I have left." That immediately turns the tables. Now it is no longer a desperate salesperson pushing a product, it is more a case of an increasingly desperate customer—you—hoping the kind, helpful salesperson will get you the product you want. You have suddenly been transformed into a very compliant customer. That salesperson was transformed into a bigger person, somebody who could do something for you rather than someone who wanted to separate you from your money.

Similarly, if you had some magical method of turning yourself into a larger, nondesperate kind of person, someone who was seen to be more of a *giver* than a taker, your business interactions would dramatically improve. If you somehow genuinely felt yourself to be a bigger person than you might really be, the perception of you would change until you had effectively made yourself bigger.

One of the popular ways to accomplish this is by spending money. Buying things does tend to make people feel good because it makes them feel larger. After all, everyone knows that the customer is king. You have wandered from store to store disbursing largesse from your wallet or by allowing imprints of your credit card. No surprise you are feeling like a benefactor. Salespeople have prostrated themselves at your feet, making you feel like a monarch. Buying things does impart a subtle feeling of control that is very welcome, particularly if you are feeling at all unsure of yourself. Acquiring things has the effect of expanding your envelope, as it were. Coming home laden down with boxes of new purchases makes me feel a little larger of a person, which is a welcome feeling. Needless to say, new purchases also satisfy that human part that seeks novelty and finds gratification in the untasted, the untouched, and the never-before previously owned.

The only problem with trying to gain psychic importance by buying things is that the effect is very short lived and is invariably followed by a psychic setback. Some call it "buyers' remorse." The novelty part of the thrill, which is similar to a drug-induced rush, quickly wears off because the purchase doesn't remain new for very long. The feeling of bigness wears off, too, because deep down, you know you have just been indulging yourself. It is hard to fool your inner self that embarking on a buying spree for some new clothing or new toys is the activity of choice for great people.

The feeling you get from buying gifts is quite different. This is why purchasing presents for others is such a popular activity. In the longer run, it imparts far more genuine pleasure than buying things for yourself. Year after year, I was told by countless callers to my radio show that their favorite aspect of the Christmas holiday season was buying presents for friends and family. How honest they were. Buying gifts for others is actually more satisfying than buying for yourself.

When trying to generate an internal feeling of magnanimity and largeness, is there an alternative to shopping? The very best way to come across to others as a fair-minded, big-spirited benefactor, rather than as a desperate little person, is to become a regular contributor to charities. To be sure, not only will this have you coming across as a larger person but, in fact, it will make you *become* a larger person. You will feel large, benevolent, and expansive, instead of desperate, mean spirited, and petty.

Of course, I'm not suggesting that mean-spiritedness is one's natural demeanor. But there are times when everyone feels intense economic pressure. At times like that it becomes easy, indeed almost natural, to begin feeling resentful toward others less pressured in this way. You can easily develop a bit of an entitlement mind set, which makes you focus on yourself and your needs, rather than on others and their needs. These conditions are easy to slide into, and they are easy for others to identify in you. They also make you far less desirable as business acquaintances and potential partners. It takes action to avoid sliding down the spiritual gravity slope of self-centeredness at times of personal need. Giving away money is one of the most powerful of all actions that defeats this dangerous tendency. It makes other people *want* to interact with you.

GIVE MONEY, NOT JUST TO DO GOOD BUT TO DO WELL

Now I must take a moment to make something very clear. While I may have my own personal beliefs, for the purpose of this book I am not urging you to be more charitable because I want to see the poor and needy provided for. I am not even suggesting that giving money away will cause God to smile on you and reward you with wealth. I am urging you to give money away because it is one of the most powerful and effective ways of *increasing your own income*. As a religious Jew, it does not surprise me at all that a benevolent God arranges things in such a way that groups who follow a Biblical blueprint tend to thrive, but that is not the point. My point right now is to discuss with you the mechanism by means of which charitable giving will effect your income and thus to astound you.

I have already presented to you the first consequence of giving some of your money away—doing so makes you feel a better person, which makes you come across as a better person. This potent point is presented in the Bible during the account of the spies returning from their furtive tour of the Promised Land to report to Moses. In general, their report was gloomy and indicated deep doubt on the part of the spies about Israel's future prospects of conquest. The land may be good, they conceded, but it is populated by mighty warriors living in fortified cities: "There we saw the great Nefilim people, giants from among them, we felt like grasshoppers in our own eyes and that is how we appeared to them in their eyes too."[9]

Jewish tradition asks how these cowardly spies could possibly have known how they appeared in the eyes of the local inhabitants? Nobody really knows how others view him or her. The answer serves as a valuable warning for all time. If you feel like a grasshopper, then you will most certainly appear to be one from the perspective of those around you. If you feel desperate and then consequently perhaps a little self-focused, then that is exactly how you will appear in the eyes of those around you. Too bad people don't really like doing business, or having any other close contact, with individuals who radiate selfishness. If you don't want to come across to others as a grasshopper, take care not to feel like one. This is easier said than done. How can you avoid feeling a bit like a grasshopper when you are feeling heavy pressures? Avoid it by giving money away.

Now at this stage, you might be thinking that you would rather find a less expensive way to adjust your internal mood so it will in turn adjust the mood you radiate to others. Good luck. By the way, should you succeed, write to me at the address at the back of this book and let me know. I will include it in future editions. Be aware, however, that the several thousand years of accumulated and recorded experience that constitutes the extant body of Jewish wisdom suggests you will be wasting your time in this quest.

BEING CHARITABLE MEANS
MAKING NEW FRIENDS

Boosting your mood is not the only way in which giving money away works to increase your own revenue by amounts way beyond the sums you donated. There is a second way in which this mechanism works its magic. You see, it is tough to give money away without becoming involved with many other people. I'm sure you could manage to find a way to help out a solitary friend in need here or to make an anonymous gift to some needy associate over there, but you need a way to give away money methodically. Don't forget, you are not running a charitable foundation; you are running your own business, You, Inc. You don't have the time constantly to be seeking worthy recipients for your largesse and to be administering the effective use of the funds. You have business to take care of, so you need help.

Fortunately, help is available in dozens of different varieties. There are religious organizations; educational organizations; cultural, medical, and civic service organizations; and many other types of nonprofit organizations. There is one additional great advantage to delivering your voluntary charitable contributions through a nonprofit organization. The Jewish legal codifier Moses Maimonides ranks various acts of charitable giving. The highest rank is putting the recipient in business for himself, thus making him independent of charity. The next highest rank is giving money to someone who needs it in such a way that neither the donor nor the recipient is aware of one another's identities. This maintains total dignity. By associating with a charitable organization, you know which groups your organization has chosen to help, but you probably don't know the identity of specific recipients. Likewise, the recipient may know she is being aided by your group, but she remains unaware of the identity of any of her specific benefactors.

Pick one organization with which to associate significantly. By "significantly," I mean that you will invest both time and money. Select one that meets regularly and whose other members are people you would like to get to know. It is not difficult to peruse the names of those who are active in each charitable organization in your city. Get to know who is who. Feel no compunction about picking an organization on the basis of which group's members are in the best position to advance your business objectives. Selfish? Of course not! I'm talking about positioning yourself to give money away. Will it benefit you, too? Obviously, it will. What do you think I have been talking about? The entire point is that God set things up so as to make human interaction beneficial for all.

So now you have joined the Rotary Club, the local hospital support group, Habitat for Humanity, the fundraising arm of a church ministry, the art museum, or some other organization. You have paid the hefty initiation fee, which is, of course, tax deductible. Now you must attend meetings, join committees, and do anything else to make yourself useful, helpful, and noticed. You will find yourself making new friends and acquaintances. If you have heeded the advice from this book's Second Commandment, you have proclaimed your professional identity quite clearly so your new friends and acquaintances know exactly what you can do for them. That is obviously very important.

Meanwhile, all this social interaction is taking place in an environment of selflessness. You are all there out of your concern for other human beings. That makes for a warm atmosphere and accounts for why so many of the most glittering events on your city's social calendar revolve around charitable causes. People all look their best when not behaving predatorily. Business is usually not conducted at these events, and rightly so. However, more than just a few business lunches are scheduled as a result of chance encounters during charitable support work. Rest assured that in very little time, you will be involved in transactions, partnerships, or collaborations that grew from your association with your charitable group. Keep accurate figures in all your accounting, and you will find that the revenue from these activities vastly exceeds the money you gave away. That is just how it works, but it is still not all there is to the magic of charitable giving.

DONATING IS LIKE INVESTING: IT INCREASES WHAT COMES BACK TO YOU

The third reason that charitable giving is a powerful tool to use in increasing your own income is that it helps you train yourself to become an effective investor. I am not suggesting that investing resembles gambling in any way, but do you recall those glamorous old James Bond movies in which 007 saunters over to the roulette table in some elegant casino? He would casually lay down the equivalent of some small country's gross domestic product on the green velvet and await the spin of the wheel. He looked very cool and appeared to be quite indifferent to the outcome of the bet; and, considering he was probably playing with British government funds, he probably was indifferent. He invariably won, but his calm confidence was always contrasted with the sweaty villain coincidentally playing at the same table. For the bad guy, it was obvious that much hung in the balance with each spin of the wheel. That is the point.

It is hard to invest effectively if you absolutely must win every single time. That is not how investing works, and it is not how business works. In fact, it is not how life works at all. Whether engaged in investing, building your own business, or any other facet of real life, you have to play each hand as if you do not really *need* to win but are sure you will win anyway. Then you have to be ready to pick yourself up from any failures and play the hand all over again.

You could join the many who have been inspired by Rudyard Kipling's poem "If." This is the third stanza (plus the poem's last two lines):

> If you can make one heap of all your winnings
> And risk it all on one turn of pitch-and-toss,
> And lose, and start again at your beginnings,
> And never breathe a word about your loss:
> If you can force your heart and nerve and sinew
> To serve your turn long after they are gone,
> And so hold on when there is nothing in you
> Except the Will which says to them: "Hold on!"
>
> . . .
>
> Yours is the Earth and everything that's in it,
> And—which is more—you'll be a Man, my son![10]

You see, some people simply cannot invest in anything. They are afraid of losing their money. They cannot comfortably invest in stocks, bonds, or any other security, and neither can they invest in their own business. Invariably, these people are equally incapable of charitable giving. It is not an accident that most of the monuments of philanthropy that dot U.S. cities—hospitals, art museums, university buildings—were invariably built by business professionals, rather than by people who saw themselves as nothing more than mere employees. Well, business professionals are the ones who had the money to erect those edifices, you might say. Exactly. That is the point. The very internal quality that enabled them to give away the money to build those impressive looking structures was the same quality that enabled them to make that money in the first place. If you have the generosity of spirit to give money away, you also have the courage to seek profit by placing your money at risk.

There will surely come a time in the expansion of your enterprise when you will need to risk money. Whether it will be something as inexpensive as printing business cards and advertising flyers or as frightening as signing a large lease on your own office, the day will come. Eventually, you will have to put your money where your convictions lie. It will be the moment of destiny. Will you be able to reach into your pocket, or actually into your bank account, and place much of the wealth you have spent the past year accumulating onto the table? Will you or won't you?

The answer may depend on how well you have been following this ninth commandment. You see, risking your hard-earned money is counterintuitive. Keeping your eyes open and firmly fixed on the ball flying toward you at 60 miles per hour is also counterintuitive, but it offers the best chance of successfully hitting the ball. Taking money out of your pocket, or out of your bank account, and placing it on the table is counterintuitive, but it offers the best chance of successfully growing it. Investing that money in stocks or bonds is a whole lot easier than investing it in your own enterprise, because you tend to have more faith in large, institutionalized companies than in yourself. Still, investing in your own efforts is exactly what you must sometimes do.

The internal quality that allows you to take your money and place it at risk on the table of your own enterprise is exactly the same quality that allows you to take your money and give it away to others. In each case, you have had to develop a willingness to remove your money from safekeeping and essentially bid it adieu.

In the case of charity, I take this money, give it away, and say to myself, "This may one day come back to me in plentiful returns, but it perhaps may not. There are no guarantees, but that is also alright." In the case of investing money in my own efforts, I also say to myself, "This may one day come back to me. It may even produce far greater returns. However, it is just possible that nothing will come of it. Still, I do it."

It is the same action and the same incantation. By methodically and regularly giving money away to charity, you are making of yourself someone who can smilingly and elegantly place an investment on the table, casually wave it goodbye, and rest confident that you made the best decision you were able to make. From this point on, whatever will happen will be. You do not remain seated at the table rigidly fixated on the spinning wheel as the sweat pours from your tense face. You are no James Bond villain. The charity habit cured you.

CHARITY FOCUSES YOU OUTSIDE YOURSELF

It may be easier to wrap yourself around this principle if you view giving charity as a way to kick-start your cash flow, as it were. I don't want to sound too metaphysical, but your object is to create a movement of money from the world around you to you. There is a sad sense in which each person lives a lonely, isolated existence. You enter the world alone and you depart it alone; but along the way everything of value flows from how effectively you battle that loneliness and how effectively you bond with others. If you retreat into yourself, you are essentially escaping the world that ends at your skin surface.

The Talmud highlights this point by emphasizing that certain traits, such as arrogance, can "take us out of the world." The point being made by this ancient Jewish insight is that behaving arrogantly isolates you from other people, who justifiably spurn you. The result is that you inevitably begin to retreat into yourself, depending ever more on your own resources, instead of building up bonds of mutual dependency with other people. Part of the very mandate of life granted you by God is the obligation to end your lonely condition and build links to others.

Like the constant to-and-fro movement of electrons that bond together the simple molecules of matter, the constant movement of money bonds together human beings. The flow of money maintains the bonds, and conversely, the bonds stimulate the flow of money. Make money flow, and you will inevitably be creating bonds. With bonds in place, more money flows. Like anything else that flows, money requires pipelines. This means that your task is to excavate pipelines that can carry money toward you.

How do you go about excavating money pipelines? The only way to construct these channels is by pumping money outward from you to the world out there. That action itself creates conduits that remain open and useable even after they have served their purpose of conveying your money, in the form of charity, from you to the world outside of yourself. Now that these pipes exist, they are able to be used for cash flow in the reverse direction, too.

Once, while engaged in my rabbinical studies in Israel, a teacher interrupted what had been an arduous few hours of analysis by suggesting that we go for a walk. As we followed the labyrinth of alleys that wind along within the walls of the Old City of Jerusalem, my mentor seemed to have an objective in mind. I was not surprised when we descended steps and found ourselves deep beneath the streets. In the gloom, I could make out a tunnel carved into the rock that led away into darkness. It was just high enough for a stooped person to pass through. Attempting to overcome my claustrophobia, I followed his hurrying figure silhouetted by the small flashlight he must have extracted from one of his pockets. We finally emerged into sunshine, and I blinked in amazement. We were outside the city walls. He replaced the flashlight into a pocket and told me a tale that has remained with me ever since: During one of the many sieges of Jerusalem about 2,000 years ago, a group of defenders needed to escape the city to fetch aid. They excavated this long tunnel and were able to emerge from behind enemy lines. In this way they were able to bring food into the beleaguered city.

The ultimate objected of digging the tunnel was obtaining food, but food on its own could not dig a tunnel into the city. The tunnel had to be initiated from within. Only then could it be used to transport in food from the outside.

Many years later, during the Six-Day-War in 1967, an advance guard of Israeli soldiers resolved to penetrate the Old City of Jerusalem, which, at the time, was held by the Jordanian army. Familiar with the history of their forebears, they were aware of the existence of this ancient tunnel. They located its opening, climbed down, and half an hour later emerged within the Old City walls to prepare for their military mission.

I remember this story well because it provided me with a model of a vital principle. A tunnel that is excavated to provide access in one direction can subsequently be used to provide access in the reverse direction, too. Sometimes, the only way to get something in is first to dig a route out.

FEEL VIRTUOUS FOR A VERY GOOD REASON

Another benefit that giving some of your money away bestows on you is that it makes you feel good about yourself. Before you protest that you already feel good about yourself, let me tell you that the human being is a marvelous machine and our subconscious is very tough to fool. You may say that you feel good about yourself, but before your subconscious part believes it, there had better be a good reason for why you think you are so good.

Let me tell you a story about how powerful the subconscious is. Soon after the conclusion of World War II, the men and women in the service returned home to try to resume normal lives. One particular congregant of my father had come home with an increasingly aggravated muscular condition in his left arm. He had undergone the entire battery of anatomical, physiological, and neurological tests, and his left arm only became more useless. Finally in despair, he consulted with his rabbi, my father. Confident that all physical causes had been ruled out by the extensive medical testing, my father felt sure that the cause lay in a spiritual condition. What he discovered would today be termed a psychosomatic disorder and might possibly be treated by a competent psychiatrist—or an excellent rabbi.

During lengthy conversations, my father indulged the ex-soldier's apparent desire to discuss his recent war-time experiences in North Africa where he served. Over many weeks of meetings, it seemed to my father as if everything always led back to one seminal day. This man seemed fixated on the dramatic allied defeat when Tobruk fell to Axis forces in June 1942. Along with thousands of British, Australian, and South African soldiers, he became a captive. As my father burrowed down into the man's subconscious and made him relive each moment of each hour of that day of crisis on the hot sands of the Sahara Desert, the answer soon emerged.

It turned out that as the Germans and Italians began overrunning the fort, his job was manning a machine gun. He recalled frantically firing to hold the invaders at bay, while his best buddy struggled to supply his machine gun with a smooth-flowing belt of ammunition. With the gun barrel glowing red from overheating and the enemy soldiers in undiminished numbers drawing close enough for him to read the expressions on their faces, his best buddy was hit.

Now he not only had to keep firing but had to feed the ammunition belt into his weapon himself. His wounded friend called out, asking for him to pass the water canteen. With neither hand free, he yelled back that he'd get him the water in just a moment. When he was able to pause and catch his breath, he reached for the canteen and passed it to his best buddy. It was too late. His friend had perished. His post was soon overrun, and he spent the rest of the war in a prisoner-of-war camp where the use of his left arm became increasingly impaired.

It didn't take my father long to reconstruct in his study the physical arrangement of that machine gun post as it existed about seven years earlier. From this, both he and his handicapped congregant were able to see that on that fateful day, he could have continued firing with his right hand while passing the canteen to his stricken comrade with his left. Note that while it took advanced spiritual forensics to bring this fact to light, the ex-soldier's subconscious knew it all along. Apparently he was punishing himself as it were by afflicting the very arm that could have supplied the water to his wounded buddy but did not do so.

After this, my father talked his congregant through the morality issues of a soldier at war. They studied the responsibilities of a military man when under attack, and they studied the question of priorities when forced to choose between defending a position and aiding the wounded. During this process, which lasted for about two weeks, the use of that left arm gradually returned until it was finally restored to normality. The word of my father's "medical triumph" quickly spread, and even his children thought him something of a miracle man.

He himself modestly explained how the Torah provided him with the insight to understand that the secrets of the human soul lay beneath one's everyday consciousness and that physical health was as dependent on the spiritual condition of the soul as it was on the chemical balance in the body. My father was my first mentor in the study of genuine holistic medicine, depending as it does on an integrated understanding of the human being comprising both body and soul.

FOR GOOD REASON, ADMIRE YOURSELF

You have to learn to make the most of everything you have. Whether you are blessed with a good singing voice, an excellent memory, or athletic aptitude, you should use these aptitudes in your business life. If used generously and self-effacingly, they can make you more memorable, more appealing, and more likeable. You have another valuable attribute: your subconscious. It can be either a help or a hindrance, depending on how well you know how to turn it into an ally.

When I say that giving charity allows you to feel genuinely good about yourself, I mean that even your subconscious gets to feel good and it is generally a lot tougher to satisfy than your conscious being. One of the great obstacles to success is when you harbor deep internal doubt about whether you deserve such success. For example, some children are accident prone: They always get hit by the fast-moving ball or are always the only one to fall and get hurt during a game in which everyone else safely clambered over a wall. It is the child who mysteriously is always the one kid to get his or her fingers caught in the door. Here is the big secret of accident-prone children: In nine such cases out of ten, the child is overindulged and underdisciplined.

Again, I turn to the reliable and ever intelligent subconscious for explanation. In many such cases, the child has sufficient moral sophistication to know that he or she gets away with things for which other children are rightly punished. Eventually, the child's subconscious takes over the parental task of punishment. The result is that the child seems constantly to be hurting himself or herself.

You see, you have to feel that you deserve good things, or else your subconscious might very well sabotage all your best efforts. If you don't truly feel that you deserve great financial success, then you are battling an almost insurmountable obstacle—your subconscious. Giving regular gifts from your income to charity is one excellent way of, once and for all, persuading your subconscious that you deserve what lies ahead. In this way it will not only end its sabotage, it will begin actively to assist you in your quest.

PEOPLE ARE CREATORS, NOT CONSUMERS, AND GIVERS, NOT TAKERS

In the entire lamentable catalog of slurs that people use to label one another, two really stand out. The fast-food industry demeaningly refers to its customers as "grazers." They actually think of the people they exist to serve as animals that gulp their food down instinctively instead of as remarkable creatures called humans whose custom can be enticed by tasty food artfully presented in inviting environments.

Other industries refer to the customer as a "consumer." You will even hear financial reports on the news refer to "consumer products." How you think of someone and how you refer to someone will ultimately impact how you relate to that person, even if you protest that you don't mean anything by the appellation. For instance, there is no doubt whatsoever that anyone who consistently refers to his wife as, say, "the old ball and chain" will gradually, and perhaps imperceptibly, come to think of her in that way. The mind is a strange entity; it tends to believe things it hears its own mouth say.

Naturally, once you think of someone in a certain way, you act in accordance with your thoughts. That is why you do not act identically toward all strangers. When encountering a stranger, your mind picks up clues from clothing, conduct, context, and occupation and draws a conclusion; and you act accordingly in your style of greeting and in how you interact with that person.

By referring to customers in disparaging terms such as "grazer" and "consumer," industries do a disservice to their own goals and missions. But wait—what is wrong with "consumer"? Well, just consider it; not even an animal is a net consumer. If it were, the farmer would not keep it. A cow may consume $300 of hay and feed each year, but it probably produces $1,200 worth of milk, butter, and cheese during the same period. It is not hard to see that even the cow is a net *producer*.

For a human, one can multiply that difference by many orders of magnitude. Active, busy, creative people produce so much more value than the food they eat and the shelter they occupy. They are far from net consumers. Even the total pay people earn does not come close to what they really produce. Part of the extra value people create beyond their pay benefits their employers. That benefit is why they were hired. Even that isn't everything. Creative people generate money beyond their pay and beyond the value that accrues to their employers. That additional value they provide to the public pot through the mechanism of taxation. When added to the contribution of everyone else, it results in broad boulevards, elegantly invisible sewer systems, parks, soaring buildings, and the other accoutrements of civilized living in a bustling and creative city. No, humans are not *consumers* at all. We humans are *creators*.

Humans are not takers by nature. Humans do far better as *givers*. They like to see themselves as givers, and they tend to be gracious as givers, rather than as takers. For example, consider the reluctance that most people have at the thought of being a burden to their children. Well, why shouldn't they become a burden to them? After all, the children were a pretty substantial burden to their parents for long enough. It really has nothing to do with justice. Of course, children owe it to their parents. That is one of the earliest of all the human compacts. Nonetheless, who wants to think of becoming dependent on anyone else, even on one's own children? Parents are happy and proud to have taken care of their children, but they do not like the thought of the children taking care of them. People prefer being givers to becoming takers.

Giving charity is another way of ensuring that you always see yourself as a giver, rather than as a taker; your drive is to achieve, your persistence, and your very zest for life are all enormously enhanced when you see yourself as a giver, rather than as a taker. Making the act of giving regular charitable donations a life habit is one way to make sure that you view yourself as a giver.

YOUR PATH TO PROSPERITY

- *Don't try to find a rational reason for giving away money:* Charity is irrational. Nevertheless, it benefits the giver in many ways. You give money away not because it is rational but because it is right. It is part of the traditional way of life in the United States.

- *Give money away because it is one of the most powerful and effective ways of increasing your own income.* More than just a few business lunches are scheduled as a result of chance encounters during charitable support work. Rest assured that in very little time, you will be involved in transactions, partnerships, or collaborations that grew from your association with your charitable group.

- *Keep in mind that giving away money is like investing.* In the case of charity, you give away money with the idea that it may one day come back to you in plentiful returns, but perhaps it may not. There are no guarantees. The same is true of investing money and effort in your own enterprise. Your investment may one day produce great returns. However, it is just possible that nothing will come of it. But you should do it anyway. Giving away money keeps your investment muscle fully exercised and ready for opportunity.

Never Retire

Integrate your vocation and your identity by thinking of life as a journey rather than a destination.

Matel "Mat" Dawson has worked for Ford Motor Company for about 60 years, and he could have retired long ago. He is 78 years old and still drives a forklift, volunteering for as much overtime as the company will allow him. He makes a base salary of $23.47 an hour, plus overtime from working 12-hour days. With his seniority, his experience, his work ethic, and his overtime, he earns nearly $100,000 a year. And he gives most of it away.[1]

On April 13, 1999, Matel Dawson donated $200,000 to Wayne State University, which brought his total contributions to Wayne State over five years to more than $1 million. He has also given nearly a quarter of a million dollars to the United Negro College Fund and $200,000 to Louisiana State University at Shreveport. Yet Matel Dawson only made it as far as the seventh grade in Shreveport before coming to Detroit in 1940. He never won a lawsuit or a lottery. He made his money by working, working overtime, saving, and investing. Although he was expected to retire years ago, Dawson still says that he has no plans to retire, and he hopes to remain at Ford and continue working and giving money away as long as he stays healthy.

RETIREMENT SHOULD NOT BE A GOAL

People have two reactions to Matel Dawson's story. The first is one of admiration. How remarkable it is for a man to remain so committed to his work and to see no end to his usefulness to his employer as well as to the beneficiaries of his charity. However, some people experience a second, simultaneous reaction: They utter a silent but fervent prayer that they won't find themselves going to work every day when they reach the ripe age of 78.

Which of these two reactions is the healthier? As is so often the case, somewhere in between the two extremes is a fairly healthy place to be. I certainly do not want to have to be working as hard as I do today when I am 78. However, neither do I want to be of no further use to anyone else when I am 78. I may want to be able to spend a little more time with the grandchildren then, should there be any; or I may want to travel a little more than I do now.

But I definitely want to have some role to play in the vast network of human cooperation that I think of as the economy. I may want to be able to volunteer some time each week to a cause that I really care about. But I do not want to be fooling myself about my usefulness when all I am really doing is keeping myself busy at some senior center pretending to be volunteering for some activity at which my absence would hardly be noted. In other words, although I may want to be able to spend a little less time at it, I do not want to ever completely cease earning money, because that is one way of making certain that what I am doing is valued by someone.

Think about retirement in terms of a golf analogy. Suppose you are being taught to play. Surely the goal of all your hard work and training is that instant when the head of the golf club strikes the ball and sends it hurtling on its way to the green. At the moment you hear that satisfying crack and watch the ball sailing down the fairway, you suspect that your work is done. Yet this is not true. Although the ball is well on its way, you should still be focused on finishing your swing with a perfect follow-through.

Like most people, you may wonder why the follow-through is important because you have already hit the ball. Nothing you do either well or badly during the follow-through is going to change the trajectory of your ball. The answer, paradoxically, is that if you view the moment when the club strikes the ball as your final goal, your drive will be deeply flawed. However, if you view the club striking the ball as an *event* on your way to the final goal of a complete swing and perfect follow-through, even without looking, you know that you've hit it perfectly down the middle of the fairway. If retirement is your goal, your entire drive will be deeply flawed. You will never create all you could have. However, if you view your creative, professional life as an exciting, ongoing *process* with no defined expiration date, you avoid limiting your potential.

Here's another analogy. Imagine you are trying to punch the nose of an assailant who thought he'd picked an easy victim. The important thing to remember is this: Visualize your fist's target area as being about nine inches *behind* your opponent's nose. If you view his nose itself as the target, your mind is already instructing your fist to start slowing down as it reaches the general area of your enemy's proboscis. However, if you view his nose as an obstacle on your fist's journey to its target, your fist will still be moving at maximum velocity when it strikes his nose.

Picture an Olympic sprinter as she wins the gold medal. Does she come to a dead stop the moment she breaks through the finish tape? Of course not; she only starts to slow down once she's through the finish line. In fact, she doesn't see the finish line as the end of her run. You should not see a retirement date as your finish line. Banish the entire idea from your mind.

Beliefs shape one's actions far more than facts do. People who give up smoking rarely do so because they discover a new fact. Hardly anyone says to himself, "Wow! I had no idea that smoking cigarettes was unhealthy. Now that I have discovered this shocking information, I had better eliminate my habit of smoking two boxes a day." No, usually people stop smoking because of a changed belief. For instance, if a woman visits her doctor and is subjected to a real health scare, she might stop smoking. However, she ended her habit not because of new information, but because of a change in her belief. Hitherto, she considered herself personally immune to the deleterious effects of smoking. Now she believes that she could become a victim of her imprudence. This is why the things that people believe have far more impact on their lives than the things that they merely know as facts.

The reason that the belief in retirement as a life goal is so destructive is that it seems to form a kind of spiritual virus that infects all your thinking. The thought of retiring becomes a distorting lens that corrupts your view of the world around you and misleads you into missteps.

If you visualize some day in your future when you will no longer "have to work," you are subconsciously slowing down already. If your goal is to reach a certain age and then retire, by the time you reach that age, your wealth will be far less than it would have been if you had reached that age with no thoughts of retirement in mind.

The traditional Jewish contempt for retirement is an important factor in Jewish economic success. Do some Jews retire? Of course they do, but seldom as part of a life plan that mandated retirement at some predetermined date. In many cases, they sold a business or came into a large sum of money and found themselves out of work. Some wisely reentered business, whereas others became idle and deteriorated. If you are working now, I say plan on never retiring. If you are currently retired, I say put down this book until you have found a job for yourself or created one. Then come back and finish this chapter.

"WE'RE GOOD UNTIL WE DIE": LIFE STORIES OF PRODUCTIVE LONGEVITY

Myrtle Thomas started teaching back in the 1920s when the only qualification necessary for a teacher was a high school diploma. Nowadays, of course, in order to teach one needs a college diploma. So at the ripe age of 100, Myrtle Thomas was recently awarded her college diploma by the University of Nebraska at Omaha.[2]

Woodie Sommers, age 90, owns a barber shop in Sacramento, California, and strides to work four days every week. About customers who have retired, Woodie says, "They all say 'I wish I'd never retired.' I see them deteriorate." People know that if his barber shop is open, Woodie is around. "We're good until we die," he said.

Charles Hoffman is 91 and still practices as an attorney in Mobile, Alabama. His recent clients: a man accused of drug possession; a husband divorcing the same wife for the third time; the estate of a deceased man with 50 beneficiaries. "There's no end," he says, "of human complication." While still in his eighties, one day in court, a young opposing attorney attacked Hoffman's integrity. "I told him, 'Why don't you just step outside with me?'" The judge leaned over and told the whippersnapper, "I'd apologize to Mr. Hoffman if I were you." Part of the delight of practicing law into his nineties, Hoffman says, is still being able, intellectually, "to scrap." He adds, "It's nice to make a little money too."

Eleanor Lambert arrived in New York from a small town in Indiana during the 1930s to begin her career as a fashion publicist. At 98, she is going strong, still heading the company that bears her name and still personally running the Annual Best-Dressed poll that she began in 1941. Does Lambert think of bringing her career to an elegant close? "Retire? At my age? It would be ludicrous," is what she says.

Dr. Walter Watson, aged 90, is chief of obstetrics and gynecology at University Hospital in Augusta, Georgia. He usually makes his rounds at 6:30 A.M. most mornings. He played college football at the Citadel and then coached football before going to medical school. He plans to keep doctoring until he can no longer be of service to patients. When that day comes, he says, "I'll go back to coaching."

Philip Johnson is a 94-year-old New York architect with credits such as New York's Seagram building, AT&T headquarters building, California's Crystal Cathedral, and The National Center for Performing Arts in Bombay, India. His motto is if architecture is not fun, don't do it. Finding the fun in turning 90 was daunting at first, he says. "If I'm going to enjoy everything, I've got to enjoy being old, don't I?"

Hazel Howard works at the McDonald's in Lynn, Massachusetts. At the age of 91, she says she loves being around people at the fast-food restaurant where she turns out 500 orders of fries each shift. She still drives her 1986 Mustang to work four days a week from the ground floor of a house she shares with one of her 11 grandchildren. A year from now she'll retire, she says, then reconsiders: "I just had my driver's license renewed. It's good until I'm 95."[3]

One of the most amazing facts about the life of *Harland Sanders* is that when he reached the age of 65, after running a restaurant for several years, he found himself penniless. He retired and received his first Social Security check, which was for $105. He looked at that check and decided that he was not made to sit in a rocking chair and await those government checks. He hopped into his car and started traveling the country peddling his fried chicken, which was seasoned with his original blend of 11 herbs and spices, just the way his mother had taught him when he was 10 years old. By the time he was 80 years old, Colonel Sanders had built Kentucky Fried Chicken into a national institution.

Sam Walton was already 44 years old when the owners of the store he worked for, the Ben Franklin five-and-dime store in Newport, Arkansas, rejected his idea of discounting prices. At an age when other men were beginning to look forward to retirement, Walton started a business. Eventually, his retailing concepts spread to other industries such as building materials, books, and videos. Despite his huge success, most people had never heard of Sam Walton until 1985 when *Forbes* magazine ranked him top of their annual Forbes 400 list. In 1991 Wal-Mart raced past Sears to become the biggest retailer in the United States. Sam worked hard expanding Wal-Mart until his death in 1992.

The Talmud[4] relates that part of the greatness of *King David* was that he was never idle. On the day he was supposed to die, the angel of death found himself obstructed from doing his job by King David's industriousness. Because death is quite incompatible with creativity, it is impossible for anyone to die while occupied in creative endeavor. After waiting around for a while in the hope that King David would take a rest (or retire), the angel of death realized he would have to take matters into his own hands. Going behind King David, the angel of death made a loud sound that startled the king. He stopped doing what he had been occupied with and wondered what could have caused the noise. In that moment, while he was idle and engaged in speculation about the sound that had distracted him, he became vulnerable, and the angel of death took him.

THE KEY TO LONGEVITY IS CARING FOR OTHERS

Dr. Donald Hensrud is the director of the Mayo Clinic Executive Health Program. He says, "Life revolves around relationships, and it shows in aging. People who maintain close relationships live longer and more healthily. It may sound corny, but caring for others helps us care for ourselves."[5] No, Dr. Hensrud, it doesn't sound corny at all. It is exactly what Judaism has been preaching for 3,000 years. Working productively means that you are caring for others. Retirement is essentially selfish. It is hard to maintain meaningful relationships with others when you are retired because you are concerned chiefly with yourself, and it shows.

Some of people's most involved relationships are in their places of work and with their colleagues at work. This is not surprising because mutual dependency creates ideal conditions for a meaningful relationship, and it is at work that people recognize their dependence on one another. For example, without effective work in marketing, the efforts of the engineering department are futile. Similarly, unless the salespeople produce results, the folks in accounting won't have a job. And so it goes. If you are getting paid to do something, rest assured you're doing something that is meaningful and valuable to at least one other person. No retired person has a reliable indicator of his or her usefulness to others. Dr. Hensrud continues, "During our working years, we are busy, stimulated, and in demand. Some people look at retirement as a time to kick back, watch the roses bloom, and drift off. In my experience, those people don't do well mentally or physically."

Let me tell you a story. A long time ago in a faraway land lived a good farmer. He provided the villagers with cheese, butter, and milk. He came home each evening from his fields and from the marketplace and helped his wife feed their children. After dinner he read to them from his book of wonderful stories, and then he tucked his family into bed for the night.

One day he was seized by the wicked duke and flung into prison on a false charge. The guards forced him to turn a heavy crank from morning to night. The rod he rotated with the sweat of his brow disappeared into the wall and he was sure that on the other side was a flour mill. A guard asked him how he could accept his fate so cheerfully. "My efforts at this crank turn a great big grinding stone on the other side of that wall. Farmers from all around bring their wheat and on account of my work, the villagers all have flour to bake into bread."

The guard laughed callously and taunted him, "There is no grinding stone on the other end of that rod." For a few days the imprisoned farmer was despondent, but then he cheered up again. Maybe there was no grinding stone at the end of the rod he rotated, but there was a merry-go-round on which children happily rode as it spun around. Again the guard laughingly disabused him of that notion. "There is no merry-go-round, and there are no children," he said. "Am I perhaps turning a water wheel to lift water from the river to irrigate the farms and fields?" the farmer hopefully asked.

The guard unshackled the prisoner and led him outside where he could see that the rod he had been so laboriously turning for so long ended in absolutely nothing—just a turning rod. The prisoner wept, lay down, and died.

I do not mean to depress you at all. In reality the story of life is precisely the reverse of my little aphorism. So many people work hard while harboring the unworthy suspicion that there is no purpose or meaning in their labors. Their lives are diminished, and the effectiveness of their efforts is reduced by lurking skepticism regarding the value of what they do. Unlike my story's prisoner, some people feel confident that there is indeed nothing at the end of the rod they faithfully rotate day after day.

Nothing could be further from the truth. When you volunteer your efforts for some worthy cause, you usually feel confident that real benefit is derived from your efforts. However, you can never be really sure. Most organizations use their volunteers responsibly, but there are some organizations that view their volunteers as a group that must be kept occupied. That is why people tend to volunteer cautiously. They don't want to be taken for granted, and they do want to know that they are doing really useful work. Good organizations have developed methods not only to use volunteers meaningfully but also to let volunteers know how useful they are being. When you are being paid for your work, you can be certain that what you are doing plays an indispensable role in the larger, invisible matrix of human cooperation that results in wealth creation. A wise employer helps his people see the vital role they play each day. Everyone needs to feel useful.

So wrapped into the human psyche is this need to feel needed and useful that it even impacts human sexuality. Particularly in the case of men, feeling unneeded can contribute to impotence. This is one of the reasons that sexual dysfunction frequently and tragically follows on the heels of a man losing his job. Losing your job is like having your tribe, your entire community, send you a telegram that reads, "Hello, you are no longer useful, and we have no further need for you." Indeed, your entire life is bound up in your need to do things for others. Retirement is a concept that is no more real than a unicorn. It attempts to suggest that one day, if you are very fortunate and if your financial planning was in good shape, you will be able to truly enjoy life without having to do anything for anyone else.

HEBREW DOESN'T EVEN RECOGNIZE THE CONCEPT OF "RETIREMENT"

It is a principle in ancient Hebrew that any concept for which no Hebrew word exists does not itself exist. The language of Hebrew is considered to be the Lord's language, and thus perfect. Obviously, words do not exist in a 3,000-year-old language for recent technological advances such as high-speed Internet connections. However, when words do not exist for timeless human concepts, it indicates that those concepts are not real.

One such concept is coincidence. It is literally no coincidence that ancient Hebrew does not recognize the concept of coincidence. In a Judaic view of reality, nothing just happens in total isolation, all by itself. Every event is tied to earlier events as it is to subsequent consequences. Even admitting the word *coincidence* to your personal lexicon misleads you into occasionally viewing events as, well, coincidences, instead of understanding them accurately to be links in a chain of occurrences.

Another concept that ancient Hebrew does not recognize is retirement. No word exists in Hebrew for *retirement*, which indicates to devotees of ancient Hebrew that the very concept of retirement is flawed.

Consider the concepts that exist but that are almost impossible to imagine. For instance, in mathematics there is the concept of imaginary numbers, such as the square root of minus one. Frankly, in spite of a deep interest in mathematics, I find it difficult to imagine this number, although I recognize that it is so useful that it has been given a name—*i*. Well, just as there are concepts that exist but are hard to describe, we also have concepts that are easy to describe but that do not exist. Coincidence and retirement are examples of concepts that can certainly be described but that do not exist. Yes, someone can decide simply to stop working, but giving a name to such an irrational action does not confer on it any legitimate reality. It is almost as ridiculous as deciding to stop breathing or to stop eating. Being alive means that you breathe, eat, and work. You do more than these basics of course, but that is where it begins.

Prior to about the 1950s, there was no such thing as retirement, as the term is used today. A 1950 poll showed that most workers aspired to work for as long as possible. Quitting was for the disabled. Life did not offer "twilight years," perhaps two decades of uninterrupted leisure courtesy of the U.S. taxpayer. In contrast today, William Diehl, who was on his company's payroll until he was 79 years old, recalls that people regarded him as a freak. They would ask whether he was trying to set some sort of a record or whether he had tragically failed to save for retirement. He told the following story:

> A man had led a long and eventful life, but the time eventually came for him to cross the deep lake. He was pleased with the skiff and the oarsman, as well as with his welcome and the accommodations furnished to him. The surroundings were beautiful, the weather pleasant, and the food more than adequate. After a few weeks, he thought he might try his hand at some gardening, but that could not be arranged. After repeated requests to work in the dining hall or on the grounds, he cried out in exasperation, "This is no better than Hell." The reply came booming out from above, "Where did you think you were?"[6]

THE VERY IDEA OF RETIREMENT ERODES THE QUALITY OF PERSEVERENCE

John Quincy Adams said, "Courage and perseverance have a magical talisman, before which difficulties disappear and obstacles vanish into thin air." Samuel Johnson once said, "Great works are performed not by strength but by perseverance." Repeated studies consistently indicate that in sales, as well as in other fields, few attributes correlate more directly with success than does perseverance. It is also one of the toughest characteristics to inculcate in oneself. Shrugging off failure and redoubling efforts takes perseverance. Picking oneself up off the ground to where one has been knocked and taking another shot at the goal takes perseverance. Resisting pain, sometimes humiliation, too, and remaining stubbornly focused on the task takes enormous reserves of perseverance.

How do you enhance your ability to persevere? Perseverance means that you have the ability to follow your head rather than your heart or your body. Using your head, you have determined that your life would be improved if you adhered to a diet and an exercise program. Perhaps you have decided to make 10 cold calls each day at work to increase your sales. It might be something else, like completing a difficult night-school credential course for career advancement. There will be many evenings when your heart will urge you rather to spend the evening with a friend. There will be evenings when your body will urge you to climb into bed and go to sleep. Each and every time you overcome one of those urgings and adhere to your plan, you not only come closer to your goal, but, even more important, you have strengthened your perseverance muscle for future occasions.

Conversely, each time you submit to the call of your heart or body, not only do you defer achieving your goal, but you have also weakened your perseverance muscle and will find the struggle even harder next time. Like any exercise regimen, it takes time and effort. The important thing to realize is this is a *spiritual* strength here; and although it is spiritual, it is strengthened just the way a physical strength would be strengthened. If you want to increase your endurance, you might decide to run several miles each week and gradually increase the distance you run. If you want to increase the strength of a particular muscle group of your body, you would commit to a work-out program that would, over time, develop those muscles.

There is little difference with spiritual "muscles." You have to design an exercise regimen that will gradually increase your ability to persevere. Start off with challenges you know you can overcome. There is nothing worse than failing in the early stages of perseverance training. Then build up gradually until you reach the point where you can fairly reliably know that you can obey your head and ignore your heart and body when it comes to knowing what you have to accomplish.

From the time you were a child, you had opportunities to develop perseverance or diminish it. Each time your parents made you finish homework before allowing you to watch television, not only were they saving you from a teacher's wrath the next day, but they were also helping you develop your perseverance muscle. Perhaps you became a runner, a swimmer, or a rower later on. These, along with other similar athletic pursuits, help to train your body to submit to your head. With any luck, by the time you embarked on your business career, your perseverance muscle was fairly well developed. If not, you didn't go very far, nor did you achieve a great deal. That much is certain. All the facts in the world drummed into your head by a diligent and determined teacher would not take you very far without a well-developed perseverance muscle. So you must have already done some good work in developing your perseverance muscle. Now it is just as important to avoid activities and attitudes that erode that muscle.

Suppose for instance, that you wanted to get your weight down to a more healthful level. You would obviously need perseverance to stick to your diet and to your exercise program. Once you had reached your target weight, however, you would need to avoid substances that would needlessly add the weight back again. You might decide to avoid soda pop with its heavy doses of sugar. Similarly, in the case of perseverance development, there are the spiritual equivalents to soda pop that undo all the good work you have already achieved.

Chief among these perseverance destroying ideas is the idea of retirement. Even a subconscious theme of retirement permeating, say, your financial planning can sometimes be enough to hurt you. Note that I am not discouraging responsible financial planning; but when your planner inquires as to the age at which you would like to retire, your firmly declared response ought to be, "Never!" You may well determine that you would like to have accumulated an investment nest egg of a certain size by the time you reach some specific date or age. That is a positive incentive to effort. But telling yourself that you would like to retire by that date or that age is quite different and very destructive.

THE THREE LIES OF THE RETIREMENT MYTH

Retirement contrasts dramatically with the ancient Jewish view of how we integrate the passage of time with our careers. Here are the three lies commonly believed about how fabulous retirement is.

Lie 1: Work Has No Value in and of Itself

The first lie is that all your work and human creativity is focused on some end, rather than having value in and of itself. By absorbing this lie, you come to believe that you are only working until you no longer need to do so. Oh, happy will be the day when I can finally turn my back on this contemptible activity called work, sings the fool. He claims to be working in order to live, rather than living in order to be able to work. He works five days a week in order to be able to live for the two days of the weekend, or he endures the terrible work day only to live for the nighttime hours.

Allowing the retirement myth into your brain encourages you to absorb the mindset that insists you work only in order to live. In reality, you do live in order to work. A life without those accomplishments that only work can bring is a life in need of constant professional psychiatric reassurance. In his encyclical on the subject of work, *Laborem Exercens*, Pope John Paul II echoes ancient Jewish wisdom when he suggests:

> Work is a good thing for man—a good thing for his humanity—because through work man not only transforms nature, adapting it to his own needs, but he also achieves fulfillment as a human being. Work expresses his dignity and increases it: It provides him with the wherewithal to have a family, and it links him with his neighbor. Not to mention also contributing to the wealth of his neighbors.[7]

What happens if you really do detest your work? People are often advised to make a profession out of what they enjoy doing. This is generally unsound advice. It is simply not always possible to make an adequate living out of what you happen to enjoy. For instance, I enjoy boating. Trying to make this my profession would probably be disastrous. As the old adage would have it, if you want to know what it feels like to go boating, stand while fully dressed under a cold shower and tear up one-hundred-dollar bills. There are undeniably a few who earn satisfactory livings by working in the vicinity of boats, but they are hardly engaged in boating. Some are running corporations like Bayliner or Searay, which are among the largest boat manufacturers in the world, whereas others may operate real estate enterprises that include marina properties in their portfolios.

Very few people, if any at all, earn their living doing nothing but what they happen to enjoy. A far more effective approach is to learn to love what you do professionally. The choice of what to do should never be made on the basis of what *you* enjoy doing. That violates the central premise of business, which is that success comes to the unselfish. Focusing on what you personally happen to enjoy doing is no way to succeed in business. You should not be so concerned with what you enjoy.

Instead, focus on what others *need* from you and that you can provide. In other words, follow the money. Find the area that pays satisfactorily. That indicates a need on the part of others. That is why there is money in that field. People are in effect saying, "Won't someone come and supply our need? Look, we have real money we are willing to pay." Locate an industry into which you have entry and that seems to be thriving. Then make it your business to enjoy working there.

How do you make yourself enjoy something? The answer is straightforward. Become accomplished and competent at it. It is a reliable fact that you tend to start enjoying anything at which you become competent and from which you derive a sense of accomplishment. Remember how you hated mathematics, chemistry, or English composition at school? You might also remember how you later came to enjoy the same subject. What changed was nothing but your level of achievement. People desperately need to feel a sense of achievement because it signals that they have been useful to others. They need to feel appreciated by others, and getting paid is one reliable way to gauge that appreciation. People can feel gratitude to their jobs for supplying this sense of achievement.

I'm not saying you should never contemplate a change of activity. On the contrary, you should be very open to the possibility of change. Maybe you ought to be in a different field. Perhaps you should have a different employer. There is nothing wrong with that, as long as you do not abandon a situation with vast economic potential and replace it with one that offers minimal monetary opportunity on the basis that at least you will enjoy what you do.

As an ambitious and successful business professional, you should always keep in mind that everything you do must benefit others as much as yourself. You are chiefly in business not only to obtain the things that you want, but also to make it possible for others to obtain the things that they want. Were this not true for everyone, even for the fabulously successful Bill Gates of Microsoft, people would cash in their chips, sell their stock, invest the proceeds in a comprehensively diversified portfolio, and retire to Fiji. Needless to say, in all probability, Microsoft workers and investors would be worse off if Bill actually did retire to Fiji. Computer users around the world may be worse off and those whose wealth is partially tied up in real estate in the locality of Redmond, Washington, would also suffer loss. The truly successful business professional is never concerned solely with his own welfare. The retirement myth sadly encourages you to believe that you are working only until you no longer have any need to do so. It entirely negates the effect your efforts have on others.

Lie 2: People Become Less Productive and Less Useful as They Age

The second lie promoted by the retirement myth is that as time goes by you become weaker and less capable of making money. It is almost self-evident that if I am indeed edging closer and closer to retirement as I age, each passing day must be robbing me of just a little more of my money-making vitality. This is a lie.

The truth is that unless my business is pounding another boxer in the ring or charging up a field while clutching a football, each passing day makes me a *more effective* wealth creator and grants me added potential to create revenue. I say this because making money depends on relationships, and with the passage of time everyone should possess a larger rolodex. With the passage of time, you ought to know an increasing number of friends and acquaintances. You ought to be a lot less self-centered, which means that you are better equipped to nurture and maintain those friendships. With growing emotional and psychological maturity, you become a more capable communicator and you become less susceptible to impulsive actions. With passing years, you often become tougher and more resilient, more experienced at rolling with the punches.

You have seen more than one roller-coaster cycle. You know how to temper the exuberance of those around you with the knowledge that things don't remain high forever; and you can boost the depression of your associates with the reassurance that things don't remain low forever either. Finally, with the passage of time, provided you have not been constantly jumping from one occupation to another, your areas of skill and your professional competence become better known to those around you.

Judaism, through the Bible, insists that you are morally obliged to accord great respect to anyone aged, even those with few academic or material accomplishments.[8] Judaism teaches that no young person, regardless of education or competence, can possibly have accumulated the experience and wisdom about life that most ordinary elderly people possess.[9]

Yet most people view an older person as someone who has started to slow down—as someone walking more slowly, driving a little less certainly than he or she used to do, and even appearing to think for a little longer during ordinary conversation. If the older person is an employee of your organization, you might conclude that it is time to replace him or her with a younger, fresher, and stronger person. It may be true that the particular function in which the older person operates does require great physical endurance. However, most organizations would be doing themselves a favor by finding a way to retain the experience and the wisdom that comes with age.

Many firms, such as mail-order clothing giant Lands End, regularly employ older people to help cope with the end-of-the-year purchasing rush. They have found these older workers to possess a work ethic and a commitment to customer service utterly lacking among their younger employees.

A person's real economic value is *spiritual*, not physical. You may have a certain economic value, which is to say a value to your fellow humans, as a ditch digger, but it is only a fraction of your real value. Henry Ford used to complain notoriously about having to hire an entire person when all he really needed was a pair of hands. Today, no successful entrepreneur would be willing to pay a salary to what was merely a pair of hands. What everyone needs from those whom they pay is total commitment of both soul and body. The full spectrum of human creativity can only emerge from a person who sees himself or herself as a totally integrated body and soul, both united in common commitment to the job.

By admitting the thoughts to your mind, even subconsciously, that "I am only 15 years away from retirement" or that "I only have to work for 10 more years," you effectively persuade yourself that your strengths are diminishing and that you are winding down your revenue-producing activities. In other words, with each passing day, you see yourself as less and less useful to your fellow humans. Nothing could be further from the truth.

If you work for a company with a mandatory retirement policy, you can hardly help reminding yourself that you only have "x" number of years left to work. Nonetheless, even in that situation, it will pay to recognize your oncoming retirement date as the date you are *switching* occupations, rather than as the date you are ceasing to work. When that date comes, or preferably well before that date arrives, you should have prepared your next landing site. Perhaps you will buy a small business, or maybe you will hang up your shingle and start consulting. What consulting means is that you continue to operate in your established field of competency, but you do so as an independent contractor, rather than as a full-time employee.

Many employees whom I have advised about this kind of transition have successfully negotiated consulting contracts with their former employers, who were as eager to retain the services of their former employees as the employees were to remain active. No matter what you do, remember that you can always fine-tune your activities to restore the reality that with passing years you are more helpful to the world, not less. Even as a football player or as a boxer, your best years may well lie ahead as coach, advisor, or consultant.

Lie 3: People Are Merely Consumers, Rather Than Creators

The third lie that springs from the myth of retirement is that people, and that includes you, are consumers rather than creators. Until you retire, you are occupying a slot at the food trough; so the only decent thing to do after an appropriate interval is to move out of the way and let someone else in to get their opportunity to feed. In this scenario, retirement is the way people are cycled through the economy in as fair a way as possible. This is the scenario that provides the moral validation for the mandatory retirement policies in place at so many companies. You have occupied the corner office for 16 years, now it's someone else's turn. If you don't retire and get out of the way, she might leave our firm and go to work for our competitor. You have had a good run. Now be a good fellow and do the decent thing—go away!

Of course, if this were true it would make no sense for any company to purchase any other company because the net sum of all that would be acquired is the responsibility to feed several hundred new mouths. When war leads one country to conquer and occupy another, it is not because the stronger country felt an altruistic impulse to feed millions of new citizens. In both cases, it is because smart leaders realize that the human being is the only creature on the planet with the capacity to create value that vastly exceeds its own needs. Provided that the corporation has been structured in a way to allow each employee to function at a level close to maximum creativity and productivity, the more employees and the larger the company, the more productive and profitable it can be.

People can create wealth, and they do it chiefly through a spiritual rather than a material process. Because a human's spiritual potential can continue increasing as he or she ages, a human's wealth-producing potential carries no expiration date. For this reason, declining populations worry statesmen. For instance, in 1986, when it first became apparent that France's birthrate had fallen to 1.8, which is well below minimum replacement level of 2.1, the French government announced a program to encourage larger families. They would award mothers who gave birth to a third or subsequent child a "temporary maternal salary" of about $300 a month for three years. West Germany has a birthrate of 1.3, and Britain and the Scandinavian countries are experiencing similar population crises. "In demographic terms, Europe is vanishing," said then French Prime Minister Jacques Chirac in 1986.[10] If people were nothing more than mouths that needed feeding, lower populations would be seen as blessings rather than as the problems they now are.

Even in the United States, the birth rate is well below replacement levels, which could result in only 1.5 workers available to support each Social Security beneficiary by the year 2030, instead of the 3.5 workers available today. The very fact that this is considered a problem reveals that people are creative and productive assets. Ben Wattenberg, a senior fellow at the American Enterprise Institute, began warning about this problem many years ago:

> There is a relationship between the size of a population and its power in the world. Belgium is not going to build a 747 airplane. Luxembourg is not going to have a Star Wars system. The only countries to launch aircraft carriers recently are the U.S. and the U.S.S.R. because it takes an enormous population base to pay the taxes to provide the money for these inordinately expensive weapons and technologies. The club of modern democratic nations now accounts for about one-seventh of the global population. At the end of World War II, these nations had about a quarter of the world's population. If present trends continue, Western countries will go down to one-tenth or one-twelfth

of the global population by 2050. On balance it is a lot more difficult to have a dominant culture when you're one-fifteenth of the world than when you're one-fourth. The history of civilization is one of nations and cultures growing and then dying. There's nothing to say that our particular democratic club will last forever. I talked to a manufacturer of baseball gloves. You don't have to look out very far—five to ten years—and the market of young boys is going to shrink substantially. After listening to me, he said, "Holy smoke, I'm in trouble." And I said, "Right, you've got it."[11]

Sustaining the retirement myth contributes to people mistakenly subscribing to the notion that humans are chiefly consumers rather than creators and that as such, the best way to run business affairs is to minimize the number of these consumers. What is worse is that with retirement an essential component of your life plan, you are far more likely to subconsciously think of yourself as a consumer rather than as a creator. If deep in your heart you suspect yourself to be nothing more than a mouth needing to be fed, the likelihood of your coming up with creative ideas is drastically diminished. Retirement feeds the materialistic myth that the only way to create wealth is by physical labor. Unless I am mining, manufacturing, or growing something, I cannot be creating wealth. Under the terms of this myth, obviously someone whose physical strengths are in decline is someone who cannot possibly be making any contribution. Not only is she not adding to the common wealth of her society, she is no longer even capable of contributing to her own needs. Society must take care of her.

In reality, if 84-year-old John spends the morning at a coffee shop helping to persuade middle-aged Tom to invest the money that will enable young Dick to buy elderly Harry's auto repair business, and if the deal is structured so that John earns a commission, John has just created considerable wealth. He has directly added to the wealth of himself and three others, and he has indirectly contributed to the wealth of the entire neighborhood. In fact, during this almost relaxed morning of conversations, John has probably created more wealth than he created all month in his earlier life as an employee of a furniture factory. Then he needed a strong back and sure eyes as he assembled high-quality office furniture. Now he may be physically less active; but by virtue of his highly developed spiritual skills, he is creating far more than he is consuming. With retirement in your mind as a step on life's road, you are far less likely to be a fountain of creativity. Your subconscious awareness of that expiration date suppresses your productivity and imposes artificial limits on your life.

THE REAL ROLE OF WORK

God placed man into the Garden of Eden to work it. Judaism teaches that this work was to be man's source of satisfaction. In this, he would fulfill his destiny as a partner of his Creator in the act of creation. Through work, he would prove that he was indeed created in God's image because he was to be earth's only creature capable of the same creativity as God Himself. There was no time limit or age limit placed on Adam's mandate to work. The book of Job later repeated and emphasized the essential link between human satisfaction and work with the words: "Man was born to work."[12]

You work not because you need the results of that work but because there is intrinsic meaning and value in the work itself. That meaning emerges from the fact that your work benefits others. That it should also benefit others is an accompanying side benefit that should not surprise anyone who sees God as benevolent. I cannot overemphasize this essential point. Business success depends on working in order to benefit others: your customers or clients, your employees, and your community. That should be your primary motivation.

The obvious question is, "How do I know that I am bringing benefit to others?" Perhaps by spray-painting graffiti on neighborhood walls, I am really bringing benefit and beauty to unappreciative locals. That is where pay and profit come in. Without these indispensable barometers of people's desires, people would all be inflicted with the involuntary consequences of activists' enthusiasms. By bestowing the gift of money on His children, God gave them the advantage of being able to be supplied with the things that *they* want rather than with the things that *others* think they should have. Pay and profit tell you that you are supplying a need and filling other people's wants. They are not the *motivation* for your work, they are the *validation* of your work.

One of the famous Talmudic stories that has embedded itself in the collective subconscious of the Jewish business professional over the centuries concerns the righteous Honi. One day Honi was journeying on a road and saw an elderly man planting a carob tree. He asked him, "How long does it take for this tree to bear fruit?" The man told Honi that it would take about 70 years. Honi asked the man, "Do you suppose that you will live long enough to eat the fruit?" The man replied that he had found mature carob trees waiting for him in the world: "Just as my fathers planted them for me, I plant these for my children."[13]

The idea that emerges from this story reaffirms that work is chiefly about how other people will benefit from your efforts. It may be today or it maybe in the future, but engaging in work is a moral, benevolent, and caring thing to do.

Jewish tradition also ascribes one additional benefit to work, and that is a sense of self-worth and independence. Discussing mutual obligations, the Talmud[14] analyzes a situation in which Jacob deposited 10 bushels of wheat with Joseph for safekeeping while he was out of the country for several months. It turned out that the value of the wheat was shrinking, perhaps due to a dropping market in wheat or maybe a fungus of some kind. The morality question was whether Joseph is obliged to sell the wheat on Jacob's behalf in order to preserve its value, knowing that he would be able to repurchase the same amount of wheat later once Jacob returned to reclaim his wheat. The answer would appear to be obvious—Joseph must do what he can to preserve and protect the value of his friend's wheat, so why even discuss it? The Talmud reminds us that no wheat on earth will ever taste as good to Jacob as the wheat he himself grew.

The analogy indicated by the Talmud is that people prefer to earn their own way instead of depending on the benevolence of others. Work is the mechanism that allows you the self-respect of knowing that when you eat, you eat as a result of having done good for others in the world. Anyone unfortunate enough to be living off the sweat and perspiration from someone else's brow is said by the Talmud to be eating "the bread of shame." Although retirees may well see themselves to be living on their accumulated savings and investments, rather than on the largesse of others, they are nonetheless contributing far less to the world than they might have were they creatively at work.

In a certain sense, to retire is to write "The End" before the story has rightfully ended. Why terminate the exciting journey prematurely? Arriving often turns out to be less than the trip itself had been. Ending your creative career is like shutting down the engines—you have arrived. Robert Louis Stevenson said, "To travel hopefully is a better thing than to arrive."[15] Continuing your business activities is the very best way of always traveling hopefully throughout your life. In this way you can prosper, and, better yet, you can help others to be doing so, too.

YOUR PATH TO PROSPERITY

- *Stop thinking of retirement as a goal, with a specific date in mind.* And stop thinking of work as a temporary or finite function, something that you should just stop doing one day. Work is valuable beyond its money-generating benefits: It keeps you vital, involved in life, and part of a community of others—all of which are necessary for survival and longevity.

- *Recognize that many people lead very productive lives long into their advanced years.* Sam Walton didn't found Wal-Mart until he was 44 years old, and Colonel Sanders didn't start selling Kentucky Fried Chicken until he was "retired" at the age of 65. Sanders didn't like retirement, and the next 15 years were the most successful and productive of his long life!

- *Understand that retirement is essentially selfish.* Working productively means that you are caring for others. It is hard to maintain meaningful relationships with others when you are retired because you are concerned chiefly with yourself—and it shows. If you are getting paid to do something, rest assured you're doing something that is meaningful and valuable to at least one other person. No retired person has a reliable indicator of his or her usefulness to others.

- *Keep in mind that retirement erodes perseverance, which is one of the most important factors to success.* Shrugging off failure and redoubling efforts takes perseverance. Picking oneself up off the ground to where one has been knocked down and taking another shot at the goal takes perseverance. Resisting pain, sometimes humiliation, too, and remaining stubbornly focused on the task takes enormous reserves of perseverance. And perseverance leads to improvement in attaining one's goals.

- *Don't believe the three lies inherent in the retirement myth.* First, reject the idea that work is only a means to an end; instead, recognize that work is valuable: You should live to work, and you should enjoy the work you do. Second, don't buy into the idea that as you age, you become weaker and less capable of making money; the opposite is actually true: You know more about your craft or area of expertise, you know more people who can help you or benefit from your work, and you are more mature in dealing with adversity. Third, ignore the misperception that people are merely voracious consumers of finite resources; instead, recognize that you are a creator of something useful and valuable: You are productive.

Epilogue

Life is business, and business is life. Learn one, and you will have also learned the other.

My Uncle Joe spent his later days driving dusty country roads in a Rolls Royce. He was a manufacturer's representative. He was a very successful manufacturer's representative. Earlier in life he had built up a business importing and servicing high-end European and Japanese audio equipment. Without even thinking about it, he practiced all the Ten Commandments of this book and became wealthy. His business prospered until he sold his growing company to a conglomerate for a great deal of money. Because he would never have violated either the tenth commandment by retiring or his non-compete agreement by opening up another business, he was in a quandary. Then he realized that nothing in his agreement prevented him from working for another company or even several companies. He approached manufacturers, importers, and wholesalers and offered to go on the road selling their products to the more remote retailers that other salespeople were reluctant to service. I was a rather unaccomplished and impecunious rabbinical school graduate at the time when I noticed that my elderly uncle was well on his way to building his second fortune.

Should I overcome both my pride and a slight intellectual disdain for business and appeal to him for the opportunity to work for him, I wondered? Testing the waters one day, I began by asking him what it was exactly that he did. His soft-spoken answer astounded me because I realized that he really believed what he told me. What he said was, "Daniel, I help hundreds of store owners around the country make a very good living." In an instant it dawned on me that he wasn't working in order to drive a Rolls Royce motor car, he was driving a fine car in order to better help other people get what they wanted. My eyes must have betrayed my inner turmoil because he continued explaining as if to a child, which I suppose in a sense I was. "I supply the desirable goods that the customers of my customers really want." He then generously offered me the chance to join him for a while.

He provided me with catalogs and descriptions of the various products we represented and gave me a list of lonely stores to visit. Upon returning from my 700-mile excursion with nary an order to show for my mileage, I began a lengthy and complicated explanation of why I had not sold any merchandise. He gently interrupted me. "Daniel, you don't have to give me the story because I am quite good at putting together the story myself. You just give me the numbers, and I'll tell you the story. How many stores did you visit? How long did you spend at each store? How many other people were in the store? Were they customers or other salespeople? How many products did you demonstrate? How many orders did you write?" Again I had an insight. My uncle, the business professional, was teaching me, the rabbi, a Torah lesson. In Hebrew the same word *Sofer* is used to describe a scribe, a scholar, and a counter, which is to say, someone good with numbers. You can never become an accomplished scholar without allowing numbers to root you in reality. Stories allow your imagination to soar unencumbered by anything as inconvenient as the laws of physics. Numbers are real and can reflect reality far more quickly and far more accurately than stories. I suspect that there may be an inverse relationship between the value of a financial report and the ratio of stories to numbers found in that report. Numbers should not need too many words to explain them. You give me the numbers, and I'll figure out the story, just as my Uncle Joe said. Numbers reflect reality, and business depends on numbers because it is reality.

Uncle Joe quickly uncovered one reason for my poor performance on that first trip. I had shown some irritation at how long I was kept waiting by store proprietors while they attended to their customers. After all, I had thought, I have come all this way to show him the latest in stereo sound equipment and he leaves me sitting around for over an hour! "You are not there for your purposes; you are there for his," reprimanded my uncle. Business is about helping other people.

I believe that the entire Torah and all the history of the Jewish experience supports the view that to achieve long-term success in business, you have to learn how to behave in the moral, ethical, and courteous way that the good Lord intended. If you are in business, then in almost everything you do, satisfying at least one other person is a prerequisite for success. You must remember that unless you are a Supreme Court judge or a tenured university professor, you are in business. I jokingly consider these two occupations to be typical of the very few modern jobs in which satisfying your customers or clients is entirely unnecessary. Being a judge, a professor, or even a university student is to be strangely isolated from reality.

It is perhaps no accident that business professionals without advanced academic degrees frequently outperform those that do. Nearly one-third of the companies on the 2002 Forbes 500 list are headed by CEOs without masters degrees. Those companies did better for their shareholders than the others on the list.[1]

In schools, for their own good reasons, professors frequently reward effort and intent. The student thus obtains an impressive grade for a mediocre product. However, in both the real world and in business, performance counts far more than intent and excuses. Whether you intended to mow the lawn, repair the car, or deliver the pizza is less important than whether you actually did those things. At least that is how it works in the real world. Business could be a better preparation for reality than school is.

In many environments, including some schools, people are encouraged to focus on their feelings and to act on them. They adoringly refer to this as honesty. In the real world, however, you often need to behave courteously and yes, occasionally even deferentially, to individuals you may loathe. This is the basis of both international diplomacy and the marketplace. The world responds favorably to you by how you actually behave rather than by what you feel. Business should remind you that most other people are not particularly interested in how you feel; they care how you act.

In the real world, you simply cannot have everything you want. You have limited energies and resources to exchange for the goods and services you want. Therefore, you must accustom yourself to deciding which things you really want and which you are prepared to forfeit. Business is one of the few cultural institutions that does impart a real-world understanding that nobody has a right to any material thing or to anyone else's labor. These can only be acquired in exchange for what you have to offer. And what you have to offer is not infinite.

The culture in the United States seems to emphasize individualism in how it idolizes stars in both entertainment and sports. Yet the real-world truth is that cooperation with others is the key to success. This is the secret of the corporation. One apple plus another apple equals two apples, but one person plus another person equals not two, but three, four, or perhaps twenty. The best ways to teach cooperation are through team sports and through business.

Today it may not really be practicable; but in theory, I would rather apprentice my son to a top-rate business professional like my old Uncle Joe than have him spend four years in the best university in the country. I suspect that in this fashion he would emerge better equipped for real life.

In this book I have provided a picture of what one would learn if apprenticed to the economic and philosophic vision of business as found in ancient Jewish wisdom. It has been painful for me to realize that for half my life I inadvertently erected a barrier between my theoretical knowledge and my practical activities. Writing this book has been anguishing in that sense. I naturally wish that I had always followed these ten commandments. If I had, my successes would have been more numerous and my failures fewer and less painful.

Learning from the tried-and-tested principles of one of history's most successful peoples is surely more prudent than working it out as one goes along. You can learn these principles, apply them, and prosper. Not only can you now start to follow the ten commandments of making money, but in so doing not only shall you prosper economically, but you shall also be improving your life and, even more important, the lives of everyone around you.

Notes

Introduction

1. Mark Twain, "Concerning the Jews," *Harper's Magazine* (September 1898).
2. Babylonian Talmud, tractate Berachot, 58a.
3. Bruce Orwall, "Hostility between Disney's Eisner and Katzenberg Explodes in Court," *Wall Street Journal*, May 5, 1999. Also see Bruce Orwall, "Katzenberg Suit Is Partially Settled," *Wall Street Journal*, November 11, 1997, B1 and B10.
4. Steven Silbiger, *The Jewish Phenomenon* (Atlanta, Ga.: Longstreet, 2000), 4.
5. Howard Schultz, *Pour Your Heart into It* (New York: Hyperion, 1997), 18.
6. Babylonian Talmud, tractate Ta'anit, 7a.

The First Commandment
Believe in the Dignity and Morality of Business

1. *Sayings of the Fathers*, chap. 4, mishna 2.
2. Rabbi Joseph Karo, "Laws of Chanuka," in *Code of Jewish Law*, sect. 673, para. 1.
3. Winston S. Churchill, *A History of the English-Speaking Peoples* (New York: Dorset, 1956), 289–290.
4. Virginia Cowles, *The Rothschilds, a Family of Fortune* (New York: Knopf, 1973).
5. Genesis 2:12.
6. Nachmanides on Exodus 25:24.
7. Genesis 48:20.
8. Numbers 6:24.

9. Babylonian Talmud, tractate Nedarim, 38a.

10. Proverbs 14:24.

11. Exodus 11:2.

12. Exodus 12:35–36.

13. Jolayne Houtz, "T. T. Minor: A School Both Blessed and Cursed," *Seattle Times*, June 19, 2000.

14. Anthony Bianco, with William C. Symonds, "Gulfstream's Pilot," *Business Week*, April 14, 1997, 64.

15. Editorial, "Asides: *Nein, Danke,*" *Wall Street Journal*, November 3, 1995.

16. Michael Medved, *Hollywood vs. America*, (New York: HarperCollins, 1992), 220.

17. *Forbes*, September 4, 2000, 82.

18. Linda Richter, Robert Richter, and Stanley Rothman, *Watching America* (New York: Prentice Hall, 1991), 201.

19. Ibid., 155.

20. Marc Gunther, "Business Is TV's Newest Bad Guy," *Fortune*, July 7, 1997, 32.

21. Timothy Lame and Alice Lynn O'Steen, *Businessmen Behaving Badly: Prime Time's World of Commerce* (Alexandria, Va.: Media Research Center, Special Reports, 1997).

22. Michael Fumento, "Businessmen Are Hollywood's Favorite Bad Guys," *National Review*, June 22, 1992.

23. Christopher Hitchins, "Ayn Randed," *The American Spectator*, September 2001.

24. Samuel II 19:31.

25. Aaron Bernstein, "Too Much Coorporate Power?" *Business Week*, September 11, 2000.

26. Diane Anderson, "The Gospel of Greed," *Industry Standard*, June 19, 2000.

27. Dinesh D'Souza, "Is Greed Good?" (lecture delivered at Grand Rapids, Mich., May 3, 2001).

28. "The Greatest Love Stories of the Century," *People*, February 12, 1996.

29. Jay Nordlinger, "Telling Adulterers' Stories," *The Weekly Standard*, April 29, 1996.

30. Allan Sloan, "The Hitmen," *Newsweek*, February 26, 1996, 44.

31. James K. Glassman, "Thank You, American Businessmen," *American Enterprise*, March 2000, 62.

32. Kemba Dunham, "Right and Wrong: What's Ethical in Business? It Depends on When You Ask," *Wall Street Journal*, January 11, 1999, 63.

33. Michael Kinsley, "The Outrage That Wasn't," *Time*, December 28, 1998.
34. Babylonian Talmud, tractate Nedarim, 64b.
35. Marianne M. Jennings, "Business Students Who Hate Business," *Wall Street Journal*, May 3, 1999.
36. Charles Oliver, "Capitalists versus Capitalism," *Investor's Business Daily*, September 17, 1997.
37. David Cay Johnston, "Management: Creating Waves in Nonprofit Sea," *New York Times*, February 2, 2000, C1.
38. New York: Penguin, 1960.

The Second Commandment
Extend the Network of Your Connectedness to Many People

1. Deuteronomy 5:16.
2. Babylonian Talmud, tractate Kiddushin, 39b.
3. Moses Maimonides, *Laws of Repentance*, chap. 9, sect. 1.
4. Leslie Alan Horvitz, in *Insight Magazine*, July 7, 1997, 38.
5. Cunnar Biorck, "Social and Psychological Problems in Patients with Chronic Cardiac Illness," *American Heart Journal* (1959), 414.
6. James J. Lynch, *The Broken Heart: The Medical Consequences of Loneliness* (New York: Basic, 1977), 14.
7. Dale Carnegie, *How to Win Friends and Influence People* (New York: Simon and Schuster, 1936).
8. Frederick Lewis Allen, *Only Yesterday: An Informal History of the 20s* (New York: Wiley, 1997).
9. Shakespeare, *Julius Caesar*, act 1, scene 2.
10. Steve Lipman, "Chai-Tech Success," *New York Jewish Week*, December 18, 1998, 88.
11. Genesis 3:8.
12. Genesis 4:9.
13. William Gilbert and Arthur Sullivan, *The Mikado*, act 2, no. 17 (1885).
14. Genesis 4:12.
15. Genesis 4:16.
16. U.S. Census Bureau, Annual Report on Income and Poverty in the United States (1998).
17. Geoffrey Colvin, "Why Execs Love Golf," *Fortune*, April 30, 2001, 46.
18. Jonah 1:8.

19. Rick Brooks, "Alienating Customers Isn't Always a Bad Idea, Many Firms Discover Banks, Others Base Service on Whether an Account Is Profitable or a Drain 'Redlining in the Worst Form,'" *Wall Street Journal*, January 7, 1999.

20. David Barboza, "In This Company's Struggle, God Has Many Proxies," *New York Times*, November 21, 2001, C1.

21. Eric Ransdell, "They Sell Suits with Soul," *Fast Company*, October 1998, 66.

The Third Commandment
Get to Know Yourself

1. Deuteronomy 11:19.

2. The Torah is written using only consonants; thus the word *them* is "oTaM," whereas the word meaning *you* in the plural is "aTeM." Had the word "oTaM" (them) been written conventionally with a consonant letter *vav* included, the word could only have meant "them." As it is written, it clearly means to say that you are obliged to teach "you" before you teach "them."

3. Babylonian Talmud, tractate Kiddushin, 29b; and Maimonides Laws of Torah Study, chap. 1, sect. 4.

4. American Psychiatric Association, *Diagnostic and Statistical Manual of Mental Disorders*, 3d ed. [DSM III] (Washington, D.C.: American Psychiatric Association, 1980), 259.

5. Genesis 22:2.

6. Genesis 22:5.

7. Three times a day, observant Jews recite the Shema prayer, which places head before heart.

8. Genesis 2:7.

9. Genesis 2:19.

10. Babylonian Talmud, tractate Berachot, 61a.

11. Rabbi Abraham J. Twerski, *Dearer Than Life* (Brooklyn, N.Y.: Shaar Press, 1997), 102.

12. *New York Times*, October 19, 1997.

13. *Wall Street Journal*, October 30, 1997, B1.

14. Robert Ardrey, *The Territorial Imperative* (London: Collins 1967).

15. A. H. Maslow, *Toward a Psychology of Being* (Princeton, N.J.: Krech Crutchfield, 1962); and *Elements of Psychology* (New York: Knopf, 1958).

16. Genesis 2:10.

17. Genesis 2:12.

18. *Sayings of the Fathers*, chap. 4, mishna 1.

19. Genesis 3:17–19.

20. Roy Baumeister, "Violent Pride," *Scientific American*, April 2001.

21. William J. Bennett, *The Devaluing of America* (New York: Summit, 1992).

22. *Personality and Social Psychology Review*, November 2001.

23. Genesis 34:21.

24. Rabbi Yitzchak of Volozhin (1780–1849).

25. Stephen Birmingham, *Our Crowd* (New York: Harper and Row, 1967), 289.

26. Psalms 34:15 (*shalom* means both "peace" and "fulfilled totality").

27. Helen Gurley Brown, "Conducting Training Needs Assessment," *Fortune*, October 28, 1996, 179–187.

The Fourth Commandment
Do Not Pursue Perfection

1. Michael Grunwald, "Unknowing Residents Have Little Left But Lawsuits," *Washington Post*, January 1, 2002, A17.

2. Editorial, *Wall Street Journal*, January 24, 2002.

3. Andrew Carnegie, "How I Served My Apprenticeship," *Youth's Companion*, April 23, 1896.

4. Burton W. Folsom Jr., *The Myth of the Robber Barons* (Herndon, Va.: Young America's Foundation, 1996), 27.

5. Robert Sobel, *The Entrepreneurs* (New York: Weybright and Talley, 1974).

6. Walter Donway, "In Defense of Decades of Greed," *Wall Street Journal*, September 4, 1992.

7. Charles Oliver, "Capitalists versus Capitalism," *Investor's Business Daily*, September 17, 1997.

8. E. Fuller Torrey, *Nowhere to Go: The Tragic Odyssey of the Homeless Mentally Ill* (New York: Harper and Row, 1989).

9. Marvin Olasky, *The Tragedy of American Compassion* (Lanham, Md.: Regnery Gateway, 1992), 211.

10. Manhattan Institute, Policy Issues in Homelessness (New York: Manhattan Institute, 1990).

11. Deuteronomy 15:4, 5.

12. Deuteronomy 15:11.

13. Leviticus 19:14.

14. Moses Maimonides, *Laws of Gifts to the Poor*, chap. 7, sect. 5.

15. Babylonian Talmud, tractate Bava Metziah, 62a.
16. William Bradford, *History of the Plimoth Plantation* (London: Ward and Downey, 1986), 12.
17. Ayn Rand, *Atlas Shrugged* (New York: Random House, 1958).
18. Brent Schlender, "The Bill and Warren Show," *Fortune*, July 20, 1998 (cover story).
19. Editorial, "The Civilizing Effect of the Market," *Wall Street Journal*, January 24, 2002, A1.

The Fifth Commandment
Lead Consistently and Constantly

1. Max Planck, *Treatise on Thermodynamics*, trans. Alexander Ogg (Cape Town, South Africa: Dover, 1926).
2. "Green Buttermilk and Some Real Leadership, Can It Be Real?" *Forbes ASAP* April 8, 1996, 110–112.
3. Sam Roberts, "La Guardia's Legacy Is Formidable But It May Be Surpassed," *New York Times*, December 31, 2001.
4. Dan Barry, "A Man Who Became More Than a Mayor," *New York Times*, December 31, 2001.
5. Hampton Sides, *Ghost Soldiers, The Forgotten Epic Story of World War II's Most Dramatic Mission* (New York: Doubleday, 2001).
6. Exodus 18:17.
7. *Sayings of the Fathers,* chap. 1, mishna 6.
8. Rich Karlgaard, "Digital Rules," *Forbes*, September 17, 2001.
9. Genesis 38:1.
10. Genesis 44:18.
11. Babylonian Talmud, tractate Kiddushin, 29a.
12. Genesis 24:3.
13. Genesis 24:37.
14. Lydia Strohl, "Why Doctors Now Believe Faith Heals," *Reader's Digest,* May 2001, 109–115.
15. Genesis 19:17.
16. Genesis 15:5.
17. John Keegan, *The Mask of Command* (New York: Viking, 1987), 308.
18. Babylonian Talmud, tractate Chagiga, 13b.
19. William Shakespeare, *Hamlet*, act 4, scene 4.

20. *Sayings of the Fathers*, chap. 4, mishna 20.
21. John Keegan, *The Mask of Command* (New York: Viking, 1987), 11.

The Sixth Commandment
Constantly Change the Changeable, While Steadfastly Clinging to the Unchangeable

1. Konrad Heiden, *Der Fuehrer*, trans. Ralph Manheim (Boston: Houghton Mifflin, 1944), 144.
2. Edward Luttwak, "The Secret the Soviets Should Have Stolen," *Business 2.0*, May 1, 2001, 83.
3. "Research News," *Science Magazine*, July 25, 1986, 417.
4. Stephen Jay Gould, "Mickey Mouse Meets Konrad Lorenz," *Natural History Magazine*, May 1979, 30.
5. Dean Starkman, "Westfield's Lowy Joins Top Ranks of Mall Tycoons," *Wall Street Journal*, January 15, 2002, B1.
6. Carrie Coolidge, "Pushing the Envelope," *Forbes*, October 19, 1998.
7. Deuteronomy 33:18.
8. Deuteronomy 33:19.
9. Deuteronomy 33:18.
10. Rashi's commentary, Deuteronomy 33:18.
11. James C. Collins, "Change Is Good—But First Know What Should Never Change," *Fortune*, May 29, 1995.
12. De Beers is the South African–based international diamond syndicate.
13. Ann Marsh, "Ice Capades," *Red Herring Magazine*, March 6, 2001, 124–134.
14. Jeffrey A. Trachtenberg and Matthew Rose, "Feeling the Stewart Effect," *Wall Street Journal*, June 26, 2002, B1.
15. "Companies Rethink Casual Clothes," *USA Today*, June 27, 2000.
16. Teri Agins and Lisa Vickery, "Heads Up—The Suits Are Coming," *Wall Street Journal*, April 6, 2001, B1.

The Seventh Commandment
Learn to Foretell the Future

1. Winston S. Churchill, *The Gathering Storm*, vol. 1 of *The Second World War* (Boston: Houghton Mifflin, 1948), 222.
2. Greg Sandoval, "Shaheen Defends Webvan Tenure" (NET News.com, April 23, 2001).

3. Cicero, *De Divinatione*, I, 118.

4. Diane Maley, "The Philosopher King—Behind the Reichmann's Mystique," *Report on Business*, December 1988.

5. Ecclesiastes 1:9.

6. *Newsweek*, October 28, 1946.

7. Genesis 5.

8. "Pass It On," *Alcoholics Anonymous World Service*, 1984, 384.

9. Nikolas Kondratieff, *The Long Wave Cycle* (New York: Richardson and Snyder, 1984).

10. Leviticus 25.

11. Richard Lipkin, "Cycles: Beating to the Same Pulse," *Insight Magazine*, March 14, 1988.

12. Foundation for the Study of Cycles, University of California at Irvine.

13. Thomas Petzinger Jr., "The Front Lines. A Professor Teaches How to Turn Xeroxes into Lucrative Profits," *Wall Street Journal*, 1998.

14. K. L. Billingsley, *The Seductive Image* (Westchester, Ill.: Crossway Books, 1989), 69.

15. Sharon Begley, "So Much for Destiny: Even Thoughts Can Turn Genes 'On' and 'Off,'" *Wall Street Journal*, June 21, 2002, C1.

The Eighth Commandment
Know Your Money

1. William James, *The Principles of Psychology* (New York: Henry Holt, 1890), chap. 10.

2. Genesis 32:25.

3. Babylonian Talmud, tractate Chullin, 91a.

4. James E. Ewart, *Money* (Seattle, Wa.: Principia Publishing, 1998).

5. Thomas A. Stewart, "Brain Power: Who Owns It . . . How They Profit from It," *Fortune*, March 17, 1997, 105.

6. Paul Johnson, *A History of the American People* (New York: HarperCollins, 1997), 640.

7. Friedrich Hayek, *The Fatal Conceit* (Chicago: University of Chicago Press, 1988), chap. 6, "The Mysterious World of Trade and Money."

8. Carl Menger, *Principles of Economics* (London: London School of Economics, 1934).

9. Extrapolated from discussions in Babylonian Talmud, tractate Sanhedrin, 38a, and Pirke D'Rabbi Eliezer, chap. 48.

10. Tiferet Yisrael, Rabbi Yehuda Loew, chap. 26.

11. Herman Minkowski, 1908, Lecture to 80th Assembly of German Natural Scientists and Physicians; quoted in Albert Einstein, *The Principle of Relativity*.

12. Generally accepted accounting principles—the rules, conventions, and practices that form the foundation for financial accounting.

13. Jewish law calculates damages in a similar way. If a man loses an arm in an industrial accident, damages are estimated on the basis of the amount of money that most people in that occupation would be willing to accept in return for losing an arm.

14. Babylonian Talmud, tractate Bava Metzia, 42a.

15. New York: Wiley, 1998.

The Ninth Commandment
Act Rich: Give Away 10 Percent of Your After-Tax Income

1. Naomi Mauer, "Tithing," *The Jewish Press*, September 7, 2001.

2. Zohar, iii, 110b.

3. Steven E. Landsburg, "Giving Your All: The Math on the Back of the Envelopes," *Slate.com* [http://slate.msn.com/default.aspx?id=2034] (on-line magazine), January 11, 1997.

4. Dan Seligman, "Is Philanthropy Irrational?" *Forbes*, June 1, 1998.

5. Study by Daniel Zizzo, Oxford University, and Andrew Oswald, Warwick University, February 2002.

6. Dan Seligman, "Is Philanthropy Irrational?" *Forbes*, June 1, 1998.

7. "Giving USA 2001, The Annual Report on Philanthropy" (The Center on Philanthropy, Indiana University, Bloomington, Ind.).

8. Genesis 47:22–26.

9. Numbers 13:33.

10. Rudyard Kipling, "If," *One Hundred and One Famous Poems* (New York: Barnes and Noble, 1993), 116.

The Tenth Commandment
Never Retire

1. Jim Irwin (Associated Press), *Seattle Post-Intelligencer*, April 14, 1999.

2. "100-Year-Old finally Gets College Degree," CNN.com [http://

www.cnn.com/2001/US/06/01/centenarian.graduate.ap/index.html], June 1, 2001.

3. Roy Hoffman, "Working Past 90," *Fortune*, November 13, 2000, 366–384.

4. Babylonian Talmud, tractate Shabbat, 30b.

5. Donald D. Hensrud, "The Mayo Clinic Doctor," *Fortune*, April 20, 2001, 210.

6. William Diehl, "I'll Never Retire," *The Free Market*, February 1997.

7. William McGurn, "Pulpit Economics," *First Things*, April 2002, 21–25.

8. Leviticus 19:32.

9. Babylonian Talmud, tractate Kiddushin, 32b.

10. "Europe's Population Bomb," *Newsweek*, December 15, 1986.

11. *U.S. News & World Report*, December 16, 1985, 67.

12. Job 5:7.

13. Babylonian Talmud, tractate Taanit, 23a.

14. Babylonian Talmud, tractate Bava Metziah, 38a.

15. Robert Louis Stevenson, "El Dorado," in *The Works of Robert Lewis Stevenson*, Vailima Edition (26 vols.), ed. Lloyd Osbourne and Fanny Van de Grift Stevenson (London: Heinemann, 1922–1923).

Epilogue

1. Matthew Herper, "Keep Your CEO Out of Grad School," *Forbes.com*, April 25, 2002.

Index